"Schwarz shows us how to become more transparent in our work with clients in a way that builds client effectiveness."
   —Mary Beth O'Neill, consultant, coach, and author of *Executive Coaching with Backbone and Heart*

"Roger Schwarz has written the perfect book to transform mediators into skilled facilitators. It is all here: the theory, the practical suggestions, the guidelines, the analysis of groups. The only thing better than this book is the book and the workshop."
   —Zena D. Zumeta, president, Mediation Training & Consultation Institute/The Collaborative Workplace

"The book arms you not only with skills for the workplace but with skills for life. At Conoco, Roger's approach has had a significant impact on our business and functional leaders—it's far more than a guide for facilitators."
   —David Nelson, manager, organization development and Conoco University, Conoco, Inc.

"Every group facilitator should be grounded in the values, assumptions, and principles underlying the practice of group facilitation. Thankfully, in *The Skilled Facilitator*, Roger Schwarz addresses these matters thoughtfully, coherently, and more comprehensively than in any other book for group facilitators."
   —Sandor P. Schuman, editor, *Group Facilitation: A Research and Applications Journal*, and moderator, The Electronic Discussion on Group Facilitation

"As a new entry to the facilitation field, I wanted to find out what the industry thought was the best resource for combining theory with the practices of facilitation. I submitted my request to the largest online discussion forum for active, professional facilitators. Roger Schwarz's book *The Skilled Facilitator* was by far the favorite choice of people in the profession. I am ordering my copy now!"
   —Malcolm Dell, former executive coordinator, Woodnet Development Council, Inc.

"The expanded, revised edition provides new, innovative approaches and insights not only to professional facilitators but also to those who want to use facilitation skills to be effective leaders, consultants, or coaches. Roger makes facilitation skills and techniques understandable and usable. These skills are particularly important in labor-management relations and other settings in which leaders must generate commitment rather than compliance and where mutual understanding is critical to productive relationships."

    —Robert Tobias, former president, National Treasury Employees Union, and
        professor of public administration, American University

"People with group and team expertise often referred to Roger Schwarz's first edition of *The Skilled Facilitator* as 'the facilitators' bible.' The enhanced revised edition will easily retain that title. The millions who have to cope with ineffective meetings on a daily basis would be wise to quickly acquire and absorb the key points. Merely using the list of behavioral ground rules would so enhance the effectiveness of their meeting process that it would pay for the book many times over. Using the rest of the ideas in the book would generate significant bottom-line return through swifter, higher-quality, more easily implemented decisions at all levels of the organization."

    —Michael M. Beyerlein, director, Center for the Study of Work Teams,
        and professor of industrial/organizational psychology,
        University of North Texas

"Roger Schwarz's approach goes far beyond the typical techniques and strategies to focus on core values that enable multiple parties with different perspectives to work together effectively. As part of the most comprehensive and long-standing education reform agenda in the country, which includes business leaders, school board members, school council members, parents, students, and state-level policymakers, thirty-five high-level leaders in Kentucky have received training in using facilitative skills as leaders. They report that they work more effectively because of the Skilled Facilitator framework."

    —Carolyn Witt Jones, executive director,
        Partnership for Kentucky Schools

The Skilled Facilitator

*A Comprehensive Resource for Consultants,
Facilitators, Managers, Trainers,
and Coaches*

New and Revised

Roger Schwarz

JOSSEY-BASS
A Wiley Company
www.josseybass.com

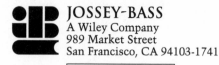

JOSSEY-BASS
A Wiley Company
989 Market Street
San Francisco, CA 94103-1741

www.josseybass.com

Jossey-Bass books and products are available through most bookstores. To contact Jossey-Bass directly, call (888) 378-2537, fax to (800) 605-2665, or visit our website at www.josseybass.com.

Substantial discounts on bulk quantities of Jossey-Bass books are available to corporations, professional associations, and other organizations. For details and discount information, contact the special sales department at Jossey-Bass.

We at Jossey-Bass strive to use the most environmentally sensitive paper stocks available to us. Our publications are printed on acid-free recycled stock whenever possible, and our paper always meets or exceeds minimum GPO and EPA requirements.

Jossey-Bass also publishes its books in a variety of electronic formats. Some content that appears in print may not be available in electronic books.

Library of Congress Cataloging-in-Publication Data
Schwarz, Roger M., date–
The skilled facilitator: a comprehensive resource for consultants, facilitators, managers, trainers, and coaches / Roger Schwarz.—New and rev. ed.
p. cm.—(The Jossey-Bass business & management series)
Includes bibliographical references and index.
ISBN 0-7879-4723-7 (hardcover: alk. paper)
1. Communication in management. 2. Communication in personnel management. 3. Group facilitation. 4. Teams in the workplace. 5. Conflict management. I. Title. II. Series.
HD30.3.S373 2002
658.4'036—dc21 2002007934

SECOND EDITION

HB Printing   10 9 8 7 6 5 4 3 2

The Jossey-Bass

Business & Management Series

To Kathleen, Noah, and Hannah,

with whom I learn about compassion . . .

and who bring so much to my life

CONTENTS

PREFACE TO THE REVISED EDITION

It has been eight years since I wrote the first edition of *The Skilled Facilitator*. The book has been successful. Many people have told me they used it to improve their work and regularly consult it. I feel good about that.

When I started to revise the book, I knew I wanted to introduce some new topics, expand others, and reframe others. As I began to write, I found that my thinking about the core ideas of *The Skilled Facilitator* has not changed; if anything, I now believe more deeply in the approach. I have also thought more deeply and broadly about some issues, including how to integrate *The Skilled Facilitator* with other methods.

But I myself have changed since the first edition. I have become aware of and appreciate more than ever the emotional side of facilitation, particularly the role that compassion plays in being a skilled facilitator. I hope this edition reflects it; if you have read the first edition, you can decide for yourself.

WHAT THIS BOOK IS ABOUT

The Skilled Facilitator is about how you can help groups become more effective, whether you are a facilitator, leader, manager, consultant, coach, or trainer. When I wrote the first edition, facilitative skills were something you would call on a facilitator for. Now, many organizations realize that the set of skills an effective facilitator has are the same skills others need when they work with groups. **Facilitative skills are increasingly becoming a core competency for leaders, consultants, and others who work with groups.** It's not just for facilitators anymore.

Throughout the book, I describe one approach—the Skilled Facilitator approach—while recognizing that others exist. Rather than include an overview of a number of approaches, **I offer one relatively comprehensive and integrated approach,** so that you can apply it and use it as a point of reference in analyzing other approaches.

The Skilled Facilitator approach has several key features. It is **based on a set of core values, assumptions, and principles.** Whether you are serving as a facilitator, facilitative leader, consultant, coach, or trainer, you can always figure out what to do in a particular situation by turning to core values, assumptions, and principles to guide your behavior. This also helps you teach others.

The approach in this book **integrates theory and practice.** Throughout, I answer two questions: "What do I say and do in this situation?" and "What are the underlying principles that explain why I say and do this?" By answering the first question, you learn the specific techniques and methods, which is a necessary process. But by answering the second question, you understand why the tools, techniques, and methods work; you can then teach them to others. You may also develop your own techniques and methods, congruent with the approach.

The Skilled Facilitator approach is **a systems approach.** In a systems view, everything is related to everything else, so you cannot change just one thing. Working effectively with a group means recognizing that you and the group function as a system. It means anticipating the potential positive and negative consequences of your actions and those of group members, both short-term and long-term.

Part of thinking and acting systemically is focusing on both the **internal and external work of facilitation.** I believe that when a situation becomes difficult, a challenging aspect of facilitation is being able to think in such a way that you can share with the group what you are thinking, to create learning without generating defensiveness in others. The Skilled Facilitator approach helps you rigorously reflect on your own thinking and feeling, to understand that how you think and feel leads you to act in a way that creates unintended consequences. The approach also enables you to begin changing how you think and feel in a difficult situation, so that you can be more effective. You can use this same set of skills to help the group examine how they create unintended consequences.

In this approach, the **same set of principles applies to you and the group members.** There is not a set of principles, techniques, or methods for you and another set for others. When you act effectively, you model effective behavior for others.

WHO THIS BOOK IS FOR

Facilitative skills are essential today, whether or not you are a facilitator. You will find *The Skilled Facilitator* useful if you work with groups and want to understand how they limit their effectiveness, and what you can do to increase the group's effectiveness as well as your own. This applies to

- **Facilitators,** internal and external, who deal with any kind of work group: a board, top leadership team, management team, work team, task force, committee, labor-management group, interorganizational committee, or community group
- **Leaders and managers,** formal and informal, who are involved in the content of conversation at the same time they need to manage group process; informal leaders include **group members**
- **Organization development consultants,** internal and external, who need facilitation skills to help a group manage the process of change, regardless of the focus of the change
- **Human resource managers,** who are often involved in difficult conversation regarding employee performance or behavior
- **Expert consultants** who work with a group in sharing their content expertise
- **Coaches** who are helping people learn by leading them to think about their behavior
- **Trainers** who facilitate discussion as part of training
- **Mediators** who want develop their facilitative skills or work with groups
- **Faculty members** who, as practical scholars, teach courses on conflict management, groups, consultation, or organization development, in the fields of management, public administration, planning, psychology, social work, education, or public health, or in other applied fields

HOW THE BOOK IS ORGANIZED

I have organized *The Skilled Facilitator* into six parts. Here are brief descriptions of the chapters within them.

Part One: How Facilitation Helps Groups

In Part One, I lay the foundation for using facilitative skills.

Chapter One, "The Skilled Facilitator Approach." In this chapter, I give an overview of the Skilled Facilitator approach, including how you can use it in whatever roles you serve.

Chapter Two, "What Makes Work Groups Effective?" If you work with groups, it is important to have a model of what makes a group effective. In this chapter, I offer a model of what groups need if they are to be effective, and I explain how you can use the model to help a new group or one facing problems.

Chapter Three, "The Facilitator and Other Facilitative Roles." Whether you are a facilitator, leader, manager, consultant, coach, or trainer, it is important that you and those you work with clearly understand and agree on your role with the group. In this chapter, I describe how you can use the Skilled Facilitator approach in any role you serve: facilitator, leader, team member, consultant, coach, trainer, or teacher. I also introduce the core values that are the foundation of the approach and that can help you develop new ways of working effectively with a group.

Part Two: Diagnosing Behavior in Groups

In Part Two, I describe how to observe a group (and yourself) and begin to determine what is happening that is limiting the group's effectiveness (or yours).

Chapter Four, "Understanding the Theories That Guide Our Actions." Your behavior and that of group members is guided by a set of values and assumptions. In a difficult situation, your values and assumptions lead you to take action that generates negative consequences for you and the group. In this chapter, I explore how this happens, and how you can help a group and yourself create fundamental change that reduces negative consequences. I illustrate this using verbatim examples of effective and ineffective theories.

Chapter Five, "Ground Rules for Effective Groups." To help a group, you have to know what behaviors contribute to or detract from effective group process. In this chapter, I introduce the ground rules for effective groups, which you can use to observe a group and lead it into productive conversation, and which the group can use to improve its effectiveness. I present verbatim examples of how to use (and how not to use) each ground rule.

Chapter Six, "Diagnosing Behaviors That Enhance or Hinder Group Effectiveness." In this chapter, I describe a six-step cycle that you can use to diagnose and intervene in a group. This chapter focuses on the first two steps of the cycle: how to accurately observe group behavior and how to decide whether, and in what way, the behavior is helping or hindering the group.

Part Three: Intervening in Groups

In the chapters of Part Two, you learn whether to intervene and, if you decide to do so, how to help a group become aware of its behavior and become more effective.

Chapter Seven, "Deciding Whether, How, and Why to Intervene." In this chapter, I explain how to decide whether to intervene at any given moment—the third step of the diagnosis-intervention cycle. I present a set of questions you can ask yourself to make the decision.

Chapter Eight, "How to Intervene." In this chapter, I discuss how to intervene in a group—literally, how you share what you are thinking, invite group members' reactions, and help them change their behavior if they decide to do so. This chapter focuses on steps four through six of the diagnosis-intervention cycle.

Chapter Nine, "Using the Ground Rules to Intervene." In this chapter, I give verbatim examples of how to intervene in a variety of situations using the ground rules and the diagnosis-intervention cycle.

Chapter Ten, "Using the Skilled Facilitator Approach with Other Processes." In this chapter, I show how to apply the Skilled Facilitator approach to get more value from other processes your group uses, such as models of problem solving, process improvement, and strategic planning.

Chapter Eleven, "Beginning and Ending Meetings." In this chapter, I describe interventions you can make at the beginning of a meeting and at the end of a meeting to increase group effectiveness.

Chapter Twelve, "Dealing with Emotions." Expressing emotions appropriately is a challenge for many people when a situation becomes difficult. In this chapter, I explain how you and the group members generate your emotions, and how you can help members (and yourself) express emotion in a way that adds value to the conversation rather than detracts from it.

Part Four: Agreeing to Work Together

In Part Four, I describe how to reach an agreement to work with a group, or a cofacilitator, and how to work together.

Chapter Thirteen, "Contracting: Deciding Whether and How to Work Together." In this chapter, I describe a step-by-step process that you and a group can use to agree on whether and how to work together.

Chapter Fourteen, "Working with Another Facilitator." In this chapter, I consider how you and a cofacilitator can work together to help a group; the chapter covers the potential advantages and disadvantages of cofacilitating, and how you can divide and coordinate your work.

Part Five: Using Facilitative Skills in Your Own Organization

In this part, I explore how you can use the Skilled Facilitator approach, as an internal facilitator and as a leader in your organization.

Chapter Fifteen, "Serving as Facilitator in Your Own Organization." In this chapter, I describe how your role as internal facilitator develops, the potential advantages and disadvantages of the role, and specific strategies you can use to be effective in your role.

Chapter Sixteen, "The Facilitative Leader." Facilitative skills are becoming a core competency for leaders. In this chapter, I illustrate some problems with traditional leadership models and show how you can use the core values, principles, and methods of the Skilled Facilitator approach to become a facilitative leader, whether you are a formal leader or an informal one.

Resources

The final part of the book contains eight resources, most of which are samples of contracting agreements or guidelines for engaging in a particular facilitation task.

FEATURES OF THE BOOK

There are a number of features of this book that will help you navigate and learn the approach:

- To help you quickly grasp the main ideas in each chapter, I begin them all with an **overview** and end with a **summary.**

- I have identified key principles of the Skilled Facilitator approach in **boldface** type.

- A book cannot substitute for the skill-building practice of a workshop. Still, I have tried to write the book in a way that gives you the kind of detail you would learn in a workshop. Throughout the book, I present **verbatim examples** illustrating how to put the principles into action. This includes real cases of how group members act ineffectively and how you can intervene in such cases.

- **I relate my own stories and my colleagues' stories** to illustrate how to apply the Skilled Facilitator approach—and how not to apply it. There are examples of my own ineffective facilitation; I have learned from them and assume you will too. In all the examples and stories, I have disguised the name and type of client organization, as well the names of individual members. I have sometimes created a composite of several stories to quickly illustrate a point.

- Part of the Skilled Facilitator approach is being aware of and effectively managing your own emotions. Throughout the book, **I describe emotions** that I have had and that you may have as you learn and practice this approach. I describe how I try to manage my emotions, so you can see how to use your emotions to help rather than hinder the group.

- The end of the book contains **eight resources** you can use to develop planning and contracting letters, and to plan for meetings with your group, manager, and cofacilitator.

WHAT IS DIFFERENT IN THE SECOND EDITION

If you have read the first edition, you may be wondering how this edition differs. There are a number of significant areas:

- Two chapters are completely new. Chapter One is an overview of the Skilled Facilitator approach. Chapter Four describes the theories that guide your actions, including the mutual learning model that underlies the Skilled Facilitator approach.

- Most other chapters are either significantly revised or expanded.
  - The discussion of facilitative roles (Chapter Three) examines five roles in which you can serve: facilitator, leader, coach, consultant, and trainer.
  - There are now nine ground rules instead of sixteen.
  - I have added a fourth core value: compassion.
  - The diagnosis-intervention cycle is integrated with the ground rules and core values.
  - The material on ground rules (Chapter Five) contains real examples of groups acting inconsistently with each ground rule and how you can intervene in each case.

- The book is easier to navigate. There are more headings, figures, and cases that make it easier to find things.

- The book is easier to read.

Regarding this last point, when I wrote the first edition I was an assistant professor trying to show my lawyer faculty colleagues that facilitation is serious, rigorous business. Unfortunately, I wrote in a stern, expert, third-person voice that unnecessarily distanced the reader. People who came to my workshops after reading the first edition of the book were sometimes surprised to find that I have a sense of humor. As one person said (in some amazement, it seems), "You're a regular guy." In this edition, I have tried to write in a more conversational, regular-guy voice, using *I* and *you* (and fewer imperatives) and putting more of who I am as a facilitator into the book.

Chapel Hill, North Carolina   Roger Schwarz
May 2002

ACKNOWLEDGMENTS

Many people helped me write this book, and it is a pleasure to thank them. Anne Davidson, Sue McKinney, Dick McMahon, Peg Carlson, Gail Young, and Tom Moore—my colleagues at Roger Schwarz & Associates—each read chapters and gave me feedback, often on short notice. It is a pleasure to have colleagues who know the subject so intimately that they can precisely point out gaps in my reasoning and find the words to express what I have been grappling to say. In addition, each of these colleagues has shaped my thinking about facilitation and facilitative leadership. Dick helped me crystallize my ideas initially and has continued to help me think clearly about fundamental issues. During the thousands of hours Anne and I have spent together consulting, co-leading workshops, and talking on airplanes, she has helped me think not only about the Skilled Facilitator approach but also how to teach others about it in a way that is clear and accessible. Sue and Peg have done this as well, each bringing a different and valuable perspective.

I am grateful to have clients who think rigorously about my work and require me to answer the difficult questions they pose. This includes clients who have attended public workshops and clients whom I have worked with in their organizations. They help me see places where my approach does not take into account the realities of their work situation, as well as encourage me to think through how I can change the Skilled Facilitator approach to do so. These clients include Sallie Hightower and David Nelson at Conoco; Ilean Galloway and Kristin Johnson at Intel; Harry Furukawa, formerly of the American Red

Cross; Jeff Litwin, formerly of Rockwell; and Carolyn Witt Jones at the Partnership for Kentucky Schools.

I have been fortunate to work with a number of colleagues integrating the Skilled Facilitator approach and their areas of expertise. Chris Soderquist of High Performance Systems has helped me apply the principles and tools of operational systems thinking; he is passionate about helping people integrate facilitative skills with systems thinking. Mark Adkins, at the Center for the Management of Information at the University of Arizona, and I have been integrating the Skilled Facilitator approach with group support systems and technology-based facilitation. In the process, Mark has helped me clarify and challenge my own thinking about the fundamental assumptions of the approach, its purpose, and its limitations. Without him, I wouldn't have spent several days on Hawaii in my hotel room looking out at the Pacific ocean and editing the final chapters of this book.

Linda O'Toole at Human Dynamics helped me see how individual differences in how people think about the world have implications for how they learn the Skilled Facilitator approach and their own strengths and weaknesses when they apply it. Steve Kay at Roberts & Kay, Incorporated has modeled for me a compassionate stance as a facilitator and helped me see things I have missed. For the past few years, Bob Putnam, of Action Design, and I have co-led a workshop at the Systems Thinking in Action conference in which we integrate our approaches to change, which are fundamentally similar but use somewhat different methods. Bob always helps me learn some subtle but powerful nuance in the work, and it is a joy to watch him in action. He also read and gave me feedback on Chapter Four, "Understanding the Theories That Guide Our Actions."

Dale Schwarz, an art therapist and organizational consultant—and most important to me, my sister—has continually encouraged me to put more of myself into the book—and just plain encouraged me in my work and life in general. She helped me think through the chapter on emotions and the role of compassion in facilitation. She is a wonderful role model for integrating thoughts and feelings.

Peter Block challenged me to find my voice as I was struggling to write. He helped me understand that part of finding my voice is using my own language. Although I didn't follow all of Peter's advice, I did use it to change the tone of the book.

Chris Argyris has given me a wonderful gift: a framework for thinking about consulting, facilitation, and human and organizational behavior in general. In the early 1980s, I was one of Chris's graduate students at Harvard. He taught me his approach to improving life and learning in organizations; he inspired me to live my life and practice my profession congruent with the same set of core values I ask my clients to apply; and he stimulated me to continue developing my own thinking about organizations.

At Jossey-Bass, my editor, Susan Williams, and assistant editor Rob Brandt are wonderful. Susan was willing to come to a five-day Skilled Facilitator workshop to learn what the approach looked like in practice, and she encouraged me to bring the workshop content and my teaching style into the book. She gave me a lot of encouragement when I got stuck and showed exceptional patience whenever I missed a deadline. Susan, along with Todd Berman, marketing manager at Jossey-Bass, repeatedly listened to my needs in regard to the book's jacket design and met them. I appreciate their willingness to create a design that is congruent with the book's content and that will attract potential readers.

This book would still be a bunch of computer files on my hard drive if it were not for my administrative assistant, Melissa Wallen. She managed the process of preparing the manuscript, dealing with figures and exhibits and making sure everything was in place. As I write this, she is making sure we meet the 7:30 Fed Ex deadline. I could not have done this without her.

Finally, I want to thank my wife, Kathleen Rounds, and my children, Noah and Hannah. They encouraged me as I was writing the second edition, and more important, they told me when the book was taking over my life and seeping into theirs. By challenging me to examine my assumptions, Kathleen helps me become the person I want to be. Noah and Hannah are learning to share their feelings openly and constructively and explain their thinking while asking me about mine. Through our conversations, they have helped me become a better father. I am blessed to have these three in my life.

R.S.

THE AUTHOR

Roger Schwarz is an organizational psychologist and founder and president of Roger Schwarz & Associates Inc., a consulting firm that helps groups, organizations, and communities use facilitative skills to create fundamental change. For more than twenty years, he has been facilitating as well as consulting, coaching, and speaking on the subjects of facilitation and facilitative leadership. His clients include Fortune 500 corporations; federal, state, and local governments; educational institutions; and nonprofit organizations. His first edition of *The Skilled Facilitator* (Jossey-Bass, 1994) is a standard reference in the field. He is currently writing *The Skilled Facilitator Fieldbook* with his colleagues Anne Davidson, Peg Carlson, and Sue McKinney.

Schwarz was formerly associate professor of public management and government and assistant director at the Institute of Government, The University of North Carolina at Chapel Hill. In 1996, he left his tenured position to found Roger Schwarz & Associates.

Schwarz earned his Ph.D. and A.M. in organizational psychology from The University of Michigan, his M.Ed. degree from Harvard University Graduate School of Education, and his B.S. degree in psychology from Tufts University. He lives and works in Chapel Hill, North Carolina, with his wife and two children.

You can learn more about Roger Schwarz & Associates, including consulting and coaching services and facilitator and facilitative leader workshops, at www.schwarzassociates.com or by calling (919) 932-3343.

PART ONE

HOW FACILITATION
HELPS GROUPS

CHAPTER ONE

The Skilled Facilitator Approach

In this opening chapter, I briefly illustrate the need for facilitation, define group facilitation, and give an overview of the Skilled Facilitator approach. We also see the key elements and how they fit together to form a values-based systemic approach to facilitation.

THE NEED FOR GROUP FACILITATION

Groups are becoming the basic work unit of organizations. Increasingly, we turn to groups to bring together differing views, produce quality products and services, and coordinate complex work. In doing so, we expect groups to work effectively so that the product of their efforts is greater than the sum of the parts. Yet our experience with groups often leaves us feeling disappointed or frustrated. Consider these examples:

• A division manager, Michael, and his department heads meet regularly to solve divisionwide problems. Michael has specific recommendations in mind but is concerned that if he shares his views early on, the department heads won't share their true opinions or buy in to his recommendations. So Michael asks the department heads a series of questions about the problems, while withholding his own opinions. The department heads begin to feel that they are being quizzed and that Michael is looking for certain answers. Uncertain what the answers are, the department heads grow careful, giving their views in vague terms so they do not commit to a position that might be at odds with their boss. Frustrated with what he considers inadequate response, Michael reacts by telling the group how the problems are to be solved. The department heads reluctantly agree, but they are not committed to the decisions, which end up being poorly implemented. After the meetings, the department heads discuss privately how Michael is not sharing decision-making authority as he had agreed. Down the hall, Michael confides to his assistant that he will be reluctant to give his department heads more say in decisions if they do not demonstrate clearer reasoning in these situations. No one ever discusses in the full group the concerns aired after each meeting.

• A board meets every other week to make policy decisions. Each time an issue comes up, members take sides and push their positions. They rarely share their reasons for taking a position, and no one asks. Each member believes that others are taking a position from questionable motives. Members leave the meetings frustrated and angry, sometimes even after winning a vote. Despite all the decisions they make, members feel the board has no unified direction.

• Members of an aspiring self-directed team believe that a couple of members, Cora and Dean, are not doing quality work. The members talk about this among themselves but never raise the issue directly with Cora and Dean because they are concerned that Cora and Dean will get embarrassed and defensive. Instead, the other team members choose to redo the work for the two. As the situation gets worse, the team members ask their leader, Leticia, to talk to Dean and Cora. She agrees and then finds herself in a conversation with them without any firsthand information about the situation, and with no other team members to respond to the pair's questions and concerns. Cora and Dean resent being talked to by Leticia without having the team members present. Little is resolved, the relationship between the two members and the rest of the team worsens, and the team's performance drops.

• A newly formed group comprising representatives from local business organizations, the police department, community groups, and the schools meet to try to figure out how to reduce crime in their community. All the members agree on the group's goals and are willing to devote time, energy, and money to solve the problem. Yet the group members' optimism quickly evaporates as they begin to blame each other for causing the problem.

• A top management team meets to solve a complicated problem that affects the entire organization. All are experienced, successful executives, and they quickly identify a solution and implement it. Just as they think they have solved the problem, it returns in another form, and the problem gets worse.

Groups do not have to function in ways that lead to ineffective performance, make it difficult for members to work together, and frustrate members. Groups can improve how they work.

This book is about helping work groups improve their effectiveness by using facilitative skills. It is about helping all types of work groups: top management teams, boards, committees, work teams, cross-functional teams, interorganizational groups, quality groups, task forces, and employee-management or union-management groups. Anyone who works with others needs facilitative skills.

Organizational consultants, internal and external, need facilitative skills when they contract with clients, diagnose problems, and recommend solutions. Leaders and managers need facilitative skills to explore stakeholders' interests and to craft solutions based on sound data that generate commitment.

Because organizations change constantly, the need for facilitative skills to support change is always increasing. This applies to a merger or acquisition, or downsizing, and to efforts to improve the quality of products and services, empower employees, develop a shared vision, develop a self-managing work team, create a learning organization, or develop an organizational culture that makes these changes possible.

Organizations typically use groups to plan and implement change, and groups typically need some form of facilitation. In addition, facilitative skills have become more important as organizations try to openly and constructively manage conflict arising from the change they try to create.

At the heart of improving group effectiveness lies the ability of group members to reflect on what they are doing, to create the conditions necessary to achieve their goals. Groups find it difficult to openly examine behavior on their own; they often need the help of a facilitator.

WHAT IS GROUP FACILITATION?

Group facilitation is a process in which a person whose selection is acceptable to all the members of the group, who is substantively neutral, and who has no substantive decision-making authority diagnoses and intervenes to help a group improve how it identifies and solves problems and makes decisions, to increase the group's effectiveness.

The facilitator's main task is to help the group increase effectiveness by improving its process and structure. *Process* refers to how a group works together. It includes how members talk to each other, how they identify and solve problems, how they make decisions, and how they handle conflict. *Structure* refers to stable recurring group process, examples being group membership or group roles. In contrast, *content* refers to what a group is working on. The content of a group discussion might be whether to enter a new market, how to provide high-quality service to customers, or what each group member's responsibilities should be. Whenever a group meets, it is possible to observe both content and process. For example, in a discussion of how to provide high-quality service, suggestions about installing a customer hotline or giving more authority to those with customer contact reflect content. However, members responding to only certain colleagues' ideas or failing to identify their assumptions are facets of the group's process.

Underlying the facilitator's main task is the fundamental assumption that ineffective group process and structure reduces a group's ability to solve problems and make decisions. Although research findings on the relationship between process and group effectiveness are mixed (Kaplan, 1979), the premise of this book is that by increasing the effectiveness of the group's process and structure the facilitator helps the group improve its performance and overall effectiveness. The facilitator does not intervene directly in the content of the group's discussions; to do so would require the facilitator to abandon neutrality and reduce the group's responsibility for solving its problems.

To ensure that the facilitator is trusted by all group members and that the group's autonomy is maintained, the facilitator should be acceptable to all members of the group; this person needs to be substantively neutral—that is, display no preference for any of the solutions the group considers—and not have substantive decision-making authority. In practice, the facilitator can meet these three criteria only if he or she is not a group member. A group member may be acceptable to other members and may not have substantive decision-making authority yet have a substantive interest in the group's issues. By definition, a group member cannot *formally* fill the role of facilitator. Still, **a group leader or member can use the principles and techniques I describe in this book to help a group.** Effective leaders regularly facilitate their groups as part of their leadership role.

To *intervene* means "to enter into an ongoing system" for the purpose of helping those in the system (Argyris, 1970, p. 15). The definition implies that the system, or group, functions autonomously—that is, the group is complete without a facilitator. Yet the group depends on a facilitator for help. Consequently, **to maintain the group's autonomy and to develop its long-term effectiveness, the facilitator's interventions should decrease the group's dependence on the facilitator.** Ideally, the facilitator accomplishes this by intervening in a way that teaches group members the skills of facilitation.

THE SKILLED FACILITATOR APPROACH

The Skilled Facilitator approach is one approach to facilitation. It is an approach I have been developing since 1980, when I began teaching facilitation skills to others. Facilitation approaches often represent a compilation of techniques and methods without an underlying theoretical framework. **The Skilled Facilitator approach is based on a theory of group facilitation that contains a set of core values and principles and a number of techniques and methods derived** from the core values and principles. It integrates theory into practice to create a values-based, systemic approach to group facilitation. Exhibit 1.1 identifies the key elements of the Skilled Facilitator approach and their purpose.

The Group Effectiveness Model

To help groups become more effective, you need a model of group effectiveness as part of your approach. To be useful, the model needs to be more than descriptive; it has to do more than explain how groups typically function or develop, because many groups develop in a way that is dysfunctional. To be useful, the model needs to be normative; that is, it should tell you what an effective group looks like. **The group effectiveness model identifies the criteria for effective groups, identifies the elements that contribute to effectiveness and the relationships among them, and describes what these elements look like in practice.** The model enables you to identify when groups are having problems, identify the causes that generate the problems, and begin to identify where to intervene to address them. If you are creating new groups, the model helps identify the elements and relationships among them that must be in place to ensure an effective group.

A Clearly Defined Facilitative Role

To help groups, you need a clear definition of your facilitator role so that you and the groups you are helping have a common understanding about the kinds of behavior that are consistent and inconsistent with your facilitator role. This has become more difficult in recent years, as organizations now use the word *facilitator* to indicate many roles. Human resource experts, organization development consultants, trainers, coaches, and even managers have sometimes

Exhibit 1.1. The Skilled Facilitator Approach

- The group effectiveness model
- A clearly defined facilitative role
- Useful in a range of roles
- Explicit core values
- Ground rules for effective groups
- The diagnosis-intervention cycle
- Low-level inferences
- Exploring and changing how we think
- A process for agreeing on how to work together
- A systems approach

been renamed "facilitators." **The Skilled Facilitator approach clearly defines the facilitator role as a substantively neutral person who is not a group member and who works for the entire group.**

The Skilled Facilitator approach distinguishes between two types of facilitation: basic and developmental. In the basic type, the facilitator helps a group solve a substantive problem by essentially lending the group his or her process skills. Once the facilitation is complete, the group has solved its substantive problem, but by design it has not learned how to improve its process. In the developmental type, the facilitator helps a group solve a substantive problem and learn to improve its process at the same time. Here the facilitator also serves as a teacher so the group can eventually become self-facilitating. Developmental facilitation requires significantly more time and facilitator skill, and it is more likely to create fundamental change.

Useful in a Range of Roles

Although I have described the Skilled Facilitator approach as having a substantively neutral third-party facilitator, the approach also recognizes that everyone needs to use facilitative skills even if not a neutral third party or not working in a group or team. So the Skilled Facilitator approach introduces roles in addition to facilitator:

- Facilitative consultant
- Facilitative coach
- Facilitative trainer
- Facilitative leader

All of these roles are based on the same underlying core values and principles as the role of facilitator. In addition, many of my clients have told me that they use the core values and principles outside the workplace, with their families and friends, and see positive results. The approach is broadly applicable because it is based on principles of effective human interaction. Consequently, if you use this approach across your roles in life, you are likely to be viewed by others as acting consistently and with integrity regardless of the situation.

Explicit Core Values

All approaches to facilitation are based on some core values. They are the foundation for an approach and serve as a guide. They enable you to craft new methods and techniques consistent with the core values and to continually reflect on how well you do in acting congruently with the values. But if you are to benefit most from the core values, they need to be explicit. **The Skilled Facilitator approach is based on an explicit set of four core values, and on principles that follow from them** (see Exhibit 1.2). The first three core values come from the work of Chris Argyris and Donald Schön.

Exhibit 1.2. Core Values of the Skilled Facilitator Approach

- Valid information
- Free and informed choice
- Internal commitment
- Compassion

Making core values explicit has several benefits. Because they form the governing ideas of skilled facilitation, rendering them explicit enables you to understand and evaluate them directly rather than having to infer them from the techniques I describe. As you read this book, you can assess whether the various methods and techniques I describe are in fact consistent with the core values. This will help you make an informed choice about whether you want to adopt this approach.

As facilitator, you need not only a set of methods and techniques but also understanding of how and why they work. As I describe the core values and the principles that follow from them, you can see the reasoning that underlies each technique and method of the Skilled Facilitator approach. Once you understand the reasoning, you can improvise and design new methods and techniques consistent with the core values. Without this understanding, you are like a novice baker, who must either follow the recipe as given or make changes without knowing what will happen.

Making the core values explicit also helps you work with groups. You can discuss your approach with potential clients, so that they can make more informed choices about whether to use you as their facilitator. If clients know the core values underlying your approach, they can help you improve your practice, identifying instances when they believe you are acting inconsistently with the values you espoused. Because the core values for facilitation are also the core values for effective group behavior, when you act consistently with the core values, not only do you act effectively as a facilitator, but you also model effective behavior for the group you are working with.

Ground Rules for Effective Groups

As you watch a group in action, you may intuitively know whether the members' conversation is productive even if you cannot identify exactly how they either contribute to or hinder the group's process. **Yet a facilitator needs to understand the specific kinds of behavior that improve a group's process. The Skilled Facilitator approach describes these behaviors in a set of ground rules for effective groups.** The ground rules make specific the abstract core values of facilitation and group effectiveness. Examples of the ground rules are to test assumptions and inferences, share all relevant information, and agree on what important words mean.

The ground rules serve several functions. First, they are a diagnostic tool. By understanding the ground rules, you can quickly identify dysfunctional group behavior, which is inconsistent with the ground rules, so that you can intervene on it. Second, the ground rules are a teaching tool for developing effective group norms. If a group understands the ground rules and commits to using them, the members set new expectations for how to interact with each other. This enables the group to share responsibility for improving process, often a goal of facilitation. Finally, the ground rules guide your behavior as facilitator.

The behavioral ground rules in the Skilled Facilitator approach differ from the more procedural ground rules ("start on time, end on time"; "turn off your pagers and cell phones") that many groups and facilitators use. Procedural ground rules can be helpful, but they do not describe the specific behaviors that lead to effective group process.

The Diagnosis-Intervention Cycle

The group effectiveness model, the core values, and the ground rules for effective groups are all tools for diagnosing behavior in a group. But you still need a way to implement these tools. Specifically, you have to know when to intervene, what kind of intervention to make, how to say it, when to say it, and to whom. To help put these tools into practice, I have developed a six-step process called the diagnosis-intervention cycle. **The cycle is a structured and simple way to think about what is happening in the group and then to intervene in a way that is consistent with the core values.** It serves to guide the facilitator into effective action.

Low-Level Inferences

As a facilitator, you are constantly trying to make sense of what is happening in a group. You watch members say and do things and then you make inferences about what their behavior means and how it is either helping or hindering the group's process. An inference is a conclusion you reach about something that is unknown to you, on the basis of what you have observed. For example, if in a meeting you see someone silently folding his arms across his chest, you may infer that he disagrees with what has been said but is not saying so.

The kinds of inferences you make are critical because they guide what you say when you intervene, and affect how group members react to you. To be effective, you need to make inferences in a way that increases the chance of being accurate, that enables you to share your inferences with the group to see if they disagree, and that does not create defensive reactions in group members when you share your inferences.

The Skilled Facilitator approach accomplishes this by focusing on what I refer to as "low-level" inferences. Essentially, this means that facilitators diagnose and intervene in groups by making the fewest and smallest inferential leaps necessary. Consider two facilitators with different approaches, working with the same group simultaneously and hearing this conversation:

TOM: I want to discuss the start time for the new project. Next week is too soon. We need to wait another month.

SUE: That's not going to work. We need to do it right away. We can't wait.

DON: I think you're both unrealistic. We will be lucky if we can start it in ninety days. I think we should wait until the next fiscal year.

A facilitator making a low-level inference might privately conclude, and then publicly point out, that members have stated their opinions but not explained the reasons for them, nor have they asked other members what leads them to see the situation differently. Observing the same behavior, a facilitator making a high-level inference might privately conclude that the members don't care about others' opinions or are trying to hide something. Making high-level inferences such as this creates a problem when we try to say what we privately think. High-level inferences are further removed from the data that we used to generate them and so may not be accurate. If the inference also contains a negative evaluation of others' motives, sharing the inference can contribute to the group members' responding defensively. **By learning to think and intervene using low-level inferences, we can increase the accuracy of our diagnosis, improve our ability to share our thinking with others, and reduce the chance of creating defensive reactions when we do so.** This ensures that our actions increase rather than decrease the group's effectiveness.

Exploring and Changing How We Think

Facilitation is difficult work because it is demanding—cognitively and emotionally. It is especially difficult when you find yourself in situations you consider potentially embarrassing or psychologically threatening. Research shows that if you are like almost everyone else, in these situations you use a set of core values and think in a way that seeks to unilaterally control the conversation, win the discussion, and minimize expression of negative feelings (Argyris and Schön, 1974). You think of yourself as knowing all you need to know about the situation while thinking others who disagree are uninformed; you think of yourself as being right and others as being wrong; and you think of yourself as having pure motives while others' motives are questionable. All of this leads you to act in ways that create the very results you are trying hard to avoid: misunderstanding, rising conflict, defensive reactions, and the strained relationships and lack of learning that accompany these results. To make matters worse, you are usually unaware of how your thinking leads you to act ineffectively. Rather, if you're like most people you typically attribute the cause of these difficult conversations to how others are thinking and acting.

The same problem that reduces your effectiveness as a facilitator hurts the effectiveness of the group you are seeking to help. Like the facilitator, the group members are also unaware of how they create these problems for themselves.

The Skilled Facilitator approach helps you understand the conditions under which you act ineffectively, and understand how your own thinking leads you to act ineffectively in ways that you are normally unaware of. It offers tools for increasing your effectiveness, particularly in situations you find emotionally difficult. This involves changing not only your techniques but also how you think about or frame situations, and the core values that underlie your approach. This is difficult but rewarding work. By doing this work for yourself, you increase your effectiveness. Then you can help the group learn to reflect on and change the ways they think in difficult situations so that they can work effectively together.

A Process for Agreeing on How to Work Together

Facilitation involves developing a relationship with a group—a psychological contract in which the group gives you permission to help them because they consider you an expert and trustworthy facilitator. Building this relationship is critical because it is the foundation on which you use your facilitator's knowledge and skills; without the foundation, you lose the essential connection with the group that makes your facilitation possible and powerful. To build this relationship, you need a clear understanding and agreement with the group about your role as facilitator and about how you will work with the group to help it accomplish its objectives. I have found that many of the facilitation problems my colleagues and I face stemmed from lack of agreement with the group about how to work together.

The Skilled Facilitator approach describes a process for developing this agreement that enables the facilitator and the group to make an informed and free choice about working together. The process begins when someone first contacts the facilitator about working with the group and continues with a discussion with group members. It identifies who should be involved at each stage of the process, the specific questions to ask, and the type of information to share about your approach to facilitation. The process also describes the issues on which you and the group have to decide if you are to develop an effective working agreement: the objectives of the facilitation, the facilitator's role, and the ground rules to be used. By employing this process, you act consistently with your facilitator role and increase the likelihood of helping the group achieve its goals.

A Systems Approach

Facilitators often tell me stories of how, despite their best efforts to help a group in a difficult situation, the situation gets worse. Each time the facilitator does something to improve things, the situation either deteriorates immediately or temporarily improves before getting even worse. One reason this occurs is that the facilitator is not thinking and acting systemically. In recent years, the field of systems thinking has been receiving the popular attention it deserves, in part through the work of Peter Senge (1990) and his colleagues. The Skilled Facilitator approach uses a systems approach to facilitation. It recognizes that a group is a social system—a collection of parts interacting with each other to function as a whole—and that groups generate their own system dynamics, such as deteriorating trust or continued dependence on the leader. As a facilitator, you enter into this system when you help a group. The challenge is to enter the system—complete with its functional and dysfunctional dynamics—and help the group become more effective without becoming influenced by the system to act ineffectively yourself. **The Skilled Facilitator approach recognizes that any action you take affects the group in multiple ways and has short-term and long-term consequences, some of which may not be obvious. The approach helps you understand how your behavior as facilitator interacts with the group's dynamics to increase or decrease the group's effectiveness.**

For example, a facilitator who privately pulls aside a team member who, she believes, is dominating the group, may in the short run seem to improve the team's discussion. But this action may also have several unintended negative consequences. The pulled-aside member may feel that the facilitator is not representing the team's opinion and may see the facilitator as biased against him, thereby reducing her credibility with that member. Even if the facilitator is reflecting the other team members' opinions, the team may come increasingly to depend on her to deal with its issues, thereby reducing rather than increasing the team's ability to function.

Using a systems approach to facilitation has many implications, a number of which are central to understanding the Skilled Facilitator approach. One key implication is treating the entire group as the client rather than only the formal group leader or the member who contacted you. This increases the chance of having the trust and credibility of the entire group, which is essential in serving as an effective facilitator.

A second implication is that effective facilitator behavior and effective group member behavior are the same thing. Taking into account that the facilitator is substantively neutral and not a group member, the Skilled Facilitator approach does not have different sets of rules for the facilitator and group members. Just as you use the core values and ground rules to guide your own behavior, you use them to teach group members how they can act effectively. Consequently, when you act consistently with the core values and ground rules, you serve as a model for the group. The more that group members learn about how you work, the better they understand how to create effective group process. Ultimately, as group members model effective facilitator behavior, they become self-facilitating.

A third key implication is that to be effective, your system of facilitation needs to be internally consistent. This means that how you diagnose and intervene in a group and how you develop agreement with the group all need to be based on a congruent set of principles. Many facilitators develop their approach by borrowing methods and techniques from a variety of other approaches. There is nothing inherently wrong with this; but if the methods and techniques are based on conflicting values or principles, they can undermine the facilitator's effectiveness as well as that of the groups they work with. For example, a facilitator who states that her client is the entire group and yet automatically agrees to individual requests by the group's leader may soon find herself in the middle of a conflict between the group and its leader, rather than helping to facilitate the entire group. By thinking and acting systemically, you increase your long-term ability to help groups.

THE EXPERIENCE OF FACILITATION

Facilitation is challenging work that calls forth a range of emotions. Part of this work involves helping group members deal productively with their emotions while they are addressing difficult issues. But it is equally important to deal with your own emotions as facilitator. **Because your emotions and how you deal with them profoundly determine your effectiveness, the Skilled Facilitator approach involves understanding how you as a facilitator feel during facilitation and using these feelings productively.**

These feelings are about yourself and the group you are working with. For example, you may feel excited after a group calls with a new request to do interesting and important work. Your excitement may turn to worry or anxiety, though, as you wonder whether you are skilled enough to really help the group.

Throughout the facilitation, various events trigger your own reactions. You may feel satisfied, having helped a group work through a particularly difficult problem, or proud to see the group using some of the skills they have learned from you. Yet, when your work goes so smoothly that the group doesn't recognize your contribution, you may feel unappreciated. When the group is feeling confused and uncertain how to proceed in their task, you may be feeling the same way about the facilitation. If your actions do not help the group as well as you would like, you may feel ashamed because your work doesn't meet your own standards. You may be frustrated by a group's inability to manage conflict even if you have been asked to help the members because they are having problems managing conflict. You may feel sad watching a group act in a way that creates the very consequences the members are trying to avoid, feel happy that you can identify this dynamic in the group, and feel hopeful seeing that the group's pain is creating motivation for change.

I have experienced each of these feelings as a facilitator. They are part of the internal work of facilitation. If I can presume that readers of this book attribute to me some expert level of knowledge and skill as a facilitator, then for some readers my disclosure may come as a relief. You yourself may be thinking, *If he wrote a book on facilitation and has these feelings himself, then what I feel must be normal also.* Or my disclosure may raise your anxiety if you are thinking something like, *If he is skilled enough to write this book about facilitation and still has these feelings, how long am I going to have to deal with these feelings?* One answer lies not so much in whether you or I have these feelings but rather in our awareness of them in ourselves and in others, and our ability to manage these feelings productively—what some refer to as emotional intelligence (Goleman, 1995; Salovey and Mayer, 1990). Although there are many ways to improve my facilitation skills that do not focus on dealing with my emotions, my use of any of these skills becomes more powerful if I am attuned to my feelings and to others and deal with them productively.

When I discuss these feelings with colleagues, I find that although the specific situations that trigger our emotions and our specific responses may vary, our own feelings are a significant part of our work as facilitators.

In this book, I do not address all of the issues related to the emotions you may experience in facilitation. But I do identify some of those you are likely to experience in certain situations, and I offer an approach for effectively dealing with your emotions. I hope this serves as both a guide to what you might encounter, recognizing that people may have varying reactions to the same situation, and as a support, so that when you experience these feelings you will know you are not alone and that it comes with the territory.

Through facilitating groups, you can also come to know yourself by reflecting on how you react to certain situations, understanding the sources of your feelings, and learning how to work with your feelings productively. In doing so, you not only help yourself but in turn increase your ability to help the groups with which you work—the people who face the same issues.

MAKING THE SKILLED FACILITATOR APPROACH YOUR OWN

Part of learning this approach is integrating it with your own style—making it your own. Throughout the book, as you read examples of what I would say in various situations, sometimes you may think that the words are natural and make sense; other times, you may think *This sounds awkward; I can't imagine myself saying those words.* You are likely to have the same experience as you begin to practice using this approach with groups. This awkward feeling is a common one, stemming partly from learning a new approach.

But it can also stem from trying to force-fit my style to yours. You can't be me (and I don't assume you would want to). When I was first learning how to use the core values in facilitation, I tried hard to imitate Chris Argyris, from whom I learned the core values in graduate school at Harvard. As deeply as I respected Chris—and still do—our styles are different; I could not intervene exactly as he did and still sound like me. (My colleague Dick McMahon would sometimes remind me of this by calling me "little Chris.") It was not until I found my own voice that the approach became mine. I assume the same is true for you. **Learning to use the core values and principles is a journey; part of the journey is finding your own voice.** Welcome to the journey.

SUMMARY

The Skilled Facilitator approach is one approach to facilitation. Based on a set of core values and using a systems thinking approach, it enables you to clearly define your facilitator role and develop explicit agreement with a group about how you will work together. Together, the core values, the group effectiveness model, the ground rules, and the diagnosis-intervention cycle help you identify functional and dysfunctional aspects of the group and intervene to help the group increase its effectiveness. The approach enables you to explore and change how you think, to improve your ability to facilitate difficult situations. It also helps groups explore and change their thinking, to help them create fundamental change. The core values, principles, and methods of the Skilled Facilitator approach are equally applicable to facilitative leaders, consultants, coaches, and trainers.

As I said earlier, one of the elements of the Skilled Facilitator approach is the group effectiveness model. Chapter Two describes the model and shows how you can use it to help a group identify problems and address them.

CHAPTER TWO

What Makes
Work Groups Effective?

Because you are called on to help groups become more effective, it is important to have a model of group effectiveness as part of your approach. To be useful, the model needs to tell you what an effective group looks like. In this chapter, I describe a group effectiveness model and how to use it. We begin by defining what makes a work group; identifying criteria for assessing a group's effectiveness; and then discussing how a group's process, structure, and organizational context contribute to effectiveness. The chapter concludes with discussion of the potential and the limits of facilitation in creating an effective group.

You probably have had a variety of experiences working in groups. For most people, the experience is mixed. In some groups, the members work well together, accomplish the task, and meet some of each member's needs. In other groups, the task is done poorly (if at all), the members do not work well together, and members feel frustrated. What factors, according to the members, might contribute to the group's success? For example, do they have clear goals? Do the members agree on how they should work together? What factors might members say contribute to the group's ineffectiveness? Is there undiscussed conflict? Are members not motivated by the tasks? Are they missing certain expertise?

The answers to these questions begin to describe a model of group effectiveness. I think of a model as a particular way to see and think about something. The group effectiveness model is like a special pair of glasses (or contact lenses, in my case) that enable you to see and understand what is determining the group's effectiveness. Each of us has a model about what makes a group effective, even if the model includes only two or three elements. Even if you are not conscious of your model, you still use it to guide your diagnosis and intervention, to decide where to look when things go wrong, and to know what to change.

As George Box, mentor of W. Edwards Deming said, "All models are wrong; some are useful." Because a model is a simplified way to describe how something works—in this case, a group—it does not need to capture all the complexities of what it attempts to model. But if your model of a group is underdeveloped, it limits your ability to help the group.

To draw an analogy, one difference between my auto mechanic and me is that when he looks at my car engine, he can figure out what is wrong because he has a model in his head of which engine parts should be present, what they should look like, how they should interact, and what the output should be. By comparing his mental model of the engine with the actual engine, he can identify what might be missing or malfunctioning. In contrast, my mental model of an engine is primitive; I don't know many of the parts or how they should function together. So I have found myself staring at the car en gine with my mechanic, without a clue about where to look, as he points out a faulty part that I didn't know should be part of the engine to begin with.

Not knowing the details of how an engine works used to bother me, but I've made peace with the fact that I can rely on others to know this for me and to fix my car. As a facilitator (or facilitative leader), you do not have this option when it comes to groups. Here, my analogy breaks down because the interaction in a group is more complex than in an engine, and because the facilitator is not a fixer. Still, **you need a model of groups that shows you what an effective group looks like, the elements that contribute to its effectiveness, and how the elements should interact.** Then you can use the model to help members of a group diagnose problems they are having, and help them make changes to improve their effectiveness.

THE GROUP EFFECTIVENESS MODEL

The group effectiveness model contains several parts. First, I define what it means to be a work group. Second, I identify criteria for an effective group. Third, I describe the factors and elements that interact to create an effective group. The model in this chapter (see Figure 2.1) draws on the work of J. Richard Hackman (1987) and Eric Sundstrom, Kenneth P. De Meuse, and David Futrell (1990).

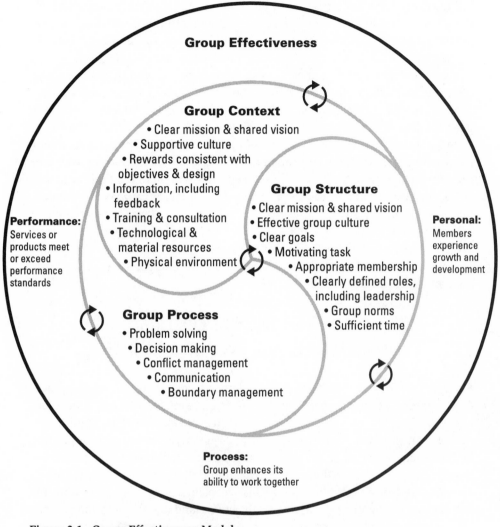

Figure 2.1. Group Effectiveness Model

Source: Adapted from Hackman, 1987, and Sundstrom, De Meuse, and Futtrell, 1990.

WHAT IS A WORK GROUP?

To discuss what makes an effective work group, we need to first consider the term *work group,* which has certain characteristics. First, a work group has a collective responsibility for performing one or more tasks, and the outcome of the tasks can be assessed. The outcome may be a product, service, or decision.

Second, a work group is a social system. It has boundaries that distinguish members from nonmembers; in addition, the members have specific roles and are interdependent in producing their work. Sometimes, a group is formed from representatives of two or more interdependent groups, as with a cross-functional team or a union-management group. A set of people working on similar but essentially individual tasks is not a work group.

Third, a work group operates in a larger context, which requires managing its transactions with other individuals, with groups, and sometimes with organizations. Examples of groups that have these three characteristics are a board of directors, a task force, or a work team.

In summary, **a work group is a set of people with specific interdependent roles who are collectively responsible for producing some output (service, product, or decision) that can be assessed, and who manage their relationships with those outside the group.** In this definition, what makes a group is the presence of key structural elements rather than the level of motivation or effectiveness of its members. In recent years, many people have used the word *team* to describe what I define as an effective group (Katzenbach and Smith, 1993). In this book, I use the terms *group* and *team* interchangeably, recognizing that either can be more or less effective.

THREE EFFECTIVENESS CRITERIA: PERFORMANCE, PROCESS, AND PERSONAL

Before answering the question of what elements contribute to a work group's effectiveness, we need to first consider what it means for a group to be effective. An effective work group meets the three criteria listed in Exhibit 2.1. Rather than simply measure the quality and quantity of the service or product against some objective or internal group standard, the first criterion—*performance*—uses the expectations and satisfaction of the group's customers to determine whether the service or product is acceptable. There are two reasons for this. First, many groups do not have objective standards of performance that can be measured clearly or easily. Second, because the group is a system, the value of its output depends greatly on those outside the group, who either evaluate its performance directly or receive its products or services, more than on any objective performance index alone. This criterion reinforces the idea that a group must respond to the demands of its customers if it is to be effective (Katz and Kahn, 1978; Zeithaml, Parasuraman, and Berry, 1990). A group must meet the demands of two types of customer: internal (those inside the organization who either receive the group's work or evaluate its performance) and external (those outside the organization who receive the group's work). The group's own standards for performance are still important, but they do not replace the assessments of others.

The second criterion, which I call *process,* takes into account that most groups work together over an extended period on a series of tasks. Consequently, the

Exhibit 2.1. Three Criteria for Effective Groups

Performance: The services that the group delivers or the products it makes meet or exceed the performance standards of the people who receive it, use it, or review it.

Process: The processes and structures used to carry out the work maintain and preferably enhance the ability of members to work together on subsequent group tasks.

Personal: The group experience contributes to the growth and well-being of its members.

Source: Adapted from Hackman (1987).

processes and structures they use must enable them to work together in a way that enhances their ability to do so in the future. For example, group processes that burn out members or that erode trust among members reduce their capability to work together on subsequent group tasks. Having a process and skills for reflecting on their behavior in order to learn from it becomes an essential tool for meeting the second criterion.

The third criterion, which I call *personal,* is that the group experience contributes to the growth and well-being of its members. Group members reasonably expect that through their work group they can meet some of their personal needs—say, doing work that is important or that makes a difference in others' lives, or the need to feel competent, or the need to learn. The members' needs can also lead them to set their own standards of quality for their service or product. In the long run, a group that does not meet its members' needs is less effective than one that does.

To be effective, the group must meet all three criteria, which are interrelated. For example, consider a group in which members manage conflict such that trust among the members is diminished. This in turn leads members to withhold information from each other. As a result, key information is not available to the full group, and the quality of the service the group produces begins to drop. Finally, members' personal needs for feeling competent suffer as they find themselves part of a group with declining quality and no means of solving the problem. As this example illustrates, if in the long run one criterion is not met, it affects the other two criteria. Groups are not, however, either effective or ineffective; their effectiveness is measured on a continuum of effectiveness.

Three factors contribute to group effectiveness: group process, group structure, and group context (Hackman, 1987; Hackman, 1990). Each factor has a number of elements (Figure 2.1). On the one hand, group process and group structure can be thought of as characteristics of a group. The group context, on the other hand, comprises elements of the larger organization that are relevant to the group's structure and process. The interrelationships among group process, group structure, and group context are complex. For now, it is sufficient to say that each element can influence the others, as illustrated by the arrows in the diagram. As I will discuss later in this chapter, **facilitators intervene primarily through a group's process and structure, enabling the group to examine and perhaps change its process, structure, and group context.**

GROUP PROCESS

Process refers to *how* things are done, rather than what is done. To be effective, a group must manage a number of processes, which are shaded in Figure 2.2. Two primary group processes are problem solving and decision making.

Problem Solving

Except for a group that has a mission to carry out orders without asking questions or making judgments, problem solving is a central part of any group's activities. A problem is simply a gap between what is desired and what exists. For example, a problem exists when a product is shipped to customers in

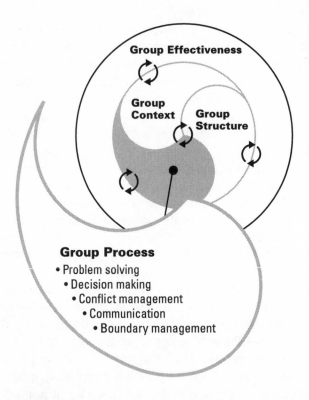

Figure 2.2. Group Process Within the Group Effectiveness Model

ten days when the customers expect the product within three days. Problem solving is the systematic approach a group uses to identify a problem, establish criteria for evaluating potential solutions, collect relevant information, identify the causes of the problem, evaluate and select a solution, implement it, and evaluate it.

A group with an effective problem-solving process meets two conditions. First, members use a systematic process for solving problems that is appropriate for the problem they are trying to solve. This seems obvious, but many groups do not use a systematic approach. Members often begin to solve the problem by suggesting solutions before agreeing on the problem or its causes. Consequently, potential causes are not considered, and the group's solution does not solve the problem. Similarly, if a group does not consider the effect of its solution over time and throughout the system, the members can solve one problem in a way that creates more difficult ones. The second condition for effective problem solving is that all members focus on the same step of the process at the same time. A group gets off track when some members are trying to identify the cause of the problem and other members are already proposing a solution.

Decision Making

Decision making involves reaching a conclusion or making a choice. In a problem-solving process, people think of the decision as the point at which the group selects the best solution from among several choices. But a group makes many decisions in the process of solving a problem, such as how to define the problem and what information should be considered in evaluating solutions. Decision making includes who should be involved when, in what decisions, and how those involved will decide.

In an effective decision-making process, a number of people are involved: those responsible for planning, those responsible for implementing the decision, those affected directly by the decision, and those affected indirectly or who can influence whether or how the solution is implemented. The core values of facilitation state that the group includes people who have the relevant information about the problem and its causes, its solutions, and potential effects.

How should members decide? Groups have various ways of deciding. In some cases, the leader of the group decides alone, with or without consulting other members. In other cases, the leader becomes a member of the group with the same influence (theoretically) as other members. In still other cases, the leader delegates the problem solving to other group members, agreeing to implement any decision they reach, given certain criteria. If more than one person is to make the decision, they need to decide whether they will do so by consensus, majority vote, or some other means. **The core values of facilitation state that a group is more effective if the group is internally committed to its choices.**

Conflict Management

An effective group considers conflict a natural part of group life; if it is managed well, conflict improves members' ability to accomplish their task, work together, and contribute to personal growth. They use conflict to learn more about the problem and how others see it, rather than to simply persuade people that they are right and others are wrong. They assume that others have relevant information they may not have, that others are well intended, and that their own solution may be missing something, instead of assuming that others are uninformed or misinformed and have ulterior motives.

To do this, members share previously hidden thoughts and feelings and openly test any difference of opinion. They can openly disagree without fear of retribution. Unlike a group that avoids conflict to help a member save face, members of an effective group openly confront each other, believing that each person is strong enough to receive negative feedback directly. Ultimately, an effective group resolves conflict so that not only does the conflict remain resolved but also members understand how the conflict arose, how they contributed to it, and how they can act differently to prevent unnecessary conflict (Eiseman, 1978). The core values and ground rules of the Skilled Facilitator approach are central to managing conflict effectively.

Communication

The communication process is embedded in all other group processes. Essentially, communication involves exchanging information such that the sender and receiver understand the meaning in the same way. An effective group communicates in a way that creates valid information. The ground rules and core values of the Skilled Facilitator approach describe elements of effective communication. I refer to several of them here.

To generate valid information, members share not just their opinions and conclusions but also how they arrived at them. In other words, they make their reasoning explicit, by sharing their intent, the assumptions and inferences they made, the information and examples they used, and the logical steps they went through to arrive at a conclusion. They encourage others to identify gaps in their reasoning and ask others to share their own reasoning as well.

Whenever possible, members communicate directly with each other, rather than using an intermediary, to ensure that their meaning has been received as they intended it and to be able to respond to questions and concerns that might arise. In a group meeting, members seek reaction to their comments to focus the conversation and move it forward, avoiding a series of unrelated monologues in which member after member states her or his views.

Members openly express disagreement with any other member, regardless of difference in position or status. The individuals offer specific examples to illustrate a view rather than communicating only in the abstract. For example, a member might say, "We had a problem with inventory. Last Friday, we scheduled assembly of Model 2800 and had only fifteen of the forty primary switches needed for assembly"; contrast this with saying "We had some problems last week scheduling production." If a member makes an inference about another, the person tests out the inference to determine whether it is valid.

In an effective group, members test out their assumptions and inferences to determine if they are valid, rather than simply acting as if they are true. For example, if the leader states that the group needs to focus on a particular project, a member would test his or her inference that the leader also wants them to give lower priority to the other group projects.

Testing inferences applies to nonverbal communication as well. Many books have been written to help in identifying what certain body language means and how to convey things to people (such as how to ask someone to stop talking) without saying anything directly. In an effective group, members communicate directly rather than use nonverbal behavior, which is easily misinterpreted. In some cultures, for instance, putting one's feet on the table is considered disrespectful; I once facilitated a meeting at which one member accused another of not having respect for her because he propped his feet on the table. It turned out that the other member had an illness that required him to keep his legs elevated.

Finally, an effective group deals with undiscussable issues—the important issues, relevant to the group's task—that members often believe they cannot discuss openly in the group without negative consequences.

Boundary Management

An effective work group manages its relationships with the organization by simultaneously differentiating itself and coordinating with the organization. Groups need to establish boundaries in order to function (Schein, 1988). In an effective group, members can articulate the group's task and what they are responsible for accomplishing, so that they do not take on tasks unrelated to their purpose and outside the group's expertise. Similarly, they know what kind of authority and autonomy the group has.

At the same time, a group must coordinate its work with other parts of the organization to produce a service or product. This includes deciding what information to share and how, what tasks each party performs, and how decisions are made. For example, a product design team needs to coordinate its work with marketing and manufacturing teams to determine whether the proposed product design meets customer needs and can be manufactured. A group also needs to manage boundaries to ensure that the larger organization provides the materials, technology, people, and information needed to accomplish the task. Some groups also have to manage boundaries directly with the external customers of the organization.

The Relationship Among Group Processes

Although this chapter discusses each process separately, in reality a group uses many processes simultaneously as its members work together. For example, in solving a problem, a group also makes decisions about who will be involved and manages conflict that arises if members disagree about what to do. Of course, all of the group's conversation is communication. Similarly, when a group manages its boundaries, it also solves problems, manages conflict, and communicates with other parts of the organization or people outside. Segmenting the group's behavior into processes simply helps a facilitator and the group understand more clearly how the group is acting effectively or ineffectively. But because the group is a system, each process is related to the other elements of the model; so any intervention to improve one process needs to take into account the effect on other parts of the model.

How Group Process Increases Group Effectiveness

A group applies its problem-solving, decision-making, and other processes to solve problems associated with the particular services or products for which they are responsible. A group of auto engineers and scientists may use a problem-solving process to determine how to improve the fuel efficiency of a car, while a group of executives may use a problem-solving process to determine how to reduce redundant personnel resulting from a merger.

But groups also use their processes to identify and solve problems that arise from their process, structure, and organizational context. The group's process is the means by which it increases effectiveness. In other words, the group relies on its processes to help identify and solve problems caused by ineffective group structure, organizational context, and even ineffective group process. **In one way, group processes, especially a group's problem-solving process, represent the group's ability to diagnose and intervene on any elements that limit its effectiveness.**

GROUP STRUCTURE

An effective group requires an effective structure. Group structure (shaded in Figure 2.3) refers to the relatively stable characteristics of a group, including mission and vision, tasks, membership, roles each member fills, the time members have available, members' shared values and beliefs, and norms. Unlike the structure of a building or the human body, group structure has no physical counterpart. In fact, group structure is simply a stable, recurring group process that results from members' constantly interacting with each other in certain ways (Allport, 1967). It is the causal relationships among the repeating cycle of activities that create structure. You do not "see" structure directly; you see the

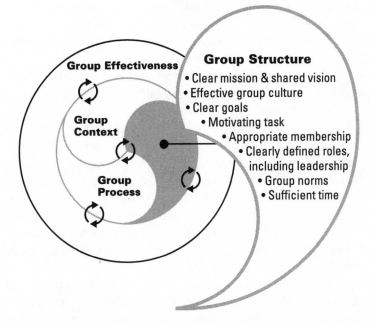

Figure 2.3. Group Structure Within the Group Effectiveness Model

resulting behavior that the structure generates. But understanding the dynamic relationships that create the structure is important because changing the relationships in the activity changes the structure.

Clear Mission and Shared Vision

A group's mission answers the question "Why do we exist?" A group attempts to achieve its mission by accomplishing various goals, which in turn are achieved by performing various tasks. A vision is a mental picture of the future that a group seeks to create. Whereas mission clarifies why the group exists, vision identifies what the group should look like and how it should act as it seeks to accomplish its mission. In an effective group, members can articulate their mission and vision, find it engaging, and use it to guide their work.

Effective Group Culture

Along with mission and vision, group culture embraces the guiding ideas for the group. Group culture is the set of fundamental values and beliefs that members of a group share and that guide their behavior. A belief is an assumption about what is true (for example, "people are naturally motivated to do a good job"). A value is an assumption about what is worthwhile or desirable (for example, "maintaining honesty at all times"). In an effective group, members can articulate the group's core values and beliefs, and they take actions and make decisions that are consistent with the shared values and beliefs. If a group's culture is consistent with effective management principles, the group can be positively influenced by the culture. For example, a group that values quality service is likely to seek and respond to customer suggestions for improving service. However, if the group's culture is inconsistent with effective management principles, the group can be negatively influenced; if a group believes that conflict is to be avoided or else won rather than seen as an opportunity for learning, then the group is not likely to learn from its own conflict.

I believe the core values of the Skilled Facilitator approach contribute to a culture of effective group process. Unfortunately, groups—and organizations generally—rarely have these core values as part of their culture. You cannot identify a group's culture simply by listening to what members say they value or believe. Members often espouse values and beliefs that are inconsistent with their actions and are often unaware of the inconsistency (Argyris and Schön, 1974). The values and beliefs that constitute the group's culture can be inferred by observing the artifacts of the culture (Schein, 1985), including how members act. An artifact is a product of the culture—a policy, a procedure, or a structure that members create. Inferring values and beliefs is a primary method that developmental facilitators use to help a group examine its process.

Clear Goals

Whether a group sets its own goals or receives them from the larger organization, an effective group has a clear goal that is consistent with the organization's mission and vision and that allows members to select the means by which they achieve the goals. Clear goals enable a group to measure its progress toward achieving them. Without clear goals, a group has difficulty solving problems and making decisions, and this often leads to conflict.

A Motivating Group Task

To claim a real group task, group members must be interdependent with each other in accomplishing the task and share collective responsibility for the group's output. The group's task is the work the group performs to accomplish its goal. However, the task and the goal are not the same. For example, if a goal is to ensure that the public has safe housing, a group may perform the tasks of inspecting dwellings and educating the public. Tasks that motivate group members meet certain conditions (Hackman, 1987):

- The group task requires members to use a variety of their skills.
- The group task is a whole and meaningful piece of work with a visible outcome.
- The outcomes of a group task have significant consequences, either for customers or for others in the organization.

- The group task gives members significant autonomy over how they accomplish the task so that they feel ownership of their work.
- Working on the group task generates regular and trustworthy feedback to group members about how well the group is performing.

Appropriate Membership

An effective group has a membership that is carefully selected according to several criteria. First, the members bring an appropriate mix of knowledge and skills to successfully complete the task. A task force formed to resolve conflict among groups should include a representative of each group to represent that perspective.

Second, the group is just large enough to handle the task. Every additional member requires that the group spend additional time coordinating activities. A group with more members than it needs to complete the task spends time on coordination that could be spent working directly on the task. In addition, as the group grows, members can lose interest in the work and reduce their effort.

Finally, the composition of the group should be stable enough that the group can maintain its continuity of effort, yet be fluid enough to ensure that members do not all think the same way and discourage new or differing ideas. A group that is perpetually losing and replacing members spends much time orienting the new members and learning how to work together (Schwarz, 1991).

The values and beliefs that members bring to the group shape the group's culture and, in turn, how it works. The Skilled Facilitator approach is based on a set of core values that contribute to creating an effective group.

Clearly Defined Roles, Including Leadership

A group comprises individuals filling interdependent roles. In an effective group, members understand clearly what role each member plays and what behavior people expect in each role. In a surgical team, members need to know who directly assists the surgeon, who monitors patient data, who gets supplies, and who handles paperwork. If roles are understood clearly and agreed upon, members can coordinate their actions to complete the task. Without clear, agreed-upon roles, members are likely to experience conflict and stress.

In some groups, each member fills only one role; in others, the members are capable of filling all the roles in the group and often shift roles. An example of the latter situation is seen when members take turns leading the group.

In theory, a position description identifies the set of behaviors expected for that role so that behavior is consistent, regardless of who fills the role. In practice, the role a person plays results from a combination of the formally defined role, the individual's personality, the person's understanding of the role, the expectations that others have for that role, and the interpersonal relationships that the person has with others in the group (Katz and Kahn, 1978). This means that different people may fill the same role somewhat differently. Consequently, an effective group clarifies its roles as the task changes or as members change.

One key role is that of leader. In an effective group, members understand and support the leader role. Defining this role includes deciding what kinds of decisions the leader is involved in and to what extent; what kinds of group tasks the leader performs; how the leader helps the group obtain resources and manage the boundaries with the larger organization; and how the leader helps group members manage conflict. Defining the leader role means defining the relationship between the leader and other group members regarding how the group handles its processes, structures, and organizational context. How the leader role is filled and whether it is filled by one person or shared by several depends in part on the extent to which the group intends to be self-directed. As a group becomes more self-directed, more elements of the leadership role are integrated into the roles of the members. Chapter Fourteen describes the facilitative leader role in detail.

Group Norms

A norm is an expectation about how people should or should not behave that all or many group members share. Norms stem from the values and beliefs that constitute the group's culture. The ground rules for effective groups are a set of group norms that are based on the core values and beliefs of the Skilled Facilitator approach.

A group can develop a norm regarding anything. It may be that members should help each other when someone is facing a deadline, that members should not talk negatively about the group to non–group members, or that members should not openly question the leader's decisions. Regarding this last norm, if it is shared then they may agree to do things they have concerns about, without understanding the leader's decisions.

Norms are important in integrating members into the group by helping them predict how others will act in a given situation and by constituting a guide for member behavior. Not all group norms help a group become effective, however; a norm might be that "the leader will take responsibility for solving group members' problems," or "don't openly state any concern you have about how the group is working." In addition, a group norm may be different from an individual member's personal view. A member may prefer not to rotate tasks among group members, believing that it reduces efficiency; but he may do so because that is the expectation. In this way, norms also influence conformity.

In an effective group, members explicitly discuss and agree on the norms that they want to guide their group. They also agree to hold each other accountable for following the norms by raising the issue if someone acts in a way that they believe is inconsistent with the norms. When a new member joins the group, it reviews the norms so that the new person does not first learn about them by violating one and being told "that's not the way we do things here." Chapter Five introduces a set of group norms, called ground rules, for effective groups.

Sufficient Time

Obviously, a group needs enough time to complete its tasks and achieve its goals. Specifically, a group needs two kinds of time: performance time and capacity-building time. During performance time, the group produces its product or service. During capacity-building time, the group engages in activities that help build capacity to improve performance. Examples are redesigning the flow of work to increase efficiency, learning to use new software to generate better performance data, or reflecting on how the group managed a conflict so as to improve its skills. Sometimes a group performs and builds capacity simultaneously, as in a facilitated meeting in which members are learning to improve how to productively resolve a real conflict they are currently facing. But if these two modes are mixed, the group's normal rate of performance slows down, in order to ultimately speed it up.

Typically, a group spends too little time on building capacity. An effective group thinks and acts systemically about the relationship between performance time and capacity-building time. The individuals recognize that to perform at a level meeting or exceeding constantly rising external standards, they must devote time to improving their group process and structure; initially, the amount of time they take from performance is more than compensated for later if they choose their capacity-building efforts well. In systems thinking, people refer to this as going slow to go fast.

GROUP CONTEXT

The group context, shown in Figure 2.4, includes aspects of the larger organization that influence the group's effectiveness but that the group usually does not control. An effective group recognizes that, although it may not control the group context, it might influence the larger organization to create a more supportive context. The group seeks to do so, rather than assuming that the larger organization cannot be influenced and that the members are powerless to effect change. Understanding the group context helps a facilitator identify how the larger organization is likely to help or hinder a group's efforts to improve effectiveness. It also helps identify the extent to which facilitation alone can help a group.

A Clear Mission and a Shared Vision

The organization's mission and vision furnish the context for the group's own mission and vision. An effective group understands and shares the organization's mission and vision and makes group decisions consistent with them.

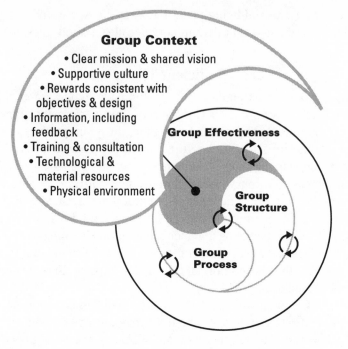

Figure 2.4. Group Context Within the Group Effectiveness Model

Sometimes, a group does not know the organizational mission or vision or does not understand the logic of it. In this situation, an effective group asks others to explain the mission or vision rather than ignoring it or complaining within their group that others have not made it clear.

Supportive Organizational Culture

Group culture refers to the set of values and beliefs that are generally shared by members of a group; *organizational culture* refers to the set of values and beliefs that members of an organization generally share and that guide their behavior. Because each group can have its own culture and because groups differ with respect to function, the professionals it may employ, and the demographic characteristics of the members, a group's culture may differ from the overall culture in the organization.

A group is more effective if the organizational culture is supportive. This means the organizational culture is consistent with effective management principles, including the core values of the Skilled Facilitator approach. Unfortunately, as I noted earlier, organizations rarely hold the core values as part of their culture (Argyris, 1990); altering an organizational culture is perhaps the most difficult kind of change to create. Therefore a strong, ineffective organizational culture can make it difficult for a group to sustain any increase in effectiveness.

Rewards Consistent with Group Objectives and Design

An organization influences groups by rewarding certain behaviors. To create an effective group, the organization rewards behavior that is consistent with the group's objectives. If, for example, a construction crew's objective is to build quality homes, then rewarding the group solely according to the number of homes it builds unintentionally encourages members to increase the reward at the expense of work quality. It would be more consistent with the group's objective to reward members also for the quality of their construction.

Rewarding the group consistently with its design means rewarding the group as a group. If the group task is designed so that it requires the effort of all members, at least part of the reward should be made to the group as a whole. If an organization espouses teamwork and then rewards only individually, it sends a mixed message, undermines credibility, and creates potential conflict among group members that is sure to reduce the group's effectiveness (Kerr, 1975).

A colleague of mine consulted to an organization that gave a financial reward for suggestions that reduced costs. A team submitted a suggestion and won a reward but was told by human resources that the reward could only be given to an individual. The team responded that they had thought of and developed the idea as a team, building on each other's ideas, and could no longer identify which individuals contributed which ideas. Having been required to make what they considered an arbitrary distinction, the group fell into conflict, and performance as a team declined. My point is not that an organization should confer only team rewards to a team (a balance of team and individual rewards seems more congruent), but rather that how the rewards are given should be congruent with how the work was done.

Information, Including Feedback About Performance

An effective group has access to the valid and relevant information needed to perform the work, whether it is information about markets, staffing, production scheduling or costs, or other topics. Similarly, an effective group has access to information about the constraints within which the members must make their own decisions and the effects that the decisions will have on other parts of the organization. A product design group has to know what constraints are placed on the design and how their design affects the ability to market, engineer, and produce the product. An effective group also solicits and receives feedback about the group's performance, including working relationships with other parts of the organization. This enables the members to continually improve their performance.

Training and Consultation

Effective groups have access to training and consultation to help them increase their knowledge, develop skills, and solve problems necessary to perform tasks. The resources may be task-related, such as learning how to improve the technical accuracy of their work, or process-related, such as learning how to manage conflict within the group.

Technology and Material Resources

Technology is the means by which a group converts or transforms its raw materials into a product or service. A health care team uses medical technology and health education to help sick people become healthy and to keep healthy people from becoming sick. A top management team uses organizational mission and vision, and information about the marketplace and the strengths and weaknesses of the organization, to make strategic choices. Faculty members use various teaching and learning methods to help uneducated students become learned students. Material resources include the tools, supplies, and raw materials needed for the finished product or service. An effective group has access to the materials and technology necessary to accomplish its goals. In particular, computer technology that enables group members to communicate and coordinate their work becomes critical as groups increasingly have members who are not located at the same physical location.

Physical Environment That Fits the Group's Needs

Within the organization, the physical environment refers to where members are physically located and how their physical space is designed. Most of us have experienced the difference between a space that makes working easy and a space that makes it difficult. The same is true for groups. An effective group has a workspace that is designed to meet the demands of the work. This may mean designing space for meetings, private conversation, viewing a large document, easy access to other groups, or other needs. Group members do not necessarily have to be physically located at the same site; in a virtual group the members are in different locations and coordinate their work largely by computer and phone. Still, the physical space in which virtual group members work is designed to meet their needs.

INTERORGANIZATIONAL GROUPS

To simplify the discussion about what makes a group effective, I have assumed that all group members work for the same organization. Clearly, this is not always the case. First, a facilitator may help a group whose members form an umbrella organization, such as an association of organizations. Here, members share a common cause, but each member represents the interests of one organization to the umbrella organization. Second, a facilitator may also assist groups that are not an organization or part of a larger organization but whose members represent different organizations; an example is a group that deals with environmental issues and includes representatives from business, labor, and environmental entities and government agencies.

An interorganizational group has structural and process elements that are similar to those of other groups. However, the interorganizational group is subject to the organizational cultural influences of each organization that the group represents. Consider a group composed of a representative from a division of state government, an environmental organization, a home builder's association, and a real estate association. The environmental organization influences the group's functioning through its representative, the state government agency shapes the group's functioning through its representative, and so on. In addition, the group is subject to the influences of related organizations not represented. In short, an interorganizational group operates in a complex organizational context, which makes group facilitation quite challenging.

HOW THE MODEL HELPS FACILITATORS

The group effectiveness model helps you determine whether a group is being effective, identify which factors and elements that contribute to effectiveness are missing or present, decide how to intervene to help a group become more effective, and determine whether facilitation alone can improve group effectiveness.

First, you can use the three criteria for group effectiveness to help determine initially whether and how a group is working ineffectively. Ineffective groups will, over time, fail to meet at least one criterion.

Next, you can consider how each element identified in the model may contribute to the group's ineffectiveness. The model implies there are predictable issues that a group must resolve if it is to be effective. **You can think of each element of the model (supportive culture, clearly defined roles, group norms, and so on) as a piece of a puzzle that has to fit together for the group to be effective. Each element also represents a foreseeable problem that a**

group must solve, and keep solved, in order to be effective. Each factor (structure, process, group context) and each constituent element plays a unique role in making a group effective. The strength of one factor or element cannot compensate for the weakness of another. For example, by itself a good structure cannot guarantee competent group behavior; it can only create conditions that make it easier for group members to take advantage of their knowledge, skills, and process. Similarly, effective group process can take advantage of a sound structure and supportive group context but cannot alone create the resources necessary to sustain a group. Finally, a supportive group context can provide ongoing resources and reinforce effective group process but by itself cannot ensure effectiveness.

It is not possible to specify which elements to focus on if a group does not meet a particular effectiveness criterion. Groups are too complex to permit such prediction. Because an element in a group can affect other elements, any element or combination of elements could be contributing to the group's ineffectiveness. The model simply gives you and the group the elements to consider.

Third, the model helps a group decide what changes to make to become more effective. Because the group is a system, **all elements of the group's process, structure, and group context can influence each other, and changes in one element can lead to changes in others.** In other words, **in a group you cannot change just one thing.** Changing how the group's task is designed is likely to change the role relationships in the group; together these changes have an impact on each of the three effectiveness criteria. **It is not enough for each element to function well; the relationships among the elements must also be congruent.**

Making changes without thinking through the effects on the rest of the system can create new problems that may be worse than the original one the group sought to solve. For example, managing group conflict in a way that relies on the leader may reduce team members' motivation to learn how to manage their own conflict and reduce the leader's ability to accomplish his or her work.

Even a systemic solution can create new problems for a group, in part because it can require greater capability from the group. Because every solution generates new problems, by thinking systemically facilitators and groups can better anticipate the problems that will arise from a particular solution. In this way, the group can actively choose which secondary problems to create and then try to solve.

You can share the group effectiveness model with the members of the group and ask them to identify how the various elements of the model work in the group. In doing so, members make explicit their mental models of how the group is working and why. Then you can help the group identify which changes will produce the greatest leverage for increasing group effectiveness. If members' views differ, you can help them inquire into these differences. Recognizing that all models are wrong, you can suggest that members modify the model itself as they build a map of their particular group. This mapping process can range from pure conversation to mapping using flipcharts and diagrams, and even to advanced methods using modeling software.

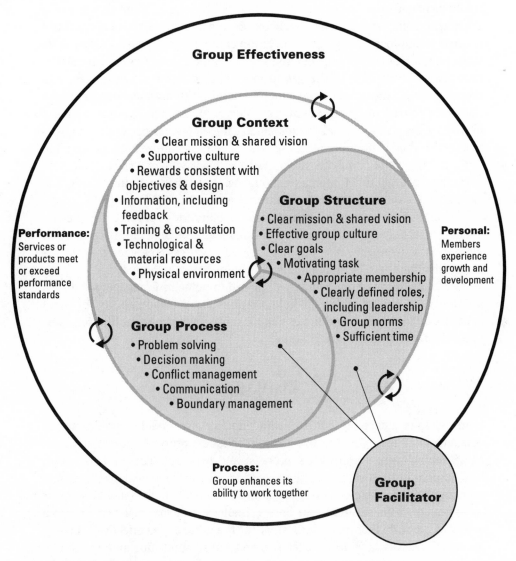

Group Effectiveness

Group Context
- Clear mission & shared vision
- Supportive culture
- Rewards consistent with objectives & design
- Information, including feedback
- Training & consultation
- Technological & material resources
- Physical environment

Group Structure
- Clear mission & shared vision
- Effective group culture
- Clear goals
- Motivating task
- Appropriate membership
- Clearly defined roles, including leadership
- Group norms
- Sufficient time

Performance:
Services or products meet or exceed performance standards

Personal:
Members experience growth and development

Group Process
- Problem solving
- Decision making
- Conflict management
- Communication
- Boundary management

Process:
Group enhances its ability to work together

Group Facilitator

Figure 2.5. The Focus of Group Facilitator Interventions to Increase Group Effectiveness

AUTHORITY AND RESPONSIBILITY: THE LIMITS OF FACILITATION

Group facilitation is a powerful method for helping a group improve effectiveness, but like any method it has its limits. Understanding the inherent limitations of facilitation helps you aid the group in making informed choices about creating change.

Group facilitators intervene largely on process and structure, to help groups improve their process, structure, and group context (see Figure 2.5). Therefore **facilitation can directly improve the group's effectiveness to the extent that there is authority within the group to change its process, structure, and group context, and to the extent that responsibility and accountability for change is shared by group members.** If the group's ineffectiveness is caused in part by elements or relationships among the elements that the group does not control (and cannot influence), group facilitation can help the group identify the problems but not solve them. Perhaps this is why one researcher (Kaplan, 1979) reported that research on group facilitation had not found that group facilitation enhances the group's performance of tasks.

Similarly, if the responsibility and accountability for improving group effectiveness rests only with the leader or with managers outside the group, it is not a group task. Group members in such a case have less free choice about the changes and are less likely to be internally committed to them.

As a group moves from being manager-led to being self-managing and then self-designing, **the group as a whole assumes more responsibility for managing its effectiveness, and it can benefit more from group facilitation, particularly developmental facilitation.**

SUMMARY

In this chapter, I have presented a group effectiveness model that helps us understand what makes an effective group. The model proposes three criteria for an effective group: performance, process, and personal. Three factors—process, structure, and context—contribute to making a group effective. Each factor comprises its own elements. We can think of the elements (such as conflict management, a motivating task, and technology and material resources) as pieces of a puzzle that must fit together for the group to be effective. The elements themselves have to be effective, and the relationships among the elements need to be congruent.

You can use the group effectiveness model to help groups explore how well they are meeting the effectiveness criteria, and what elements and relationships among elements may need to change to improve effectiveness. Like all approaches, group facilitation has its limits. The approach becomes powerful first to the extent that the group has authority to change the elements that contribute to effectiveness and second to the extent that responsibility and accountability for this change is shared by the full group.

In the next chapter, we explore the role of the facilitator in helping a group increase its effectiveness.

CHAPTER THREE

The Facilitator and Other Facilitative Roles

In this chapter, I begin by describing several facilitative roles—facilitator, facilitative consultant, facilitative coach, facilitative leader, and facilitative trainer—and explain how to choose an appropriate one. Then there is a description of the core values that guide these facilitative roles. For the rest of the chapter, I explain how to perform these roles in a way that is consistent with the core values.

CHOOSING A FACILITATIVE ROLE

Many of you reading this book need to use facilitative skills but are not (or at least sometimes are not) a substantively neutral third-party facilitator. Instead, you are involved in the group's discussions and decisions as an expert consultant, a team leader or member, a coach, or a trainer. Increasingly, people who serve in these roles are recognizing that facilitative skills are essential for working effectively with groups. If you serve in any of these roles, you can apply the same core values, principles, and ground rules discussed throughout the book in working with groups. **You do not have to give up your leadership role or your expertise to use facilitative skills. On the contrary; using facilitative skills enhances your leadership or consulting role and expertise.**

It is important to understand how the facilitative roles are similar and different and to select the appropriate facilitative role—the one that accu-

rately represents your relationship with the group. If group members see your facilitative role as appropriate, they are likely to be legitimately influenced by you. If members think you are filling an inappropriate facilitative role, they may not be open to being influenced by you, even if your observations and suggestions make sense within that role. For example, a group sometimes rejects the help of an expert consultant who, by inappropriately serving as a neutral facilitator, leads the members to wonder whether the consultant is trying to subtly steer them in a certain direction without saying so. Table 3.1 shows the five facilitative roles and how they are similar and different.

The Facilitator Role

As I described in Chapter One, a facilitator is a substantively neutral third party, acceptable to all members of the group, who has no substantive decision-making authority. The facilitator's purpose is to help a group increase its effectiveness by diagnosing and intervening largely on group process and structure.

Substantively Neutral. By *substantively neutral,* I do not mean that you have no opinions on the issues that the group is discussing. That would be unrealistic and inhuman. Rather, I mean that you facilitate the discussion without sharing your opinions and so that group members cannot tell what you think about the group's issues; consequently, you do not influence the group's decisions. Group members are easily and justifiably annoyed by a facilitator who claims to be neutral and then acts in a way that is not.

To remain neutral requires listening to members' views, and remaining curious about how their reasoning differs from others (and from your private views), so that you can help the group engage in productive conversation. If you

Table 3.1 Facilitative Roles

Facilitator	Facilitative Consultant	Facilitative Coach	Facilitative Trainer	Facilitative Leader
Third party	Third party	Third party or group member	Third party or group member	Group leader or member
Process expert	Process expert	Process expert	Process expert	Skilled in process
Content-neutral	Content expert	Involved in content	Content expert	Involved in content
Not substantive decision maker, nor mediator	May be involved in content decision making	May be involved in content decision making	Involved in content decision making in class	Involved in content decision making

trade your curiosity for a belief that some members are right and others are wrong, or that the group as a whole is going in the wrong direction, you give up your ability to help group members explore their own views and differences and replace it with your desire to influence the content of discussion. **If you find yourself invested in an issue or in having the group reach a particular outcome, or if you have expertise on the subject that makes it difficult for you to remain neutral, then consider serving in one of the other facilitative roles.**

Third Party. A facilitator needs to be a third party because it is difficult to act neutrally in your own group. If you are a group member or leader, an individual would reasonably expect you to be involved in the content of discussion and to have a role in decision making.

The term *third party* is open to interpretation. Even if you are not a member of the immediate group that requests facilitation, members may not consider you a third party. This may happen, for example, if the group is seeking facilitation to address concerns with the division it is part of and you are an internal facilitator working in the larger division. To serve as a facilitator, the group requesting help needs to consider you a third party.

Process Expert. A facilitator is content-neutral but also a process expert and advocate. As a process expert, you know what kinds of behavior, process, and underlying structure are more or less likely to contribute to high-quality problem solving and decision making, and you know which elements contribute to making an effective group. If you ask a group to use certain ground rules or if you identify certain ineffective behavior in the group, it is on the basis of this process expertise. Process expertise makes each of the four roles a facilitative role.

As a process expert, you advocate for processes, structures, and behaviors necessary for effective facilitation, such as appropriate membership, useful problem-solving methods, sufficient time, and ground rules. You inquire whether the group you are working with sees any problems with your design for the facilitation. For all of these decisions about the facilitation process, you are a partner with the group.

The Facilitative Consultant Role

Unlike the facilitator, a facilitative consultant is used for expertise in a particular area. The facilitative consultant is a third-party expert whose purpose is to help the client make informed decisions. The consultant does this by applying the area of expertise (marketing, management information systems, service quality, and so forth) to the client's particular situation, recommending a course of action, and in some cases implementing it for the client. Any substantive decision-making authority the consultant has results not from the role per se but from its being delegated by the client. A facilitative consultant uses facilitative skills while serving as an expert in a particular content area. Like the facilitator, the facilitative consultant may be external or internal to the organization. Internal human resource or organization development consultants often serve as facilitative consultants in an organization.

Facilitative skills are essential for expert consulting, which typically requires developing effective relationships, working with groups, and dealing with difficult conversations. The issues on which the expert consultant is called in are often ones on which members have strong and differing views. Consequently, the ability to help the group address the issues depends partly on the consultant's ability to effectively manage the process of exploring the issues. To paraphrase one of my clients, who is an expert consultant, "What do I do when I am talking to the client about what I found and what I recommend, and people start disagreeing with each other in front of me?" When this occurs, the facilitative consultant can help in the conversation while still being a participant in the content of the discussion. By integrating facilitative skills with expertise, the facilitative consultant increases the value provided to the clients.

The Facilitative Coach Role

In recent years, organizations have made coaches available for many of their executives and managers. A coach usually works one-on-one with people, helping them improve their effectiveness. Depending on his background, a coach may bring subject-area expertise in certain areas. At the heart of the facilitative coaching role is the ability to help people improve their effectiveness by helping them learn to rigorously reflect on their behavior and thinking.

When I coach clients—whether facilitative leaders, facilitators, or someone serving in another role—we explore difficult situations that they face, the outcomes they seek, and what it is about the situation that makes it difficult for them. Using the core values and principles described in this book, I help them think about how the way they are thinking and acting (or have thought and acted) contributes to the outcomes they seek as well as creating negative unintended consequences. Over time, clients develop the ability to do this kind of analysis themselves and produce the outcomes they seek with few unintended consequences.

A facilitative coach jointly designs the learning process with the client instead of assuming that she knows how the client can best learn. She also models mutual learning by exploring with the client how her coaching methods are helping or hindering the client's ability to learn. Facilitative coaches and clients explore the coaching relationship itself as a source of learning for both the client and the coach.

The Facilitative Trainer Role

Like the expert consultant, a trainer also has knowledge to share with participants; like the facilitative consultant, the trainer models the core values and ground rules and uses facilitative skills to enhance the participants' learning experience. When feasible, a facilitative trainer should work with the participants to design the training so that it meets their interests. During the training, the facilitative trainer regularly inquires whether the training is meeting the participants' needs and is flexible enough to modify the design if not. The facilitative trainer also considers the training setting an opportunity for her own learning, not just for participant learning. This means she is open to changing her views and inviting participants to challenge her assumptions, just as the trainer herself challenges participants. The facilitative trainer also facilitates the interaction among participants to enhance learning.

In recent years, some trainers have changed their title to facilitator. To the degree that this signals a shift in trainers' recognizing the value of facilitative skills and integrating them into their work, it makes me hopeful. Yet calling a trainer a facilitator obscures the fact that the individual is expert in and has responsibility for teaching some particular topic. I use the term *facilitative trainer* to recognize both sets of responsibilities and skills.

The Facilitative Leader Role

The facilitative leader uses the core values and principles to help groups increase their effectiveness, which includes helping to create the conditions in which group members can also learn to use the core values and principles. The facilitative leader may be the formal leader of the group or just a group member. In either case, **the facilitative leader role is the most difficult to fill because he needs to use his facilitative skills at the same time that he has strong views about the issue being discussed.** For example, this requires that the facilitative leader openly state his views on a subject, explain the reasoning underlying those views, and then encourage others to identify any gaps or problems in his reasoning. Underlying the facilitative leader role is the premise that a group increases its effectiveness as members take on more responsibility for the group and increase their ability to learn from their experiences. In Chapter Sixteen, I discuss the facilitative leader role in detail.

Choosing the Appropriate Role

The appropriate facilitative role is the one that accurately represents your relationship with the group; if you select an inappropriate role, you create problems for yourself and the group. One common problem occurs when an internal or external consultant or leader tries to serve as a facilitator, rather than as a facilitative consultant or facilitative leader.

Consider, for example, an internal HR manager who works with groups across the organization to develop and implement HR policy. The manager begins the group meeting by describing her role as a facilitator and asking for each group's thoughts about a particular policy. But the manager is an expert in the area of HR and has her own thoughts about what makes effective HR policy.

When she realizes that the groups have ideas differing from those of HR, the "facilitator" begins asking leading questions in order to influence the group members' views without saying so explicitly, or she simply identifies some problems with others' proposals. Other group members begin to feel set up, believing that the HR person misled them about her role. At the same time, the manager is frustrated because she feels she cannot openly influence the group's ideas in the facilitator role. In this case, serving as a facilitative consultant or facilitative leader enables the manager to share subject-matter expertise, be involved in the decisions, and still use facilitative skills to improve the quality of the group's interaction.

A leader faces a similar problem in trying to serve as a neutral facilitator with his or her own group, or other groups in the organization. As a facilitator, the leader does not get a chance to openly share thoughts and feelings about the issue, to influence others and to be influenced, or to be involved in making decisions in which the leader has a legitimate role. Group members may need the leader's relevant information on the issue and find it hard to believe that the leader has no opinions. Acting as a facilitator, the leader may see a decline in the quality of the group's decisions, as well as his or her own commitment to group decisions. This can cause the leader to change group decisions that were made while he or she was serving as facilitator, which undermines both the leader's credibility and the role of a genuine facilitator. Serving in the facilitative leader role eliminates these problems.

In short, **the facilitator role is appropriate for a situation in which you are not a member of the group, you have no stake in the issues, and no role in the group's decision making given your roles in the organization.**

SERVING IN MULTIPLE FACILITATIVE ROLES

At times, you may serve in two or more of these facilitative roles. You may be a facilitative leader in your own group, a facilitator or facilitative consultant to other parts of the organization, and a facilitative trainer as well. Because all five facilitative roles are based on the same core values and principles, you can move among the roles as necessary with integrity. Whether serving in one facilitative role or more than one, the underlying principle is the same: **select the appropriate role given the situation, accurately and explicitly describe to the group the facilitative role you plan to fill, seek agreement with the group, and then fill the role according to that agreement.** If you plan to use facilitative skills in a nonfacilitator role, say so, being clear to distinguish between using facilitative skills and serving as a substantively neutral third-party facilitator.

THE CORE VALUES OF THE SKILLED FACILITATOR APPROACH

Every third-party role is based on a set of assumptions about human behavior. Assumptions include values (things worth striving for) and beliefs (things considered to be true) that typically are accepted as valid without testing. Because assumptions clarify biases, identifying them is important.

Core Values

The Skilled Facilitator approach is based on four values: valid information, free and informed choice, internal commitment to those choices, and compassion (see Table 3.2). The first three core values come from the work of Chris Argyris and Donald Schön (Argyris, 1970; Argyris and Schön, 1974); I have added the fourth.

Valid information means that you share information in a way that enables others to understand your reasoning and, ideally, to determine for themselves whether the information you have shared is accurate. This means sharing all information relevant to an issue, including your assumptions and your feelings about how the issue is being addressed. It means using specific examples so that other people can understand clearly what has been said and can determine independently whether the information is accurate. Valid information also means that others understand the information that you share with them. This means that you share not only your conclusions but also the reasoning by which you reach them. Having done so, you inquire whether others have information that is different from yours.

Free and informed choice means that you and others can define your own objectives and the methods for achieving them, and that these choices are based on valid information. When you make a free choice, you are not coerced or manipulated. Consequently, **the facilitator does not change people's behavior. The facilitator provides information that enables people to decide whether to change their own behavior. If they decide to, the facilitator helps them learn how to change.**

Internal commitment to the choice means that you feel personally responsible for the choices you make. You are committed to the decision because it is intrinsically compelling or satisfying, not because you will be rewarded or penalized for making that choice. If people are internally committed to a decision, there is little need for traditional over-the-shoulder monitoring to make sure they are really doing what they said they would do.

Compassion means adapting a stance toward others and ourselves in which we temporarily suspend judgment. It involves having a basic concern for the good of others that leads you to be concerned about their suffering. By *suffering* I mean simply the pain that people feel when their needs are not met. When you act with compassion, you infuse the other core values with your intent to understand, empathize with, and help others.

Compassion literally means "to suffer with" and is sometimes mistakenly thought of as having pity for others. Unfortunately, this pity-based compassion leads people to help others in a way they do not want to be helped, and to protect others in a way they do not want to be protected. **The kind of compassion I am describing enables you to have empathy for others and for yourself in a way that holds you and others accountable for your actions, instead of unilaterally protecting yourself or others.** This kind of compassion strengthens rather than diminishes the other core values.

Table 3.2 Core Values

Core Value	Description
Valid information	• People share all relevant information.
	• People share information in such a way that others understand their reasoning.
	• People share information in such a way that others can independently validate it.
	• People constantly seek new information to determine whether past decisions should be changed on the basis of new, valid information.
Free and informed choice	• People define their own objectives and methods for achieving them.
	• Choices are not coerced or manipulated.
	• Choices are based on valid information.
Internal commitment	• People feel personally responsible for their choices; they own their decisions.
	• Commitment to action is intrinsic, rather than based on reward or punishment.
Compassion	• People temporarily suspend judgment.
	• People are concerned for others' and their own good.
	• People appreciate others' and their own suffering.

Source: The first three core values come from the work of Chris Argyris and Donald Schön (Argyris, 1970; Argyris and Schön, 1974); I have added the fourth.

If you act out of compassion, rather than out of fear and guilt, you are able to move beyond defensiveness and to be vulnerable. This vulnerability in turn enables you to create conversation in which you can mutually learn with others how to increase effectiveness.

The kind of compassion I am describing enables you to have empathy for others and for yourself in a way that still holds people accountable for their actions rather than unilaterally protecting others or yourself. With a systemic view, this involves understanding how people, presumably acting in good faith, each contribute to creating or sustaining a problem, rather than placing blame. It means exploring what other people see that you do not, rather than assuming that those who do not share your view "just don't get it" or have questionable motives.

The core values create a reinforcing cycle. People need valid information to make an informed choice. Compassion creates an environment in which people are willing to share valid information. When they make free and informed choices, they become internally committed to the choices. Compassion leads people to be concerned about others' free and informed choices, aside from their own. If people are internally committed to their decisions, they take responsibility for seeing that the decisions are implemented effectively. Internal commitment leads people to continue seeking new information to determine whether their decisions remain sound or should be revisited. Compassion leads people to avoid focusing on blame when things are implemented in a way that creates unintended consequences.

Guiding Facilitator and Group Behavior

Central to the Skilled Facilitator approach is the assumption that the same core values that increase your effectiveness as a facilitator increase the group's effectiveness. This means that when you act effectively, you are modeling effective behavior for group members. The notion that using the core values leads to effective process is not an untested assumption. It has been borne out by more than twenty-five years of research (Argyris, 1982, 1985, 1987, 1990; Argyris, Putnam, and Smith, 1985; Argyris and Schön, 1974). To examine how values serve as a guide for effective behavior, consider what happens when a group's actions are inconsistent with core values.

To take an example, group members often try to influence a decision by sharing information that supports their position and by withholding information that is inconsistent with it. They place a higher value on winning the discussion or protecting their own interests than on sharing valid information. Because valid information has been withheld, the group often makes poor decisions. The *Challenger* space shuttle disaster—caused by the failure of an O-ring, which some organizational members already believed might malfunction—is a vivid and tragic example of what can happen when valid information is withheld and choices are not as informed or free as they could be.

Group members are often asked to commit to achieving a goal without having any control over how they will accomplish the goal—or what it should be. They often become compliant, doing only what is minimally necessary to complete the task, expending extra effort only when they believe others are monitoring their work. Because of the lack of internal commitment, the group may fail to accomplish the goal.

The facilitator helps the group improve process by acting consistently with core values. **In developmental facilitation, the group members develop the ability, over time, to identify when they have acted inconsistently with the core values and to correct their behavior—without a facilitator's help. In basic facilitation, the group uses a facilitator to help it act consistently with the core values, temporarily, while working with the facilitator.**

You use the core values to guide your own behavior. You create valid information by sharing your observations and checking with the group about how members have acted consistently or inconsistently with core values and other principles of group effectiveness. By helping group members see the consequences of their behavior and by asking them whether they want to change, you enable the group to make free and informed choices. Consequently, members become committed to the choices they make during facilitation. By acting with compassion, you model your intent to understand, empathize, and help.

Core Values Are Ideals

Core values are ideals to strive for, recognizing that in some situations optimization is not possible. For example, a group sometimes needs to make a decision without full valid information because it may not be available. Similarly, a strategic choice that members at one level of an organization make might limit the free choice that members at lower levels of the organization can make.

Because we are human, there are times when you as facilitator and the group you work with miss the mark and act inconsistently with the core values. As facilitator, perhaps you withhold valid information and act so as to reduce the group's ability to make an informed free choice to which the members can commit. Or you respond out of fear or guilt rather than compassion. When this inevitably occurs, your ability to reflect on your behavior keeps you on the path of learning, to close the gap between what you say you value and how you act.

THE ROLE OF THE FACILITATOR

Having briefly described five facilitative roles, let us explore the facilitator role in detail. Essentially, **the facilitator's role is to help the group improve its process in a manner consistent with the core values.** The facilitator accomplishes this by helping the group establish ground rules for effective group process, identifying behavior that is inconsistent or consistent with the ground rules and core values, and helping members learn more effective behavior.

BASIC AND DEVELOPMENTAL FACILITATION

I divide facilitation into two types on the basis of the group's objectives (Table 3.3). **In** *basic facilitation,* **the group seeks only to solve content problems, such as reducing the time for responding to customers or developing a strategy for marketing a new product.** The group uses a facilitator to temporarily improve its process to solve the problem. Once the group solves its problem, the facilitation objective has been achieved. But the group has probably not improved its ability to reflect on and improve its process. Consequently, if other difficult problems arise, the group is likely to require a facilitator again.

In *developmental facilitation,* **the group seeks to develop its process skills while solving problems.** The group uses a facilitator to learn how to improve its process and applies newly developed skills to solving the problem. Once the group accomplishes its objectives, as in basic facilitation it has solved the problem. But the group will also have improved its ability to reflect on and manage the process. Consequently, if other difficult problems arise, the group remains less dependent on a facilitator than before. In practice, facilitation occurs on a continuum from purely basic to purely developmental, rather than as two discrete or pure types.

Table 3.3. Basic and Developmental Facilitation

Characteristic	Basic Facilitation	Developmental Facilitation
Client objective	Solve a substantive problem	Solve a substantive problem while learning to improve the group's process
Facilitator role	Use facilitator's skills to temporarily improve group's process; take primary responsibility for managing the group's process	Help group develop its process skills; share responsibility for managing the group's process
Process outcome for client	Same dependence on facilitator for solving future problems	Reduced dependence on facilitator for solving future problems

Choosing the Type of Facilitation

To help a group decide where on the basic-developmental facilitation contin-uum it needs help, it is useful to consider how your role differs with the ap-proach. **In basic facilitation, although the group can influence the process at any time, in general it expects you to guide the group, using what you consider effective group process. In developmental facilitation, members expect to monitor and guide the group's process and expect you to teach them how to accomplish this goal.**

Basic and developmental facilitators intervene for different reasons. In gen-eral, **as a basic facilitator you intervene when the group's process or other factors affecting the group interfere with its accomplishing a specific goal.** Your intervention is designed to help the group accomplish the goal without necessarily learning how to improve process.

A developmental facilitator intervenes under the same conditions as a basic facilitator. But in addition, as a developmental facilitator you inter-vene when the group's process or other factors affecting the group hinder the group's long-term effectiveness, or when reflecting on the process will help members develop their process skills. Your intervention is designed to help the group learn how to diagnose and improve process. A fundamental dif-ference between basic and developmental facilitation is doing something for a group in the former case and teaching a group how to do the same thing for it-self in the latter case.

Throughout the book, I use the terms *basic facilitator* and *basic group* to re-fer to a facilitator and a group using basic facilitation. Similarly, I use *develop-mental facilitator* and *developmental group* to refer to a facilitator and a group using developmental facilitation.

Given that ineffective group process hinders a group's ability to solve sub-stantive problems, basic facilitation is essentially limited. It helps a group solve one problem without exploring why it has trouble solving problems in general. In contrast, developmental facilitation identifies why the group, functioning as it does, has difficulty solving problems and helps the group learn how to ad-dress the fundamental causes. In doing so, developmental facilitation requires a group to reflect on its behavior and often change the basic values and beliefs that guide behavior in the group. In this sense, developmental facilitation is more systemic and produces deeper learning than basic facilitation.

When Is Developmental Facilitation Appropriate?

Still, developmental facilitation is not always the more appropriate choice for every group. The extent to which you use a basic or a developmental approach with a particular client depends on several factors. Obviously, the group's primary goal is a major one. A second important factor is time; a group unable to devote the time necessary for developmental facilitation should not pursue it. Even with adequate time available, if the group is a temporary one (such as a task force) then the investment required for developmental facilitation may not be worthwhile. A third factor is group stability. Even with a group initially learning to facilitate itself, if membership changes frequently or drastically the group may not be able to sustain the skills. A final factor is control over process. Unless the group has control over process, including how it makes decisions, developmental facilitation may be of limited use.

Even so, developmental facilitation is essential for some groups given their stated identity. For example, **a truly self-directed work team must be self-facilitating; an organization that purports to be a learning organization has to have groups that can reflect on their actions in a manner consistent with developmental facilitation.**

THE GROUP IS THE CLIENT

One significant implication of the core values and your objective to help groups improve their effectiveness is that your client needs to be the entire group rather than only the group leader. When you choose the group as your client, you are telling your clients that your responsibility is to help the group as a whole rather than only the leader (or a subset of the group). This simple choice has many implications. In practice, it means you offer valid information that enables the group to make a free and informed choice about whether to work with you, so that if they choose to do so they are likely to be internally committed to the process. It means that you do not automatically agree to the group leader's requests (say, to use a certain agenda or process) simply because they come from the group leader.

It can be scary to choose the group as your client. The leader has more authority and often more power than other group members. You may be afraid that if the group is your client you will alienate the leader and jeopardize future work with the group or the larger organization. But if you meet the leader's needs at the expense of other group members, you lose your credibility with the group and your ability to facilitate. Viewed in this either-or way, you find yourself in a dilemma; either choice creates problems. The challenge is to recognize that the leader's role in the group is different and still treat the group as your client. I explore this issue in detail in Chapter Thirteen.

Facilitator's Responsibility for Group Outcomes

One challenging part of your facilitator role is deciding what responsibility you have for the group's outcomes. Some facilitators believe they are largely responsible; they reason that they are hired to help the group accomplish a task, such that if the group does not accomplish its objective then the facilitator considers himself at fault. Other facilitators believe that they have little responsibility for outcomes, reasoning that they are hired to help the group improve its process, so if the group does not accomplish its desired outcome, the facilitator is not at fault.

The Facilitator's Contribution. Thinking about this systemically means thinking about your role and potential contribution rather than what you can be blamed for. As a facilitator, your contribution involves acting effectively so that you help the group accomplish its goals. To the extent that you act ineffectively, you contribute to the group's ineffective behavior and its consequences.

Consider, for example, a top management team that commits to making decisions by unanimous agreement but then votes six to four to install a new organizationwide intranet, although several members insist that the intranet will not meet divisional needs. Once installed and debugged, the computer intranet remains underused, largely because it cannot perform critical tasks needed by several divisions. As the facilitator, you are partly responsible for the effect of the group's poor decision if you have not shared with the group that several members' interests are not met in the decision, that the group is acting inconsistently with its own ground rule by voting, and that negative consequences can develop as a result of these behaviors.

A basic facilitator fulfills her responsibility to the group by designing an effective process for the group to accomplish its work, acting consistently with the core values, identifying for the group when members have acted inconsistently (or consistently) with principles of effective group behavior, and letting the group make free and informed choices on the basis of the facilitator's interventions. In addition, a developmental facilitator helps group members learn how to identify when they have acted inconsistently with principles of effective group behavior, how to explore the conditions that create the ineffective behavior, and how to change these conditions to generate more effective behavior.

Although you are not directly responsible for *what* the group decides, you are responsible for helping the group consider *how* its process leads to more or less effective decisions. Imagine that a group is trying to decide what data to use to predict the size of the market for a service. As facilitator, you do not offer an opinion about which are the best data to use. But you do help the group consider which criteria it uses to make the decision. If members disagree about the best data to use, you help them design a way to test their disagreement.

If the group makes a decision that creates a problem, you are responsible for helping the members analyze the process they used in making that decision. By determining where the group went wrong (perhaps there was an erroneous assumption), members can agree on what they will do differently next time.

Process Is Necessary But Not Sufficient. If the content of a group's decisions improves as the process improves, it would seem to follow that all problems in a content decision flow from poor process—and therefore are partly the facilitator's responsibility. But they are not, for several reasons.

First, effective group process, and problem solving in particular, is based on assumptions that all relevant information is available and accurate and that the consequences of actions can be predicted accurately. Obviously, such assumptions are often incorrect. If the assumptions are violated, a group can make a content mistake even though the process is effective.

Second, as Chapter Two describes, effective group process is necessary but not sufficient for creating an effective group. An effective group also requires an effective structure and a supportive organizational context. An effective structure includes such elements as members who have appropriate knowledge and skills; well-designed, motivating jobs; and adequate time for members to complete the task. A supportive organizational context includes aspects of the larger organization that influence the group: a supportive culture, rewards consistent with the group's objectives, and various resources.

Finally, **even if you facilitate effectively, the group may engage in ineffective process, because part of facilitating effectively is enabling the group to make free and informed choices, including choices about their own process.** Sometimes you may feel you are abandoning a group by allowing it to make a free and informed choice that you are certain will have negative consequences. Or you may feel frustrated that a group does not seem to understand what you understand. For some facilitators, this is the hardest test of whether they enable the group to make a free and informed choice. Yet it may also be the most important test. If, by trying to help a group avoid poor process, you prevent the group from making its own choice, you act inconsistently with the core values being espoused. Ultimately, this reduces your credibility as facilitator. Also, it may suggest incorrectly to the client that the core values can be ignored if they are inconvenient or if the stakes are high.

Colluding with the Group

Collusion is a secret agreement or cooperation between parties that affects others. When you collude with a group, you are explicitly or implicitly asked (or you ask others) to act in a particular way but not to reveal that you are doing so, or why. **Collusion is inconsistent with the facilitator's role, because it requires you to withhold valid information in a way that unilaterally places the interests of some group members above the interests of the group as a whole, which prevents the full group from making a free and informed choice.** You can collude in several ways: with one or more members against one or more other members, with one or more members against a non-group member, and with a non-group member against one or more group members. Here are illustrative examples of the three forms of collusion:

- Jack, a group member, approaches you before a meeting. Jack says he wants to raise an issue in the meeting but does not want the group to know it is his issue. He is concerned that the issue will not get the attention it deserves if the group thinks he is raising it. Jack asks you to raise the issue "at an appropriate time" but to not tell the group where it originated. You agree.

- A task force is about to meet with Erika, the department head to whom it reports, to recommend changes in the department. (Erika is not a member of the task force.) It has been agreed that as the task force facilitator, you will facilitate the meeting. Before the meeting, the task force members realize they have made some assumptions about Erika that were not confirmed with her. The recommendations will work only if the assumptions are true. But they are reluctant to ask her about the assumptions, because a sensitive issue is involved. They ask you not to raise the assumptions in the meeting or to pursue them if the Erika mentions them. You agree.

- Sven, a manager, tells you that a team that reports to him (and that he is not a member of) is spending too much time on an issue. Sven is especially concerned that the team is spending time discussing issues that are not in its charge. He asks you to attend fewer group meetings and, when facilitating, to steer the group away from those issues. You say, "OK, I'll see what I can do."

Colluding with group members is a solution that creates new problems and often makes the situation worse. In an attempt to help the group by colluding, you act inconsistently with the core values you espouse, reducing your effectiveness and credibility. Further, by shifting the responsibility for raising issues from a group member to you, you miss the opportunity to help group members develop their skills in dealing productively with difficult issues, and you reinforce ineffective group behavior. Over time, you may wonder why the group is overly dependent on you, without realizing how your own actions contributed to the very outcome you set out to avoid.

Even if you agree with this rational explanation, in any of these situations you may still feel a lot of emotion. You may feel angry if you attribute to a member that he intends to deceive others by asking you to act collusively. You may feel trapped if faced with choosing between meeting the request of a powerful member (who might pay your bill or salary) and acting inconsistently with your role and not helping the group. If members ask you to raise issues for them because they are worried about the consequences if they raise the issue themselves, you may feel sorry for them and want to protect them. In some of these situations, you may be naturally more compassionate than in others. The challenge is to respond out of compassion when it is not your immediate re-sponse—and to do so in a way that does not shift member responsibility onto you, because of how you are feeling about yourself or about others.

Dealing with Collusion

One way to avoid colluding with the group is to discuss, as part of the con-tracting process, what you as facilitator can and cannot do, explaining your reasoning. You can give examples of requests that you cannot fulfill because they would lead to collusion.

When you receive a request that requires you to collude with the group, you can explain how fulfilling the request obligates you to act inconsistently with the role of facilitator, which in turn reduces your ability to help the group in the long run. You can then ask the individual if he sees the situation differently. In this way, you can work with the person making the request to find a way for him to raise the issue directly with relevant individuals. You might begin by say-ing, "I think it's important that the group hear your concern, and I think it's ap-propriate for you to raise it with them because it's your concern. If I raise the issue in my role as facilitator, people might think I'm steering the conversation, which is inconsistent with my role. I can't raise the issue for you. But as soon as you raise it, I'll actively facilitate to help you and the other group members have as productive a conversation as possible. Do you see any of this differ-ently? If not, do you want to talk about how you can have that conversation with the group?"

LEAVING THE ROLE OF FACILITATOR

I have emphasized how important it is to clarify your facilitator role and to act consistently with it. Yet sometimes it is appropriate to temporarily leave the fa-cilitator role and serve in another role. This section considers the other roles, when it is beneficial to take them on, and what risks you face in doing so.

The Facilitator as Mediator

When is it appropriate to serve as a mediator? Before we discuss that question, let us explore the similarities and differences between the roles of facilitator and mediator.

Comparing Facilitation and Mediation. People sometimes use the words *facilitation* and *mediation* interchangeably. According to Christopher Moore (1996, p. 15), "mediation is the intervention in a negotiation or a conflict of an acceptable third party who has limited or no authoritative decision-making power but who assists the involved parties in voluntarily reaching a mutually acceptable settlement of issues in dispute."

Although there are similarities between facilitation and mediation, there are also important differences. Both facilitation and mediation involve intervention by a neutral third party who is acceptable to the clients and who has no substantive decision-making authority. Both seek to help people reach a decision acceptable to all who are involved. The facilitator and the mediator share many of the same skills and techniques, but they apply them in varying situations and sometimes to accomplish different objectives. In general, mediation is more similar to basic facilitation than to developmental facilitation.

I see several distinctions between facilitation and mediation. First, they have differing objectives. Parties seeking a mediator have a conflict they have been unable to settle, so traditionally the objective of mediation has been to help the parties negotiate a settlement to a particular conflict. Note, however, that at least one approach to mediation (by Bush and Folger, 1994) also focuses on transforming relationships among participants and the participants themselves.

The objective of facilitation is to help a group improve its process for solving problems and making decisions so that the group can achieve goals and increase overall effectiveness. Although dealing with conflict can be a significant part of facilitation, it is not necessarily the primary focus. In addition, developmental facilitation seeks to help the group develop its own ability to improve the process for solving problems by teaching facilitative skills to the group.

Second, because a mediator helps parties resolve their conflict, the parties typically seek a mediator after they reach an impasse—that is, once they believe they can progress no further without third-party help. When a facilitator helps a group resolve conflict, she too is sometimes called in after the group has reached an impasse. But the facilitator often becomes involved earlier. For example, a group may seek basic facilitation because members understand that they do not have skills sufficient to manage the process of what is expected to be a difficult or complex discussion. A facilitator might also enter the process after the group has gone through a critical incident, such as a significant change in group membership or group mission.

Third, a facilitator works in the presence of the entire group, whereas a mediator may work with the parties together as well as separately. The potential problem with a facilitator playing the role of mediator is illustrated by the differences in the roots of the two words. *Mediate* comes from a Latin word meaning "to come between"—in our context, to come between group members. *Facilitate* comes from a Latin word meaning "to make easy"—in our context, to make it easy for the group to be effective. **One of the facilitator's goals is to help members improve their ability to work together effectively; serving as an intermediary usually limits achievement of this goal if members do not develop the skills for dealing directly with each other.**

Temporarily Becoming a Mediator. There are three common situations in which I am asked to move from facilitator to mediator by coming between members of the group: (1) in the beginning of a facilitation, when subgroups have concerns either about working with me as a facilitator or about working with the other subgroups; (2) during a facilitation, when a member or members want information raised in the group or some action taken without it being attributed to them; and (3) in a conflict, when the facilitation breaks down and one or more subgroups are unwilling to continue.

Acting as a mediator in these situations, I face a common risk of acting inconsistently with the core values, similar to collusion. Members share information with me outside of the group conversation and want me to use it to intervene in the full group. But because the members do not want the full group to know the source of the information (or even that it was shared with me), the members ask me to share the information for them or else act on their information without explaining that I am doing so (much like what is seen in the earlier examples of collusion). If I explicitly or implicitly agree not to share the information that was shared with me, and this becomes the basis of my intervention, then I cannot explain why I am intervening, and so I am withholding relevant information from the group. In addition, if the person who shared the information with me is not willing to identify herself in the full group, neither the group nor I can determine whether the information is valid.

The risk is actually a dilemma. If I act on the information given me without testing its validity or explaining my intervention, I act inconsistently with the core values I am espousing and may make an intervention that is ineffective. On the other hand, if I do not act on the information given me, the group and I miss an opportunity to get the group together initially or keep it from completely breaking down.

Returning to the three common situations I described earlier, in each one if certain interests are met then I can temporarily serve as a mediator without reducing the integrity of my facilitator role. In each situation, I seek first to serve as a facilitative coach, helping one or more members of the group raise concerns or questions about the other members in the full group (as I illustrated in the section on avoiding collusion). This role is still consistent with the facilitator role, as long as I am helping the group members raise their own issues. In any event, I do not agree to raise the issue for the members. Doing so could lead to a situation in which, after I raise the issue for the members, the members claim that they did not raise the issue with me. It also increases the group's dependence on me as the facilitator.

I may also meet with subgroups when I am beginning to work with a group, and one or more subgroups might have a concern about whether I am impartial and sensitive to their needs. Initially, I ask the subgroup what makes them reluctant to share this information in the full group, share my reasoning on the advantages of doing so, and ask what would need to happen for them to be willing to do so. If they are not yet willing to share these concerns in the full group, I consider it reasonable to meet separately with them to hear their concerns. If the concerns are relevant for the other subgroups, I help the subgroup figure out how to share these concerns in the full group, if they are willing.

I may temporarily act as mediator if conflict between subgroups threatens a complete breakdown in communication. I facilitated a union-management cooperative effort in which the seven union members of the union-management committee simultaneously closed their notebooks and walked out in the middle of a meeting. The discussion had become tense, and union members were frustrated by what they perceived to be management's efforts to undermine the process. As the facilitator, I saw two choices. I could stay in the room, let the union leave, and see the process unravel, along with the progress the committee had made. Or I could temporarily assume the role of mediator and talk with the union members, trying to find a way to help union and management members to work together again. I chose the latter course and spent the next six hours mediating in meetings and phone calls. The next morning, the union and management subgroups were back in the room, discussing why the process had broken down and exploring ways to prevent it from recurring.

When the facilitator meets with a subgroup, especially if the facilitator decides to mediate by conveying information between subgroups, the facilitator needs to state clearly that she or he is serving in the mediator role and the facilitator and subgroups need a clear agreement about what information, if any, the facilitator will share with the other subgroups. Without this agreement, a subgroup can easily feel that the facilitator has not acted neutrally, violated confidentiality, or colluded with another subgroup.

The facilitator acting as mediator entails advantages and disadvantages. Mediating can sometimes prevent a difficult conflict from escalating to the point where the group essentially breaks down and ceases to function. However, by agreeing to mediate, the facilitator may reduce the likelihood of the group developing the skills to resolve conflict. Also, working with a subgroup may lead group members to question the facilitator's neutrality. Therefore, before serving as mediator the facilitator should consider whether the advantages outweigh the disadvantages.

The Facilitator as Evaluator

As a facilitator, you face a role conflict whenever someone in the organization asks you to evaluate the performance of one or more members in the group. For example, a manager who is outside the facilitated group may be concerned about the performance of one of the members. She may ask you to evaluate the member to help her decide whether to take any corrective action. Alternatively, she may be considering promoting one of several members of the group and ask you to evaluate the members to help her make the promotion decision.

You face a potential role conflict in this situation because evaluating group members can jeopardize the members' trust in you. One reason members trust you is that the facilitator has no authority and adheres to the principle that **the facilitator does not use information obtained within facilitation to influence decisions about group members that are made outside facilitation, except with the agreement of the group.** Evaluating group members increases your power in the organization and therefore decreases the likelihood of members discussing openly information that they believe could prove harmful to them.

Still, it can be difficult to tell a manager that you cannot share information about subordinates, especially if you want to share positive information that can be used to help the subordinates' careers.

One way a manager can obtain this information from you, the facilitator, in a manner consistent with core values is to have the group member about whom the evaluation is being sought agree that you can share your observations with the manager. In this case, you would provide specific examples that you observe about the group member's behavior. You share these observations in the presence of the group member—ideally, in the presence of the entire facilitated group—and ask the evaluated group member (and other group members) whether they would make a different evaluation. Making your information available to all group members such that they can validate or disagree with it enables the members to make an informed choice about whether you have shared valid information with the manager. This can reduce member concerns about trust to the extent that they are based on concern about your sharing valid information. If you share all relevant information with the group, the information that you share during the evaluation session has already been discussed with group members as part of your facilitator role.

The Facilitator as Content Expert

Earlier in this chapter, I discussed when it is appropriate to serve as a facilitative consultant more than as a facilitator. Even if you decide to serve as a facilitator, the client may still ask you questions in an area in which you have expertise (marketing, performance management systems, finance, and so on).

The group is able to quickly obtain information when you serve as a content expert; doing so helps you feel good by showing the group you are knowledgeable about their work and that you can add value to their conversation. But offering this information also creates risks. One is that the group begins to see you as a *non*neutral third party, which reduces your credibility and ultimately your effectiveness. A second risk is that the group becomes dependent on you. Group members may grow sensitive to whether you approve of their decisions, which then affects the decisions they make.

The facilitator as content expert or information resource is an appropriate role if you and the group explicitly contract for it. In this situation, you can take several steps to reduce the risk that imparting expert information will negatively affect your facilitator role. First, acting as a content expert only when asked by the group, and only when the group reaches consensus to do so, reduces the prospect of meeting the needs of only some group members. Second, announcing to the group when you are temporarily leaving the role of facilitator and afterward that you are returning to the facilitator role reduces confusion about the role you are currently serving in. Finally, by avoiding serving as a content expert in the early stages of working with a group, you reduce the likelihood of the group coming to depend on you in this role.

People who facilitate groups in their own organizations are often asked by group members to play an expert role. Chapter Fifteen discusses how an internal facilitator can offer expert information and facilitate effectively.

When the Content Is About Group Process: The Myth of Total Neutrality

It is a myth that you can always be neutral about the substance or content of a group's discussions while being partial about what constitutes effective group process. Recall that "substantively neutral" means a facilitator conveys no preference for any solution the group considers.

You are partial about what constitutes effective group process because that is your area of expertise. As a skilled facilitator, you know what kind of behavior is more or less likely to lead to effective problem solving and other important group outcomes—and you convey this knowledge through your actions as facilitator.

When I ask group members to follow certain ground rules (such as sharing all relevant information) or when I identify how members act inconsistently with the core values, I am also identifying my beliefs about what constitutes effective group process. When I use the core values to guide my own behavior, my behavior is a reflection of my theory of effective interpersonal process. In fact, embedded in each of my interventions is some prescription for effective behavior. In other words, because as facilitator I am always striving to model effective behavior, and because embedded in my behavior are beliefs about effective group process, I am constantly conveying my beliefs through my actions.

Consequently, **the facilitator cannot be neutral about the content of a group's discussion when it involves how to manage group or interpersonal process effectively.** In this case, your theory about what makes group process effective can be used to address the group's discussion of how to manage process effectively. As the group process becomes the subject of discussion, your comments about process focus on the group content. Consequently, you become involved in the content of the discussion. Because many management issues involve some aspect of interpersonal or group process, your theory of group effectiveness has implications for how groups handle many issues.

However, your role is not to impose upon the solution the principles that guide your intervention with the group. To do so is inconsistent with the facilitator's role. The chapters on intervention describe some ways to address this issue.

SUMMARY

Group facilitation is the process by which a person who is acceptable to all members of the group, is substantively neutral, and has no substantive decision-making authority intervenes to help a group improve the way it identifies and solves problems and makes decisions, in order to increase the group's effectiveness. Basic facilitation seeks to help a group solve an important problem. Developmental facilitation seeks to help members solve a problem while learning to improve their group process. Both types of facilitation are based on core values of valid information, free and informed choice, internal commitment, and compassion. The facilitator's role is designed to help a group act consistently with the core values. Although temporarily leaving the role of facilitator is appropriate at times, it may also jeopardize the facilitator's (and the group's) ability to act consistently with these values.

Anyone needing to use facilitative skills while being involved in the substance of a conversation can do so by serving as a facilitative consultant, a facilitative leader, or a facilitative trainer.

In the next chapter, we explore why it can be so difficult to act consistently with core values and to remain in your facilitator role, especially when you are faced with a difficult situation.

PART TWO

DIAGNOSING BEHAVIOR IN GROUPS

CHAPTER FOUR

Understanding the Theories That Guide Our Actions

This chapter is about the most fundamental work in facilitation: the internal work you do with yourself to help a group as much as you can. I discuss how the way you think can lead you to act less effectively than you would like, and what you can to do to fundamentally change your thinking so that you can better help groups become more effective.

THE CHALLENGE

Facilitation is difficult work because it is mentally demanding, cognitively and emotionally. Many of us espouse core values similar to those of the Skilled Facilitator approach and embody them, we hope effectively, in a variety of situations. But if we find ourselves in a difficult situation—one we consider potentially embarrassing or psychologically threatening—we still think and act in a way that reduces our competence. Our own ineffectiveness diminishes the effectiveness of the groups we serve.

Group members face the same challenge as you. **The same kind of thinking that leads you to act ineffectively as a facilitator also leads group members to act ineffectively.** Like you, the group members are probably unaware of how they create these problems for themselves. Part of being a developmental facilitator is helping group members reflect on and change their thinking to increase their effectiveness.

This is not simply a matter of learning new strategies, tools, or techniques. Your ineffectiveness results from the core values and assumptions you hold. You use these core values and assumptions to design and select strategies and techniques that create your ineffectiveness. In other words, if you change strategies and techniques without changing the underlying core values and assumptions that give rise to them, you simply have new strategies that generate the same negative consequences. In addition, you remain unaware of the core values and assumptions that you use to design your ineffective behavior.

The challenging internal work of facilitation is to identify and explore the core values and assumptions that guide your actions, to rigorously reflect on how they increase or decrease your effectiveness, and to develop a new set of values and assumptions that you can use to increase your effectiveness and that of the groups you work with.

The "Creating a Vision" Case

How you think can lead you to act in a way that is ineffective. To see this, consider a real case. Emily, a facilitator for a group of senior information technology managers, has met with them to develop a vision. The group's leader, Joe, was absent from this particular meeting because of a family medical emergency, but he stated that the group should meet without him, and Emily agreed. (When Emily agreed, she created a problem, one that I address in Chapter Thirteen, on contracting.) Prior to the meeting in question, Emily talked individually with members and inferred that they were dissatisfied and untrusting of Joe.

In the real-life case that Emily wrote up as a participant in one of my workshops, she said her goals were "to get the group to feel accomplished in their vision and be able to follow-up with Joe on barriers and plans to achieve the vision; to get the group to not be cynical and bored, but engaged and motivated; and for them to be open about their frustrations." Her strategy in the conversation was "not to directly confront the issues around Joe, since he wasn't there, but to get them to work better together and perhaps mitigate the problems with Joe's management by being a real team." Reflecting on the case, she stated, "The difficulty was that nobody would openly discuss his or her issues—only by innuendo. We never got to the core issues."

Exhibit 4.1 reproduces the conversation Emily had in her meeting with the group when Joe was absent. It includes two columns. In the right-hand column is a difficult part of the verbatim conversation that Emily had with the group as best she recalled it. In the left-hand column are Emily's thoughts and feelings—her internal conversation—that she had during the public conversation, whether or not she expressed them. As you read the case, notice how Emily is thinking about the situation and how she chooses to act as a result.

Exhibit 4.1. Unilateral Control Model: Emily's Case

Emily's Thoughts and Feelings	The Conversation
Wow. She's not liking what I've got them doing.	BARBARA: Why are we doing this [work on developing a vision]?
I think this stuff is not very exciting. And they've done this kinda stuff before, and it goes nowhere. Without Joe here, it's rather futile. It's another [useless] exercise. Plus, they have such reservations about working for him.	EMILY: This is the process we laid out, given the purpose and goals of the day. Is there another suggestion you have for achieving our vision?
They won't tell the truth. I wonder how many of them really have had it, too.	BARBARA: Well, we seem to not be getting anywhere. Maybe it's just me and my mood today. I'm not sure what this is going to do for us.
I'd like to tell them I wanted Joe to do the "undiscussables" and he vetoed it, saying they can talk about anything with me. But that would be turning against him and doing so in his absence. Not good to do that. But they might trust me more. Nah! Can't trust them!	EMILY: What could I do to make it more useful?
Oh boy, now they won't want to use me as a facilitator in their organizations, if they think I can't handle them. Maybe I should have talked to them each one-on-one to build more trust. Too late for that now!	BARBARA: I don't know, you're the facilitator. I just know I have so many things to do and I don't think this is getting us where we need to go.
They participated in saying what to do today, and the agenda reflects that. Why is she acting like she wants no part of it?	EMILY: We built the agenda around the deliverables that everyone agreed to. Is this not reflecting what you thought we'd do?
Joe was so late in getting back to me, he didn't finalize the agenda until three days before, which didn't give them much time. Everything always is so rushed around there! Maybe she didn't look at the agenda. Probably not. But I can't blame them, since they are	BARBARA: No, no. Maybe it's just me. I can't see this getting us anywhere.

Exhibit 4.1. *(continued)*

Emily's Thoughts and Feelings	The Conversation
so overworked and undervalued. And I know Barbara particularly wants to get a reorg going, so maybe we're not moving fast enough for her on that right now.	
Let's see what anyone else thinks. Moe had suggested this overall flow, which I adjusted, so what is he thinking?	EMILY: How about the rest of you?
They are defending me, but I somehow don't completely buy it!	MOE: Well, this is a process that takes time, and I think we need to play it out.
I think I need a break myself to see what to do now. They are just going through this by rote, although some of them seem to be engaged or enjoying it a bit. They did, after all, do a pretty good job on their vision posters, which showed some commitment on their part.	EMILY: Well, let's try to finish this piece and break for lunch and see how we do.

Emily's Contribution to the Group's Problem

What may be difficult to see at first reading is that Emily acts in ways that reduce the chance of creating the kind of open conversation she seeks in the group; on the basis of my discussing the case with her, I would say she was unaware of how she was doing this as she was doing it. Even with the best of intentions, Emily was undermining her own effectiveness by operating from a set of values and assumptions that are incongruent with the Skilled Facilitator approach. Emily is typical of almost all the facilitators I have worked with and taught, when they find themselves in a situation that they consider threatening or embarrassing in some way. What leads a facilitator to seemingly undermine the values that she openly espouses? How do we explain this puzzle? First, let's look at Emily.

As part of her goals, Emily wanted the group to be engaged and motivated and open about their frustration. Yet, reflecting on her case, she noted that "the difficulty was that nobody would openly discuss his or her issues—only by innuendo. We never got to the core issues." She inferred that they were about why some members seemed reluctant to engage in the process. I agree with Emily's assessment in that Barbara expressed general concern about the process but did not state the source of her concern.

But Emily also contributed to this result in ways that she was unaware of until we discussed her case in the workshop. Essentially, she thought that the process was not very exciting, that they had done this before, and that it goes nowhere; yet she withheld all of these thoughts from the group and acted as if there were no problem with the activity. This is the same thing that she was critical of the group for.

If Emily does not model the behaviors she expects of the group, it is unlikely that she can create the kind of environment that enables others to demonstrate those behaviors.

YOUR THEORIES OF ACTION

One way to think about this puzzle, developed by Chris Argyris and Donald Schön, is that you have in your head *theories of action* about how to act effectively in various types of situations. You need these theories of action to respond quickly to a situation; without them, you would have to invent a new response to every situation you face and never be able to act in time. You have two types of action theories in your head: your espoused theory, and your theory-in-use. To oversimplify, there is what we say we do, and what we actually do.

Espoused Theory

Your *espoused theory* **is what you say you do.** It is how you tell others you would act in a given situation; you usually express it in general terms, including your values and beliefs. In my experience, facilitators often have an espoused theory that reads like a good group-process textbook; they often espouse the need for people to have the same information, understand different perspectives, and use a decision-making process that can generate commitment to a group decision. One way to recognize your espoused theory is to say, "I believe . . ." and finish the sentence. In Emily's case, she espouses the value of having people be engaged and motivated and the belief that people should be open about expressing their frustration.

Theory-in-Use

Your *theory-in-use* **is essentially reflected by what you actually do. It is called theory-in-use because it is the theory you actually employ to design and act out your behavior.** Theory-in-use can only be inferred from watching your actual behavior. It includes (1) a set of core values and assumptions, (2) strategies that follow from the core values and assumptions and that specify how you should act, and (3) the consequences of your interaction with others. One way to recognize it is to phrase it as "When I'm in situation X and Y happens, I do Z"; for example, "When I'm facilitating a group of my peers and people start to express negative feelings about each other, I defuse the conflict by looking for common goals." In Emily's case, I inferred that part of her theory-in-use was "when we are going through a process I developed and people raise concerns about it, I do not fully inquire into their concerns. And if I have similar concerns, I act is if I do not."

You are unaware of your theory-in-use. Part of what makes your theory-in-use so powerful is that it operates quickly, skillfully, and effortlessly. Most significant, it operates outside of your awareness. You are often acting or reacting using core values and assumptions, yet you are typically unaware of what your theory-in-use is or how you are using it to design your behavior. All of this is a benefit if you get the kind of results you seek. In fact, if you had to think about your theory-in-use while acting, it would slow you down considerably and, at least temporarily, make you less skilled. For example, consider how your skill in driving a car quickly drops if while driving you start thinking about all the things you are doing in driving. You can't respond quickly and your thinking about driving gets in the way of your driving.

You can, however, become aware of your theory-in-use. There is a time to become aware of and question your theory-in-use. **Although we all have various espoused theories, when we find ourselves in an embarrassing or psychologically threatening situation, almost all of us activate just one theory-in-use to guide our behavior,** one which I am about to describe (Argyris and Schön, 1996). Your theory-in-use leads you to create misunderstanding, conflict, and defensiveness; it reduces your ability to help the group. Unfortunately, now the speed, effortlessness, and unawareness of your theory-in-use becomes a liability and compounds your problem. Not only are you acting ineffectively but your theory-in-use is leading you to do it quickly, skillfully, and effortlessly, without even being aware that you are doing so. Consequently, you are blind to the inconsistency between your espoused theory and your theory-in-use, and to how your theory-in-use is reducing your effectiveness. You are not walking the talk, so to speak.

This blindness makes it difficult for you to discover inconsistency for yourself and then reduce the negative consequences that stem from your theory-in-use. Fortunately, others can often see you being inconsistent and help you become aware of what is going on. Let's explore what the theory-in-use is that you implement in determining your behavior in a difficult situation.

UNILATERAL CONTROL MODEL

The *unilateral control model* refers to the theory-in-use with which we design our behavior in a psychologically threatening or embarrassing situation (see Figure 4.1). I have adapted the model from the work of Argyris and Schön (1974), who developed the model and called it Model I, and Robert Putnam, Diana McLain Smith, and Phil McArthur at Action Design, who adapted Model I and refer to this as the unilateral control model.[1] I use the term *unilateral control model* because it captures the essence of the model.

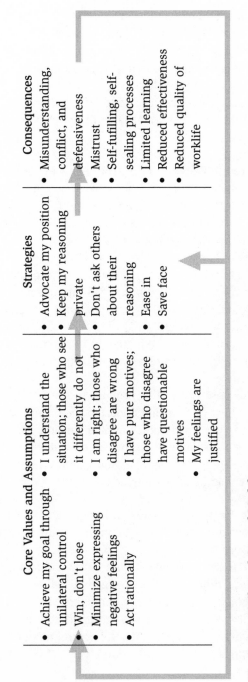

Core Values and Assumptions

- Achieve my goal through unilateral control
- Win, don't lose
- Minimize expressing negative feelings
- Act rationally

- I understand the situation; those who see it differently do not
- I am right; those who disagree are wrong
- I have pure motives; those who disagree have questionable motives
- My feelings are justified

Strategies

- Advocate my position
- Keep my reasoning private
- Don't ask others about their reasoning
- Ease in
- Save face

Consequences

- Misunderstanding, conflict, and defensiveness
- Mistrust
- Self-fufilling, self-sealing processes
- Limited learning
- Reduced effectiveness
- Reduced quality of worklife

Figure 4.1. Unilateral Control Model

Source: Adapted from Argyris and Schön, 1974, and Action Design, 1997.

Core Values

When you use a unilateral control model, you design your behavior using this set of core values (Argyris, 1993; Argyris and Schön, 1974, 1996): (1) achieve your goals through unilateral control, (2) maximize winning and minimize losing, (3) minimize generating or expressing negative feelings, and (4) act according to what you consider rational.

People use a mix of these core values and to differing degrees. **You can only infer the presence of these values by observing people's behavior and testing your inferences with them.**

Achieve My Goal Through Unilateral Control. Achieving a goal through unilateral control essentially means to get others to do what you want them to do. It includes conceiving of the purpose of the meeting, task, or activity by yourself, rather than jointly deciding the purpose with others. Once you have defined your goal, you try to achieve it by acting unilaterally to control the conversation.

In Emily's case, one of her espoused goals is for the group to develop its vision. When Barbara asks why the group is doing this and notes that it is not getting the group anywhere—comments that call into question the goal of developing the vision—Emily continues to facilitate with the goal of developing the vision. For example, by asking Barbara "Is there another suggestion you have for achieving our vision?" and "What could I do to make it more useful?" Emily never asks explicitly, "Do we need to revisit the goal for this meeting?"

Win, Don't Lose. This core value is a corollary to the first value and means defining winning as achieving your intended purpose. Anything that leads to either changing the purpose or not achieving it is considered losing and a sign of weakness. In talking with Emily about her case, I understood that she considered success as developing the vision; as she saw it, if the group did not develop the vision, she would be acting ineffectively.

Minimize Expressing Negative Feelings. Minimizing expression of negative feelings means keeping your unpleasant feelings out of the conversation, in the belief that to show anger or frustration, for instance, is to act incompetent or undiplomatic because it can hurt people and make it difficult to accomplish goals. Similarly, allowing others to express negative feelings is also considered ineffective. Emily espouses that the group members should be "open about their frustrations," but she too is frustrated and neither inquires into Barbara's frustration nor shares her own. In the unilateral control model, raising negative feelings can lead to things getting out of control.

Act Rational. Acting rational means remaining objective, not becoming emotional, and thinking of any discussion of the issues as being purely objective, regardless of the emotions that might underlie them.

Together, the core values are a basis for shaping how you think.

Core Assumptions

In conjunction with core values, there is a set of assumptions that everyone using the unilateral control model makes: (1) I understand the situation, but those who disagree do not; (2) I'm right, and those who disagree are wrong; (3) I have pure motives, but those who disagree have questionable motives; and (4) my negative feelings are justified.

I Understand the Situation; Those Who See It Differently Don't. The first assumption means that whatever information you bring to understanding the situation is valid and complete, as are the conclusions you draw. In other words, how you see things is how things really are. Those who disagree with you are misinformed and just do not get it. If they understood what you understand, they would agree with you. In Emily's case, her belief that others won't tell the truth, that they can't be trusted, and that some people seem to be enjoying the conversation is considered truth; she does not test the validity of the belief. It does not occur to her during the conversation that it would be valuable to test whether her belief is valid.

I Am Right, Those Who Disagree Are Wrong. You assume that there is a right and wrong perspective to begin with and that if you are right then others who disagree or see it differently must be wrong.

I Have Pure Motives; Those Who Disagree Have Questionable Motives. You assume you are acting in the best interests of the group or organization and that those who disagree with you are motivated by self-interest or other motives inappropriate for the situation.

My Feelings Are Justified. Because others do not understand the situation as it is (meaning, as you see it) and because their lack of understanding results in part from their questionable motives, you are justified in being angry or feeling whatever you feel toward them.

In the unilateral control model, you consider your feelings as the natural and inevitable result of others' actions toward you. You do not consider the possibility that your feelings result from your own thoughts and that, to the extent your thinking may not be reflecting the full situation, neither do your feelings reflect it.

Strategies

You use the combination of the core values and assumptions to develop strategies for dealing with conversation. These are strategies that you use to guide your actions, whether or not others use them. The unilateral control strategies are (1) advocate my position, (2) keep my reasoning private, (3) don't inquire into others' reasoning, (4) ease in, and (5) save face.

Advocate My Position. "Advocate my position" means to tell people what decision should be made or which course of action should be taken.

Keep My Reasoning Private. As you advocate your position, you are careful to *keep your reasoning private.* The position you advocate is a conclusion that results from the values and beliefs you hold, the assumptions you make, the data you are using, and the inference you draw from the data. How you put all these pieces together to draw a conclusion makes up your reasoning process. Yet you share little of your reasoning with others. Notice that at the end of Emily's case, she advocates the group continuing to finish the piece of work, but she does not explain what leads her to advocate this, given Barbara's unaddressed concerns.

A key part of sharing your reasoning is explaining the strategies you use in working with the group. In Emily's case, part of her unilateral control strategy was "I'll ask the group questions about their concerns and withhold my own relevant information about concerns. This way, I won't have to tell the group about my conversation with Joe and I won't have to share information I don't trust them to have." Given that Emily's strategy is designed to unilaterally control the situation and minimize expression of negative feelings, she needs to keep it private. Sharing it with group members would reduce her ability to implement the strategy. **The ability to implement a unilateral control strategy often depends on the ability to withhold the strategy from those on whom you are using it.**

Do Not Inquire into Others' Reasoning. You also do not inquire into others' reasoning. As others advocate their point of view, you may respond by telling them why they are wrong, but you typically do not ask them to explain how they reached their conclusion. If you do inquire into another's reasoning, you do so in a way that does not fully answer your private questions. For example, Emily privately wonders what Moe is thinking, given that she adjusted the overall process that he suggested the group use. Yet Emily simply asks, "How about the rest of you?" without asking Moe directly what his reactions are.

Ease in. You often ease in, to indirectly convey your point of view. Easing in can involve asking others questions or making statements that are designed to get others to figure out and state what *you* are privately thinking without your having to say it. It is an indirect approach designed to get others to see things your way for themselves. For example, Emily subtly eases in when she says, "We built the agenda around the deliverables that everyone agreed to. Is this not reflecting what you thought we'd do?" Essentially, Emily is indirectly stating her point of view: "This does reflect what we said we would do." In another form of easing in, you make a general statement of the sort "I think it's important that everyone take initiative on this project" when you are thinking of two people in particular but do not want to identify them by name.

Save Face. Together, these strategies enable you to save face in order to unilaterally protect yourself and others. If you fully explain your reasoning—including the assumptions you are making, the data you base your conclusions on, and your inference—you make yourself vulnerable by enabling others to question your reasoning and identify a place where your reasoning has a gap or inconsistency. If you allow others to point out that your reasoning has gaps in it, this makes it difficult to continue to advocate for your original position and achieve your goal.

Had Emily shared her full reasoning with the group about why it made sense to her to finish the piece of work, she would have stated that she needed a break herself at that point to figure out what to do. By withholding this information, she unilaterally protects herself from letting the group know she is not sure what to do at this point. Of course, after Emily shared this with the group, it would make it more difficult for her to continue to unilaterally control the situation to achieve her goal.

In addition, you do not share the specific examples that you use to reach your conclusions because that would require identifying people by name, which you believe makes people defensive and raises negative feelings.

For similar reasons, you do not inquire genuinely into others' reasoning to understand how they have come to advocate their position. Instead, you might engage in rhetorical inquiry by asking a leading question ("Don't you think it would be better if we tabled this conversation till later?"). This is simply a statement dressed up to look like a question.

If you were to inquire into others' reasoning, you might find out that their reasoning makes more sense than yours, or at least it takes into account some things that your reasoning does not. This again makes it more difficult for you to prevail. Second, if you inquire into others' reasoning, they will probably expect and feel free to inquire into yours. Third, by inquiring into others' reasoning, you fear making public what you have privately thought: that there are gaps and flaws in the other person's reasoning. You assume this would embarrass or threaten the other person or yourself, and that this would lead to raising negative feelings, which you are trying hard to suppress.

Rather than inquiring into others' reasoning or behavior, you simply assume that you know what they are saying and why they are saying it. Instead of testing with the other person whether your inference is accurate, you privately conclude it is and then use your untested inference to respond to the person. For example, when Barbara says, "I just know I have so many things to do and I don't think this is getting us where we need to go," Emily thinks, *Why is she acting like she wants no part of it?* In this way, Emily transforms her untested inference that Barbara wants no part of it into what she considers hard data that she then uses to guide her future interaction with Barbara.

If Emily tests her inference by saying something like, "From what you said, Barbara, I'm thinking you don't want to do this vision piece. Is my inference accurate?" Barbara might say, "No, I think it's so important that I don't want us to do it in a way that's not working."

But in the same way that Emily acts on her untested inference, assuming it is accurate, your untested inferences form the faulty foundation for all sorts of conclusions you make and actions you take toward others. In short, you build a compelling but potentially flawed database about others.

Consequences

All of these strategies are designed to unilaterally control the situation and to suppress negative feelings and defensiveness. Ironically, by attempting to control the situation you also create the very consequences you say you are trying to avoid: (1) misunderstanding, conflict, defensiveness, and mistrust; (2) self-fulfilling and self-sealing processes; (3) limited learning and reduced effectiveness; and (4) diminished quality of worklife. Your core values and assumptions and strategies interact in a complex way to create these consequences.

Misunderstanding, Conflict, and Defensiveness. For example, you create misunderstanding because you assume that the situation is as you see it, and you base your actions on untested inferences about others instead of testing your inferences with others. To the extent that you make negative attributions of others' motives and do not test them, you generate your own mistrust of others and their mistrust of you. For example, Emily attributes to the group that they won't tell the truth and can't be trusted, which leads her to withhold information, increasing the chance that *she* will not be trusted by the group.

Self-Fulfilling and Self-Sealing Processes. Similarly, by attempting to control the conversation and simply pushing your point of view, and by not being open to being influenced by others, you are seen as defensive. Believing that openly sharing your reasoning with others makes them defensive, you ease in by asking others questions without explaining why you are asking them. This reasonably leads them to be wary and cautious in their response, which you see as defensive. In this way, you create a self-fulfilling process, generating the very consequence you set out to avoid.

Others recognize that you are withholding information but acting as if you are not doing so, and this leads them to mistrust you. Of course, others are unlikely to point this out to you because that would be potentially embarrassing, so they play along and withhold their concern about you. If you sense that they have a concern about you but are not raising it, you do not bring up the issue with them either. In this way, you create a self-sealing process, eliminating the opportunity for learning how your own behavior may be contributing to the group's reduced effectiveness.

Emily thinks that Moe is defending her, but in a way that she does not find persuasive. Yet she does not test with Moe whether her inference is true because to do so could be embarrassing for her. It would also publicly raise the issue that group members have a concern about her performance.

Getting results that you did not intend leads you to be even more controlling and focused on winning. You try to suppress negative feelings, thus reinforcing your unilaterally controlling approach.

Reduced Learning and Effectiveness. In this approach, you reduce the opportunity for learning about content and process. By focusing on unilaterally controlling the conversation and having your point of view prevail, you reduce the opportunity to learn how others see the issues differently and to learn about flaws or gaps in your own reasoning. In addition, you reduce the opportunity to learn how your own behavior may be contributing to the group's reduced effectiveness. Emily misses this opportunity by not asking Barbara and Moe specifically about things she is doing that they may find ineffective. This reduces effectiveness in working with the group.

Diminished Quality of Worklife. The unilateral control model also reduces the quality of worklife. It can be stressful if you cannot say what you are thinking without creating negative consequences. It can be difficult to make untested inferences about others that lead them to get defensive. It can also be difficult when others use the unilateral control model in dealing with you.

I am capable of the same unilaterally controlling behavior I have been describing throughout the chapter. To take a simple example, I was conducting a facilitation for a prestigious international consulting firm. The group included some of their internal consultants and the internal consultants' valuable clients, along with world-renowned external organizational development consultants. The stakes were very high for me. At one point, in response to my question about how things were going, one of the internal consultants said, "This is the most overfacilitated session I've ever been to." My immediate thought was that he was talking about my facilitation approach and that I had been ineffective. Seeking to control the conversation to protect myself, I made a joke and changed the subject. If I had acted ineffectively, I responded even more ineffectively by trying not to be vulnerable in front of the client. As a result, I never learned what I had done, if anything, that led the client to say that. The client also never asked me back to facilitate again.

Creating a Left-Hand Column Dilemma

Using a unilaterally controlling approach creates a set of dilemmas in which there is no good answer to the question "What should I do with the thoughts and feelings in my left-hand column?" As Table 4.1 shows, there are several options when your left-hand column contains unilateral control thinking: be direct, self-censoring, or indirect. In the direct option, if I say exactly what I am thinking and feeling in the form in which I am thinking and feeling it, it is likely to create a defensive reaction in others. Emily does not use this option in her case. On the other hand, in the self-censoring option, if I do not share at all what I am thinking and feeling, others do not hear my views. Emily uses this option when she decides not to raise the issue that she cannot trust the group members.

The third option, being indirect, which people adopt as a solution to resolving the dilemma of the first two options, is to say what I am thinking and feeling, but to make it sound nice. This involves easing in, saving face, and not being specific. However, being indirect still creates some defensiveness in others, and it still prevents others from hearing my views specifically. This approach combines the negative results of both previous solutions, although perhaps in a less severe form. In addition, it requires that others correctly read between the lines to understand my view and prevents me from checking directly to see whether I have been understood as I intended. Emily uses this option when she thinks *Why is she acting like she wants no part of it?* and says, "We built the agenda around the deliverables that everyone agreed to. Is this not reflecting what you thought we'd do?"

Using a unilateral control approach creates an unsolvable dilemma: no matter which option you use to share or not share your thoughts and feelings, you create a problem. Emily's case is typical of almost all facilitators. It is also consistent with the research showing that when faced with an embarrassing or threatening situation, 98 percent of professionals use a unilaterally controlling approach to work with others (Argyris and Schön, 1996).

Because as a facilitator you are charged with helping a group become more effective, your own ineffectiveness reduces group effectiveness. The group may see

Table 4.1. The Dilemma of Dealing with Unilateral Control Thinking

Strategy	What I Say	Element of Dilemma
Direct	Exactly what I am thinking and feeling	Others will get defensive.
Self-censoring	Nothing	Others will not hear my views.
Indirect	Part of what I am thinking and feeling, but indirectly, alluding to what I do not say	Others will still get somewhat defensive and will not hear my views directly; they will have to correctly read between the lines to understand my view, and I will not be able to find out if they have interpreted my views correctly.

you espousing a particular way of acting but then acting in a unilaterally controlling manner. If they see you use a unilateral control approach, they may use your behavior to confirm that it is legitimate to use a unilateral control approach.

GIVE-UP-CONTROL MODEL

When people recognize that they use the unilateral control model, they often want to change. Unfortunately, they often shift from one form of control to another—the give-up-control model. (The give-up-control model was developed by Argyris [1979], who called it Opposite Model I. Robert Putnam, Diana McLain Smith, and Phil McArthur at Action Design [1997] adapted it and refer to it as the give-up-control model.)

The core values of the give-up-control model are (1) everyone participates in defining the purpose; (2) everyone wins and no one loses; (3) express your feelings; and (4) suppress using your intellectual reasoning (Argyris, Putnam, and McLain Smith, 1985). An assumption in the give-up-control model that differs from the unilateral control model is that in order for people to learn and be involved and committed, they must come to the right answer by themselves. Of course, the right answer is the one you have already come up with. When others don't see the answer that you see, a common strategy is to ask easing-in or leading questions to help the people get the answer by themselves. The results of the give-up-control model are the same as those of the unilateral control model: increased misunderstanding, conflict, and defensiveness, as well as reduced learning, effectiveness, and quality of worklife.

The easing-in strategy of the give-up-control model is often part of the unilateral control model. I think of the give-up-control model as a subset or variation of the basic unilateral control model.

People often move from the unilateral control model to the give-up-control variation and back. A common occurrence is with managers who seek to empower their employees. After recognizing that he has been micromanaging and unilaterally controlling the group, the manager shifts to letting his group make decisions. He delegates an important decision to the group and in an effort not to influence them, does not share relevant information he has, including criteria that need to be met in the solution. When the group proudly returns with a solution, the manager rejects it because it does not meet the criteria (which he did not share) or take into account the information he withheld. As a result, the group infers that the manager doesn't want to give up control and that the manager thinks the group is not ready to be empowered. The manager responds by shifting back to a unilaterally controlling approach.

Facilitators use the give-up-control model when they get frustrated with a group's lack of responsiveness. A facilitator may think to herself, *They seem not to want to my help. I'll just let the group continue to make assumptions about each other and get off track and take cheap shots. Eventually they'll implode and figure out something's wrong.*

In the unilateral control model you take control; in the opposite model you give up control. But because you take control and give up control unilaterally, fundamentally both models are unilaterally controlling.

Let us explore an alternative to the unilateral control and give-up-control theory-in-use, one that resolves the problems we have just seen.

MUTUAL LEARNING MODEL

The *mutual learning model* is the theory-in-use that enables you as a facilitator and the group you are working with to enhance your effectiveness, particularly under difficult conditions. The Skilled Facilitator approach is based on the mutual learning model. I have adapted the model from the work of Argyris and Schön (1974), who developed it and called it Model II, and Robert Putnam, Diana McLain Smith, and Phil McArthur at Action Design, who adapted it and call it the mutual learning model. Like the unilateral control model, it has three components: (1) core values and assumptions, (2) strategies, and (3) consequences.

In Exhibit 4.2, I show what Emily's left-hand column case might look like if she used more of a mutual learning approach. As you read this, you may wonder why Emily would say or think certain things. I explain this in the rest of the chapter.

Exhibit 4.2. Mutual Learning Model: Emily's Case

Emily's Thoughts and Feelings	The Conversation
Hmm. I wonder what leads her to ask. Does she have concerns, is she just unclear, or what? Let me check.	BARBARA: Why are we doing this [work on developing a vision]?
	EMILY: Barbara, I'm not sure what you're asking. Are you not sure about the purpose of doing it, or do you have concerns about doing it, or is there something else that leads you to ask?
Yeah, I agree. They seem stuck. And this isn't the first time. It's beginning to look like a pattern.	BARBARA: Well, we seem to not be getting anywhere. Maybe it's just me and my mood today. I'm not sure what this is going to do for us.

Exhibit 4.2. *(continued)*

Emily's Thoughts and Feelings	The Conversation
	EMILY: So, I'm inferring that you're thinking that even if the group accomplished the vision work, you're not sure it would be useful. Have I got that right?
So this is not just an issue of the process being poor. This is a bigger issue. What does she mean by "dragging"?	BARBARA: Yeah, I just can't see this getting us anywhere, and the group just seems to be dragging.
	EMILY: When you say "dragging," can you give me an example of a time when you thought it was dragging? That'll help me understand what you mean. . . .
Yeah, I agree. I didn't intervene on that either. Too bad. Oh well, I can't see everything.	BARBARA: Well, a few minutes ago when we were talking about creating a workplace that values risk taking, we kept on repeating ourselves. And we never came up with something we were all willing to support.
	EMILY: Moe, what are your thoughts about what Barbara said?
I'm not sure what he means by that. Is he saying the process has problems or not?	MOE: Well, this is a process that takes time, and I think we need to play it out.
	EMILY: Moe, I agree that the process takes time. Are you also saying that you don't see any problems with the process and have no concerns about what it will get you when you complete it?
Moe seems less concerned than Barbara about the issue.	MOE: That's what I'm saying. I think there will be value for us in the vision. The process is dragging a little, but I think that's because it's just before lunch.
Let's check to see what people agree on here.	EMILY: Barbara, I share your concerns about the session dragging. I agree that when the group was discussing creating a vision of a risk-taking organization, each of you repeated your point of view and the group was not able to identify

Exhibit 4.2. *(continued)*

Emily's Thoughts and Feelings	The Conversation
	a solution that everyone could support. Does anyone see that differently?
OK, let people know my contribution to this.	[All team members agree with Emily]
	EMILY: I think I contributed to your not doing as well as you could have by not intervening sooner when people were repeating themselves. Was there anything else you think I did or did not do that contributed to the group dragging?
	DAVID: Yeah, one thing. I think you could have checked sooner to see if the conversation was still on track—like the time when we got into a conversation about workflows.
Wait a second. A few minutes ago Barbara agreed that even if the group develops a vision, it won't be useful. That seems to suggest that there's a problem beyond the vision process itself. I'm curious why that would be. I wish I had picked that up earlier, but I didn't. It's still not too late to find out.	EMILY: I agree with you. I will try to do that sooner.
Let me check to see if I remembered it accurately.	EMILY: Barbara, a few minutes ago you said that even if you complete the vision it won't be useful. Yes?
	BARBARA: Yeah.
	EMILY: I'm curious, what would lead the vision to not be useful?
Why is that? What does Barbara see that I don't?	BARBARA: We've had visions in the past and they just never got implemented.
	EMILY: And what do you think led to them not being implemented?
I wonder where the differences are. They've made a number of comments earlier about things being too forward thinking for Joe, and Joe seeing it differently. It might be related to Joe.	BARBARA: Like I said earlier, I think there are different views about how to implement.

Exhibit 4.2. *(continued)*

Emily's Thoughts and Feelings	The Conversation
I wonder what prevents them from reaching agreement? I think I see some relationships here with Joe and lack of progress and things dragging. I'm going to lay this out and see what people think. If people are concerned about Joe implementing any vision, I can see why this session would drag for them.	DAVID: And we don't reach agreement on them.
	EMILY: I have some thoughts about why this session is dragging and how it relates to what you've been saying about the vision not getting implemented. Let me explain what I'm thinking and get your reaction. First, this is not the first time you have tried to create a vision for the group. In fact, I worked with you before on one. And each time the vision does not get implemented. Yes?
OK, I can continue.	[Team members nod in agreement]
I wouldn't want to be in the position they are in. Come to think of it, I helped create it. Well, I need to tell them.	EMILY: I think it is difficult for you to try to agree on a vision for the group when Joe, who is the leader of the group, is not here. I know he had a family emergency, but as the facilitator, I think I contributed to the problem by agreeing to facilitate when Joe couldn't make it. Barbara and David, I'm thinking that you also thought that was a problem, given your comments about "having the same meeting again" when Joe returns. Have I inferred correctly?
	BARBARA: Yeah, it's happened before.
Sounds like David is seeing this as an ongoing problem. OK, I need to raise the issue about Joe and the group. See if that's what's going on. This may be difficult, but if I don't raise it, I'm just letting the group falter.	DAVID: And I think it will happen again.
	EMILY: I think your comments relate to what I'm inferring is the more fundamental issue here. My inference is that at least some of you have concerns that Joe is never going to implement a vision that includes risk taking, despite setting up this visioning process. Let me give some examples of things you

Exhibit 4.2. *(continued)*

Emily's Thoughts and Feelings	The Conversation
	have said that led me to make this inference and find out if you see it differently. This may be a difficult issue, but I want to raise it because if my inference is correct, it will be very hard for you to accomplish the task today. My intent is not to put you on the spot but to figure out what needs to happen so you can work effectively as a group.
	Here's what I've heard that led me to raise the issue. Barbara and David, after each of you presented ideas you are excited about, you dropped them, saying, "Joe will never agree to that; it's too forward-thinking." Moe, you've said several times in this meeting that you thought it was hard to implement a vision without a visionary. Have I remembered this accurately?
OK.	BARBARA AND DAVID: Yeah.
OK, he's still with me.	MOE: Well, I don't think that's exactly what I said, but it's close enough.
	EMILY: Those comments are what lead me to think that you are concerned that Joe won't implement a vision you develop, and that makes this a useless exercise. "Useless exercise" are my words, not yours. Have I misinterpreted your comments, or am I missing anything?
	BARBARA: No, I didn't feel comfortable raising it, but since you did, I think that was in the back of my mind when I said, "I don't think the process will get us anywhere."
It sounds like Barbara and David are pretty frustrated about this. I can understand that. They just spent another half a day on visioning that they think will be useless.	DAVID: That pretty much captures it. It's like, does this train go anywhere?

Exhibit 4.2. *(continued)*

Emily's Thoughts and Feelings	The Conversation
This doesn't surprise me. It's consistent with what Moe has been saying throughout. Still, all three believe that it's an issue.	MOE: Well, I wouldn't say that Joe won't implement any vision we develop. But his limits are different than mine. I don't think I'm as concerned as David and Barbara; it's a smaller issue for me.
	EMILY: Barbara and David, from the tone of your voice I'd say you sound frustrated. Yes?
	BARBARA: Yeah, it's a pain to spend time on something that is not going to happen, when I could be working on other things I need to get done.
	DAVID: I feel the same way.
	EMILY: Well, let's figure out together where we go from here, given your concerns. My interest as your facilitator is to help you accomplish what you think you need to accomplish, not to keep you on a task if it doesn't make sense anymore. Let's craft an approach that all of you can support. I can think of a couple of options. If you want, you can talk about how to address the concerns about Joe that you just raised. I can help you think about addressing the issue with Joe if you want. Or you can continue the visioning if you think having this conversation changes things for you. Or we can stop meeting if you think that makes the most sense. I'm sure there are other options I haven't thought of. The choice is yours. What are your thoughts?

Although the case begins with the same comment, it immediately changes from Emily's actual conversation. When you use a mutual learning approach, it is not just what you say that changes, but how you think. As a result, the conversation quickly takes another course.

Core Values

The core values that guide the mutual learning model are those of the Skilled Facilitator approach that I described in Chapter Three: (1) valid information, (2) free and informed choice, (3) internal commitment, and (4) compassion. (See Figure 4.2.)

Valid Information. By valid information, I mean that you share all information relevant to an issue, including your assumptions and your feelings about how the issue is being addressed. It means using specific examples so that other people can understand clearly what you mean and, ideally, determine independently whether the information is accurate. Valid information also means that others understand the information you share with them. This means that you share not only your conclusions but also the reasoning by which you reached them. Valid information is the primary core value, on which the next two are built.

In the mutual learning version, Emily generates valid information in a number of ways. She shares her own concerns about the process, including how she contributes to the group's problem. When she wonders why someone is saying something, she asks them about it rather than assuming she knows the answer. She also checks with people to make sure she has heard them correctly.

Free and Informed Choice. When you make an informed choice, it is based on valid information. You make a free choice to the extent that you can define your own objectives and the methods for achieving them. In making a free choice, you do so not because you are being coerced, manipulated, or acting out of defensiveness, but because the choice is related to fulfilling some important personal need. Emily enables the group to make a free and informed choice when she asks them how they want to proceed, given their concerns about Joe.

Internal Commitment to the Choice. You are internally committed if you feel personally responsible for the choice you make. You are committed to the decision because it is intrinsically compelling or satisfying, not because you are rewarded or penalized for making that choice. If you are internally committed to a decision, you take ownership for implementing it. As a result, there is little need for traditional over-the-shoulder monitoring to make sure you are really doing what you say you will do. In Emily's case, the group is likely to feel committed to the decision they make, given how she raises the issue and enables them to make the choice.

Compassion. Compassion involves adapting a stance toward others and yourself in which you temporarily suspend judgment. In acting with compassion, you infuse the other core values with your intent to understand, empathize

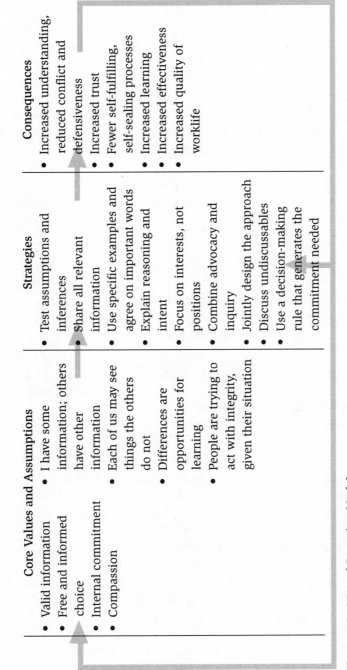

Figure 4.2. Mutual Learning Model

Source: Adapted from Argyris and Schön, 1974, and Action Design, 1997.

with, and help others. Compassion means "to suffer with"; it is sometimes mistakenly thought of as having pity for others. Pity leads you to help and protect others such that in the long run it is not helpful and leaves people less protected.

The kind of compassion I have in mind enables you to have empathy for others and for yourself while holding yourself and others accountable for action rather than unilaterally protecting others or yourself. This kind of compassion enhances the other core values, rather than diminishing them.

Compassion comes from the heart. If you act out of compassion, rather than out of fear and guilt, you are able to move beyond defensiveness and be open and vulnerable. This enables you to create conversation in which you can mutually learn with others how to increase your effectiveness.

Emily demonstrates compassion for the group by recognizing that they are in a difficult and frustrating situation, rather than blaming them for not accomplishing the vision work. She demonstrates compassion for herself by recognizing that, although she has missed some potential interventions, she can't see them all.

Core Assumptions

The mutual learning core assumptions are that (1) I have some relevant information, and other people also have relevant information; (2) each of us may see things the others do not; (3) differences are opportunities for learning; and (4) people are trying to act with integrity, given their situation.

I Have Some Relevant Information, and Other People Also Have Relevant Information. In the mutual learning approach, you assume that you have only part of the information necessary to understand and address the issue. You assume that others have relevant information that would affect how you think about the subject if they shared the information. In other words, you know that you don't know all that you need to know. Information includes many things: what you believe to be facts, your point of view, the reasoning by which you come to a point of view, and your feelings. Emily assumes this when she shares her view on the issues and checks to see if people have other views.

Each of Us May See Things the Others Do Not. In a mutual learning approach, you assume that just as you may know or see things that others do not, others may see things that you miss. You see a conversation partly as a puzzle in which each person brings different pieces; the task is to jointly figure out what pieces each person is bringing and how the pieces fit together. You recognize that, whether you are working with another person, a group, or an organization, you are part of a system, and that the information and perspective you bring is limited; you can see only certain things from your vantage point in the system. Emily demonstrates this when she asks whether she has missed anything in her description of what is occurring. In a unilateral control approach, you assume that you have all the pieces of the puzzle and that if other people have pieces differing from yours, their pieces are not part of the same puzzle.

A key part of this mutual learning assumption is the idea that *I may be contributing to the problem and not seeing it.* In a unilateral control approach, it is the behavior of others that is the problem, not your own behavior. In a mutual learning approach, by starting with the assumption that you may be contributing to the problem and be unaware of it, you are recognizing your own limits. This leads you to be curious and to ask about how others see you as contributing to the problem. Emily demonstrates this when she asks if there is anything else she does that contributes to the group dragging.

Another part of this assumption is that *my feelings may be one of the ways I am contributing to the problem and not seeing it.* In the unilateral control model, you consider your feelings as the natural and inevitable result of others' action toward you. In the mutual learning model, you consider the possibility that your feelings have resulted from your own conclusions being based on untested inferences, assumptions, and attributions. You recognize that to the extent you act on these feelings, you are contributing to the problem. Using the mutual learning model does not preclude your feeling angry or disappointed; it asks you to reflect on the thinking you use that generates the feelings.

In the unilateral control model, if someone has a different point of view you consider it an obstacle to overcome. You may try to persuade the person that she is wrong or avoid the issue; in either case, you want to have your view prevail. In the mutual learning approach, you consider multiple points of view as an opportunity for learning. This means that if a group member holds a contrasting point of view, you help him or her figure what leads to seeing the situation differently. If you have a view unlike that of a group member, you jointly discover what leads you both to see things differently. By exploring how people see things, you can help the group create a common understanding that enables them to move forward in a way that everyone can support. In Emily's case, the group members do not differ significantly in their views. If, however, Moe says that he does not see Joe's behavior as a problem, Emily can help Moe, Barbara, and David explore what leads them to see Joe's behavior differently.

Differences Are Opportunities for Learning. In the unilateral control approach, differences in points of view are threats to be dealt with. If someone sees something differently than you do, you try to ignore the differences, minimize them, or even exaggerate them—all strategies for ensuring that your point of view will prevail. In the mutual learning approach, you are curious about others' perspectives because you consider differences in points of view as opportunities for learning. You are eager to explore differences because you see them as possibilities for developing greater understanding and solutions that integrate multiple perspectives. Emily assumes this when she thinks to herself, *What does Barbara see that I don't?*

People Are Trying to Act with Integrity, Given Their Situation. In the mutual learning model, you begin with the assumption that people's motives are pure rather than suspect. If people are acting in a way that does not make sense to you or that you think you understand but disapprove of, you do not assume that they are acting that way from a dubious motive. Instead, you begin with the assumption that people are striving to act with integrity; part of your task becomes understanding the reasons for their action rather than assuming you know and evaluating them accordingly. Implicit in Emily's actions is the notion that the group is trying to work but is getting stuck.

This assumption is the corollary to the value of compassion. **If you have compassion, you can understand that, just like you, others may act in a way that has negative effects even though that is not their intent.** If you have compassion for yourself, you accept that you may create problems for others, even if that is not intentional.

Strategies

You use the combination of core values and assumptions to develop strategies for dealing with a conversation. These are strategies you use whether or not others use them. The strategies for mutual learning are the ground rules of the Skilled Facilitator approach. I discuss the ground rules in detail in Chapter Five; for now, let us settle for brief descriptions of them.

- *Ground rule one: Test assumptions and inferences.* When you test assumptions and inferences, you ask others whether the meaning you make of their behavior is the meaning they make of it. Emily tests her inference when she says, "So, I'm inferring that you're thinking that even if the group accomplished the vision work, you're not sure it would be useful. Have I got that right?" By testing an assumption, you create valid information.

- *Ground rule two: Share all relevant information.* When you share all relevant information, you share all the information that affects how the group solves a problem or makes a decision. The next several ground rules identify specific ways of sharing all relevant information. Emily uses this ground rule when she describes how she contributes to the group's problems.

- *Ground rule three: Use specific examples, and agree on what important words mean.* Using specific examples means sharing detailed relevant information, including who said what and when and where it happened. By agreeing on what important words mean, you make sure that you are using words to mean the same thing that others mean when they use those words. Emily applies this ground rule when she asks Barbara, "Can you give me an example of a time when you thought it was dragging? That will help me understand what you mean."

- *Ground rule four: Explain your reasoning and intent.* As you explain your reasoning and intent, you share relevant information about the logic and motives behind your statements, questions, and actions. Emily shares her reasoning and intent when she says, "My intent is not to put you on the spot but to figure out what needs to happen so you can work effectively as a group." **A key part of explaining your reasoning is to make transparent your strategy for working with the group.** Notice that Emily makes her private strategy explicit to the group.

- *Ground rule five: Focus on interests, not positions.* An interest is a need or desire you have in regard to a given situation (Fisher, Ury, and Patton, 1991). A position or solution is how you meet your interests. Emily shares her interests when she says, "My interest as your facilitator is to help you accomplish what you think you need to accomplish, not to keep you on a task if it doesn't make sense anymore."

- *Ground rule six: Combine advocacy with inquiry.* When you combine advocacy with inquiry you (1) explain your point of view including the reasoning you use to get there, (2) ask others about their point of view, and (3) invite others to ask you questions about your point of view. Emily uses this ground rule when she describes how the group's concern about Joe is affecting their work in the session and then asks, "Have I misinterpreted your comments, or am I missing anything?"

- *Ground rule seven: Jointly design next steps and ways to test disagreements.* When you use this ground rule, you discuss and agree with others what next steps to take, including how you can test your disagreement. Emily jointly designs next steps with the group when she says, "Let's figure out together where we go from here. . . ."

- *Ground rule eight: Discuss undiscussable issues.* An undiscussable issue is one that is relevant to the group and reducing the group's effectiveness; people believe that they cannot discuss it without creating defensiveness or other negative consequences. By using this ground rule and the others, you can discuss these issues fruitfully and reduce the level of defensiveness. Emily raises a potentially undiscussable issue when she says, "This may be a difficult issue, but I want to raise it because if my inference is correct, it will be very hard for you to accomplish the task today."

- *Ground rule nine: Use a decision-making rule that generates the level of commitment needed.* This ground rule recognizes that the extent to which group members need to be internally committed to a decision for it to be implemented effectively is often commensurate with their involvement in making the decision. Emily uses this ground rule when she says, "Let's craft an approach that all of you can support."

Consequences

All of the mutual learning strategies—the Skilled Facilitator ground rules—are designed to create valid information, free and informed choice, and internal commitment, and to do so with compassion. Together, the mutual learning core values and assumptions and strategies (1) increase understanding and trust while reducing conflict and defensiveness; (2) reduce self-fulfilling and self-sealing processes; (3) create mutual learning; (4) increase effectiveness; and (5) increase the quality of worklife. These results are quite in contrast to those of the unilateral control model.

Increase Understanding, Reduce Conflict and Defensiveness. With the mutual learning approach, you increase understanding because you seek to create valid information, you assume that others have information you do not, and you accept that they may see things you are missing. This leads you to test inferences with others so that you determine whether they are valid before acting on them. By assuming that people are striving to act with integrity, you reduce the negative attributions you make about others. When you do make attributions, you test them. By doing so, you reduce the conflict arising from acting on untested or inaccurate assumptions and inferences and you reduce the defensive behavior associated with it. Similarly, you increase trust.

By using a mutual learning approach, Emily is able to understand the group members' concerns underlying their comments and see whether her inferences are accurate before acting on them. Using a mutual learning approach does not ensure that others will not respond defensively; however, it does reduce the chance of your creating or contributing to another's defensive reaction.

Reduce Self-Fulfilling, Self-Sealing Processes. You also reduce self-fulfilling and self-sealing processes by using a mutual learning model. In the second case (Exhibit 4.2), Emily thinks in a way that enables her to share what she is thinking and raise a difficult issue, instead of assuming that the group is not honest and then privately collecting data that confirms her inference.

Increase Learning. All of this enables you to increase *your* learning and help the group enhance its own. This includes learning how you and the members each contribute to group effectiveness or ineffectiveness. By sharing how the group's dragging is related to concerns about Joe, Emily helps the group learn about the impact of their behavior on their task. When Emily asks about whether she has done anything else that contributes to the problem, she learns that she has not always intervened soon enough when the group gets off track. Using the core value of compassion enables Emily to have this conversation, focusing not on who is to blame but rather on understanding how each person, acting in good faith, creates unintended consequences and how the group can reduce unintended consequences next time.

Increase Effectiveness. All of these results contribute to group effectiveness. By raising the issue of whether the visioning exercise makes sense given the group's concerns, Emily helps the group make an informed free choice about how to use its time effectively in the meeting. More significant, they can now discuss how to address an important issue for the group.

Increase the Quality of Worklife. Using a mutual learning approach also increases the quality of people's worklives. The values and assumptions of mutual learning enable you to increase understanding and trust and reduce defensive behavior. This reduces feelings of anxiety, fear, and anger that create stress. Even though the unilateral control approach is a natural response to a difficult situation, and even though it operates outside our awareness, it can still generate negative internal feelings not only in others but also in ourselves.

Consequences Reinforce the Model. The mutual learning consequences you create feed back to the mutual learning core values and assumptions, reinforcing the approach. In a difficult conversation, for instance, you temporarily withhold judgment to test inferences and inquire into others' reasoning; you learn more about yourself and others while minimizing defensive behavior, and you are more likely to continue using the approach.

MOVING TOWARD MUTUAL LEARNING: CHANGING OUR THINKING TO CHANGE OUR CONVERSATION

A central point of this chapter is that simply changing what you say and how you say it—the ground rules you use—is not sufficient to significantly change the unintended consequences you get. Because you apply the values and assumptions of your theory-in-use to design and implement what you say, if you try only to learn new mutual learning phrases, your unilateral control theory-in-use overrides them when it is active. As a result, your conversation has a unilateral control form. It is how you think when using a unilateral control approach that is the source of the dilemma of what to do with your left-hand column thoughts and feelings. **In the unilateral control model, you think in ways such that you cannot say what you are thinking without creating problems.** This is why many programs that teach only techniques to improve leadership, communication, or conflict management do not work in difficult situations. When I hear my clients wondering why the ground rules have stopped working for them, upon joint reflection we often discover that they were using the ground rules in a unilaterally controlling way.

The Skilled Facilitator approach uses a mutual learning model, which resolves the dilemma of how to manage your left-hand column thoughts and feelings. It involves **two levels of learning that happen concurrently. First, you learn how to move your thoughts and feelings from your left-hand column into the conversation in a way that is productive and does not contribute to others' defensiveness. This involves using the ground rules. Second, you learn to reflect rigorously on and redesign your core values and assumptions in order to think differently and use the new ground rules effectively.** To engage in this level of learning (what Argyris and Schön call double-loop learning), you need to explore the question, "What is it about the values and assumptions that I hold that leads me to design the kind of strategies that create unintended consequences for me and others?" This is the difficult but rewarding internal work of facilitation.

Although I have described the unilateral control model and the mutual learning model as if you are using one or the other, in practice I think of them as occupying the end points of a continuum. In my ideal view of myself, I am able to use a pure mutual learning model. In practice, my approach will likely be some mix of unilateral control and mutual learning. Although I may begin by mostly using a mutual learning approach, if a situation grows particularly difficult for me, my unilateral control approach begins to kick in. As the situation becomes more difficult for me, my approach becomes more one of unilateral control and less one of mutual learning. The challenge for me and for all of us is to increase the range and degree of difficult situations, and the length of time, in which we can sustain a mutual learning approach.

REFLECTING ON THEORY-IN-USE AS YOU READ THIS BOOK

Moving toward a mutual learning approach is difficult to do on your own, in part because you are usually unaware of your own unilateral control theory-in-use. For example, Emily was aware that her conversation was less effective than it could be, but she was unaware of how specifically she contributed to its ineffectiveness until we discussed it in a workshop. However, after understanding the differences between the two models, she began to see how her unilateral control theory-in-use had created consequences she had not intended.

This book can help you understand the distinction between using a unilateral control approach and using a mutual learning approach and can help you begin the journey toward using the Skilled Facilitator approach—if you choose to learn it. But reading about the mutual learning model is not a substitute for learning in a workshop or working with a coach.

My clients experience a range of feelings as they begin to practice the Skilled Facilitator approach. In subsequent chapters I identify some of the feelings that a facilitator commonly experiences. I hope this serves both as a guide to what you might encounter (recognizing that people may have their own reactions to a given situation) and as a support, so that when you experience these feelings you will know you are not alone and that the feelings come with the journey. This book can also help you consider how thinking anew about a situation and your role as facilitator may help you deal with your feelings.

Through facilitation, we come to know ourselves by reflecting on how we react to certain situations, understanding the sources of our feelings, and learning how to work with our feelings productively. In doing so, we not only help ourselves but also increase our ability to help the groups with which we work, whose members are facing the same issues.

SUMMARY

Your behavior is guided by your theory-in-use. In difficult situations, you employ a theory-in-use in which you unilaterally control the situation. As a result, you create many unintended negative consequences. An alternative and more effective theory-in-use is the mutual learning model, which is the basis for the Skilled Facilitator approach. The mutual learning approach helps you think and act in a way that is likely to increase learning and effectiveness and reduce unintended consequences, including defensive behavior. The mutual learning model presents tools for increasing effectiveness, particularly in situations that are emotionally difficult. The strategies for implementing the mutual learning model are the ground rules of the Skilled Facilitator approach. Employing a mutual learning theory-in-use involves changing not only your techniques but also how you think about situations—the core values and assumptions that make up your thinking. This is difficult but rewarding work. By doing this work for yourself, you increase your effectiveness. Then you can help groups learn to reflect on and change how their members think in difficult situations as well, so they can work more effectively together.

In the next chapter, we discuss the ground rules that you and your groups can use to put the mutual learning model core values and assumptions into practice.

Note

1. Action Design, founded by Robert Putnam, Phil McArthur, and Diana McLain Smith, is an organizational and management development firm that has built on the work of Argyris and Schön. Putnam and McLain Smith are coauthors, with Chris Argyris, of *Action Science*, published by Jossey-Bass.

CHAPTER FIVE

Ground Rules for Effective Groups

In this chapter, I present the ground rules for effective groups, describe what each of the nine ground rules means, and show how you can use them as a group leader, member, or facilitator to help a group become more effective.

USING THE GROUND RULES

As you watch a group in action, you may intuitively know whether their conversation is productive even if you cannot identify exactly how members contribute to or hinder the group's process. **The ground rules for effective groups describe specific behaviors that improve group process.** The ground rules make specific the abstract core values of the Skilled Facilitator approach, the mutual learning theory-in-use, and effective groups.[1] If you are familiar with the set of sixteen ground rules presented in the first edition of *The Skilled Facilitator*, you may want to read Resource A, which explains the relationship between the previous set and the current, smaller set of ground rules (listed in Exhibit 5.1).

What the Ground Rules Do

The ground rules have several purposes. First, **they serve as a diagnostic frame.** By becoming familiar with the ground rules, you can watch a group and identify specifically what is happening that is enhancing or hindering the group's process.

96

Exhibit 5.1. Nine Ground Rules for Effective Groups

1. Test assumptions and inferences.

2. Share all relevant information.

3. Use specific examples and agree on what important words mean.

4. Explain your reasoning and intent.

5. Focus on interests, not positions.

6. Combine advocacy and inquiry.

7. Jointly design next steps and ways to test disagreements.

8. Discuss undiscussable issues.

9. Use a decision-making rule that generates the level of commitment needed.

Second, **the ground rules guide your behavior as a facilitator.** You use the ground rules to guide your talk and increase your own effectiveness; by modeling the ground rules, you demonstrate how group members can do the same. You also use the ground rules to identify times when group members are acting less effective than they could, and to intervene to help them use the ground rules.

Finally, **the ground rules serve as a learning tool for developing effective group norms.** When a group understands the ground rules and commits to using them, they set new expectations for how the members will interact with each other. This enables the group to share responsibility for improving their process, which is often a goal of developmental facilitation. In other words, you can help groups learn to use the ground rules just as you do: to guide their own behavior and to serve as a diagnostic frame for improving their behavior.

Behavioral Ground Rules

The Skilled Facilitator ground rules may differ from some other ground rules you have seen or used. Some ground rules focus on procedural matters: "we will start on time and end on time," or "turn off pagers and cell phones." Procedural ground rules are useful, but they do not help the group understand what makes for productive conversation. Other sets focus on desired behavior but at a relatively abstract level, such as "treat everyone with respect" or "be constructive." They may create problems if group members differ in their understanding of what behavior is desirable (say, treating people with respect) or if members define terms according to a unilateral control model.

Sometimes facilitators ask me why I do not have the groups I work with develop their own ground rules. They reason that members commit to ground rules they develop and that they can develop useful ones. I have several reasons for introducing a set of ground rules rather than having them created within the group.

First, as a facilitator, I know that groups hire me for my process expertise, which includes knowing what kind of behavior helps a group become more effective. **Because I use the ground rules to diagnose behavior and to intervene, changing the ground rules would also mean changing the types of behavior that I diagnose and intervene on.** Second, **I do not assume that members have to develop the ground rules themselves to be committed to them; rather, I assume that they can be committed to them if they make a free and informed choice to use them.**

Third, in my experience **members are often not able to identify behaviorally specific ground rules**—the kind needed to improve group process. In addition, they sometimes generate ground rules that are designed to unilaterally protect themselves and others and reduce the group's ability to make a free and informed choice.

Finally, **in basic facilitation, a group is reasonably asking the facilitator to manage the process.** Asking a group to develop its own ground rules—behaviorally specific ground rules—takes time and shifts the focus from content to process.

Consequently, I choose to present the ground rules to the group, explain how they work, encourage members to raise questions and concerns they have, and identify any ground rules they think might be missing or need to be changed. (For example, groups often add a ground rule about keeping information confidential.) I use this approach for both basic and developmental facilitation, although in developmental facilitation the group and I spend considerably more time exploring this issue.

If you do choose to ask the group to develop or modify the ground rules, the basic principle is that the rules need to be consistent with the core values if you are to use the ground rules as a basis for diagnosing and intervening in the group.

Contracting to Use the Ground Rules

The ground rules are not the group's ground rules until its members have agreed to use them. There are two choices the group faces with respect to using the ground rules. First, the group needs to decide whether it wants to use me as a facilitator, understanding that a central part of my approach is to use the ground rules to diagnose group behavior and intervene in it. This includes asking group members to use the ground rules when I think doing so improves the process. Second, group members have to decide whether they want to take responsibility for practicing the ground rules themselves and for giving other group members feedback about using them. A group interested in learning to improve its process typically wants to do this. Even if the group as a whole does not choose to take responsibility for using the ground rules, individual members can still choose to do so.

To help the group make these decisions, I talk about the ground rules, how I would use them, what it would mean for them to use the rules, and inquire about concerns that they have about using the rules. This conversation is part of contracting with the group, which I discuss in detail in Chapter Thirteen.

GROUND RULE ONE: TEST ASSUMPTIONS AND INFERENCES

When you assume something, you take for granted that it is true without verifying it. When you infer something, you draw a conclusion about what you do not know on the basis of things that you do know. The effect is the same whether it is an assumption or an inference that goes without testing.

Jim, a group leader, observes that Hank, although productive, has considerably more work than any other group member. To lighten Hank's workload, Jim begins transferring some of Hank's work to other members. One day in a team meeting, Jim says, "Hank, your group's been working really hard and doing good work, but the analyses have been slowing your group down. I'm going to give Donna's group the weekly sales figures to analyze. You won't need to do it."

Hank replies with some sarcasm, "Thanks a lot. We bust our guts to fix others' mistakes, and we end up paying for it."

Jim responds, "You're not paying for it. I appreciate the hard work your group has done. I'm giving you some slack. Now, here's how I'd like to shift the work to Donna. . . ."

Jim has assumed that Hank will know why he is trying to lighten Hank's workload, and Hank incorrectly infers from Jim's statement that Jim is dissatisfied with his work. Furthermore, Jim does not test his assumption with Hank, and Hank does not test his inference with Jim; thus, neither can find out that he is incorrect. Here is how this happens.

The Ladder of Inference

How you make inferences is illustrated in the ladder of inference (Figure 5.1), which I have adapted from Argyris and Schön and from Action Design, which modified Argyris and Schön's work.

Directly Observable Data. In a conversation, you are faced with a lot of directly observable data, including what people are saying and their nonverbal behavior. I think of directly observable data as whatever a video camcorder can record.

Observe and Select Data. You cannot attend to everything, so at the first rung of the ladder of inference you observe and select certain data to pay attention to while ignoring other data. Some of what you choose to pay attention to is

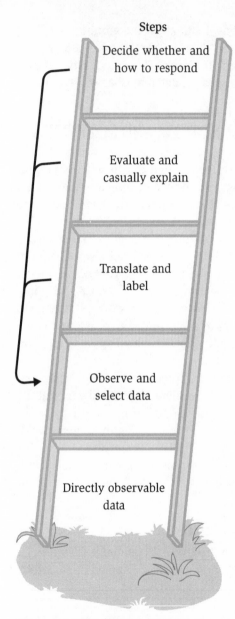

Steps	Internal Questions
Decide whether and how to respond	What should I do?
Evaluate and casually explain	What is leading the person to say or do this? How is this positive or negative?
Translate and label	What does it mean when the person says or does this?
Observe and select data	What data am I paying attention to? What data am I excluding?
Directly observable data	What data are available to me?

Figure 5.1. The Ladder of Inference

Source: Adapted from Argyris, 1985, and Action Design, 1997.

selected consciously, but much of it happens out of your awareness. In the case of Hank, he pays attention to the part of Jim's comment that says "but the analyses have been slowing your group down. I'm going to give Donna's group the weekly sales figures to analyze." He ignores entirely Jim's comment that "your group's been working really hard and doing good work" (Figure 5.2).

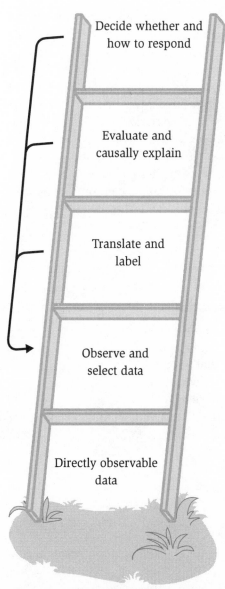

He's already made up his mind, but I still need to let him know it's not fair.

He thinks I can't handle the sales analyses because we were late the last four weeks. It's not my fault that Donna's unit has been giving us data sets full of errors that take two days to clean up. Jim is doing this because he doesn't want to confront Donna with the problem. I'm angry. We get the blame for her group's mistakes.

He's saying that I haven't done the job well and that we're not going to be responsible for the sales analysis anymore. He is taking away part of my job.

Jim said, "The analyses have been slowing your group down. I'm going to give Donna's group the weekly sales figures to analyze."

Jim says, "Hank, your group's been working really hard and doing good work, but the analyses have been slowing your group down. I'm going to give Donna's group the weekly sales figures to analyze. You won't need to do it."

Figure 5.2. Hank's Ladder of Inference

Source: Adapted from Argyris, 1985, and Action Design, 1997.

Translate and Label Data. At the second rung, you begin to infer meaning from the data by translating it into your own words and labeling it. Essentially, you say to yourself, *What does it really mean when this person says or does this?* Hank thinks to himself, *Jim is saying that I haven't managed the job well and that we're not going to be responsible for the sales analysis anymore. He is taking away part of my job.* Notice that in translating and labeling Jim's comment, Hank infers that Jim thinks he has not done the work well, and also that the change is permanent.

Evaluate and Explain. At the third rung, you evaluate and explain what you have translated and labeled at the second rung. Whereas on the second rung you describe what is occurring, on this rung you judge it and create a causal explanation. You ask yourself, *In what way is this positive or negative?* You also ask yourself, *What is leading the person to say or do this?* Hank thinks, *He thinks I can't handle the sales analyses because we were late the last four weeks. It's not my fault that Donna's unit has been giving us data sets full of errors that take two days to clean up. Jim is doing this because he doesn't want to confront Donna with the problem. I'm angry. We get the blame for her group's mistakes.*

Notice that the causal explanation that Hank creates includes an attribution about Jim (that he is doing this because he doesn't want to confront Donna with the problem)—that is, an inference about what is motivating Jim to do this.

Exhibit 5.2. Not Testing Inferences and Assumptions

Hank's Ladder of Inference	The Conversation	Jim's Ladder of Inference
Jim said: "I'm going to give Donna the weekly sales figures to analyze." He's saying that I haven't done the job well and that we're not going to be responsible for the sales analysis anymore. He is taking away part of my job. He thinks I can't handle the sales analyses because we were late the last four weeks. It's not my fault that Donna's unit has been giving us data sets full of errors that take two days to clean up. Jim is doing this because he doesn't want to confront Donna with the problem. I'm angry. We get the blame for her group's mistakes. He's already made up his mind, but I still need to let him know it's not fair.	JIM: Hank, your group's been working really hard and doing good work, but the analyses have been slowing your group down. I'm going to give Donna's group the weekly sales figures to analyze. You won't need to do it.	

Decide How to Respond. On the fourth and final rung, you decide whether and how to respond. Hank decides, "He's already made up his mind, but I still need to let him know it's not fair." Like Hank, you go up the ladder of inference in milliseconds without even being aware that you are doing so.

Of course, while Hank is inferring, so is Jim. In a group conversation, each person makes inferences, and they are going to differ. If you could combine Hank's and Jim's left-hand columns, they might look like Exhibit 5.2. As you can see, Hank makes inferences on the basis of Jim's comment and responds. Jim, in turn, infers from Hank's comment and responds. In this way their conversation arises from an accumulated set of inferences that each makes about the other.

Our Inferences Become Data

The ladder of inference is not linear. You turn the inferences that you make into facts that influence what you observe, and this becomes the basis for further inference. This is called a reflexive loop. For example, Hank will use his inference—that Jim thinks Hank's team can't do the work and that Jim doesn't want

Exhibit 5.2. (*continued*)

Hank's Ladder of Inference	The Conversation	Jim's Ladder of Inference
	HANK: Thanks a lot. We bust our guts to fix others' mistakes and we end up paying for it.	"Thanks a lot?" That's a sarcastic comment. He's complaining when he should be thanking me. Jim just wants to analyze the sales figures because that information puts him in a position of power and he thinks that everyone else makes it difficult for his group to do its work. That's one problem with Jim. But I'm not going to get into that with him. I'll just let it pass and get to the details.
	JIM: You're not paying for it. I appreciate the hard work your group has done. I'm giving you some slack. Now, here's how I'd like to shift the work to Donna. . . .	

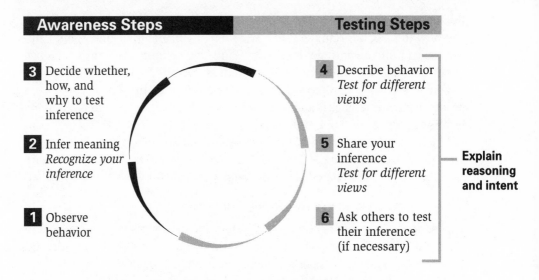

Figure 5.3. Cycle for Testing Inferences and Assumptions

to confront Donna—to systematically select data from future interactions with Jim to confirm his inference. If Jim makes an ambiguous comment, Hank is likely to interpret it as another example of the same. This reflexive loop leads a person to create what he or she *thinks* is a solid basis for a conclusion. In fact, what is created is a large set of untested inferences that may be completely flawed.

It happens quickly. It takes just milliseconds to make an inference. You do it throughout the day and act without being aware of doing so. The problem is not that you make inferences; you must do that to make sense out of what people are saying. Rather, it is how you make inferences and what you do with them. First, **you are usually unaware that you are making inferences,** so you consider them facts rather than hypotheses. Second, **the inferences you make are often high-level inferences,** greatly removed from the data you have. Therefore, there is a logical gap in the steps of reasoning, which you are typically unaware of. For example, if someone disagrees with what you are proposing, you may make a high-level inference that the person is trying to undermine your plan, rather than a low-level inference that the person's needs are not being met by your plan. Third, **you do not test out with the people about whom you are making an inference whether it is accurate; you simply act on it as if it is true.** Consequently, you take action on the basis of an inference that may not be valid.

Testing Your Inferences and Helping Others Test Theirs

Testing inferences generates valid information that you can use to make informed choices. The cycle for testing inferences and assumptions (see Figure 5.3) describes the steps for using the ground rule.

Figure 5.4. Testing Inferences and Assumptions

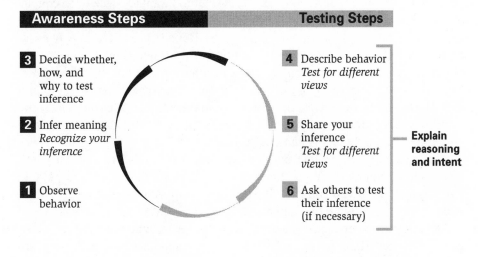

Awareness Steps	Testing Steps

3 Decide whether, how, and why to test inference

2 Infer meaning *Recognize your inference*

1 Observe behavior

4 Describe behavior *Test for different views*

5 Share your inference *Test for different views*

6 Ask others to test their inference (if necessary)

Explain reasoning and intent

---

3 I'm going to test my inference because if we don't have a common understanding of the situation, we will not be able to solve the problem.

2 I'm inferring that the cause of the problem is Donna's group, and I'm also inferring that Jim thinks the cause of the problem is my group.

1 Jim says, "Hank, you have been working really hard and doing good work, but the analyses have been slowing your group down. I'm going to give Donna the weekly sales figures to analyze. You won't need to do it."

4 "Jim, I want to check out a couple of inferences I made. I think you just said that the analyses have been slowing my group down and that you are going to give Donna's group the weekly sales figures to analyze. Do you remember it differently?" [*if Jim remembers it the same way, Hank continues*]

5 "From what you've said, I'm inferring that you think the sales analyses were late because of my group. Is that what you are thinking, or am I off?"

6 [*not needed*]

Figure 5.4 shows how Hank could use the cycle to test his inferences with Jim.

Steps one through three are awareness steps; they are private thoughts. In step one, Hank observes Jim's behavior, namely the words he says to Hank, his tone of voice, and his nonverbal behavior. In step two, Hank infers that the cause of the problem is Donna's group; he infers that Jim thinks the cause of the problem is Hank's group. In step three, Hank decides to test these inferences because a common understanding of the situation is necessary in order to solve the problem. Hank tests the inference with Jim by using the rest of the cycle.

Steps four through six are the testing steps. They are public—that is, they are spoken. In step four, Hank begins by stating his intent, describing the behavior he sees that leads him to make an inference, and checks to see whether Jim remembers the behavior differently. Hank says, "Jim, I want to check out a couple of inferences I made. I think you just said that the analyses have been slowing my group down and that you are going to give Donna's group the weekly sales figures to analyze. Do you remember it differently?" If not, Hank moves to step five and says, "From what you've said, I'm inferring that you think the sales analyses were late because of my group. Is that what you are thinking, or am I off?" If Jim says he does make that inference, Hank has tested his inference and found it accurate. If Jim says that he does not think Hank is the cause of the problem, Hank finds out that his inference is inaccurate.

In this example, Hank does not need step six of the cycle. He would use it if Jim made an inference about someone other than Hank. In that case, Hank would say, "Jim, would you be willing to check with Allen to see if your inference is accurate?" Step six is used to ask the person if he or she is willing to test out an inference about someone other than the person who is asking for a test of the inference. Hank doesn't need to use this step because he is testing out an inference that Jim has made about him.

If Hank does not test his inference, the facilitator can intervene to ask him to do so. Figure 5.5 shows the steps of an intervention.

Again, steps one through three are awareness steps and are private thoughts. Assume you are the facilitator. In step one, you observe Hank's behavior, which comprises the words he says to Jim, his tone of voice, and his nonverbal behavior. In step two, you infer from his saying "thanks a lot," and from the rest of his comment, that he thinks he would not be slowing down if others were not making mistakes, and that he has inferred that Jim does not understand this. In step three, you decide to test your inference because if correct then it is important that Hank find out whether Jim understands it as Hank does. You decide to test the inference with Hank using the rest of the cycle.

Steps four through six are the testing steps; you make them public. In step four, you begin by stating your intent, describing the behavior you see that leads you to make your inference, and check to see whether Hank remembers the behavior differently: "Hank, I'd like to check something out. I think you said, 'Thanks a lot. We bust our guts to fix others' mistakes and we end up paying for it.' Did I get that?" If Hank does not remember it differently, you can move to step five and say, "From what you said, I infer that you're thinking your group wouldn't be in this situation if others hadn't made mistakes, and that you have inferred Jim doesn't understand that. Are my inferences off track?" If Hank says that he does make that inference, you can move to step six and say, "Would you be willing to check your inferences with Jim to see whether he understands it differently from you?" Assuming Hank agrees, you have completed the cycle. As Hank tests out his inference with Jim, you use the cycle to decide whether Hank may be making other untested inferences.

Figure 5.5. Intervening on Testing Inferences and Assumptions

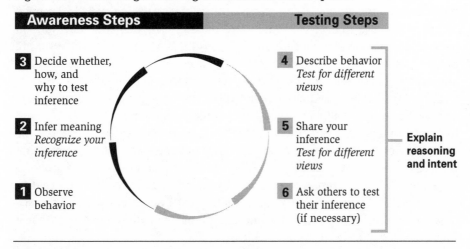

3 I'll intervene on this because if my inference is correct, then it is important that Hank test his inference with Jim to see if he understands it differently.

2 I'm inferring from Hank's tone of voice when he says "Thanks a lot" and from the rest of his comment that he thinks he would not be slowing down if others had not made mistakes and that he has inferred that Jim does not understand that.

1 Jim says, "Hank, you have been working really hard and doing good work, but the analyses have been slowing your group down. I'm going to give Donna the weekly sales figures to analyze. You won't need to do it." Hank says, "Thanks a lot. We bust our guts to fix others' mistakes and we end up paying for it."

4 "Hank, I'd like to check something out. I think you said, 'Thanks a lot. We bust our guts to fix others' mistakes and we end up paying for it.' Did I get that?" [*if the answer is yes, continue*]

5 "From what you said, I infer that you're thinking your group wouldn't be in this situation if others hadn't made mistakes and that you have inferred that Jim doesn't understand that. Are my inferences off track?" [*if inference is accurate, continue*]

6 "Would you be willing to check your inferences with Jim to see whether he understands it differently from you?"

As a facilitator, you also use the cycle to test any inference that you think others are making about you and your facilitation. Whether you are a facilitator or a group member, **when using any of the ground rules, you do not have to use the words *infer* and *inference*.** If these words sound unnatural or like jargon, you can say, "I'm thinking that . . . ," "It sounds to me like . . . ," or something similar.

The Diagnosis-Intervention Cycle

Earlier I distinguished between using the ground rules myself and helping group members use them. When I intervene with group members, I use the diagnosis-intervention cycle (see Figure 5.6). It is a structured way to diagnose behavior and then to intervene. It is essentially a generic version of the cycle for testing inferences and assumptions. The inference testing cycle is designed to test inferences that you or others are making. The diagnosis-intervention cycle is designed to test your inferences that others are not using one or more of the ground rules. Because testing inferences is one of the ground rules, you can use the diagnosis-intervention cycle for testing inferences and assumptions (as I illustrate in Chapter Nine). Like the testing cycle, the diagnosis-intervention cycle has two sides: diagnosis and intervention.

I use the diagnosis side of the diagnosis-intervention cycle to observe the group conversation, infer which ground rules members are not employing that they could benefit from using, and decide whether to intervene in the group to help them use the ground rule. I use the intervention side of the cycle to explain the intent of my intervention, share what I observe, test my inference that they are not using a ground rule that would be helpful, and ask them if they are willing to use the ground rule.

In Chapters Six through Eight, I explain in detail how to use each step of the diagnosis-intervention cycle. I have briefly introduced it here so that I can show you examples of interventions you can make when you want to help group members use each ground rule.

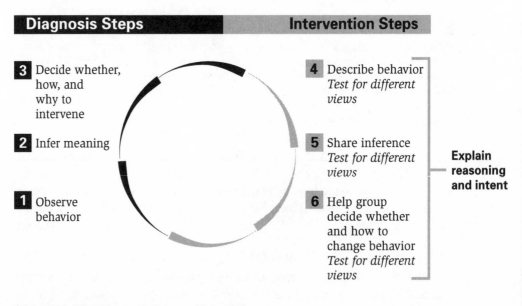

Figure 5.6. The Diagnosis-Intervention Cycle

GROUND RULE TWO: SHARE ALL RELEVANT INFORMATION

Ground rule two means that each member shares all the relevant information she or he has that affects how the group solves a problem or makes a decision. Sharing relevant information ensures that members have a common base of information on which to make an informed choice and generate commitment. If people make a decision and later find out that others have withheld relevant information from them, they feel they were prevented from making an informed choice; sometimes they withdraw their agreement. Even if they do not, they may implement the agreement with little commitment.

Sharing relevant information includes whatever does not support your preferred position. For example, a top management team of a small consumer goods company is deciding how to restructure its organization and move into a new facility. Sandra, the head of one manufacturing process, wants very much to maintain her role. Yet she also knows that in the new facility a number of manufacturing processes could easily be merged for greater efficiency. Here, sharing all relevant information means telling the group about the benefit, even though doing so may reduce her chance of achieving the role she wants.

Group members' feelings are also relevant information to share. For example, a member of an organizational development (OD) group in a global financial services organization is frustrated because he believes his manager is assigning him work that is not within his responsibility. At the same time, he is reluctant to raise this issue because of concern that the manager thinks he isn't a team player. In this case, sharing all relevant information includes the OD person saying something like, "I want to talk with you about some concerns I have about being given the white paper to write. But I'm also concerned that you may think it's inappropriate for me to question being given the assignment. So I'd like to check that out before we talk about the work. Is that OK?"

In a difficult conversation, there is often a large gap between what you say and what is in your left-hand column. You are likely to talk about the content or substantive issue and keep unexpressed your thoughts and feelings regarding the people you are having the conversation with. It is relevant to share both types of information, in part because your feelings about others affect how you view the content of the conversation.

Exhibit 5.3 illustrates how you withhold relevant information. Consider a conversation between Ted and Paula, in which she is trying to get him to understand that he has been ineffective in presenting a project proposal to the senior management team.

Notice all the relevant information in Paula's left-hand column that she does not share with Ted. The point is not that she should share her thoughts and feelings exactly as they appear on the left. As we saw in Chapter Four, this would

Exhibit 5.3. Withholding Relevant Information

Paula's Thoughts and Feelings	The Conversation
I thought it was abysmal; I wanted to crawl under my chair at the meeting. I had three others tell me it was a waste of their time.	PAULA: How do you think the presentation to the senior management team went yesterday?
Does he really believe it went OK, or is he just trying to put a good spin on it? Nitpicky! You couldn't answer some basic cost questions.	TED: I think it went OK, although there were some rough spots. Some of those execs can really get nitpicky.
I don't understand why you didn't emphasize the need for the project. The team won't approve a project if they can't get answers to some basic questions.	PAULA: We've got some really important reasons for doing it. Do you think the team will support the project now, or do you think maybe we need to give them more answers?
I don't want to wait while this project dies on the vine. Besides, my reputation is at stake here, too.	TED: I think we're in OK shape. A couple of the members came up to me afterward and said they appreciated the presentation. I think we should just wait and see.
I hope the team doesn't think I'm responsible for your not having the answers to those questions. Why didn't you use the information I gave you? I've got to get you to understand what you've done.	PAULA: Maybe, but I think we might want to give them some more information.

be inconsistent with many of the other ground rules. To be effective, Paula should share the relevant information by using the other ground rules (such as testing assumptions and inferences, and using examples).

To share some relevant information in her left-hand column, she might say, "Ted, I have some concerns about the presentation you did yesterday. I'd like to give you some specific examples about what concerned me and get your reaction. OK?" Assuming Ted agrees, Paula continues, "One thing that concerned me was that when Tanya asked you what the cost savings would be, you said you hadn't calculated them. Do you remember it differently?"

If Paula does not share the relevant information, you can intervene to ask her for it. Obviously, you cannot directly observe Paula's private thoughts and feelings to make your intervention, but you do not need to. Figure 5.7 shows how to intervene using the diagnosis-intervention cycle.

Figure 5.7. Intervening on Sharing Relevant Information

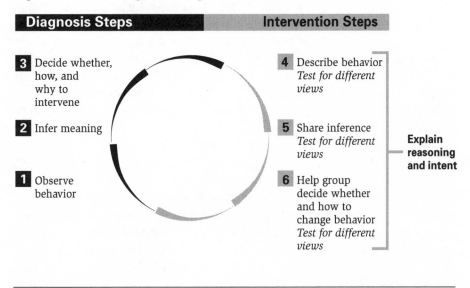

<table>
<tr><td>

3 I'll intervene on this because Paula has not shared the information she is talking about.

2 I'm inferring that Paula has some information to share that leads her to ask her question and has some specific ideas of how Ted could have given them more information.

1 Paula said, "How do you think the presentation went today? . . . Maybe, but I think we might want to give them some more information."

</td><td>

4 "Paula, a minute ago I think you said a couple of things to Ted: 'How do you think the presentation went today?' 'Maybe, but I think we might want to give them some more information.' Did I get it accurately?" [*if yes, continue*]

5 "When you said that to Ted, I thought you had your own views about how the presentation went and had an idea about some information that he could have shared. Was my thought correct?" [*if yes, continue*]

6 "Would you be willing to share that information with Ted?"

</td></tr>
</table>

GROUND RULE THREE: USE SPECIFIC EXAMPLES
AND AGREE ON WHAT IMPORTANT WORDS MEAN

Using specific examples and agreeing on what important words mean is one way of sharing relevant information that generates valid data. Specific examples use directly observable data to name people, places, things, or events. Unlike a general statement, a specific example yields valid information because it enables other members to determine independently whether the example is valid.

For example, if Henry makes the general statement to the group, "I think some of us are not doing their share of the work," other members cannot determine whether the statement is valid. Members cannot observe who "some of us" are; neither can they directly observe whether someone is "not doing their share of the work." As a result, the people Henry is referring to may incorrectly infer that he is not talking about them, and the people that he is not referring to may incorrectly infer he *is* talking about them. In contrast, if he states specifically, "Selina and Joe, you did not complete and distribute your section of the report," other members can determine whether the statement is valid by directly observing whether Selina and Joe's section of the report is complete and has been distributed.

Some group members and facilitators have a concern about naming names in the group. They follow the principle to "praise in public, criticize in private." Unfortunately, following this principle prevents sharing valid information. If Joe and Selina's not completing their report section creates a problem for other group members, and if Henry pulls Joe and Selina out of the meeting to share his concern, the other group members do not get a chance to directly share their own concern and Joe and Selina do not get a chance to talk about how others' work habits may have contributed to their not completing their section. Talking to Joe and Selina in private essentially removes the data from the system (the group) in which it arose, which increases the chance of the problem being solved in a way that contributes to more problems in the system.

Of course, the principle of praising in public and criticizing in private has a unilateral control set of assumptions embedded in it: discussing your concerns about others' behavior is criticism. As you shift toward a mutual learning approach, you begin to think of these situations as an opportunity to learn something you may have missed or to help the group understand how together they may have acted in a way that makes sense individually but creates unintended consequences at the group level.

Another way to think about specific examples is that they help people agree on what important words mean. When a member unintentionally agrees or disagrees with another, it is often because the same word means different things to them. Suppose a group decides to make decisions by consensus. To some members, the word means that a mere majority of people support it, while to others it means unanimous support. The first time the group makes a decision that has majority (but not unanimous) support, it will learn that it has not agreed on the meaning of consensus.

One way to determine whether all group members are using a word to mean the same thing is to ask them the first time the word is used. You can say, "You used the word *consensus*. To me, consensus means unanimous support and not majority support. In practice, this means everyone in the group can say that they will implement the decision, given their role. It doesn't mean that people are silent about their concerns. It does mean saying something like, 'Even though I have these concerns, I support the decision to implement it.' How does your definition differ, if at all?" Notice that giving an example is part of describing what a word means, and that it helps also to give an example of what it does not mean.

To think about how to use this ground rule, consider a real conversation, which took place in a publishing company (Exhibit 5.4). Sarah is a senior editor; Linda is the director of sales. Sarah is expressing concern about the design of a book jacket.

Notice that Sarah describes the book jacket in such general terms as "too flashy and blah," "not simple and more sophisticated," "dated and old." She does not illustrate what elements of the book jacket lead her to describe it in these terms. Linda, by contrast, does focus on specific examples when she asks, "What if we changed the type?" However, Sarah responds simply by saying it's a start and then suggests that if the type change doesn't work she will look for ways to "tweak this"; but again she does not give an example of what she means by tweaking. Without hearing Sarah explain what she has observed that leads her to describe the book as too flashy and blah, Linda cannot decide whether she sees it differently; nor can she decide whether she thinks she should talk to the designer about it.

To use this ground rule, Sarah could say, "Let me give you a couple of examples of what I mean by too flashy, and get your reaction. The fonts are all uppercase, in primary colors, and the letters are shadowed in a contrasting color. Is there anything I've said so far that's unclear about what I mean by flashy?"

If Sarah does not share specific examples, you can intervene to ask her to do so. Figure 5.8 shows how to intervene using the diagnosis-intervention cycle.

GROUND RULE FOUR: EXPLAIN YOUR REASONING AND INTENT

If you do not explain your reasoning, the people you are talking with will often generate their own explanation of your reasoning, and their explanations may differ greatly from your own explanation. **Using this ground rule means explaining to others what leads you to make a comment or ask a question or take an action.** Reasoning and intent are similar but different. Your intent is your purpose for doing something. Your reasoning—like the ladder of inference—represents the logical process that you use to draw conclusions on the basis of data, values, and assumptions.

Explaining your reasoning and intent includes making your private reasoning public, so that others can see how you reached your conclusion and can ask you about places in your reasoning where they may reason differently. This includes making transparent your strategy for managing the conversation. In a unilateral control approach, explaining your reasoning is a problem because it enables others to point out flaws in your reasoning, which reduces the chance

Exhibit 5.4. Not Using Specific Examples or Agreeing on What Important Words Mean

Sarah's Thoughts and Feelings	The Conversation
Be open and friendly; do not attack. Dear God, I can't sleep because of this hideous design.	SARAH: Linda, I know you feel like this design is fine for the book, but I have big reservations. I think we need a new design.
I knew she would blow up—but I detect an opening here. . . . Her words sound inflamed, but she seems to know I have to be on board.	LINDA: WHAT?! I thought you liked this! What are you talking about? What's wrong with it? It's fine!
Yeah, I screwed up. I should have known. But you and the design director are the supposed experts here, and you're blowing it! This project deserves the best, and this is just not it yet. I'm worried that even if we go back to the drawing board, it won't get better. But it can't get worse . . . can it?	SARAH: I know. I think at the beginning I felt we were going through a few rounds of design . . . and in retrospect I should have probably axed them immediately . . . but I thought I was letting the process run its course. I'll tell you honestly, I feel very strongly about this—I think we need to go back to the drawing board. I think we should hire a completely new designer.
Hmm, she is opening up. I was afraid there would be little room to negotiate; was I overly afraid?	LINDA: What don't you like about it?
She is trying to work with it—a good sign, and her tone has come down a few notches. Good. But she is trying to work within the design. . . . I still think we need to throw it out.	SARAH: Well, it's too flashy and blah. It does not have the feel of the book . . . simple and more sophisticated. It feels dated and old. The design is not modern—it says this book is nothing new—and it's new and exciting.
	LINDA: What if we changed the type?
Can't we just send this out, damn it?!	SARAH: Well, that's a start. I think we may want to farm it out to a new designer. If that doesn't work, then I'd be willing to look at ways to tweak this.

Figure 5.8. Intervening on Using Specific Examples and Agreeing on What Important Words Mean

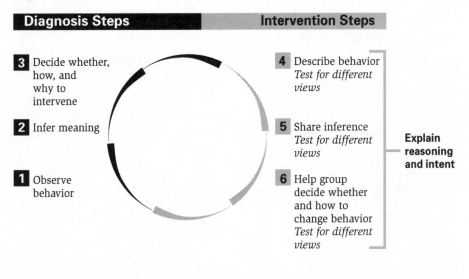

Diagnosis Steps	Intervention Steps

3 Decide whether, how, and why to intervene

2 Infer meaning

1 Observe behavior

4 Describe behavior *Test for different views*

5 Share inference *Test for different views*

6 Help group decide whether and how to change behavior *Test for different views*

Explain reasoning and intent

---

3 I'll intervene on this because Sarah and Linda are each unlikely to understand how the other is thinking about the jacket unless they get to specifics.

2 I'm inferring that Sarah has not been specific in describing what makes the jacket seem flashy and blah to her.

1 Sarah said, "Well, it's too flashy and blah."

4 "Sarah, I think you described the jacket in a number of ways. One of the things you said was that it was 'blah and flashy.' Did I get that?" [*if yes, continue*]

5 "When you said that to Linda, I inferred that you had specific examples of how the jacket was blah and flashy, but I didn't hear them. Have I inferred correctly?" [*if yes, continue*]

6 "Can you give Linda some specific examples of how it's blah and flashy?"

---

that you can win in the discussion. Instead, your reasoning often seeps out indirectly, sometimes in the form of a cheap shot, in which you indirectly surface your concern by making an oblique or sarcastic comment. In the unilateral control model, making your strategy transparent is a problem because your strategy is to be unilaterally controlling; sharing your strategy reduces your ability to implement it.

In a mutual learning Skilled Facilitator approach, explaining your reasoning and making your strategy transparent are opportunities to learn where others have differing views or approaches and where you may have missed something that others see. Sharing your intent to unilaterally control others reduces your chance of accomplishing it; in contrast, sharing your mutual learning intent is likely to increase your ability to accomplish that purpose.

Exhibit 5.5. Not Explaining Your Reasoning and Intent

Leslie's Thoughts and Feelings	The Conversation
OK, that's your starting position. Let's see what options we can work out.	JACK: I really need a full-time person dedicated to this project.
Boy, it would really help me and my resources if this can wait. How time-critical is it?	LESLIE: How soon will it start? Can it wait two months until next quarter?
Well, if you don't find anybody, you'll sure have to wait, won't you?	JACK: The project's got to be worked on right away. I can't wait any longer than I already have.
Let's see if I can buy some time for me and still get some of the project done for him.	LESLIE: Well, I know one of your people has the experience for this; how about if she works on it part-time until next quarter?
People don't always get to do what they want to.	JACK: I don't think she wants to do that. In fact, I'm pretty sure she really wants to work on my other projects.
OK, what if we spread the hit across multiple people instead of creaming just one?	LESLIE: Couldn't we have more people work on smaller pieces of the project instead of just one person?
Strike two.	JACK: No, I don't think that would work out.
Let's look at the data. Is this project really documented well enough that Jim's reasoning stands up?	LESLIE: Can we look at the Gantt chart to see? Maybe there are specific topics that can be dealt out.
Geez, here we go again. What's the deal with him?	JACK: No, I don't think this project would work well without a dedicated person; something might drop through the cracks.

Exhibit 5.5 shows a real conversation between Jack and Leslie, two managers in a semiconductor corporation, in which Jack is asking for some of Leslie's people to work on a project he directs. Jack wants one person full-time; Leslie wants to give Jack several people at less than full time to work on the several parts of his project.

To share her reasoning and intent, Leslie can say something like, "Jack, the reason I'm asking you if you can wait until next quarter is that I have a project due next month, and I need input from all of my staff to complete it. Giving you a person full-time will make it difficult for me to complete the project."

Figure 5.9. Intervening on Sharing Your Reasoning and Intent

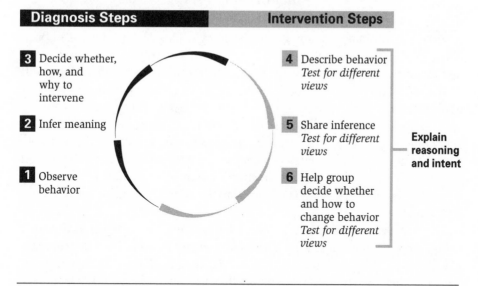

3 I'll intervene on this because Jack can't help it if he doesn't know what's leading Leslie to ask him the questions.

2 I'm inferring that Leslie has reasons for asking Jack these questions that she has not yet shared.

1 Leslie asked, "How soon will it start? Can it wait two months until next quarter?" and "Couldn't we have more people work on smaller pieces of the project instead of just one person?"

4 "Leslie, I think you asked Jack, 'How soon will it start?' 'Can it wait two months until next quarter?' and 'Couldn't we have more people work on smaller pieces of the project instead of just one person?' Yes?" [*if yes, continue*]

5 "When you asked Jack that, I was thinking that you had reasons for asking about changing the time frame and the number of people, but I didn't hear them. Was my thinking correct?" [*if yes, continue*]

6 "Would you be willing to share your reasoning with Jack?"

If Leslie does not share her reasoning and intent, you can intervene to ask her to do so. Figure 5.9 shows how.

GROUND RULE FIVE: FOCUS ON INTERESTS, NOT POSITIONS

Focusing on interests is another way of sharing relevant information. **Interests, we have seen, are the needs and desires that people have in regard to a given situation** (Fisher, Ury, and Patton, 1991; Graham, 1995). Solutions or positions are how people meet their interests. In other words, people's interests lead them to advocate a particular solution or position.

Identify Interests

An effective way for members to solve problems is to begin by sharing their own interests. Unfortunately, many groups begin by talking about solutions or positions. For example, if the group is trying to solve the problem of when to meet, one member may start by saying, "I suggest we meet every other Monday at 7:30 A.M." Another may respond, "I think that we should meet the second day of each month." Their positions do not help the group identify each member's real needs, desires, and concerns. Here, the person who suggested meeting every other Monday at 7:30 A.M. is interested in meeting early in the morning, before some important clients call. The person who wants to meet the second day of each month is interested in meeting immediately after a relevant bi-weekly report is made available. Each takes a position that meets his or her individual interest.

The trouble with solving a problem by focusing first on positions is that people's positions are often in conflict even when their interests are compatible. This occurs because people tend to offer their position after they have attended to their own interests, but before they have included the other members' interests. In the meeting example, each member's solution is rejected by the other because it fails to meet the other's interest. However, if each member is aware of the other's interest, either one may be able to offer a solution that satisfies both.

One way to think about interests is as criteria that need to be met in order to solve the problem in a way that people support. To help the group focus on interests rather than positions, you can begin by asking each member to list the criteria that must be met for that member to accept a solution. Take a simple example of a group buying a car. One member is interested in a car that can hold all six group members, so that they can work together as they travel. Another is interested in a car that uses fuel efficiently, while a third member is interested in a car that requires little expense for maintenance. Notice that none of these interests specifies a particular make and model of car (position). If a member states a position ("I want to buy a Grand Caravan"), then this can be identified as a position and the person can be asked, "What is it about the Grand Caravan that leads you to suggest that as a solution?"

In the conversation between Leslie and Jack, both focus on positions. Jack's position is that he needs a full-time person immediately; Leslie's position—which she does not state directly—is that she can only give people part-time and beginning only next quarter. Neither explains the need he or she faces that has led to offering a particular solution.

Jack could share his interests by saying, "Leslie, I have a need for the kind of project support that will ensure that all the tasks are accomplished with a minimal amount of coordination among my project staff."

Figure 5.10. Intervening by Focusing on Interests, Not Positions

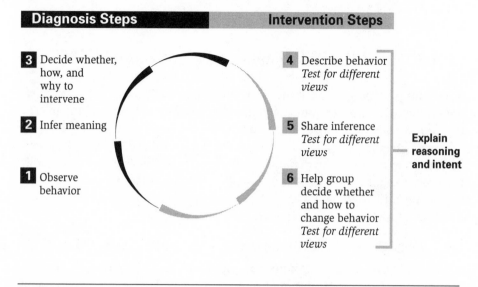

| Diagnosis Steps | Intervention Steps |

3 Decide whether, how, and why to intervene

2 Infer meaning

1 Observe behavior

4 Describe behavior
Test for different views

5 Share inference
Test for different views

6 Help group decide whether and how to change behavior
Test for different views

Explain reasoning and intent

---

3 I'll intervene on this because Jack and Leslie seem to be at a stalemate.

2 I'm inferring that Jack has a set of interests underlying his positions that he has not shared. They may be to minimize the amount of coordination and ensure that all the tasks are covered.

1 Jack has said, "I really need a full-time person dedicated to this" and "No, I don't think this project would work well without a dedicated person; something might drop through the cracks."

4 "Jack, I think you said that you need a full-time person dedicated to the project and that without it something might drop through the cracks. Did I miss anything?" [*if no, continue*]

5 "I'm inferring that you have some particular needs that lead you to suggest your solution, but I didn't hear them. Have I inferred correctly?" [*if yes, continue*]

6 "Can you say what it is about having a full-time person that is important to you?"

If Jack does not share his interests, you can intervene, as Figure 5.10 illustrates.

Craft a Solution That Meets Interests

After all members have shared their interests, you can check to see whether group members are willing to generate solutions that take into account all the interests identified. If members identify some interests that they believe should not be considered in generating solutions, then you can ask them to share their reasoning. Once the members agree to the set of interests, they can begin to generate solutions or positions. In the car example, a solution is to name specific cars (Ford Taurus, Dodge Caravan). When offering a solution, it helps to have the person identify how the solution meets the interests on which the group members have agreed.

GROUND RULE SIX: COMBINE ADVOCACY AND INQUIRY

Combining advocacy and inquiry means expressing your point of view, which includes sharing your reasoning and intent and then inviting others to inquire into your comments (Argyris and Schön, 1974). For example, a group member might say, "I think it would help to give division heads their own budgets to work within, so that their accountability will be commensurate with their responsibility. Here's the reasoning that led me to suggest this. [Explains reasoning] I'd like to hear what each of you thinks about this idea. What are your thoughts? What, if anything, do you see differently?"

What Combining Advocacy and Inquiry Accomplishes

Combining advocacy and inquiry accomplishes several goals. First, it shifts a meeting from a series of monologues to a focused conversation. In some meetings, one person speaks after the other, but no one's comments seem to directly address the previous person's. This happens partly because when one person finishes talking, he or she does not invite others to inquire. Without an explicit invitation to inquire or comment on the previous person's remarks, the meeting switches focus with each person who speaks.

Second, combining advocacy and inquiry creates conditions for learning. When you share your reasoning and then ask others to inquire into it, they can determine for themselves whether they agree with your reasoning or see parts of it differently. By identifying where group members' reasoning differs, you can help the group explore what has led people to reason differently; are they using other data, are they making other assumptions, or are they assigning different priorities to certain issues?

Some facilitators tend to focus the group on where the members agree and minimize discussion of where members disagree. These facilitators are often concerned that focusing on different views creates unnecessary conflict and defensive group member behavior that the facilitator will not be able to handle effectively. Because the Skilled Facilitator approach starts with the assumption that multiple views are an opportunity for learning, focusing on differences is essential. The mutual learning approach increases the chance that you can intervene on disagreement without creating unproductive conflict and defensive behavior.

As this rule implies, combining advocacy and inquiry requires that you both advocate and inquire. If you only advocate, you do not create the conditions for learning about a gap in your reasoning. If you advocate without inquiring, other people respond by advocating their own point of view, which leads you to respond with more advocacy. This creates a reinforcing cycle of rising advocacy in which each party tries to convince the others.

If you only inquire, you do not help others understand your reasoning and why you are inquiring. Advocacy and inquiry alone are both ways of unilaterally controlling the conversation; both can easily contribute to defensive behavior in others.

Inquiry, Genuine and Rhetorical

Not all inquiry is genuine. **In genuine inquiry, you ask a question with the intent of learning. In rhetorical inquiry, you ask a question with the intent of implicitly conveying your point of view.** The question "Why don't you just try it my way and see how it works out?" is not genuine inquiry because embedded in the question is the implicit advocacy "just try it my way." In contrast, a genuine inquiry would be, "What kind of problems do you think might occur if you were to try it the way I'm suggesting?" Notice that in the genuine inquiry there is no intent to embed your own point of view in the inquiry.

The difference between genuine and rhetorical inquiry is not simply in words; it is a difference in intent and meaning and the kind of response you help to generate. If you use rhetorical inquiry, people infer that you are withholding information or trying to persuade them with your question. In the extreme, rhetorical inquiry feels like an inquisition and can lead those being questioned to become cautious, withhold information, and turn defensive.

Easing in sometimes takes the form of rhetorical inquiry. When you ease in, you indirectly try to raise an issue or advocate your point of view. One way of easing in is to use your question to get the other person to see your point of view without explicitly stating it. For example, you might ask, "Do you think it would be a good idea if we . . . ?" while privately thinking, *I think it would be a good idea if we. . . .*

Managers often ease in with their direct reports. A manager may be concerned that sharing her own view first will influence or simply reduce the input from their direct reports. The manager reasons that if she asks people what they think first, she will get the direct reports' opinions without their being influenced by her point of view. However, in this situation, direct reports might be reluctant to share their views because when they have done so in the past she responded with her own advocacy in order to show them that they were wrong. So, when the manager asks her question, the direct reports are wary about responding. They remain noncommittal in order to leave themselves room to change their views depending on the manager's response. This leads the manager to infer that her direct reports don't really know about the issue, which may prompt her to revert to advocacy, thinking that inquiry doesn't work. By using the ground rules and the mutual learning approach, a manager does not need to worry about whether to speak first or last, because genuine inquiry increases the chance of the manager learning how others really think about an issue.

An Example

Exhibit 5.6 presents an actual conversation between Brad, the director of an agricultural support organization, and Paul, who reports to Brad. Brad considers Paul a highly educated and talented professional who nevertheless is resisting changing his work in response to changing client demands. Brad wants to offer suggestions without putting Paul on the defensive.

Notice that Brad decides to make his point in the form of a question, so it won't sound critical and so Paul won't get defensive. But Brad's question is

Exhibit 5.6. Not Combining Advocacy and Inquiry

Brad's Thoughts and Feelings	The Conversation
He's kind of a defensive guy. I need to offer options and suggestions, but he probably won't take it right away.	BRAD: Let's take a look at your current plan of work.
In this new program plan, all he did was change the dates. There's nothing new here.	PAUL: That's fine with me. I'm proud of the work I've done this year.
I'll let him control this part of the meeting. I can listen for weak spots and make specific suggestions. Maybe having him share his accomplishments will let him know I do respect his work.	BRAD: Why don't you go through your current plan for me, and share why you chose these objectives? Also, tell me the areas where you have the greatest pride in your accomplishments.
Oh, boy, now I've done it. I hope this doesn't reinforce his position that he doesn't need to change.	PAUL: Here are the objectives I wrote this year. I know they look a lot like years past, but you know, people don't really change, and I'm proud of what I've accomplished.
Maybe if I talk about the big picture, he'll realize that we have to change. I'll put it in the form of a question so I don't sound critical.	BRAD: Paul, you work hard. I know these programs have been effective for years, but don't you think as quickly as our client base is changing, you need to change along with it?
Here comes the defense. I knew he'd react this way.	PAUL: What are you saying? Are you claiming that my work isn't good and I'm old-fashioned?

simply advocacy in the form of a question; Paul responds defensively, creating the very result that Brad hopes to avoid by easing in.

If Brad used the ground rule combining advocacy and inquiry he could say, "Paul, I'd like to talk with you about your work plan. I have some concerns that your new plan doesn't address the changing needs of our clients. Let me give you a couple of examples of what I mean and get your reactions. [Brad then turns to the ground rule "use specific examples" to illustrate his point.] What are your thoughts, Paul? What, if anything, do you see differently, or have I missed anything?"

If Brad does not combine advocacy and inquiry, you can intervene, as Figure 5.11 illustrates.

Figure 5.11. Intervening on Combining Advocacy and Inquiry

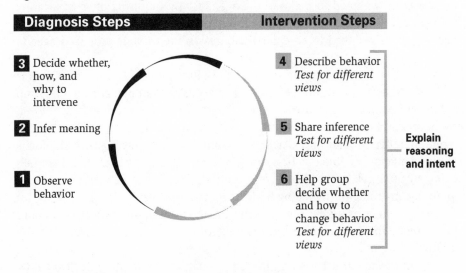

3 I'll intervene on this because if Brad has his point of view about this, it is important for Paul to understand it. Assuming Brad is easing in, it's also contributing to Paul's defensive response.

2 I'm inferring that Brad's question is not simply an inquiry and that Brad has his own view that he has not expressed.

1 Brad has said, "Don't you think as quickly as our client base is changing, you need to change along with it?"

4 "Brad, you asked Paul, 'Don't you think as quickly as our client base is changing, you need to change along with it?' Did I get that?" [*if yes, continue*]

5 "It sounds to me from your question like you believe Paul is not changing along with the clients. Am I off?" [*if no, continue*]

6 "Can you explain to Paul how you reached that conclusin and then ask Paul if he sees it differently?"

GROUND RULE SEVEN: JOINTLY DESIGN NEXT STEPS AND WAYS TO TEST DISAGREEMENTS

Jointly designing next steps and ways to test disagreements means deciding with others what topics to discuss, when to discuss them, how to discuss them, and when to switch topics, rather than making a decision privately and unilaterally. Group members routinely make unilateral decisions about the next step if they state what the agenda is without input from others or if they tell another group member that his comment is off topic. That is part of using a unilateral control approach to win.

If you use this ground rule to jointly design next steps, you might still draft the agenda, but you would explain to others what leads you to include the items that are on the agenda and exclude others, and then ask, "What changes, if any, do you think we need to make to the agenda?" By inquiring after advocating your proposed agenda, you may learn, for example, that there are other items needing to be resolved to adequately address some of your proposed agenda items.

A common way for a group member to unilaterally control the next step is by trying to keep the group discussion focused. For example, consider a group talking about how to increase sales to current customers. Yvonne says, "I think we have a problem with our billing cycles" and Arthur responds, "That's a different topic for another day." Arthur's comment unilaterally controls the focus of the conversation on the basis of his untested assumption that Yvonne's comment is unrelated to the current topic. If she thinks her comment is on topic, she may stop participating in the meeting. As a result, the group does not get the benefit of using her relevant information in deciding a course of action. In addition, she may end up not committed to the course of action that the group decides on.

If Arthur wants to use the ground rule, he can say, "Yvonne, I don't see how your point about the problem with billing cycles is related to increasing sales to current customers. Maybe I'm missing something. Can you help me understand how you see them being related?" Notice that in using the ground rule he assumes (and states explicitly) that he may be missing the relationship, not that she is off track. When she responds, Arthur and other group members might learn about a connection between the two topics that they have not previously considered. For example, the organization's billing cycles may create a long enough time lag that salespeople do not have real-time data about their customers' inventory. If there is a connection, the group can decide whether it makes more sense to pursue Yvonne's idea now or later. If it turns out that her comment is not related, Arthur can ask her to place it on a future meeting agenda.

In general, **jointly designing next steps means (1) advocating your point of view about how you want to proceed, including your interests, relevant information, reasoning, and intent; (2) inquiring about how others may see it differently; and (3) jointly crafting a way to proceed that takes into account group members' interests, relevant information, reasoning, and intent.** Jointly designing the next step creates valid information that enables the group to make an informed free choice about how to proceed.

Jointly designing a way to test disagreements is one specific type of next step. If members find themselves in a disagreement, each person may try to convince the others that his or her own position is correct, engaging in an escalating cycle of advocacy. Each offers evidence to support his or her position, and the others do the same for theirs. Each doubts the other's data, and none are likely to offer data to weaken their own position. Even after the disagreement is over, the "losers" are still likely to believe they are right.

A Developer Disagreement

Consider the disagreement laid out in Exhibit 5.7, between Jonathan and Parker, investment partners and developers in a large, complex real estate development that uses principles of traditional neighborhood development (TND), a high-density mixture of residential, commercial, office, and retail space in a tight pattern of pedestrian-oriented streets. Both want the greatest return on their joint investment. To maximize the return, Jonathan wants porches on the houses and Parker wants brick houses without porches.

Notice that both Jonathan and Parker cite their own sources to advocate their point of view. Each has gathered these sources unilaterally, without involving the other in collecting the information or assessing its validity. Jonathan does share the relevant information that there is not a lot of hard evidence yet to support his view, but he still advocates it. Both try to convince the other that he is wrong; neither engages in genuine inquiry.

To use the ground rule of jointly designing next steps and ways to test disagreements, Jonathan could say to Parker, "It looks like we disagree about whether porches will increase the value of the homes, and if they do, whether it is possible to have porches and brick together. Do you see our disagreement differently?" If Parker agrees that that is the disagreement, then Jonathan can continue: "Rather than each of us trying to convince each other, how about if together we figure out a way to find out whether porches will increase the value of the homes, and if they do, whether it is possible to have porches and brick together? We would agree beforehand on what data we need to look at and who to talk with. What do you think?"

If Jonathan does not use the ground rule, as facilitator you can intervene (Figure 5.12).

Exhibit 5.7. Not Jointly Designing Ways to Test Disagreement

Jonathan's Thoughts and Feelings	The Conversation
This argument was used by critics when TNDs first started, but no one except Parker has used it in the last four years.	PARKER: Let me tell you, where I grew up, we associate porches with poverty. Look at the poor parts of Washington. Very few of the houses built in the last forty years have porches.
Where is the hard evidence when I need it?	JONATHAN: Porches have made a huge comeback in recent years. Virtually every TND has a porch, and I understand porches are starting to bring a premium for builders.
Can't he find a way to use language to indicate that there is some middle ground? How can we reach a compromise when he needs to state his case in black and white?	PARKER: Well, builders have told us that they will not build both brick and porches. It's too expensive to do both. It's either brick or porches, and I want to have mostly brick.
The architect's plan is so logical. What is it he does not get about it?	JONATHAN: Yes, I know the builders have told us that. The reason why the architects' plan works so well, in my opinion, is that they have taken that into consideration. They have come up with a plan that balances brick and porches, putting brick townhouses with no porches where they are most prominent and using siding on the houses whose façades are mostly covered up by a full porch.
He states everything as a "fact." He just does not give an inch.	PARKER: Let me tell you, we are headed for disaster if we do not have more brick. I've been a builder in this region for more than forty years. Residents expect brick. It gives them a sense of having a good solid house. If we don't have a preponderance of brick, the builders will never be able to successfully sell these townhouses for the prices they need to get.
His apartment buildings that he built look like an engineer designed and built them. They have no redeeming architec-	JONATHAN: I really respect that you have been at this a lot longer than I have, but I have spent the last two

Exhibit 5.7. *(continued)*

Jonathan's Thoughts and Feelings	The Conversation
tural quality, though they provide him with a healthy cash flow.	years studying this new concept of TND. It is very new, and there is not a lot of hard evidence of its value. At the same time, many of the developers and designers I have talked with say that there are all kinds of details that are critical to the success of a TND, but we do not have absolute evidence of what is critical and what is not. From everything I have read, all new urbanists agree that porches are critical.

To conduct a joint test, Jonathan and Parker must be willing to accept the possibility that their information is inaccurate or incomplete.

Designing the joint test entails deciding who they should speak with, what questions to ask, what statistical data to consider relevant, and how to collect the data. Whatever method they use, it is critical that both agree to it and agree to use the information that comes from it.

After Jonathan and Parker collect their information, they discuss the data, interpret it together, and reach a joint decision about porches and bricks. Two important questions to ask when jointly testing disagreements are "How could it be that we are both correct?" and "How could we each be seeing different parts of the same problem?" Members of a group often have contrasting sets of facts because they are talking about various times, places, and people. By jointly resolving disagreement, members generate information that can be validated; they are more likely to be internally committed to the outcome because they have jointly designed and agreed to the test.

When I think of this ground rule, I imagine two scientists with competing hypotheses who are able only to design a joint experiment to test their competing hypotheses. To conduct the experiment, the research design needs to be rigorous enough to meet the standards of both.

Some disagreements are easier to address than others. Deciding what a particular memo says may be as simple as opening the file and looking at it. Agreeing on what has been said in previous meetings may require talking to a number of people and trying to reconstruct the conversation. Particularly difficult is deciding what the effects will be of implementing a strategy or policy. Still, if the effects of the choice are significant, group members can collect data from other organizations that have already implemented a similar strategy or policy; or you can help the group simulate the effects by using systems-thinking modeling.

Figure 5.12. Intervening on Jointly Designing Next Steps and Ways to Test Disagreements

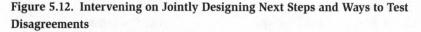

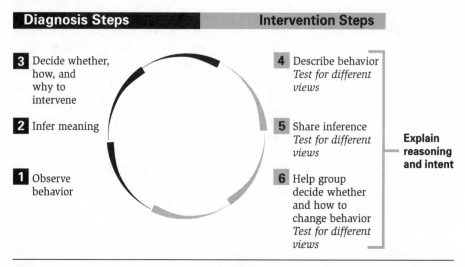

3 I'll intervene on this because if my inference is correct, they will not be able to jointly make a decision that both can support.

2 I'm inferring that each is using different data and that each may not agree with the validity of the other's data.

1 Parker has said, "Builders have told us that they will not build both brick and porches. It's too expensive to do both" and "If we don't have a preponderance of brick, the builders will never be able to successfully sell these townhouses for the prices they need to get." Jonathan has said, "I understand porches are starting to bring a premium for builders," "From everything I have read, all new urbanists agree that porches are critical," and "The architects' plan works well, in my opinion, because it balances brick and porches."

4 "Let me see if I can capture how the two of you are seeing it differently and then suggest a way of addressing the differences. Parker, you've said that builders have told you they will not build both brick and porches and that it's too expensive to do both. You are also thinking that if you don't have a preponderance of brick, the builders will never be able to successfully sell these townhouses for the prices they need to get. Yes? And Jonathan, you've said that you understand porches are starting to bring a premium for builders, that from everything you've read, all new urbanists agree that porches are critical, and that the architects' plan works well because it has a way to include both brick and porches. Have I misstated anything?" [*if no, continue*]

5 "From your comments, it looks to me like each of you is using different information to arrive at your conclusions. I'm thinking that each of you may question whether the other person's information is accurate. Have I inferred correctly?" [*if yes, continue*]

6 "Let me suggest a way that the two of you can decide together how to reach a decision about porches and bricks and then get your reactions. How about if together you decide what information you will use to make the decision and then jointly decide how to get the information so that both of you will consider it valid? Do you see any problems with this approach?"

GROUND RULE EIGHT: DISCUSS UNDISCUSSABLE ISSUES

Undiscussable issues are those that are relevant to the group's task but that group members believe they cannot discuss openly in the group without some negative consequences. Examples of undiscussables are a member who is not performing adequately and the effect on the group, or members not trusting one another, or a member reluctant to disagree with his manager since she is also a group member. Unfortunately, because such issues often raise feelings of mistrust, inadequacy, and defensiveness, members usually deal with the issues by talking about them not at all or outside the group meeting with people they trust.

The Problem with Not Discussing Undiscussables

Group members often choose not to discuss undiscussables, reasoning that to raise these issues makes some group members feel embarrassed or defensive; they therefore seek to save face for the group members (and for themselves as well). In short, they see discussing undiscussable issues as not being compassionate.

Yet people often overlook the negative systemic—and uncompassionate—consequences that they create by not raising an undiscussable issue. Consider three team members who are concerned about the poor performance of two others, and how the pair's performance affects the ability of the rest to excel as a team. If the concerned trio does not raise this issue with the two peers, the trio is likely to continue talking about the others. This creates a situation in which the two team members do not know the other three have concerns, so the pair cannot make a free and informed choice about whether to change their behavior. But because the pair are not changing their behavior, the trio continue to privately complain while simultaneously withholding information that could change the situation. Over time, the entire team's performance, its process, and its members' ability to meet their needs for growth and development are likely to suffer. This does not strike me as particularly compassionate, either for the pair in question or for the trio.

The Skilled Facilitator approach offers another perspective. By discussing undiscussable issues, you share relevant but difficult information with team members so that they can make a free and informed choice about whether to change their behavior. By raising these issues with the assumption first that you may be missing things, second that you may be contributing to the problem, and third that others are trying to act with integrity, you demonstrate your compassion for others and yourself.

A Challenging Ground Rule

The reason discussing undiscussable issues is a more difficult ground rule to use than the others is that this ground rule ties strongly into our unilateral control theory-in-use. When we try to discuss an undiscussable issue, the fact that we think of it as undiscussable means we are likely to bring a unilateral control approach to the conversation. That is, we may be assuming that others will get defensive, we may be feeling defensive ourselves, and we may believe strongly that we know what the truth is. Further, because an undiscussable issue often has been around for a while, we may believe that our feelings are justified. All of these conditions make using this ground rule difficult.

Even though this ground rule is emotionally difficult to use, the process for employing it is contained in all the previous ground rules (which is why this ground rule comes late in the list). This means that when you are discussing an undiscussable issue, it is important to test assumptions and inferences, share all relevant information, use specific examples and agree on what important words mean, share your reasoning and intent, focus on interests, combine advocacy and inquiry, and jointly design next steps and ways to test disagreements.

Sharing your feelings about raising the undiscussable issue is relevant information here. You may say, "I want to raise what I think has been an undiscussable issue in the group. I'm raising it not to put anyone on the spot, but because I think we can be a much more effective team if we address this issue. I'm worried about discussing the issue because I'm concerned I may get defensive, or others may get defensive. If you see me getting defensive, please let me know."

Group members can also explore their feelings about discussing such an issue without actually discussing its specific content. For example, a member might say, "I want to raise an important issue for the group, but I'm afraid that there may be reprisals toward me if I do. I'd like to talk about this possibility before I decide whether to identify the undiscussable issue." If a member has some assurance that his fear will not be realized, he may be more willing to talk openly about a previously undiscussable issue.

If as a facilitator you infer that there is an undiscussable issue, you can raise the issue to check whether your inference is correct. Figure 5.13 shows how to do so. In this example, Allison, an OD manager, is meeting with Stephanie, Bob, and Juan of the marketing function to explore how OD can help their function improve service quality.

GROUND RULE NINE: USE A DECISION-MAKING RULE THAT GENERATES THE DEGREE OF COMMITMENT NEEDED

Ground rule nine makes specific the core value of internal commitment. It increases the likelihood of group members supporting the decision that is made and implementing it.

Figure 5.13. Intervening to Discuss an Undiscussable Issue

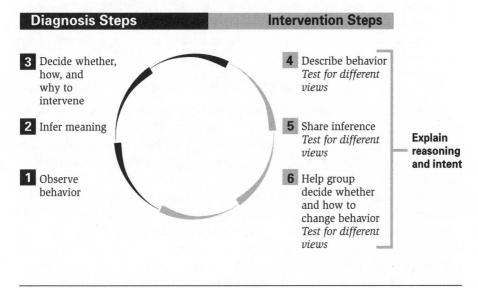

I think it's important to raise this because if my inference is correct and the issue isn't raised, marketing may need OD help that they believe the OD people may not be able to provide. OD may also have a credibility problem that they are unaware of.

2 I'm inferring that Stephanie, Bob, or Juan have some concern about OD providing them consultation and that they are reluctant to raise this issue.

1 During the meeting, Stephanie, Bob, and Juan said that the group needs some help on improving service quality. Several times, Allison has said her human resource team can provide the help, and each time Stephanie, Bob, or Juan said that the OD team is already overcommitted to other important work. Stephanie and Bob also looked at each other before declining OD's offer.

4 "I want to share some observations and raise what may be an undiscussable issue. I'm raising it not to put people on the spot, but to see if there is an unaddressed issue that is preventing you from being as effective as you want to be. Here's what I've observed. During this meeting, several of you—Stephanie, Bob, and Juan—have commented that the group needs some OD help on improving service quality. Have I gotten anything incorrect?" [*if no, continue*] "And each time Allison has offered her OD team to provide the service, at least one of you has said that the OD team is already overcommitted to other important work. Am I correct?" [*if yes, continue*] "Stephanie and Bob, I also noticed one of you looking at the other before declining OD's offer. Yes?" [*if yes, continue*]

5 "From all of this, I am inferring that at least the three of you may have some concern about OD's ability to adequately provide the consultation. Is my inference accurate, or do others have another interpretation?"

6 [*not needed*]

Underlying this ground rule is the premise that the members' level of commitment to a decision is in part a function of the degree to which they make an informed free choice to support the decision. The more the group members are able to make an informed free choice, the more they are likely to be internally committed to the decision.

Decision-Making Rule Types

A group can use a number of decision-making processes. A decision-making process specifies who in the group makes a particular kind of decision, and how other members are involved in the process of that decision. Exhibit 5.8 shows four types of group decision-making processes, adapting the work of Victor Vroom and his colleagues.

In *consultative* group decision making, the leader or a subgroup makes the decision for the group after discussing with them ideas about the issue and possible solutions. In *democratic* decision making, the full group discusses the issue and is involved in making the decision; a decision is made when some percentage of the group agrees. Rather than a one-person, one-vote democratic approach, sometimes this vote is weighted in a way that gives influence preferentially to a powerful member or members (somewhat like national elections in the United States, in which the most populous states have greater influence through the electoral college).

In *consensus* decision making, everyone in the group is involved in making the decision. A decision is reached when all group members can support it and agree to implement it given their roles. In this definition of consensus, if one person does not support the decision then the group does not yet have consensus.

In *delegative* decision making, the leader gives the decision to the group or to a subgroup to make. The leader may specify conditions within which the decision must be made, such as limits on cost, time, or other criteria. In delegative decision making, the leader may or may not specify what decision-making rule to use.

Exhibit 5.8. Group Decision-Making Process Types

Type	Decision-Making Process
Consultative	Leader consults with group members, then leader makes decision.
Democratic	Leader and group discuss issue, then vote. Some possibly weighted percentage of group members is needed to agree on a decision.
Consensus	Leader and group members discuss issue and reach unanimous agreement.
Delegative	Leader delegates decision to group or subgroup to make, sometimes within leader's identified constraints.

Source: Adapted from Vroom and Jago, 1988; Vroom and Yetton, 1973.

Matching the Rule to the Commitment Needed

These group decision-making processes generate differing responses. Exhibit 5.9 shows the level of acceptance for implementing a decision.

As Vroom and Jago (1988) have described, group member commitment is necessary when implementation of a decision requires the support and cooperation of the group members. If commitment is needed and there are differing perspectives among members (or between group members and the leader), the decision-making process needs to help members (including the leader) explore their perspectives and create a shared understanding. Consensus decision making accomplishes this by ensuring that a decision is not reached until each group member can commit to the decision as his or her own. It equalizes the distribution of power in the group, because every member's concerns must be addressed and every member's consent is required to reach a decision. Making a decision by consensus can take more time than other methods, but because people are then internally committed to the decision, it will usually take less time to implement effectively.

Consensus implies that if group members do not have relevant information about the decision and they will implement the decision or will be affected by it, the leader has the responsibility of giving them the information that will enable them to make an informed choice.

Ground rule nine does not state that all decisions should be made by consensus. It recognizes that some decisions do not require the internal commitment generated through consensus; a decision-making process other than consensus can be appropriate. However, with divergent perspectives on an issue, you create a mismatch if you use a democratic or consultative process to try to generate internal commitment from group members.

If you use a consensus decision-making process, the approach to determining if there is consensus is simple. Once the group thinks it is close to reaching

Exhibit 5.9. Degree of Acceptance of a Decision

Internal commitment	Believes in the decision and sees it as his or her own; will do whatever is necessary to implement it effectively
Enrollment	Supports the decision; will work within his or her role to implement the decision
Compliance	Accepts the decision but does not believe in it; will do what is formally required within his or her role
Noncompliance	Does not support the decision; does not follow through on formal requirements within his or her role
Resistance	Actively undermines the decision

Source: Adapted from Senge, 1990; Vroom and Jago, 1988.

consensus, a member can state the decision under consideration, and then each member can say whether he or she consents. This avoids the mistake of assuming that silence means consent. Voting is inconsistent with consensus decision making, but the group can take a straw poll to see whether it is close to consensus and to see which members still have concerns. Some groups (say, a governing board) have bylaws that require that decisions be made by voting, which may seem to exclude consensus. Nevertheless, a group can attempt to reach consensus even if ultimately it must decide by vote.

Consensus can be used throughout the time a group is solving a problem, not just at the end when members select the best alternative. Whenever the group is about to move to the next step of the problem-solving process, it is appropriate to reach consensus to do so.

You may be reluctant to use consensus because in your experience, groups are rarely able to reach consensus and you are worried that key decisions will not get made. Many groups *are* unable to reach consensus because they do not use an effective set of ground rules. By using all the other ground rules, the group increases the likelihood that it can reach consensus.

USING THE GROUND RULES TOGETHER

The ground rules are like dance steps; each one is part of the foundation, but the power and elegance you see usually results from combining the steps to create movement with a purpose. I have focused on the ground rules individually as a way to introduce them and show how to use each one. However, as you can see from the case examples in this chapter, when I use one ground rule I am often using several others at the same time. As a group member or a facilitator, you can practice combining the ground rules to increase your ability to help the group move forward effectively.

The ground rules are necessary but not sufficient for effective group process. I think of the ground rules as each being a micro process, in the sense that it creates effective group behavior in the moment. But a group also needs a macro process to impart direction; consider problem-solving models, root cause analysis, and systems-thinking models for understanding complex systems. In Chapter Ten, I describe how to integrate the ground rules with this kind of macro process.

LEARNING TO USE THE GROUND RULES

You may feel awkward as you start using the ground rules. You may feel this doesn't sound like you; instead, it sounds like you imitating something you read in a book (well, actually you have) or heard in a workshop. It is natural to feel unnatural in beginning to use the ground rules. The unnaturalness comes from a number of sources, notably trying to translate your left-hand column into sentences that use the grammatical structure of the ground rules, trying to integrate the ground rules with your own natural speech pattern and word choice, and trying to put it all together so you can talk at the speed of normal conversation.

It takes practice to find your own voice in using the ground rules. With regular practice, you will probably find that you can use the ground rules in a way that sounds like you and that doesn't require you to talk at an unnaturally slow pace to find the words that you are looking for.

As you practice using the ground rules and understanding their implications, you may have new or renewed concern about whether it makes sense to use them. This is also natural. When you start practicing the ground rules, you do not—and cannot—make a fully informed choice. It is not possible to know in advance of practicing the ground rules all the risks you will see and concerns you will have. Exploring these concerns is an important part of the process of learning the ground rules.

SUMMARY

In this chapter, I have described the set of ground rules at the heart of the Skilled Facilitator approach. I explained how you can act inconsistently with the ground rules, use them yourself, and intervene to help others use them. In showing how to intervene to help others use the rules, I introduced the diagnosis-intervention cycle. In the next chapters, we explore in detail how to use this essential tool.

Note

1. In general, the ground rules are derived from Argyris (1982) and Argyris and Schön (1974). Ground rule five is from Fisher, Ury, and Patton (1991), which was based on the work of Mary Parker Follett in the early 1990s (Graham, 1995).

CHAPTER SIX

Diagnosing Behaviors
That Enhance or Hinder
Group Effectiveness

In this chapter, we consider how to diagnose behavior in groups. I address the question, How do you watch a group in action and figure out exactly what members are doing that is reducing or increasing their effectiveness? I begin by describing the diagnosis-intervention cycle, which structures how you observe group behavior and draw meaning from it. I show how to use the core values, ground rules, group effectiveness model, and theory-in-use to diagnose what is happening in a group. I end the chapter by considering some challenges in diagnosing behavior.

Before you can intervene to help a group, first you need to determine whether the group is functioning effectively. *Diagnosis* **is the process by which you observe a group's behavior, infer meaning from the behavior, and causally relate it to your models of effective group behavior.**

To diagnose, you need two sets of knowledge and skills. **First, you need to know what type of behavior to look for.** When you watch a group in action, there are many behaviors that you could pay attention to. But you are limited in the number you can attend to at any time, and some behaviors are more important than others because they reflect key dynamics that influence the group's effectiveness. To be able to quickly understand which types of behaviors are important to focus on and why, you need to have a model of the effective group in your head.

The ground rules for effective groups are one set of behaviors to look for. To the extent that group members are using the ground rules, their process is effective. When we see group members acting inconsistently with the ground rules, we are identifying ineffective behavior. The group effectiveness model offers another set of behaviors to look for. Each element of the model must be in place for the group to function most effectively. For example, the group needs clear goals, clearly defined roles, and a way of managing its boundaries with the rest of the organization. Consequently, you can observe the group's behavior for signs of whether these elements are in place.

Second, you need a process for diagnosis—a method for observing and making sense of behavior, regardless of the specific behaviors involved. Diagnosis begins with observing behavior and ends with inferring the cause of behavior. When diagnosing causes in group behavior, facilitators often deal with concepts involving high-level inference (such as control and trust) that cannot be observed directly but must be inferred. A useful process of diagnosis helps you move from observation to inference in a way that minimizes distortion and increases the likelihood that an inference is valid. In this chapter, I present a diagnosis-intervention cycle that you can use regardless of specific behaviors; I also discuss problems and pitfalls in diagnosing behavior.

The need for a model of diagnosis to guide your analysis is part of a fundamental principle that underlies the Skilled Facilitator approach: the effective facilitator bases her thinking and action on a model of effective groups and on models of diagnosis and intervention, all of which are internally consistent.

THE DIAGNOSIS-INTERVENTION CYCLE

The diagnosis-intervention cycle is a structured way to diagnose behavior and then intervene on it. The cycle (shown in Figure 6.1, with the diagnostic steps in black) has six steps, three for diagnosis followed by three for intervention. In this chapter, I briefly describe all six steps and then focus on the first two diagnostic steps. Chapter Seven explores the third diagnostic step, deciding whether, how, and why to intervene. In Chapter Eight, we consider the intervention steps in the cycle.

The diagnostic steps (one through three) are private; they denote your thoughts (Schein, 1987). The intervention steps (four through six) are public; they denote what you actually say to the group. The three diagnostic steps structure how you think. You can picture the diagnostic steps as part of your left-hand column, which is why they are on the left side of the cycle.

Step One: Observing Behavior

In step one, you directly observe the behavior in the group. Directly observable behavior comprises the verbatim words that people speak and the nonverbal actions they make. I think of directly observable behavior as the data my videotape recorder captures. For example, I might observe this interaction:

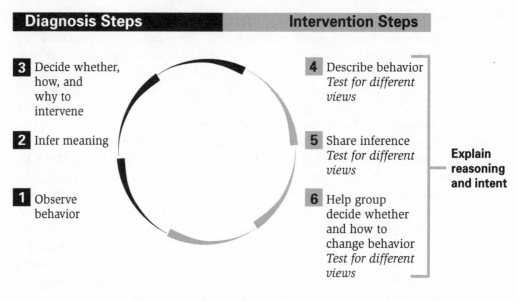

Figure 6.1. The Diagnosis-Intervention Cycle

DON: I think we should hold off on the new project until fourth quarter.

SHARON: That's too late. It has to start no later than second quarter.

DON (IN A LOUDER VOICE): We just don't have the luxury to wait that long.

SHARON (ROLLING HER EYES): We don't have the ability to do it sooner.

Step Two: Inferring Meaning

In step two, you infer some meaning from the behavior. An inference is a conclusion you reach about something unknown, on the basis of some things that are known to you. In this example, I infer that Sharon and Don are acting inconsistently with several ground rules. For example, they are stating their positions (start the project in the fourth quarter, or the second quarter) without sharing their interests, and they are not explaining the reasoning underlying their statements. I might also infer from Sharon rolling her eyes that she is somewhat frustrated with Don's comment.

Step Three: Deciding Whether, How, and Why to Intervene

In step three, you decide whether, how, and why to intervene in the group. In this example, I need to decide whether the inferences I have made in step two, if accurate, warrant my intervening or whether I should remain silent. Is Sharon and Don's focus on positions, or their failure to explain their reasoning, or Sharon's seeming frustration enough of a problem that I should intervene? If I decide to do so, I must design my intervention by deciding to whom I will address my comments, exactly what I will say, and when I will say it. In this example, I would probably decide to address their focusing on positions.

Step Four: Describing the Behavior

In step four, you publicly describe the behavior that you observed and that led you to intervene. Then you ask the group member or members whether they observed the behavior differently. Here, I might say, "Don, a minute ago I think you said we should hold off on the new project until fourth quarter. Do you remember it differently? And Sharon, I think you said that you needed to start the project in the second quarter. Am I correct?" If they agree with my descriptions, I have accurately described their behavior; then I move to the fifth step.

Step Five: Sharing Your Inferences

In step five, you share the inference that you privately made in step two and test with the group member or members whether they have a different inference. I might say, "Don and Sharon, it seems to me that each of you is stating a position without explaining the interests that led you to take your position. Do either of you see it differently?" Or if I choose to refer to the ground rule without identifying it by name, I might say, "Don and Sharon, it looks like each of you has said what you want to happen but not what led you to favor that solution. Do either of you see it differently?" In any case, if neither Don nor Sharon sees it differently, then I move to the sixth step.

Step Six: Helping Group Members Change Their Behavior

In step six, you help group members decide whether and how to change their behavior to be more effective. Here I might say, "Don and Sharon, would each of you be willing to say what it is about the solution you are proposing that meets your interests (or needs)?" Assuming that they agree to do so, the cycle begins again, and I continue to observe whether their behavior (and that of the other group members) is contributing to or hindering the group's effectiveness.

Sharing Your Reasoning and Intent

At steps four, five, and six you may share your reasoning and intent. This helps the group members better understand why you are intervening at all, especially why you are asking them to redesign their behavior in a particular way. For example, at the beginning of step four you might say, "I want to make some observations about something that I think is slowing the group down, so I can get your reactions." Or at step six you might say, "Would you be willing to share your interests? The reason I'm asking is because if you can identify each of your interests, I think you will be better able to find a solution that integrates your different needs."

The diagnosis-intervention cycle is designed to structure how you think so that your diagnosis is based on directly observable behavior. It is also designed to intervene so that you share with the group the directly observable data and test inferences to see if they are valid. In this way, the diagnosis-intervention cycle enables you to create conditions for valid information in the group.

You repeatedly use the six-step cycle throughout facilitation with the group. In developmental facilitation, over time the group learns to conduct its own diagnosis and interventions, becoming less dependent on you. In basic facilitation, the group usually relies on you to diagnose and intervene.

Let us examine the first two diagnostic steps in more detail.

STEP ONE: OBSERVING BEHAVIOR

Diagnosing group behavior begins with direct observation. This seems obvious, but it has large implications. For group members to understand the reasons for your diagnosis and intervention, you must base these actions on the raw materials of group interaction that everyone has access to—the words and actions of the group.

Remembering Behavior as Behavior

Observing behavior means listening to group members' words and watching their actions. Step one requires that you be able to remember the exact words that group members said and the nonverbal behaviors that accompanied them. The challenge is to be able to remember the behaviors without changing them or adding your own meaning.

In this scenario, we have an example of nonverbal behavior in Sharon rolling her eyes. If, as you read that Sharon rolled her eyes, you describe her behavior to yourself as frustration or impatience, you have gone beyond describing her directly observable behavior and instead are inferring meaning. You cannot directly observe frustration or impatience; you can only infer it. You can, however, observe people rolling their eyes, crossing their arms, or talking in a louder voice. Similarly, you do not directly observe people focusing on positions or withholding relevant information; you infer this from their specific words and actions. Doing step one well means training yourself to distinguish between behaviors and the inferences you make from them.

In practice, it is almost impossible to observe behavior without making meaning of it. The reason you notice certain behavior is you believe it *is* meaningful; that is, it makes a difference in the group's process. You use—and should use—the diagnostic frames you have in your head, such as the ground rules and the group effectiveness model, to pay attention to and identify certain behaviors.

Consider Arnie, who responds to a plan developed by his group by commenting, "Let's just say not everyone will be willing to support our plan." Using the Skilled Facilitator approach, you find Arnie's sentence meaningful because it suggests that he has relevant information to share (about who will not support the plan and why) that he has not shared with the group. In contrast, in a facilitation approach with another set of diagnostic concepts, the facilitator might initially make some other meaning out of the same sentence—perhaps considering Arnie to be undermining the solution.

The point is that even though you use your diagnostic frames to look for certain behaviors, you still need to remember the group behavior in its original form. For some of us, after we have made meaning of behavior, we have difficulty remembering the specific behavior that led us to make our interpretation. We may be able to remember that Sharon was frustrated but not recall the rolling of the eyes that led us to infer it. Our brains are designed to quickly make meaning out of behavior because it is the meaning of behavior that is important, not the behavior itself. But as a facilitator **it is important that you remember the behavior because it is the raw data for your inferences, diagnoses, and interventions.** If group members do not agree with the inference you have made, and if you cannot recall the behavior from which you made the inference, then you have no way of explaining how you moved from the data to your inference.

Diagnostic Frames: Behaviors to Look for

What kinds of behaviors are important to attend to in observing a group? There are a huge number of behaviors you could look for, and it is beyond your (or any human's) cognitive capacities to catch every behavior in the group. Even if you were a human video recorder—capable of remembering every word and action that every member said—that by itself would not tell you which behaviors are *important,* or how to use them. You need a way to categorize or code group members' conversation and actions so you can search for a few, general types of behavior.

The ground rules for effective groups, the group effectiveness model, and the unilateral control model and the mutual learning model are diagnostic frames for identifying behavior that has a significant impact on the group's process and overall effectiveness. As Figure 6.2 shows, you use these diagnostic frames in step one to attend to certain behaviors, and you use them again in step two to make particular meaning out of the behavior you have observed. In this way, steps one and two are inextricably linked.

Using the Ground Rules to Observe Groups. In the Skilled Facilitator approach, the ground rules for effective groups are a central tool for observing and diagnosing group behavior. I use the ground rules as a template for

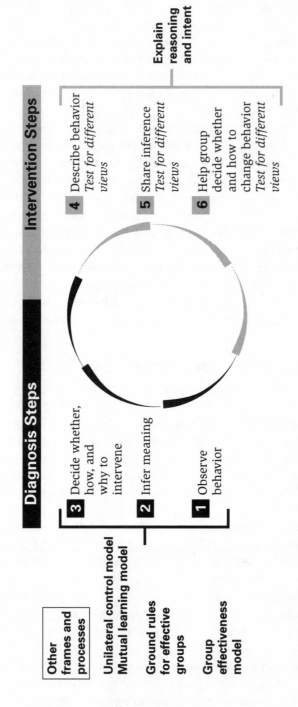

Figure 6.2. Diagnosis-Intervention Cycle with Diagnostic Frames

observing behavior. As I watch group members, I mentally compare their conversation and actions to the ground rules and notice which behaviors are consistent or inconsistent with each ground rule. In a given comment, a group member might act consistently with certain ground rules but inconsistently with others.

Take, for example, a team that has been trying to solve a problem of customers waiting too long to receive service. Having agreed on a definition of the problem and criteria for a solution, the team decides to move to the next step: brainstorming potential causes. After several members have each identified a potential cause, this conversation occurs:

AL: One reason may be that we don't have adequate coverage throughout the workday. For example, yesterday at 10:00 A.M., using our standard response time analysis, we calculated an average wait time of twenty minutes for customers across all areas. I have the individual department numbers if you want them. That's fifteen minutes longer than our acceptable standard for adequate coverage, and we had 10 percent fewer people covering the phones at that time of day.

TED: I agree that's the cause. Let's increase the coverage 10 percent, at least during the peak periods.

SUE: Yeah, I agree with Ted. That should make a big difference.

SAM: Well, I think our people are just tired of working.

AL: Well, I think we've just got some people who are burned out.

PAT: Al and Sue, it sounds like your suggestions to increase coverage are solutions, but I understood that we were still talking about causes. Do you see this differently?

AL AND SUE: No, you're right.

PAT: Are you willing to focus only on potential causes and hold the solutions until we finish identifying causes?

Analyzing the conversation, we see that Al begins by using a specific example of inadequate coverage with data and describes what he means by adequate coverage (ground rule three). By doing so, he explains the reasoning behind his belief that the cause of the problem is inadequate coverage on the phones (rule four). However, he does not inquire about whether others see any flaws in his reasoning or have different data (rule six). Next, Ted and Sue, by discussing solutions, switch the focus of the conversation without checking with the group (rule seven). Sam returns to the focus of the conversation (rule seven) by addressing another potential cause, but he makes an untested inference about people being burned out (rule one), and he does not share any specific examples (rule three) or the reasoning (rule four) that leads him to his conclusion. Like Al, he does not inquire whether others have other information or see it differently (rule six).

In Pat's two comments to Al and Sue, Pat gives the specific example of their suggesting solutions (rule three) as a way of illustrating that they have changed the focus of the group (rule seven). Notice that, having stated that Al and Sue seem to be off track, Pat specifically asks them whether they see it differently (rule six). After they agree with her, Pat asks if they are willing to refocus on discussing causes of the problem (rule seven) instead of simply telling them that they are off focus and to refocus.

Pat acts consistently with the ground rules; she is also using the ground rules to ask Al and Sue to act consistently with a ground rule they have not used. By intervening with those two, Pat is acting as a facilitative leader. When group members intervene with each other, it is significant because this indicates that members are taking responsibility for their own group process.

To the extent that members are acting inconsistently with the ground rules, I decide in step three whether to intervene. Because the ground rules are principles for effective group process, I use them to guide my observation, whether the group has agreed to practice the ground rules themselves or they have instead chosen not to practice the ground rules but agreed to my using them.

Using the Group Effectiveness Model to Observe Behavior. The group effectiveness model presents another set of behaviors to look for. Each element of the group effectiveness model needs to be in place for the group to function well. The group needs clear goals, clearly defined roles, and a way of managing its boundaries with the rest of the organization. Consequently, we can observe the group's behavior for signs of whether these elements are in place.

To take a simple example, consider a conversation about a report (produced by a group) that has errors:

JIM: The numbers literally did not add up. We had blank cells and columns without totals. Ken, you were supposed to do the final check on the copy; what happened?

KEN: I was just handling the text. I got the tables from you; that was your job.

You might reasonably infer from watching this interaction that Ken and Jim have not clearly agreed on their roles and responsibilities for this project. In step three, you may decide to intervene on this issue, depending on its importance in the overall conversation and on the frequency with which it happens in the group. Typically, it requires more data than presented in this example before you can infer that the group has a problem that relates to an element of the group effectiveness model.

Employing Theory-in-Use to Observe Behavior. Observing group members' behaviors to see if they represent a unilateral control or mutual learning theory-in-use is a central part of developmental facilitation. This goes beyond observing whether the people are using the ground rules; here, you consider the core values and assumptions they use to design their behavior.

Consider, for example, a conversation in which members are trying to persuade each other to choose a particular solution. If a group member says, "You just don't get it. What you're proposing makes no sense!" we might consider that the member's behavior reflects a core assumption that the situation is as he sees it and that others who see it differently are wrong. Of course, you usually need more than a single sentence to make this kind of inference. Ultimately, when identifying part of a member's theory-in-use, you have to ask him what he was thinking during the conversation. Still, the process is the same; you use the concepts that constitute theory-in-use to help look for behaviors that may illustrate the concepts in action.

Using Other Diagnostic Frames and Processes to Observe Behavior. There are many other diagnostic frames you can use to guide you in observing group behavior. For example, groups often use some kind of problem-solving model that includes steps for agreeing on problem definition; developing criteria for a solution; identifying causes; and then brainstorming, selecting, and evaluating a solution. The steps are typically followed in order, and there are certain actions that a group is expected to take in each step. Given this, you can use a problem-solving model as a diagnostic frame to watch for group behavior that indicates whether the group is following the model in sequence, and whether it is performing each step. In this way, **you can use the diagnosis-intervention cycle with any model of group process (other examples being strategic planning or process redesign) for which you can identify behavior that indicates whether the group is acting consistently or inconsistently with the model.** Chapter Ten addresses this issue in detail.

The diagnostic frames I describe are not exhaustive; they are the ones I find most useful in diagnosing behavior. You may have other diagnostic frames that you use to make sense out of group behavior. In deciding whether to use other diagnostic frames, it is important to select one that is consistent with the core values of the Skilled Facilitator approach. If you select one that is inconsistent (say, a frame that treats using specific examples as putting people on the spot rather than sharing valid information), the conflicting frame makes it difficult for you to diagnose behavior, and group members may then view your intervention as inconsistent as well.

Using Agreement with the Group to Observe Behavior. The agreement I make with the group about how I will help them also affects what kind of behavior I look for. If a group seeks my help because members say they cannot resolve conflict without bitter argument, I look for behavior that lets me determine whether I agree with the group's diagnosis. If the group seeks my help because it spends a lot of time discussing plans but never accomplishes them, I look for behavior related to that diagnosis. However, as I discuss in Chapter Thirteen, on contracting, although the agreement with the client may specify particular behaviors that the client wants me to focus on, it does not limit what I can observe and diagnose. To act consistently with core values, I have to consider all the behavior of the group, so that I can help the group identify what is reducing its effectiveness, confirm or disconfirm the group's own diagnosis, and enable the members to make a free informed choice about whether to change.

STEP TWO: INFERRING MEANING

In step two of the diagnosis-intervention cycle, I use the diagnostic frames to make meaning out of the behavior observed in step one.

Making Inferences

As I described in Chapter Five, an inference is a conclusion you reach about something unknown on the basis of some things that are known (Hayakawa, 1972). For example, if in looking out my office window I see smoke billowing up from the trees in the distance, I may infer there is a fire. Even if I cannot directly observe the fire, I infer that it is present because I know that smoke is often accompanied by fire. Similarly, if you observe a group leader tapping a pencil on the desk and saying "Go on, go on" in response to her subordinate's explanation, you may infer that the boss is impatient. You cannot observe impatience; you conclude its presence from the meaning you make of the behavior you observe.

Like everyone else, as a facilitator you need to make inferences because they create the meaning you use to decide how to react. If, in the example of the boss, you infer that when she taps her pencil and says "Go on, go on" it is meant to encourage the subordinate to talk, then you may choose not to intervene. If, however, you infer that the tapping means she is trying to move the conversation faster than other group members want to go, you may intervene.

Inferences can also save you time by aggregating and abstractly conveying a large number of behaviors. It can be more efficient to say "She was very angry" than to describe the manager's multiple behaviors that led you to infer the anger ("In a loud voice she screamed, 'You've ruined the project'"; "She threw the report on the floor"; "She left, slamming the door"). Similarly, rather than saying "It was 10:15 when I saw Frank enter his office and take off his trench coat. Frank is due at work at eight," people say, "Frank was late this morning."

As a facilitator, you make many kinds of inferences. Here are some of the key types.

Inferring the Causes of Behavior. We use inferences to identify the causes of behavior. When an auto mechanic announces that "your car's timing is off" after listening to the engine and hearing complaints of engine hesitation, the mechanic has inferred the cause of a problem from its symptoms. Similarly, when you suggest that the group is lacking focus after observing failure to reach a decision within an hour, you are making a causal inference after observing a number of behaviors. A causal inference is about what has led to something happening. As a facilitator, you need to make causal inferences because a group can solve a process problem only after identifying what caused the problem, and the cause is often not directly observable.

Inferring Emotion. Sometimes we may make inferences about members' emotions. Someone who has asked a number of questions that the group has not answered may respond by sitting back in her chair, crossing her arms, tightening the muscles in her face, and furrowing her eyebrows. I may quickly infer that the behavior reflects anger, but it may also reflect some other emotion.

By making an inference about (and intervening on) an emotion on the basis of behavioral cues, you both broaden and deepen how you observe and help the group. Because we generate our emotions from our experiences, embedded in group members' emotions are their stories about experiences in the group that have led them to feel whatever they feel. When you pay attention to a members' emotions, you are attending to things that they consider important. In doing so, you are also attending to the third criterion of group effectiveness, the extent to which experiences in the group meet personal needs. By inferring and intervening on emotion, you can quickly find out about important issues in the group that have not been addressed, such as an unexpressed interest, an untested assumption someone is making about others, or an undiscussable issue.

Anytime there is a mismatch between the emotions you infer that group members are feeling and what you would expect, you have an opportunity. For example, if you infer that a group member is feeling angry and you are surprised, essentially you are thinking to yourself, *Given the behavior I've seen in the group, I don't see how this would lead the member to respond with anger.* You can consider several possibilities. First, you may have missed important behavior in the group that, had you observed it, would not leave you surprised to find that a member is angry. This may prompt you to return to step one of the cycle to look for this kind of behavior. Second, you may not have missed any behaviors in the group relevant to the feeling you have inferred, in which case you might begin to consider whether the feeling inferred results from members having concerns they have not yet expressed in the group, or from things that have happened outside the group meetings. Finally, you may have incorrectly inferred what the member is feeling.

In developmental facilitation, you can use emotions to help group members explore their theories-in-use. Embedded in every emotion is a theory-in-use. By identifying what a member is feeling, you can then help him explore how his values and assumptions led him to make meaning of the situation and respond in a way that generated the emotion. You can also help him explore how his emotions are based on an event that occurred in the group, or on an event unrelated to the group, or on an untested assumption or inference.

Attending to emotion is part of bringing compassion into your work. Emotion is always part of the group conversation, whether or not members are aware of their emotions or expressing them. By attending to members' emotions, you may affirm what they are feeling, help them recognize that their emotions are natural, and advocate for discussing them as a necessary element of building effective group relationships.

But you can also go beyond that. You can help them see how their thinking generates their feelings, how their feelings may be based on an untested inference or attribution about others, and if so, how by changing their thinking they have the ability to make new choices about what they are feeling. In short, by helping group members become more aware of their feelings and the sources, you strengthen their ability to make choices about their response. We examine this more in Chapter Twelve.

I offer one caution about believing in the universality of body language as it relates to inferring emotion. A number of books describe various aspects of body language—the position of a person's arms, head, or hands—and describe what each position means. I hope it is clear that in the Skilled Facilitator approach a given behavior does not necessarily always mean one thing. Across cultures, the same body language can have many meanings. Even within a culture, a particular nonverbal behavior can have numerous meanings. If each time you see me cross my arms in front of my chest you infer that I am feeling defensive or am closing out your views (as some books suggest), your inference is often incorrect. Not that I never get defensive, but I also get cold easily and this frequently leads to my crossing my arms.

Attributing Motives. Sometimes, you make a causal inference about other people's motives. Consider a facilitator who is helping an executive team that is experiencing several conflicts. At one point Hans, the team leader says, "Why don't we put this issue aside so we can give it some careful thought." This leads the facilitator to think—but not say—*Typical Hans. This isn't about time; he's not willing to take on the difficult issues.* In thinking this, the facilitator is attributing to Hans the motive of avoiding difficult issues.

Attribution often involves high-level inference. After you have attributed a motive to a group member, you are likely to begin coding her behavior in a way that is consistent with the motive you have attributed to her. As with other inferences, it becomes important to test your attribution.

Making a Value Judgment. Many inferences also involve value judgment— that is, whether you consider the behavior in question to be positive or negative. If you observe a conversation and think *Bob was obnoxious to Joan,* you not only are summarizing a large number of behaviors but likely are also stating implicit disapproval of Bob's behavior. In the example of the executive team, the facilitator's attribution of the leader's motivation includes a negative judgment about it; the facilitator does not approve of the leader avoiding a difficult issue and covering it up with a false explanation.

Making Process and Content Inferences

When you work with a group, you make inferences about both the process and the content of a conversation.

Making Inferences About Process. *Process* inferences are about the quality of conversation and the effectiveness of the group's process and structure. You make a process inference when you privately conclude that group members are acting consistently or inconsistently with a particular ground rule, having difficulty with an element of the group effectiveness model such as boundary management, operating out of a unilateral control theory-in-use, not following some aspect of a problem-solving model, or acting inconsistently with some other model of effective group process.

In making a process inference, you try not to focus especially on the content of the conversation. In other words, you are interested in how the group members say whatever they say. Whether the group is talking about problems with losing market share or retaining employees, I can make the same inference that the members are focusing on positions rather than interests. When you infer that some aspect of process is hindering the group, you make a decision about whether to intervene.

Making Inferences About Content. In contrast, as the name states, *content* inferences are about the substantive meaning of the conversation. For example, consider an interaction in a meeting about a project deadline:

SHERRY: We really need your projections by 5:00 P.M. Friday if we are going to get the final report to corporate by next Tuesday. Can you guarantee that you'll meet that deadline?

LEWIS: That's a stretch, but we'll do the best we can.

Hearing Lewis's response, I would infer that he has promised a good effort but not guaranteed meeting the deadline. Having made this inference, in step three of the diagnosis-intervention cycle I might decide to intervene to test whether he *is* guaranteeing to meet the deadline. By making a content inference and then intervening on that basis, I could help group members clarify their meaning.

There is a link between making content inference and group process. If I decide to intervene on a content inference, it is because I believe that if I do not, the untested inference may negatively affect the group's process.

Making Inferences About Others Making Content Inferences. Sometimes, as you observe a conversation you think that a group member is making an inference; that is, you are inferring that someone else is making an inference about the content of the conversation.

Consider this brief interaction in a conversation about job performance:

ALEX: Sandy, I've got some concerns about your covering both of your regions. I want to talk about it and see if we can agree on something that will work.

SANDY: Well, if I can't handle both regions, I doubt anyone else will be able to do the job.

Here I would infer that Sandy is inferring that Alex thinks Sandy is not capable of handling both regions.

When you infer that a group member is making a content inference and not testing it out, then you may decide to intervene so that the members do not continue their conversation on the basis of what might be an incorrect inference. In this kind of situation, you are making both a content inference and a process inference; you are inferring that a group member might be incorrectly inferring a particular meaning, and you are also inferring that the group member is doing so without testing the inference, which is inconsistent with the ground rule to test assumptions and inferences.

Recognizing Our Inferences as Inferences

Everyone makes inferences. **Step two of the diagnosis-intervention cycle requires that you recognize the content and process inferences you are making as you make them.** It is this awareness that enables you to reflect on whether your inferences have a basis in any data and decide whether you should intervene to test them. Without this awareness, you assume that your inference is accurate and intervene without testing it. You treat your inference as valid data, and if you are incorrect you could create negative consequences.

For example, consider a facilitator who observes that one man in the group is responsible for every other comment offered. She infers that he is talking too much, but she is unaware that this is an inference. She might say, "John, how about letting others share their thoughts?" If the facilitator has inferred incorrectly, other group members may respond, "No, John's not talking too much. He may be talking a lot, but we need to hear his information before we can make a decision." Using the Skilled Facilitator approach, the facilitator would recognize that her belief that John is talking too much is a process inference (and a judgment) that she should check with the other members of the group. She might say to the group, "I've noticed that during the last ten minutes, John has made every other comment. Has anyone noticed anything different? If not, I'm wondering whether people feel that his comments are relevant and whether any of you have been trying unsuccessfully to share your thoughts."

Moving Back and Forth Between Observations and Inferences

In practice, you do not always simply move from step one to step two to step three of the diagnosis-intervention cycle. Sometimes you use your diagnostic frames to observe behavior, make an inference about what the behavior means, and return to observe more behavior to confirm or disconfirm your working hypothesis, until you decide whether to intervene. For example, I might observe a group and begin to infer that there is an undiscussable issue in the group. If I am uncertain, I may continue to observe the group, looking for more data that either confirm or disconfirm my inference. If I believe I have enough data for my inference, I may choose to intervene.

Making Low-Level and High-Level Inferences

You can think of the inferences you make as being on a continuum or ladder. As you move up the rungs of the ladder, you move from lower-level to higher-level inferences. Low-level inferences require adding only a relatively small amount of unknown information to observable behavior. As you make higher-level inferences, you add more conclusions about what members are feeling, the cause of their behavior, their motives, and your judgment about these things. Exhibit 6.1 shows three levels of inference for both process and content and the observable behavior used to generate them. Note that, in the example, the mid-level and high-level inferences have assumptions embedded in them that cannot be directly linked to the observable data.

The Skilled Facilitator approach seeks to diagnose behavior by making inferences at the lowest level possible in order to avoid attributing more meaning to behavior than is warranted. Unnecessarily high-level inferences can reduce the effectiveness of your interventions because group members reasonably infer that your inferences are not grounded in the data. To reduce this problem, most of the ground rules are designed to produce relatively low-level process inferences.

The Skilled Facilitator approach recognizes that there are times when you need to make high-level inferences as part of your diagnosis. In

Exhibit 6.1. High-Level and Low-Level Inferences

High-level inference	(content) Leslie doesn't want Jack's project to succeed.
	(process) Leslie is trying to manipulate Jack.
Mid-level inference	(content) Leslie won't give Jack any of her people because she believes Jack's people can do the project themselves.
	(process) Leslie is unwilling to tell Jack her concerns.
Low-level inference	(content) Leslie wants to delay giving Jack a full-time person.
	(process) Leslie is asking questions but not explaining the reasoning for her questions. She is not sharing her own interests.
Observable behavior	JACK: I really need a full-time person dedicated to this project.
	LESLIE: How soon will it start? Can it wait two months until next quarter?
	JACK: The project's got to be worked on right away. I can't wait any longer than I already have.
	LESLIE: Well, I know one of your people has the experience for this; how about if Jill works on it part-time until next quarter?
	JACK: I don't think she wants to do that.
	LESLIE: Couldn't we have more people work on smaller pieces of the project instead of just one person?

developmental facilitation, if I infer a group member's core value or assumption as part of his or her theory-in-use, I am making a relatively high-level inference. Suppose I infer from a member's behavior that he values unilaterally controlling the conversation to make sure that solutions other than his own do not get selected; I am actually making several inferences about the cause of his behavior that involve high-level attribution as to his motive.

Issues of trust, power and control, equity, and defensiveness usually involve making relatively high-level inferences on the basis of behavior in the group. To the extent that you think these issues have a significant impact on a group's effectiveness and you have an agreement with the group to explore these issues, you should consider inferences of this kind.

When you make a high-level inference, it needs to be logically connected to the behavior observed. In high-level inferences, you are actually making a series of nested inferences, with each at a successively higher level and adding more meaning, attribution about motive, and judgment to the behavior you observed. For group members to understand how you arrived at your high-level inference, you have to be able to fully explain your reasoning. This means that you can describe each step of your inferential process—beginning with the level closest to the observable behavior—and that you do not make any inferential leaps to reach your conclusion. If you are unable to do this privately in step two of the diagnosis-intervention cycle, you will not be able to explain your reasoning when you intervene.

Seeing at Different Levels

As you watch a group and try to understand what is happening, you see a number of things depending on what you focus on. We can look at things at three levels: behavior and interaction, a pattern of behavior, and structure (Hirokawa, 1988; Senge, 1990; Watzlawick, Beavin, and Jackson, 1967). Regardless of the level you focus on, you are still starting with the same directly observable behavior as your data. So when you look at these three levels you are not seeing different things; you are seeing the same thing in different ways. Yet what level you pay attention to affects how you intervene in the group. As you move from seeing only behaviors or interactions to seeing structure, your ability to make high-leverage diagnoses and interventions increases.

Behavior and Interaction. At the first level, you focus on *behavior and interaction*. Focusing on this level, you are attending to who is saying what to whom, how others respond, and with which ground rules members act consistently or inconsistently.

Consider a team conversation in which the leader begins the meeting by identifying a problem communicating with field staff: "The way to solve this problem is by giving all of our people online computers on board their vehicles." The finance and budget director responds, "That's not necessary. People don't need computers. Cell phones will work just as well." You notice other team members are rolling their eyes after the leader speaks, but you say nothing. Looking at the behaviors and interactions, you infer that both the leader and the finance director are focusing on positions and that other members are withholding some relevant information.

This might lead you to intervene, by asking them to focus on their interests and share all relevant information.

Patterns of Behavior. At the second level, you focus on *patterns of behavior.* You take the behavior you noticed at the first level and note how it recurs over time. In addition, you pay attention to other behaviors and interactions and note how they recur over time. You also pay attention to the correlation among these behaviors.

Continuing with the example, you would begin to note the frequency with which this type of interaction occurs and the other conditions present around the time of the interaction. You might, for instance, note that the leader and finance person focus on positions after the finance person shares information that the team is over budget. You might also note that members are silent whenever the team leader initiates a new conversation, but they speak up when the finance director initiates the conversation.

This could lead you to intervene by pointing out the recurring behaviors, which is a more powerful intervention than simply identifying a single occurrence of an ineffective behavior.

Structure. At the third and deepest level, you notice the underlying *structure*. **Unlike focusing on behavior and interaction or on pattern, noticing structure means proposing a causal explanation for part of how the group is operating.** The causal map includes how members are thinking (their left-hand column, including their values and assumptions), how their thinking leads to them to act or react, how these actions and reactions generate consequences for the group, and how these consequences feed back to people's thinking to maintain the structure. In many ways, seeing structure is like seeing part of a group's theory-in-use. By describing this causal map to the group, you can test it, and the group can make a choice about changes to reduce the negative consequences.

At this level, you begin to make inferences about what group members are thinking and how this leads them to create the patterns you have seen. For example, you might infer that members assume their budget director is not likely to approve their budget if they disagree with him. This leaves members reluctant to state views differing from the budget director's if their own budget is on the line. So they respond through nonverbal behavior. You might also note that as a result of not raising their concerns with the director, they create a cycle in which the director makes decisions without the full input of the other members, which then lead the members to continue to be frustrated with the director. The director may contribute to this by recognizing the members' discontent but not raising it for fear of precipitating expression of negative feelings.

By intervening on structure, you can help the group members explore how their thinking leads to action that creates unintended consequences, by contributing to maintaining the system that each is dissatisfied with. In this way, you help the group explore the underlying dynamics that keep their more superficial but ineffective behavior and pattern in place. This means engaging in developmental facilitation and intervening in theory-in-use.

CHALLENGES IN DIAGNOSING BEHAVIOR

In becoming skilled at diagnosing behavior, you face several challenges. Some are inherent in the nature of facilitation; others have to do with learning the Skilled Facilitator approach.

Diagnosing at the Speed of Conversation

When I teach people the diagnosis steps of the diagnosis-intervention cycle, I show them a videotape of a group in action; I ask them to observe the group behavior and infer which comments are consistent or inconsistent with which ground rules. Being able to do this at the speed of conversation is essential. When participants first try this, they sometimes feel overwhelmed. The conversation seems to move so quickly that, by the time they have figured out which ground rule is reflected in a particular comment, they have missed several comments that followed it. People often report getting better at this after just their second try, though. Still, the challenge of inferring the ground rules in real time exists.

This concern recedes with practice. After learning the ground rules, people can quickly access them. As people continue practicing steps one and two of the diagnosis-intervention cycle, the ground rules become a template through which they naturally hear and see the group, and this enables them to quickly match behavior with ground rules.

The Need to Attend Constantly to the Group

One reason facilitation is such mentally demanding work is that you need to attend unceasingly to the group during the entire time you are working with it. Consequently, you have to learn to diagnose behavior while simultaneously continuing to observe the group (Schön, 1983). Unless you are cofacilitating a group, it is difficult to mentally take time out from the group to diagnose behavior.

One way to increase this ability is to reduce the distractions that fill up your left-hand column and that keep you from being able to fully attend to the group. This may mean resolving issues unrelated to the facilitation before it begins, or resolving to put the issues out of your mind until you are no longer facilitating. If possible, not having to respond to voice mail, e-mail, and cell phone calls during the facilitation is a major way to reduce distraction. A second method is to increase your ability to focus for a long period of time by practicing your diagnostic skills. As your ability to diagnose behavior increases, you can do it with less effort and therefore attend to the group longer before tiring. Of course, you can explain to group members that you have temporarily lost focus and ask them to repeat what they have said.

The Principle of Repeating Opportunities

To diagnose accurately, you need to observe multiple behaviors simultaneously—a formidable task. Because it is not possible to observe everything simultaneously, you are likely to miss some important behaviors or patterns that occur during a particular time period. Fortunately, group behavior is often repetitive. If a member or the group as a whole has a particular issue, it will show up more than once. Consequently, you do not need to worry about missing a single critical behavior. **If the behavior is genuinely part of the group's process, you will have more than one opportunity to observe it.**

Being Comfortable with Ambiguity

At times, you may be unable to make sense out of what you are observing in the group. You may feel uncertain, confused, or overwhelmed, and even wonder how you can help the group. This is a natural feeling for even an experienced facilitator, especially when just beginning to work with a group. A natural response to confusion is to try to impose some order. The challenge is to become comfortable with ambiguity and not impose order prematurely by rushing to inference and diagnosis. Diagnosing behavior prematurely increases the probability of missing important aspects of the group's behavior.

One reason group behavior seems ambiguous at times is that you are observing a complex pattern, but the group has displayed only part of it. Like a mystery that seems impossible to solve until the last page of the book, the entire pattern may need to appear before you can interpret it. Sometimes, you may feel confused because you have missed the beginning of the pattern, much like walking into a movie theater after a film has begun; a conflict between members just before the meeting begins might be played out during the meeting.

Apart from accepting that ambiguity and confusion are inevitable, you can try to make sense of the situation without imposing order prematurely. By generating alternative hypotheses about what is happening, you can observe behavior that either confirms or disconfirms the hypotheses. Of course, you can also share your ambiguity and confusion with group members and ask them to help diagnose the situation.

Reducing Distortion

To be a skilled facilitator, you need to accurately diagnose behavior. However, your own personal issues and biases lead you to see groups through a distorted lens. As a result, you may systematically attend to certain behaviors and not see others, make inaccurate high-level inferences and attributions about group members' behavior, and respond to the group with emotions that have no basis in the group's experience. For example, a facilitator who has a strong desire to control the situation may tend to interpret client disagreement with him as resistance and respond with frustration or anger, rather than considering the possibility that the client has become independent enough to challenge the facilitator.

Becoming aware of your theory-in-use helps you understand how your core values and beliefs lead you to distort your diagnosis. By identifying your systematic biases and personal issues (need for control or approval; fear of being wrong; and so on), you can begin to monitor your behavior. Also, by working with a cofacilitator with whom you have shared these issues, you can get feedback from the cofacilitator and also reduce the chance of your issues affecting the group.

Being Drawn in by the Content

As a facilitator, you have to pay attention to the content of the conversation to help group members explain their views and test their assumptions and inferences about an issue. The challenge is to pay attention to the content without being drawn into it and losing your ability to help the group.

When you are drawn in by the content, you stop attending to the group's process; you might even find yourself participating in the content of a conversation. You can get drawn in if you are interested in the content, if you are completely unfamiliar with the content, or if you feel overwhelmed by the group's process. For obvious reasons, if you have a special interest in the content you may be particularly susceptible to being drawn in by it. If you are completely unfamiliar with the content, you can still be drawn into it by trying to understand what group members' comments mean. Finally, you might seek refuge in the group's substantive discussion if you feel overwhelmed by the group process, especially if the content is familiar to you.

One way to avoid being drawn into content is to attend to it for the purpose of examining the process. When I attend to the group, I am looking for whether group members are using the ground rules. If I infer they are not, I then attend more closely to the content of the conversation to see specifically how the potential process problem is affecting the content. It is as if the group conversation is a piece of music. The group process is the melody, and the content the specific notes. I pay attention to the melody until some part of it sounds off key, at which point I listen to the specific notes.

Expanding Your Diagnostic Frames

Your effectiveness is determined partly by the range of your diagnostic frames. The law of the instrument (Kaplan, 1964) essentially states that if the only tool you have is a hammer, everything will look like a nail to you. Applying this to diagnosis, you naturally construe the behavior you observe to fit the diagnostic frames you have. If, for example, you are able to diagnose when group members are acting inconsistently with the ground rules, but you are less able to use the group effectiveness model to diagnose the group's problems, or to diagnose problems that stem from members' theories-in-use, then you may continue to make interventions that address only part of the cause of the behavior and that miss the root cause.

To make the situation more difficult, you have your favorite diagnostic frames and look for opportunities to use them, even when another frame may be more appropriate. All of this, of course, reduces your ability to help a group.

The challenge is to develop the ability to diagnose the comprehensive set of behaviors related to group effectiveness and to learn to use an equally comprehensive set of interventions related to these behaviors.

SUMMARY

This chapter has introduced the six-step diagnosis-intervention cycle and explored its first two steps: observing behavior and inferring meaning. I have described various diagnostic frames that you can use to observe behavior and infer meaning. The chapter concludes with consideration of some challenges we face in observing and inferring meaning.

In the next chapter, we consider the last diagnostic step of the diagnosis-intervention cycle: deciding whether, how, and why to intervene.

PART THREE

INTERVENING
IN GROUPS

CHAPTER SEVEN

Deciding Whether, How, and Why to Intervene

In this chapter we consider whether, how, and why to intervene. First, I describe types of interventions you can make with a group. Next, I propose a set of questions you can ask yourself to decide whether, how, and why to intervene. I end the chapter by discussing issues to consider in deciding how to intervene.

In step three of the diagnosis-intervention cycle, you decide whether, how, and why to intervene. In practice, intervening means entering the group's conversation to help it become more effective. An intervention is any statement, question, or nonverbal behavior of yours designed to help the group.

Step three is the last diagnostic step in the diagnosis-intervention cycle (see Figure 7.1); it represents a transition between the diagnosis and intervention parts of the cycle. In this step, if you decide to intervene, you also decide whom to intervene with, on what issue, and how you will craft your opening lines.

TYPES OF INTERVENTIONS

To decide whether and why to intervene, you must know your intervention options. There are a number of types that you can carry out in a group (see Exhibit 7.1). I have already discussed the group effectiveness model, the ground rules for effective groups, and theory-in-use as diagnostic frames. They are also

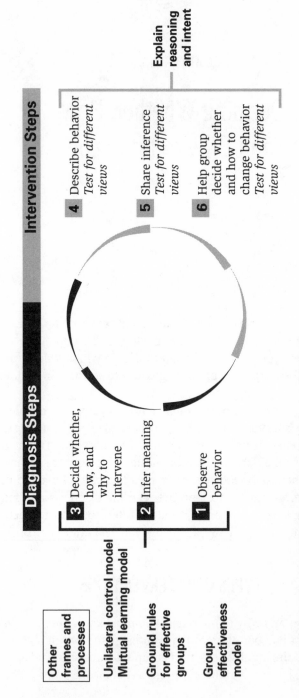

Figure 7.1. Diagnosis-Intervention Cycle with Diagnostic Frames

the basis for differentiating the type of intervention. In this section, I describe general types from which you can choose.

Ground Rules

You intervene on the ground rules when you see some behavior in the group that is inconsistent with the ground rules and that you believe reduces group effectiveness. The purpose of intervening on the ground rules is to improve group process by identifying members' behaviors and inviting them to change their behavior to be consistent with the ground rules. You make a ground rule intervention when you ask a member to explain his reasoning, test his inference, or give a specific example. You may also intervene to identify when a member is using the ground rules effectively.

Compared with other types of intervention, when you intervene solely on the ground rules your focus may be relatively narrow. That is, you are often focusing on a single behavior of one or two group members.

Group Effectiveness Model

You intervene using the group effectiveness model when you believe there is some larger process, structural, or contextual issue reducing effectiveness. For example, you may infer that the group is unclear about its goals or roles, or that it may not have sufficient support from the larger organization. This intervention is broad in scope in that the issues often involve the group has a whole.

Theory-in-Use

You intervene on theory-in-use when you want to help members explore their core values and assumptions, or explore how the core values and assumptions lead them to design a strategy that creates unintended consequences. Theory-

Exhibit 7.1. Types of Interventions

- Ground rules
- Group effectiveness model
- Theory-in-use
- Other diagnostic frames
- Managing group process and structure
- The facilitator's role and performance
- Teaching concepts and techniques for improving group process
- Making content suggestions
- Reframing

in-use intervention is the deepest type in that it may lead members to reveal privately held values and beliefs. Theory-in-use interventions can also be the most powerful, because members' theories-in-use are often a significant source of group process problems.

Other Diagnostic Frames

You may use any diagnostic frame as the basis for your intervention. Some facilitators use individual difference models, such as Myers-Briggs or a model of conflict, to make sense of group process. Some diagnostic frames (say, a model of group problem solving or decision making) fit well with specific elements of the group effectiveness model. Other diagnostic frames can be used well with the Skilled Facilitator approach if they are based on core values that are congruent with the approach and have a foundation in directly observable data. Chapter Ten describes how to diagnose and intervene with other diagnostic frames.

Managing Group Process and Structure

In a group process or structure intervention, you decide with the group what process and structures to use during the facilitation. Because this is your area of expertise as facilitator, you make the decision jointly with the group. This entails advocating for a process that fits the group's needs, whether it is a particular problem-solving process, a strategic planning process, or some other. In a large group, managing process may also involve recognizing people to speak and monitoring the time. Advocating structure includes helping the group clarify its meeting objectives and agenda, suggesting what kind of people may need to participate to generate valid information, and estimating how much time may be needed for various discussions. In developmental facilitation, you and the group jointly manage the process. In basic facilitation, you manage much of the process for the group, although ultimately the group and you jointly control the process.

The Facilitator's Role and Performance

In an intervention oriented toward the facilitator, your role or performance is the subject of discussion. For example, a group member may express concern that you are acting inconsistently with the facilitator role, say by taking sides in the substance of a discussion. Or a member may see that you are acting inconsistently with the core values and ground rules. In some cases, you may infer that members are concerned about how you are fulfilling your role.

The purpose of this type of intervention is to identify whether and how you have acted ineffectively, and if so, to identify what if anything needs to happen for you and the group to continue to work effectively.

Teaching Concepts and Techniques
for Improving Group Process

At times, you may need to teach the group about a particular method or technique for improving process, so that it can decide whether to use the method. You do this when you explain the core values and ground rules and ask the members whether they want to adopt them as their own. Other examples include teaching a group to use the effectiveness model or a general problem-solving model, or how to identify system dynamics. Technically, when you make this intervention you are serving as a facilitative trainer. Still, this intervention is consistent with the facilitator's role if it focuses on improving group process. However, if you teach concepts related to the substance of the group's issues (such as marketing methods or product development), you are moving outside the role of facilitator and into the role of facilitative consultant.

Making Content Suggestions

In the content type of intervention, you share some information or suggest how the group can address some substantive aspect of the issue. As you saw in Chapter Three, this type of intervention is generally inconsistent with the facilitator's role. One exception may be when the group has tried unsuccessfully to identify a solution that meets all the members' interests. Here you may suggest a solution if you first receive the group's permission and afterward ask whether the suggested solution meets all the members' interests.

Let's look at an example: "Tawana, you said your interest behind sending a memo now was to let the department know what progress the group has made, correct? [Continuing, assuming Tawana agrees] Ted, you said your interest behind not sending a memo now was to avoid having people falsely conclude that the group has made a decision, correct? [Continuing, assuming Ted agrees] If the group sends out a memo stating very clearly that the memo reflects the group's current thinking, but that the group has not made any decision, would this meet everyone's interests?"

Technically, all content suggestions are inconsistent with the facilitator's role. However, as I discussed in Chapter Three, when the content of a group's discussion involves how to manage process effectively, you are nonneutral about the content because you are a process expert. Consequently, a content suggestion closely related to group or organizational process and therefore closely related to the group's ground rules is less inconsistent with your role. The intervention about sending a memo is an example of this situation. However, content suggestions that have no relation to group or organizational process are more inconsistent with the facilitator's role, as with suggesting that a department buy rather than lease equipment.

Reframing

A reframing intervention helps members change the meaning they ascribe to an event. As the meaning of the event changes, people's response and behavior also change (Bandler and Grinder, 1982; Bateson, 1972). For example, group members are often reluctant to give each other negative feedback, because they say they care about members and do not want to hurt them. I often help members address their reluctance by helping them reframe what it means "to care." I suggest that genuinely caring about members means *giving* others feedback about their behavior such that the data can be validated and the person receiving the feedback can make an informed free choice about whether she wants to change her behavior. Further, I suggest that by *withholding* information, members hurt each other by precluding each other from making an informed choice about whether to change ineffective behavior.

When you help members reframe something, you are also helping them change their values or beliefs. Consequently, a reframing intervention is useful in conjunction with intervention on the core values and ground rules as well as theory-in-use.

CONSIDERING WHETHER TO INTERVENE

You consider whether to intervene once you have inferred in step two that the group can improve its effectiveness, on the basis of one or more of your diagnostic frames. Members may be acting inconsistently with ground rules, or acting in a way that suggests a problem with an element of the group effectiveness model, or employing a unilateral control theory-in-use, or having difficulty using some other process model.

It is not feasible or even desirable to intervene every time a group member acts ineffectively or each time you identify some element of the group's process, structure, or organizational context that hinders its effectiveness. If you did, in some groups you would be intervening after each person's comment! This would prevent the group from ever accomplishing its real tasks. An overall consideration in deciding whether to intervene is determining how much time to take temporarily from the group's focus on its task so as to focus on improving group process, in order to ultimately improve overall effectiveness. This is an issue that you can decide jointly with the group.

There are a number of questions you can ask yourself to decide whether to intervene (see Exhibit 7.2).

Observation and Diagnosis

"Have I observed the behavior enough to make a reliable diagnosis?"

Sometimes you need to repeat steps one and two of the diagnosis-intervention cycle before you are relatively sure that your inference is sound. If you

Exhibit 7.2. Questions for Deciding Whether to Intervene

- Have I observed the behavior enough to make a reliable diagnosis?
- To what extent is the behavior hindering the group's effectiveness?
- What are the consequences if I do not intervene?
- Have I contracted with the group to make this type of intervention?
- Do I have the skills to intervene?

think that group members are focusing on interests rather than positions but are not quite sure, then you may decide to observe the group a little more to either confirm or disconfirm your hypothesis.

However, waiting to intervene also has potential disadvantages. If you wait until you are quite confident about what you have observed, group members may infer that you are not performing with vigilance. In addition, early intervention shows the group what it can expect from you and can help members become quickly aware of behavior. You can reduce this potential problem if you state early in the facilitation why you may not intervene at times when others believe it would be appropriate. You can also invite the group members to intervene.

Behavior Hindering Effectiveness

"To what extent is the behavior hindering the group's effectiveness?"

Not all ineffective behavior has the same impact on a group's effectiveness. For example, consider a group in which Tom is not fully explaining the reasoning and intent behind his statements, questions, and actions. Even if he is acting inconsistently with the ground rule, I might choose not to intervene unless I observe some other behavior in the group that leads me to infer that not sharing his reasoning is contributing to a problem. I might notice that in response other group members are making negative inferences about Tom's motives.

Sometimes I decide to intervene because I anticipate that the behavior will have a negative impact on the group in the future. Suppose I infer that group members are making plans on the basis of some significant untested inferences; I will decide to intervene. Making this kind of judgment requires understanding how ineffective group process is causally connected to various negative group outcomes. Essentially I am saying, "When I see this kind of behavior under these conditions, I can predict that it will have a negative impact on the group."

Behavior that hinders the group keeps it from achieving any of the three group effectiveness criteria: producing services and products that meet or exceed the standards of those who receive, use, and review them; working together so as to enhance members' ability to do so in the future; and satisfying the growth-and-development needs of the members. Keeping in mind all three effectiveness criteria is important when deciding whether an issue is critical enough to warrant intervention.

Consequences of Not Intervening

"What are the consequences if I do not intervene?"

There may be positive and negative consequences if you do not intervene. Here are two general issues to consider. First, **if I do not intervene, will a group member do so?** One principle of the Skilled Facilitator approach is to reduce unnecessary dependence on you as the facilitator. In other words, don't do for the group what the group can do for itself. This principle leads you not to intervene if group members can intervene themselves. Determining what the group can and cannot do at any point requires continual testing. It is reasonable to assume that the group is unable to intervene in difficult issues until it has intervened in simple ones.

Not intervening can be a strategy for further diagnosis and group development. If you believe that members have the skills to recognize and intervene on their own behavior, you can give them time to intervene first. Especially in developmental facilitation, you may decide not to intervene immediately so as to determine whether members will intervene on their own. If a member does intervene effectively, you learn that the group has developed the ability to diagnose and intervene on that type of behavior or issue.

The second issue is this: **if I do not intervene now, what is the probability that I can intervene later and still help the group avoid any negative consequences of its ineffective behavior?** Ineffective group behavior reduces a group's effectiveness. But in some situations, if you do not intervene there are great negative consequences for the group, and they occur quickly; for example, the group's process may be growing increasingly more ineffective, the quality of the group's decisions is suffering, or there is insufficient commitment to implement a decision.

Consider, for example, a group that has made a decision without realizing it has not reached consensus and is about to move on to the next agenda item. If I do not intervene immediately, the group is likely to realize they have not reached consensus only after they begin to commit resources and implement the decision.

In contrast, if members are discussing a problem and are not giving specific examples to illustrate their points, the consequences for the group are likely to be less severe if I do not intervene immediately. Group members will probably have a more difficult time understanding what exactly each member means, and as a result the conversation may take time. I will surely have other chances to intervene before the results of not sharing specific examples become severe. If, however, by not giving specific examples members begin to dig into their positions and make negative attributions about others, the consequences become greater.

Because group process repeats itself, like the horses on a merry-go-round, you have repeating opportunities to intervene on the same ineffective behaviors or patterns. If members do not test inferences on one issue, they are likely not to test those inferences throughout their discussion of the issue at hand, as well as other issues. However, once a group makes a decision on the basis of ineffective process (such as an untested inference), you may not have another opportunity to help the members deal with the content of their decision if you do not intervene at that time.

The Contract with the Group

"Have I contracted with the group to make this type of intervention?"

Part of your agreement with a group is to delineate the kinds of interventions you will make with them. In basic facilitation, your agreement with a group may not include making an intervention about fundamental group dynamics or theory-in-use. Although you may see process issues arise in the group, it may not be necessary to address them for the group to accomplish its stated objectives.

However, if you need to make a type of intervention that you have not contracted for in order for the group to accomplish its stated objectives, you have a dilemma. If you simply intervene, you act inconsistently with the agreement. If you do not intervene, the group may be unable to meet its objectives. One way to try to resolve the dilemma is to recontract with the group—in the moment. You can state the dilemma to the group and ask to make whatever intervention is necessary.

Requisite Skills

"Do I have the skills to intervene?"

Some interventions, such as those dealing with defensive behavior, require significant skill. To be helpful, you need to intervene within the limits of your skills. This does not mean that you should totally avoid intervening if you are not completely proficient; that would prevent you from taking a reasonable risk in order to become more effective—a behavior worth modeling for the group. However, you need to limit the risk by choosing interventions that are within the range of your current level of skills. If you decide to pursue an intervention that is new and challenging for you, you might begin by saying, "I'm going to take a risk here and do something I haven't tried before. . . ."

CONSIDERATIONS FOR INTERVENING

At any time, you may have the opportunity to make various interventions. How do you decide? When choosing how to intervene, as with many choices in facilitation, there is no one correct answer. Faced with the same situation, two facilitators may make different interventions. In addition, making one intervention does not preclude making another. In fact, the various types of interventions are often linked or nested within one another. For example, I may begin by intervening on several ground rules, which then leads to teaching a concept on the ground rule, which then leads me to make a theory-in-use intervention. I know of no simple rule for mechanically deciding which interventions to make. Still, there are a few principles you can use to help you decide how to intervene.

You Get More Than One Chance

Interventions are not one-step solutions. It is rare that you can make a single intervention that goes directly to the cause of a problem and helps the group improve process. Do not misunderstand me; I love a well-crafted intervention, one that addresses the group's issues succinctly, powerfully, and compassionately. But if you think of crafting only the ideal intervention, you place unreasonable pressure on yourself to get everything right the first time you open your mouth. Ironically, focusing on getting it completely right distracts you from doing the good work you are capable of.

Instead, I find it helps to think of interventions as a series of unfolding steps. I start with one, and then depending on the members' responses I move to other related interventions. Each time I intervene, I learn more about how the members are thinking and feeling and about how my interventions work, all of which enables me to better craft my next intervention. In shifting my thinking this way, I also show compassion for myself.

Address Concerns About the Facilitator's Role First

Sometimes the group has concerns about your role or performance as facilitator. People may be concerned that you are paying attention to some members more than others, that you are becoming involved in the content of the conversation, or that you are colluding with certain members. Or the group may be concerned that the process is not helping them achieve their objectives. **If members do have concerns about you, it is important to address them as soon as possible, because your ability to facilitate credibly may be reduced until you satisfactorily address the concerns. It can feel threatening to have group members question your facilitation, but only by encouraging them to describe their specific concerns can you address them.** Chapter Thirteen deals with the issue of handling your emotions as well as those of group members.

Consider the Basic-to-Developmental Facilitation Continuum

One factor that influences your choice of interventions is the extent to which the facilitation is basic or developmental. In the former case, you help the group temporarily improve its process so as to accomplish some significant task. In the latter case, you also help the members accomplish a task, but in addition you help them learn how to reflect on and improve process.

Basic Facilitation. In basic facilitation, you choose interventions that are narrowly designed to help the group directly address the task at hand. This includes managing group process and structure, intervening on the ground rules, and focusing on elements of the group effectiveness model that are essential for the group to accomplish its task, such as clear goals and appropriate membership. While you help group members articulate their core values and assumptions about the task they are working on, you are less likely to intervene on their theory-in-use. Nor are you likely to intervene on the more fundamental elements of the group effectiveness model such as group culture, in part because you may not have contracted to make these interventions, but also because they are typically not required in helping the group accomplish its task.

Developmental Facilitation. As facilitation becomes more developmental, you draw on the full range of interventions. You teach the group concepts and techniques for improving process, including helping them become proficient in using the ground rules. If, for example, you find yourself intervening on the same ground rules, this might lead you to begin to intervene on theory-in-use as a way to understand what people are thinking that leads them to continue acting inconsistently with the ground rules.

In basic facilitation, when a conflict arises in the group, you may choose to intervene by asking members to focus on their interests, test their assumptions, and share their reasoning. In developmental facilitation, you are likely to go beyond such intervention on action and interaction, instead examining the pattern of group conflict and how members contribute to creating the structure of the conflict. In doing so, you help group members learn how they create unproductive conflict in general and how they can change it.

Intervene with People Who Have the Data

Part of deciding how to intervene is deciding to whom you should address your interventions. **The basic principle is to intervene with the person or people who have the data to respond to the intervention.** For interventions on the ground rules, this usually means intervening with the person or people whose behavior is inconsistent with the ground rules. If I infer that someone has not shared her reasoning with the group, I would address my intervention to her, because she is the person who can best explain her reasoning. If several members are focusing on positions rather than interests, I would intervene with each of them, addressing each by name.

When intervening on a pattern of behavior, I would address all members who contribute to the pattern. First, I identify the full pattern so group members understand the point of the intervention. Then, in the order in which they have entered the pattern, I address each member's contribution. This allows the group to see how the pattern develops.

Identify People by Name. It may seem like an obvious point, but when making these interventions it is essential to identify the members by name. Some facilitators address the group in general terms when they observe certain members acting in a way they consider ineffective: "I notice some members focusing on positions rather than interests. I think it would be helpful if you would focus on your interests." The facilitators reason that by not addressing members specifically, they avoid embarrassing people or putting them on the spot. However, because they have not been addressed directly, the members concerned may not know that the facilitator is addressing them, and it prevents the facilitator from finding out whether the group members agree with the facilitator's inference. As a result, members may not respond to the facilitator's intervention, either because they do not understand it is meant for them or because they disagree with the facilitator's inference about their behavior.

There are times when it is not necessary to address specific group members, as when you are helping to manage group process and structure. You might say, "What are some ways to solve this problem?"

Intervening on Current and Past Events. In this section, I have been describing interventions on events that take place in the meeting you are currently facilitating. But you can also focus your interventions on events that occurred in a previous meeting or outside the current session. Perhaps group members are describing a difficult conversation they had outside the facilitated meeting; I would ask them to repeat the part of the conversation that made it difficult. Then I might intervene further, for example by asking members what it was about the conversation that was difficult or by identifying how I think each member contributed to making the conversation less productive than it could have been. Through this type of intervention, the group and I are able to reflect on experiences that occur outside the facilitated meeting. Obviously, intervening on past data is useful if members want to discuss issues that have come up outside the facilitated meeting. It is also useful when looking for data that may confirm or disconfirm patterns that members exhibit within the meeting.

Consider Macro Interventions Before Micro Interventions

Most interventions are designed to structure members' behavior to some degree. When I ask a group member, "Do you see it differently?" I am intending to structure the group member's answer to respond to my question. When I suggest that the group develop a meeting agenda, however, I am intending to broadly structure the group's discussion for that entire meeting.

Macro Interventions. An intervention that tends toward the *macro* (such as developing an agenda) addresses structure; an intervention that is *micro* (such as asking one member a question) involves less structure. Although macro and micro represent two ends of a continuum measuring structure, I sometimes refer to them as discrete choices for the sake of simplicity. For example, you make a "relatively macro" intervention when you suggest that the group use a problem-solving model to discuss its problem. Other relatively macro interventions are establishing roles, ground rules, and expectations for a meeting, or setting an agenda. Macro interventions entail greater structure by limiting the range of appropriate actions that members may take while the macro intervention is in effect. For example, by agreeing to use a set of ground rules during a meeting, members limit themselves to certain behaviors throughout the meeting. In other words, a macro intervention creates structure that affects member behavior after the facilitator's intervention is over. Macro interventions also tend to create structure for the entire group. Establishing ground rules and developing an agenda, for example, apply to all group members.

Micro Interventions. In contrast to macro interventions, micro interventions incorporate relatively little structure. When you point out similarities among members' comments or ask members to define important words, the intervention limits the range of behavior only in immediate response to the facilitator's intervention. Whereas a macro intervention tends to structure all members' behavior, a micro intervention tends to structure individual behavior (or that of a subgroup). When a micro intervention does structure all group members' behavior, it does so for a relatively short time.

When choosing between macro and micro interventions, it helps to make the macro intervention first. This approach sometimes makes micro intervention unnecessary. Imagine you are facilitating a group and infer that they have begun discussing issues that are completely off the agenda. At the same time, you infer that a group member has made an inference that seems untested. If you intervene first to determine whether the group is off task and then help the group return to the agenda (macro intervention), once the group is back on task the untested inference may become irrelevant. However, if you intervene first on the untested inference (micro intervention), the group spends time on an issue that is off task.

SUMMARY

In this chapter we have considered the last diagnostic step of the diagnosis-intervention cycle: deciding whether, how, and why to intervene. This step represents the transition between private diagnosis and public intervention. I began by considering the types of interventions you can draw on: ground rules, the group effectiveness model, theory-in-use, other diagnostic frames, managing group process and structure, the facilitator's role and performance, teaching concepts and techniques for improving group process, making content suggestions, and reframing.

Because you need to strike a balance between focusing exclusively on the group task and focusing on process to improve the ability to perform tasks, you need to decide when to intervene and when not to. By asking yourself several questions about how important the intervention is and the consequences of not intervening, you can quickly make a good choice.

Finally, we have considered several issues for shaping how you intervene: addressing issues of the facilitator's role or performance first, considering the basic-developmental facilitation continuum, intervening with people who have the data, and choosing macro before micro interventions.

If you decide to intervene, the next step is to make your intervention. In Chapter Eight, we consider how to craft an intervention so that it follows logically from your diagnosis. This includes identifying exactly what you might say at each intervention step of the diagnosis-intervention cycle.

CHAPTER EIGHT

How to Intervene

This chapter explores how to use the diagnosis-intervention cycle to intervene once you have decided to do so. I describe each step of an intervention and explain what to say, how to say it, who to say it to, when to say it, and when not to say it. At the end of the chapter, I describe how to carefully choose your words in intervening.

THE INTERVENTION STEPS OF THE DIAGNOSIS-INTERVENTION CYCLE

The three intervention steps of the diagnosis-intervention cycle parallel the three diagnostic steps (Figure 8.1). **In step four, you describe to the group what you privately observed in step one that led you to intervene, and you test whether the group agrees with the observations. In step five, you describe the inferences you privately made in step two and test whether group members agree with the inferences. Finally, in step six, you help group members decide whether and how to redesign their behavior to be more effective, describing the consequences of changing the behavior that you privately identified in step three.** Assuming group members have decided to change their behavior, the cycle begins again, and you observe whether the group members have in fact changed their behavior. You use the diagnosis-

175

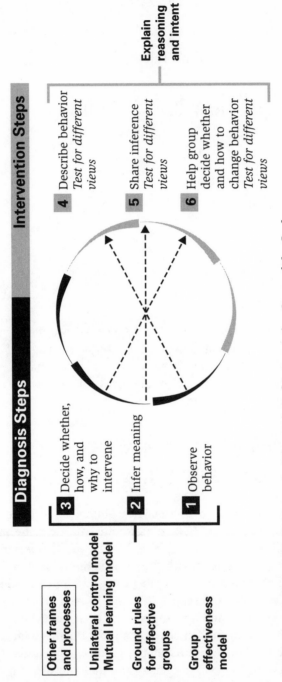

Figure 8.1. Relationship Between the Diagnosis and Intervention Steps of the Cycle

intervention cycle continually to determine whether there is any group behavior for you to intervene on.

The parallel steps of the diagnosis and intervention parts of the cycle accomplish a couple of things. First, they present a general structure for diagnosing group behavior. Second, they are a way to intervene that is transparent; specifically, in the intervention steps you share what you are privately thinking, including your reasoning, and you test with others whether they see your reasoning differently.

The ground rules and core values of the Skilled Facilitator approach are embedded in the intervention steps of the cycle. As Figure 8.1 shows, in step four, as you describe observable behavior, you apply the ground rule of using specific examples and agreeing on what important words mean. In step five, by sharing your inference, you are using the ground rule about testing assumptions and inferences. In step six, when you ask others whether they are willing to change their behavior (perhaps to apply a ground rule they have never used), you are jointly designing next steps.

In each step, you can use the ground rule of explaining your reasoning and intent. In step four, you use it to briefly explain why you are intervening. In step five, you explain how the person's behavior may create a problem. In step six, you explain how, if the person involved changes his behavior, it can create a more effective process. Steps four through six each have two parts; the second part is testing for different views. When you carry out that test, you are using the ground rule of combining advocacy with inquiry.

Of course, the ground rules are a way of operationalizing core values. So when you intervene using the steps of the cycle, you share information in such a way that group members can validate it for themselves; you let them make a free and informed choice about whether to change their behavior; and you help them be internally committed to the changes they choose. Employing the mutual learning theory-in-use increases the chance of intervening with compassion.

Compassion is an essential element in intervening. It is relatively easy for group members to agree to use the ground rules, or agree that I can intervene when they act inconsistently with the ground rules or other elements of group effectiveness. But it can become relatively difficult for group members when I actually intervene on their behavior, especially in the beginning of the facilitation. They may feel bad about their ineffectiveness and believe they have been put on the spot by my intervention. If I see the group primarily as having made a promise to act effectively, then I will view my interventions simply as a way to police their transgressions. If they continue to act ineffectively, I will become frustrated with them for not having the skills that they hired me to help them with. At this point, my interventions shift from being helpful to being hurtful.

Instead, if I see the group as simply trying to work together without the necessary set of skills, I view my interventions as a way to help provide (or teach them) the skills they are missing. If they continue to act ineffectively, I can have compassion for them, thinking about the difficulty they are having in learning this set of skills, just as I learned them.

Exhibit 8.1 shows an example of intervening using the diagnosis-intervention cycle. Three executives are discussing how to redesign part of the organization's performance management system. The right-hand column shows the conversation, and the left-hand column presents notes about the conversation.

Exhibit 8.1 Intervening Using the Diagnosis-Intervention Cycle

Notes	Conversation
I infer that Ronald has stated a position and begun to discuss an interest of being able to budget for the system *(step two)*. I consider whether to intervene to ask Ronald to fully identify his interest. I decide to wait to see how others respond, given that he has begun to identify an interest *(step three)*.	RONALD: I think the performance management system needs to have a cap on the payout and a forced distribution with a predefined percentage of people who will be rewarded. This way we can budget for it in advance.
I consider whether to ask Cynthia to check whether others share her assumption *(step two)*. I decide not to make this intervention because she has clearly stated the assumption and the next person may respond to it without my intervening *(step three)*.	CYNTHIA: But a forced distribution assumes that only a predetermined number of people can be excellent performers. It's hypocritical for us to say that we expect everyone in this organization to be excellent and then design a system that assumes that's not possible.
I infer that Andrew may be discussing another topic and therefore unilaterally designing the next step in the conversation *(step two)*. I wait until the next person speaks to see if the conversation will return to what I understood to be the original topic *(step three)*.	ANDREW: Cynthia, if anyone is hypocritical, it's the employees. Remember how they were complaining last year that their managers didn't give them enough autonomy, and then when it was given to them, they said their managers were too distant?
I infer that Ronald continues on the same different topic as Andrew *(step two)*. I decide to intervene because the group seems not to be returning to the original topic as I understand it *(step three)*.	RONALD: Yeah, no matter what we did, it wasn't right.
I briefly explain my reasoning for intervening and then describe the directly observable data and test whether Ronald and Andrew see it differently *(step four)*.	FACILITATOR: I want to check whether the conversation is still on track. A minute ago, you were talking about the forced distribution. Then Andrew

Exhibit 8.1 *(continued)*

Notes	Conversation
	said, "Cynthia, if anyone is hypocritical, it's the employees. Remember how they were complaining last year that their managers didn't give them enough autonomy, and then when it was given to them, they said their managers were too distant?" And Ronald, you said that you agreed. Did I misstate anything?
With Ronald and Andrew agreeing, I move to step five.	RONALD AND ANDREW: No, that's right.
I share my private inference from step two that I don't see the relationship between Andrew and Ronald's comment and the comments before they spoke. I check to see if they see a relationship I don't see *(step five)*.	FACILITATOR: Andrew and Ronald, I don't see the relationship between your comments and conversation about the forced distribution. Can you say how your comments are related, if they are?
Andrew agrees that his comment represents a different topic and that it is not going to affect discussion on the current topic *(step five)*.	ANDREW: Well, it's a different topic. We have to find ways of getting people to accept more responsibility, but I don't think that's going to affect whether we have a fixed distribution.
With Ronald agreeing, I move to step six.	RONALD: Yeah, I agree.
I ask the group whether they want to return to the distribution topic or continue on the shifting-responsibility topic *(step six)*.	FACILITATOR: What do you want to do? Do you want to continue the conversation about distribution or shift to the issue of responsibility?
	RONALD: Let's go back to the distribution issue.
I check for consensus from the group *(step six)*.	FACILITATOR: OK. Anyone have a different suggestion?
	ALL: No.
	FACILITATOR: OK. Cynthia, you were the last person to talk before the topic changed. Would you repeat what you said so people can respond?

Step Four: Sharing Observations

In step four, you describe to the group the data that you have privately observed in step one that leads you to intervene, and you test whether the group agrees with the observation. Sharing observations means sharing directly observable data. To return to the camcorder metaphor, a way to think about directly observable data is as the information the camera (with sound) records if it simultaneously captures all the group members' verbal and nonverbal behavior.

It is important to share observations without making an inference or attribution. Table 8.1 shows several statements I can make to share my observations with the group and to test whether they agree. Notice that the only way I can share my observation without making an inference or attribution is to repeat the words I heard the group members use. Once I add an inference or attribution, I move beyond observation to interpretation. A video camera simply observes; it does not interpret.

Facilitators sometimes confuse inferences with observations when intervening on a group member's feelings. Saying "I notice that you are angry" is stat-

Table 8.1. Embedding Inferences in Sharing an Observation

Nature of Inference	Facilitator's Statement
High-Level Inference and Attribution	
I infer that Andrew is shifting the topic unilaterally because he wants to control the conversation.	"Andrew, you changed the subject. I think you are trying to control the conversation."
Medium-Level Inference and Attribution	
I infer that talking about responsibility is not talking about distribution, and I attribute the cause to Andrew's not listening to what Cynthia was saying.	"Andrew, you changed the subject. I don't think you heard what Cynthia was saying."
Low-Level Inference	
I infer that talking about responsibility is not talking about distribution.	"Andrew, you're not talking about the same topic as Cynthia."
Directly Observable Data	
I make no inference.	"Andrew, you said, 'Cynthia, if anyone is hypocritical, it's the employees. Remember how they were complaining last year that their managers didn't give them enough autonomy, and then when it was given to them, they said their managers were too distant?'"

ing an inference. The observable behavior might be that the group member's face is red, his brow is furrowed, and he has pushed away from the desk and crossed his arms. Of course, these same observable data may also imply something other than anger.

It is important to share my observations without making an inference or attribution, because the observable data are the basis of my intervention. If the group member does not see the observable data as I see it, then the group member is not likely to agree with my inference, which is based on the observable data.

Sometimes I find it useful to begin step four by briefly explaining the intervention I am about to make, before the members share the directly observable behavior. In this example, I begin my intervention by saying, "I want to check whether the conversation is still on track" before describing the observable behavior. I find this particularly useful when I am about to describe a complex pattern that requires me to share and test a large number of behaviors. I might say, "I've noticed a pattern of behavior in the group that I think makes it difficult for you to reach consensus. Let me share what I've observed, check it out with you, and see whether you agree." The statement gives members a context in which to understand each behavior that goes into the pattern that I then describe and test with the group. Without a context, I would be describing and testing many behaviors, and group members would be wondering what my point is.

When I begin step four, I address the group member by name so the group knows to whom I am speaking. I also include a phrase such as "I think I heard you say . . ." or "I think you said. . . ." Using such a phrase sets me up to complete the sentence by quoting what the group member said—which is exactly what I want to do in step four.

Be prepared for group members to see things differently. The second part of step four involves asking the person whether you have accurately captured what the person said. If I ask, "Have I misstated anything you've said?" and the person simply answers yes, then I follow up by saying, "Tell me what I missed." Finding out that I have misheard a group member is not a mistake; on the contrary, it is a success. Using the diagnosis-intervention cycle well means learning that others see things differently than I do.

After the person tells me what she actually said, I can then decide if it still makes sense to proceed with my intervention. If the corrected version no longer leads me to infer that the person has acted inconsistently with the ground rule, I stop my intervention. I can say, "I was going to follow up on what I thought you said, but given what was actually said, it's not relevant."

Sometimes, from the time a person has spoken to the time I start to intervene, I forget exactly what the person said that led me to intervene. In this situation, I simply say something like, "Sheryl, would you repeat what you just said? I wanted to follow up on it, but I forget exactly what you said." Group members do not expect you to be infallible; it is OK to occasionally ask people to repeat themselves.

Step Five: Testing Inferences

In step five, you share the inference that you have privately made in step two and test with the group member or members whether they have a different inference. When I intervene on behavior that is inconsistent with the ground rules, I test my inference that what a member says or does in fact represents behavior inconsistent with a ground rule.

Publicly testing inferences with the group prevents me from unilaterally acting on inferences that are inaccurate. Many research studies have found that after developing a hypothesis about what is happening in the group, people tend to seek data consistent with the hypothesis and avoid or discredit data disconfirming it (Nisbett and Ross, 1980). This leads people to a self-fulfilling prophecy (Merton, 1957). In facilitation, the facilitator may inadvertently misinterpret behavior in the group such that it supports his initial hypothesis (see, for example, Snyder and Swann, 1978).

I observed this tendency one day in a group facilitation workshop I taught. The facilitation students were watching videotapes of a group that was simulating various kinds of dysfunctional behavior. In the first videotape, the group leader's ineffectiveness was an undiscussable issue, and the facilitation students accurately identified the problem from various behavioral cues. In the second videotape, several students also saw signs of group leader ineffectiveness, although none was there. In discussing the second videotape, one student mentioned that he was looking for places where the leader was acting ineffectively, as he had done in the previous videotape. Having found the leader ineffective in the first videotape, he "found" ineffective behavior in the second videotape. Only after publicly testing his inference did he find that his data were missing.

As I mentioned in Chapter Four, **I make inferences at the lowest level needed for the intervention.** In the example with Andrew and Ronald (Exhibit 8.1), my inference that Andrew's comment doesn't seem related to Cynthia's comment is a relatively low-level inference. I do not have to make a higher-level inference to intervene on the ground rule of jointly designing next steps.

There are times, particularly in developmental facilitation, when I do make high-level inferences—for example, regarding a group member's theory-in-use. Under certain circumstances, I might for instance infer not only that Andrew's comment is unrelated to Cynthia's but also that Andrew is introducing this comment by design to purposely shift the conversation away from Cynthia's topic, which he finds threatening in some way.

However, to make such a high-level inference, I would need to share the data that led me to make it. The data would come from previous group conversations in which the group and I explored with Andrew his reasons for regularly shifting the topic of conversation before checking with group members. I also

need to have seen a pattern of this behavior before making the high-level inference. If Andrew has changed the topic of the conversation only once or twice
in the meeting, the data are probably insufficient for me to make such a high-
level inference. Also, to make a high-level inference intervention (such as
theory-in-use), I must be sure the group agrees to this kind of intervention. We
discuss this in Chapter Thirteen, on contracting.

When I do make a high-level inference or attribution about a group member's motives or emotions, I attribute it to the person but not to his personality.
For example, I would say, "David, given what you just said, I'm inferring the
reason you do not want to give your consent is that you don't trust that Lucinda
will help you complete the project. Is my inference off?" (rather than "You are
not very trusting toward Lucinda" or "You aren't a very trusting person"). The
difference is important. The former statement is more closely related to the observable data. It makes an attribution about trusting behavior in a particular
situation rather than overgeneralizing and implying that the person has a mis-
trustful personality. Also, attributing the behavior to personality implies that it
is less likely to change, because aspects of personality are relatively stable. Consequently, the former statement is less likely to elicit defensive behavior than
the statements in parentheses.

As part of step five, I may explain how a member's behavior can create a problem. In the conversation with Andrew, the problem with his changing the topic
of the conversation is likely to be apparent, and I probably would not offer an explanation. However, if a member is making an untested inference or assumption,
I might intervene by saying, "I'm inferring that you are thinking that the problem needs to be solved using the current staffing available. Is my inference correct? The reason I raise this is because if it turns out that your assumption is
incorrect, you may end up designing a solution based on a faulty assumption."

Sometimes I share my inference in a way that calls direct attention to the
ground rule that I believe the group member is not using: "Brett, your statement
sounds like a position rather than an interest. Do you see it differently?" If I
want to emphasize the group's agreement to use the ground rules, I might say,
"Brett, one of the group's ground rules is to focus on interests rather than positions. Your statement looks like it's focusing on positions. How do you see it?"
Naming the specific ground rule is useful when I am helping the group learn to
use the ground rules themselves. My intent in doing this is to help them see the
ground rules clearly, not to sound like the ground rules police.

Be prepared for group members to see things differently. The second part
of step five involves asking the person whether your inference is accurate. As
with step four, if I ask, "Is my inference off in any way?" and the person simply answers yes, then I follow up by asking what meaning he makes of his statement. Here too, finding out that a group member's meaning is different from
mine is not a mistake; it is a success. Using the diagnosis-intervention cycle well
means learning that others see things differently than I do.

Whether I am testing out an inference about content or process affects how I respond if a group member does not share the inference I have made. If I am testing a content inference—one about the meaning of the person's words—I am likely to accept the person's interpretation if it makes sense to me as a possible explanation. I accept it because it is difficult for someone other than that person to independently know what he or she means.

If, however, I am making a process inference—for example, that a group member is acting inconsistently with a ground rule—then I pursue our differing interpretations because as a process expert I have relevant information and can logically explain the reasoning by which I made my inference. For instance, if in step five I share my inference that Amal has advocated without inquiring and Amal disagrees with my inference, I would then say, "Amal, would you explain how you see your statement as combining advocacy with inquiry so I can understand where we see it differently?" After listening to Amal's explanation, I may explain as a process expert how I think his understanding is incomplete, or I might learn from his explanation that he has in fact inquired and I missed it.

Some facilitators make their interventions in the form of a question (see, for example, Schein, 1987). The facilitator might begin an intervention by asking, "Andrew, do you think you're off track?" Edgar Schein states that the question format is generally more helpful "because it encourages, even forces, the client to maintain the initiative. If the goal is to help the client to solve his own problem, to own the responsibility, then the question is the best way to communicate that expectation" (1987, p. 158).

I share Schein's goal of helping the client to own responsibility, and I think his approach can be appropriate for a group in developmental facilitation that is becoming skilled at diagnosing its own behavior. However, I see several potential problems with the question format. First, it requires me to withhold relevant information. If I am thinking, *I heard Lois say "X," which leads me to infer that Lois is not explaining her reasoning,* but I say to the group "Do you think Lois is explaining her reasoning?" or "What do you think of Lois's comment?" then I am withholding relevant information and easing in. Unless I state the relevant information, I cannot check whether the group shares my point of view.

This leads to the second problem: the group can feel set up. If the group answers, "Yes, Lois is sharing her reasoning," then unless I share my differing view or drop the intervention, I need to continue asking leading questions until the group figures out the supposed answer. Eventually, the group may infer correctly that I am looking for the so-called right answer, but for whatever reason I am unwilling to share it with them.

Finally, using the question format can send the message that the group needs to take responsibility for its observations but that I do not have to take responsibility for mine. This message is inconsistent with the Skilled Facilitator assumption that the facilitator is a model of effective behavior. Therefore, unless the group understands that my question is designed to help the group learn to diagnose its own behavior, I think it is more effective to share my inference about the member's behavior and then ask whether the member or others view it differently.

Step Six: Helping the Group Decide
Whether and How to Change Behavior

In step six, you help group members decide whether and how to redesign their behavior to be more effective, describing the consequences of changing the behavior that you privately identified in step three. When I carry out step six, I ask group members to do what they have agreed to in step five that they have not done. For example, I may ask them to check an untested inference or share their interests instead of their positions. By doing so, I help the group move the conversation forward. Asking group members whether they are willing to change their behavior is not simply a behavioral nicety; it maintains members' free choice and responsibility for changing their behavior.

Helping group members decide whether and how to redesign their behavior means saying something like, "Would you be willing to test out your inference to see if it's accurate?" If I have not explained in step five the potential problem with making inferences but not testing them, I can do so in step six. I may say, "The reason I'm suggesting this is that by testing your inference you can be sure you are designing the solution on the basis of accurate information." My explanations for steps five and six are similar. In step five, I describe the potential problem with the group member's current behavior; in step six I describe the advantage of changing the behavior. I usually do not need to offer both explanations.

Sometimes group members need help redesigning their behavior. If they have just been introduced to the ground rules, they may not know how to test an inference, focus on interests, or combine advocacy with inquiry. Here I help the members redesign their behavior either by coaching them or by modeling the behavior for them.

Even if members redesign their behavior, it may still be inconsistent with the ground rules. In this situation, I use the diagnosis-intervention cycle again, sharing my observation, testing my inference that they are, for instance, still focusing on positions (explaining why I believe that), and asking the members whether they want to try again.

I have assumed that members are willing to redesign their behavior to be consistent with the ground rules. **In practice, group members rarely choose not to redesign behavior that is inconsistent with the ground rules if they have validated my observations and inferences.** But what if, for example, a member says no when I ask whether he would be willing to give a specific example? First, I ask, "Can you say what leads you to say no? I'm asking not because I want to pressure you, but to find out if there is something that is keeping you from giving an example so that the condition might be changed. The choice is still yours." If the person is willing to share his concern, I can then explore that concern with the person and the group and ask, "What needs to happen for you to be willing to share an example?" Ultimately, to preserve the group's free choice, I must respect members' decisions about whether they want to change their behavior.

Viewing a reluctant group member as resistant is not a particularly useful frame. It attributes to the person that he is unreasonable—even if I do not understand his reasons—and questions his motives. Instead, if I view a reluctant group member as having unmet needs—needs that I may not fully understand— I can maintain my compassion even if he chooses not to change his behavior.

Repeating Intervention Steps

I have described the diagnosis-intervention cycle as a one-way process in which I move from step four to five and six (sometimes skipping part of a step along the way). However, sometimes I repeat steps. For example, if I am intervening on a pattern of behavior, I may identify several people's observations and test them in step four. Then I move to step five and test the several inferences I have made from the observations.

When to Skip Intervention Steps

So far, I have described how you can use the three intervention steps in their full form. Although each step of the cycle serves a purpose, sometimes you can skip a step—or part of a step—and still intervene effectively. One reason to skip a step is that using the full diagnosis-intervention cycle repeatedly when it is not needed can sound unnatural, awkward, or laborious. However, skipping a step inappropriately can create problems.

Deciding when to skip a step is a judgment call. Steps four, five, and six are each designed to share your reasoning and check with group members to see if they see the situation differently. Skipping a step creates two risks. First, you increase the chance that group members will not understand part of your reasoning for asking them to change their behavior. Second, if you skip the part of the step that tests for differing views, you end up assuming that members agree with your observation or inference. If your assumption is incorrect, then you move to the next step of the cycle without the members having agreed to a previous step.

There are several conditions under which I sometimes skip a step.

A Member Has Just Spoken. If a group member has just said something and I intervene immediately after she has spoken, I may skip step four and begin with step five. For example, in a group meeting discussing the effects of the economy on the organization, Tara says "I've been through this before. Believe me, there will be layoffs." If I intervene immediately after Tara speaks, I can skip to step five and say, "Tara, hearing you say that, I'm thinking that you have some relevant information about previous situations like this one. Is my inference correct?" However, if Tara has just spoken but said a number of things, I will repeat the part of what she said that I want to focus on, so that she and others understand, but I may skip the part of step one in which I test for differing views. I would say, "Tara, you said a number of things just now. One thing you said was X. From that, I infer that you have some relevant information about previous situations like this one. Is my inference correct?"

The Intervention Creates an Ordinary Request. If the group member has just spoken and I am asking him to follow a ground rule that is a generally accepted request in meetings, I may skip directly to step six. For example, if Ellis has said, "We miss the deadlines because we don't have full cooperation from other divisions," I would say, "Ellis, can you talk about a time when that happened?" Here, I am intervening to ask Ellis to use specific examples and agree on what important words mean. Because asking people for specific examples is typically seen as an ordinary request, I feel that my risk is relatively low if I skip to step six. Other ground rules that may fall in this category, depending on the group culture, are explaining your reasoning and intent, and focusing on interests and not positions.

Group Members Have Agreed to Redesign Their Behavior. In developmental facilitation, when a general agreement exists that members will redesign their own behavior, I do not need to ask each time. Instead, in step six I can simply ask, "How would you say that so it is consistent with the ground rules?"

I Want to Paraphrase What a Group Member Said. Paraphrasing involves taking a group member's words and using different words to convey essentially the same meaning. When I paraphrase, I am combining steps four and five because by changing the words that a group member has used I may be adding my own meaning. I may paraphrase in order to summarize and capture the essence of a person's comments: "Jessica, I'm going to paraphrase what I heard you say; then tell me if I misrepresented you in any way. I understood you to be saying that creating a new division will shift the responsibility for quality away from manufacturing without creating any benefits. Is there anything I said that didn't accurately capture what you meant?"

I may also paraphrase in order to emphasize certain points that the person has made, perhaps to contrast them with others' comments: "Jessica, let me see if I can paraphrase, emphasizing the key issue as you see it. These are my words, not yours; let me know if I misrepresent what you've said. You're saying that, unlike Ian, you do see a lack of cooperation between the units, and you are frustrated that he doesn't see it. Have I misstated anything?"

When Not to Skip Intervention Steps

There are also conditions under which I do not skip an intervention step.

The Group Is Beginning Developmental Facilitation. Early in developmental facilitation, using the complete intervention cycle helps members learn all the steps. After members become familiar with the entire cycle, collapsing becomes less risky. Then members know which steps I have skipped and can respond if they believe the missing steps need to be discussed. If skipping a step creates a problem, I return to using the full cycle.

The Intervention Is Complex. A complex intervention requires that I share more of my reasoning than with a simple intervention. Discussing undiscussable issues and jointly designing next steps and ways to test disagreements are complex ground rule interventions. Testing assumptions and inferences can also be complex. Other complex interventions involve reframing and theory-in-use.

Group Members Are Misunderstanding Each Other. When group members misunderstand each other, I use the full cycle to ensure that I do not misunderstand them. This often occurs in a high-conflict situation, particularly if a group member is responding defensively. In this situation, I may begin step four by saying, "Pierre, I know you just said this a second ago, but I want to repeat it to make sure that I have heard it accurately, because there have been a number of times when people said they had been misquoted."

The Facilitator Is Learning to Use the Diagnosis-Intervention Cycle. When you are first practicing the diagnosis-intervention cycle, it is useful to use the full cycle without skipping any steps. By learning all the steps in the cycle, you develop a sense of what each step contributes. This helps you make an informed choice about when it is sensible to skip a step.

MAKING JARGON-FREE GROUND RULE INTERVENTIONS

Some facilitators find the language of the ground rules relatively jargon-free. Others see considerable jargon; equally important, they are concerned that the groups they work with also consider it jargon and are put off by it. For example, if the phrase "Based on what you have said, I am inferring . . ." does not sound natural in your workplace, you can say "From what you've said, I'm thinking that . . ." or "It sounds to me as if. . . ." Chapter Five has examples of how you can intervene on each ground rule without using jargon.

Still, be careful about making an untested assumption that a group with relatively little formal education will find the language of the ground rules to be jargon. In my experience, such groups have quickly understood the ground rules and used them in their current form.

Choose your words carefully. The specific words you use are important; they are the fundamental elements of interventions. A small difference in your choice of words can lead to a large difference in meaning and in the group's reaction. By using language that states exactly what you mean—no more and no less—you can intervene clearly.

Some guidelines for categories of words to use and to avoid are given in Exhibit 8.2.

Use Words with One (Correct) Meaning

Use words and phrases that have one meaning—the meaning you want to convey. Certain phrases carry more than one meaning. You may use a phrase intending to convey a particular meaning, but clients may interpret it to mean something else. As part of a union-management cooperative effort, I served as the facilitator in a three-member training team that included union and management representatives. At one point, employees were clarifying instructions we had given them as part of a training exercise. When an employee asked whether the exercise could be approached in several ways, the union representative on our training team said, "I don't care which way you do it." Later, the employee said he was annoyed that the union representative was not interested in answering the question. He interpreted the union representative's statement to mean "I'm not interested in your problem." However, the representative meant "I have no preference for how you conduct the exercise."

Exhibit 8.2. Guidelines for Words to Use and Avoid

- Use words and phrases that have one meaning—the meaning you want to convey.
- Use descriptive words when they can be substituted for evaluative words.
- Use proper nouns or other nouns rather than pronouns.
- Use active voice unless the identity of the actor is not clear.
- Use words that give equal recognition to all members and tasks.
- Choose words that distinguish the facilitator role from group members' roles.
- Avoid imperatives; focus instead on cause and effect.
- Avoid facilitator jargon.
- Avoid humor that puts down or discounts members or that can be misinterpreted.

Use Descriptive Words

Use descriptive words if they can be substituted for evaluative words. Words that identify directly observable behavior are more easily validated than judgmental words. The ground rule to "use specific examples and agree on what important words mean" is based partly on this principle. It is easier for a group to agree whether a member did not hand in a report by 5:00 P.M. than to agree whether the member was irresponsible.

Descriptive words are consistent with the facilitator's neutral role. Judgmental words contain some built-in evaluation, implying that the facilitator either approves or disapproves of a behavior or idea. For example, in facilitating a conflict between teachers and administrators, I intervened to summarize the two alternatives posed by members, saying: "You have identified two alternatives. The radical one is X. The other alternative is Y." As soon as the word *radical* left my lips, I realized I had made a mistake, even though some group members had used that term. By labeling one alternative with the adjective *radical*, I loaded it with all the political connotations with which that word has come to be associated. For some group members, *radical* probably had a positive connotation, while for others it was negative. In any case, by framing the alternative as radical, I added an unnecessary evaluative component. Had I intervened in a purely descriptive way, I would have said, "You described two alternatives. One is X. The other is Y."

Using judgmental verbs can have the same consequence. If, in summarizing an interaction between Sidney and the group you say "Sidney refused to participate," the implication is that Sidney's behavior was uncooperative. A descriptive alternative would be, "I did not see Sidney participate."

Sometimes, two words are synonyms but one is more judgmental than the other or is more easily misinterpreted. In asking whether a group member knew about a situation, you could ask, "Were you unaware of the situation?" or "Were you ignorant of the situation?" Although *ignorant* means unaware, people often associate the word ignorant with *stupid.* So *unaware* is a better word choice.

Use Proper Nouns

Use proper nouns or other nouns rather than pronouns. Consider this interaction between a facilitator and José:

JOSÉ: I talked with Peter about how to handle my conflict with Fred. Peter said he wasn't the kind of person who was particularly good at resolving conflicts and that I should try to solve the problem on my own. Or, I could work something out with Jack, Beth, or Nancy. Frankly, I don't think I can get help from any of them.

FACILITATOR: Do you think you can solve the conflict without him?

JOSÉ: I don't have any choice.

FACILITATOR: Are you saying that you don't have the choice to talk with Fred about what's going on?

JOSÉ: No, I wasn't talking about Fred.

FACILITATOR: When you approached Peter, didn't he say he wasn't good at handling conflict?

JOSÉ: No. Peter didn't say Fred wasn't good at handling conflict. He said *he* wasn't any good.

FACILITATOR: Oh, I misunderstood. I thought when you said, "Peter said he wasn't any good," *he* referred to Fred.

JOSÉ: And when you asked me whether I could "solve the problem without him," I thought *him* meant Peter.

FACILITATOR: No, by *him* I meant Fred.

If the conversation seems confusing, it is. The confusion occurs largely because José and the facilitator unknowingly use the pronouns *he* and *him* to refer to different people. When pronoun confusion becomes complicated, it begins to sound like the famous Abbott and Costello routine "Who's on First?" By using individual's names or their distinctive titles, you can avoid confusion.

The pronoun *that* (or *this*) creates similar confusion. Imagine a discussion in which you are helping a group move from positions to interests. Various members have each identified several positions. If you say, "Dan, would you be willing to explain what your interest was behind that?" *that* could refer to any of several positions recently discussed. However, if you say, "Dan, would you be willing to explain what your interest was behind meeting with Andrea alone?" the ambiguity is reduced.

One exception to avoiding pronouns is the singular form of the word *you*. When you look directly at a group member, and say "Do you think X?" there is little ambiguity. Of course, saying, "Terry, do you think X?" further reduces ambiguity. However, using *you* to refer to a subset of the group can be confusing. Identifying the individual group members by name or by some appropriate label (for example, "all of you first-line supervisors") reduces the ambiguity.

Use Active Voice

Use active voice unless the identity of the actor is not clear. Active voice identifies who or what is taking the action; passive voice does not. "Sue decided to promote Glen" uses active voice. "It was decided to promote Glen" uses passive voice. When you use active voice, you provide valid information to the group, reduce potential ambiguity, and act consistently with the belief that individuals should take responsibility for their actions.

However, it is sometimes helpful to intentionally use passive voice, when the identity of the actor is not clear. Consider this interaction:

TED: We've got a problem. Jan called the director and told him there was no way we could get the job done today.

JAN: No, I didn't call the director about that. When I spoke to him in the afternoon, he already knew we couldn't meet the deadline. Maybe Sue told him when she dropped off the plans. He mentioned that Sue had come by.

SUE: I didn't even see him when I dropped off the plans. I just left them on his desk.

FACILITATOR: When the director was told that the deadline couldn't be met, how did it create a problem?

Here, several members disagree about who told the director that the group would not be able to meet a deadline. By using passive voice ("the director was told"), you are able to focus on how telling the director creates a problem without making an assumption about who told the director and thereby continuing the disagreement. If it is important to determine who told the director, you would return to the disagreement. Using passive voice to ignore conflicts or issues that need to be discussed is inconsistent with the mutual learning model, which is at the core of the Skilled Facilitator approach.

Use Words Bestowing Equal Recognition

Use words that give equal recognition to all members and tasks. Organizational members can be divided into various groups according to their position or title (for example, customer service representatives), functional area (marketing department), work status (full time, permanent), professional training (psychologist, engineer, physician), sex, or race. Facilitated groups are rarely completely homogeneous. You may often have occasion to refer to subgroups.

Remaining neutral and credible with all subgroups includes referring to each subgroup in a way that maintains its identity and does not subordinate it to other groups. The principle is to **refer to each subgroup in terms that reflect its independent identity rather than in terms that use another subgroup as a point of reference.** My colleague Peg Carlson and I used to be members of a university department faculty made up mostly of lawyers. At faculty meetings, faculty members would refer to "the lawyer faculty" and "the nonlawyer faculty." Peg, who like me is an organizational psychologist, commented that until she came to this department she had not realized that she was a nonlawyer. She then said that she realized that she was also a nonastronaut, a nonphysicist, and so on.

The point is that when you identify people in terms of a reference group that they do not belong to, you minimize part of their identity. The reference subgroup is often those with the highest status or power in the group, even if that subgroup does not represent a majority. In the example with Peg, if you refer to psychologists as nonlawyers you are also using the language of the high-power subgroup to define a low-power subgroup. In a subtle way, this can lead others to infer that as the facilitator in such a situation you are aligning with the high-power subgroup members, which can lead the low-power subgroup members to doubt your neutrality.

Use Words That Distinguish the Facilitator Role

Choose words that distinguish your facilitator role from group members' roles. One way to clarify your content-neutral third-party role is to use language that distinguishes you from group members; refer to the group as *you* or *the group* rather than as *we* or *our group*. If you are part of the decision-making process (for example, if the group and you are deciding about the meeting process), it is appropriate to use the term *we*.

Avoid Imperatives

Focus on cause and effect instead of using imperatives. An imperative is a command. Imperatives such as "Make a decision" or, more loosely, "you must make a decision" ("Avoid imperatives" is also an imperative!) reduce group members' free and informed choice. An example is, "Check out your assumption before acting on it." Instead, focusing on the relationship between member behavior and the effects of the behavior helps people see the consequences of their actions, without telling them they must change. For example, you might say, "When you act on your assumption without checking it out, you miss generating some valid information, and that in turn reduces the group's ability to make a more informed choice. Do you see it differently?" Focusing on cause and effect also helps people see the systemic nature of their actions.

Avoid Facilitator Jargon

The guideline of avoiding facilitator jargon is more relevant for basic facilitation than developmental facilitation. Terms such as *intervention, role conflict,* or *directly observable data* are shorthand that some groups may not understand; indeed, a group using basic facilitation has little need to learn them. Using everyday language instead of jargon lowers the barrier of language. In developmental facilitation, teaching the group the language of facilitation is an appropriate task because group members are developing their self-facilitation skills.

Be Careful with Humor

Avoid humor that puts down or discounts members or that can be misinterpreted. Humor can be a valuable tool for relieving tension in the group, emphasizing a point, and helping members examine their behavior. However, certain types of humor can reduce your effectiveness. Sarcastic humor about a member's ineffective behavior can decrease trust in you because people are likely to interpret the humor as unsupportive. Sarcastic humor can create problems because it requires the listener to interpret your meaning as the reverse of the literal meaning of the words. The sarcastic statement "I can see there is a high level of trust in this group" means "there is *not* a high level of trust in this group." If members do not detect the sarcasm, they will question your diagnostic skills if they believe there is low trust in the group. Even if they do detect the irony, you have not modeled transparent communication.

SUMMARY

In this chapter, I have described the intervention steps of the diagnosis-intervention cycle: sharing observation, testing inference, and helping the group decide whether and how to change its behavior. The cycle is designed to publicly share your reasoning such that you can test it with group members. By using the cycle to intervene, you help the group create effective group process. In the next chapter, we consider how to use each of the ground rules to intervene in a group.

CHAPTER NINE

Using the Ground Rules
to Intervene

I n this chapter, I give verbatim examples of how to use the diagnosis-intervention cycle to intervene using each of the ground rules.

INTERVENING ON GROUND RULES

The ground rules are basic elements for improving group effectiveness. Consequently, many of my interventions focus on helping people use the ground rules.

As I mentioned in Chapter Five and discuss in detail in Chapter Thirteen, I always explain the ground rules to the group before beginning the facilitation. Even when a group member or members decide not to take the initiative to use the ground rules themselves, they have still agreed that I will intervene in their behavior if they are not using the ground rules and it hinders the group's functioning.

In Figures 9.1 through 9.18, for each ground rule I show one or more typical comments that a group member or members might make and how to use the diagnosis-intervention cycle to intervene in their behavior. To save space, I have assumed accurate identification of the behavior (step four of the diagnosis-intervention cycle) and that they agree with the inferences I have made (step five of the cycle). In practice, if someone has a different view of the behavior or my inferences, I stop at that point, inquire into how they see it, and proceed accordingly. I have varied the examples to show how to skip and combine intervention steps. Each example can be thought of as a separate move made under particular circumstances. When facilitating, I combine various moves to respond to the members' previous comments.

TEST ASSUMPTIONS AND INFERENCES

Figure 9.1. Asking Someone to Test an Inference He or She Is Making

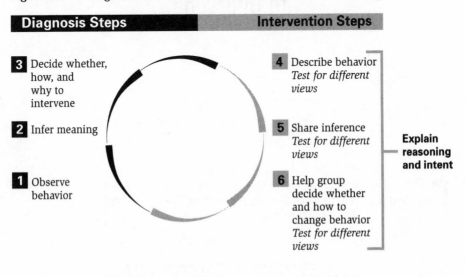

Diagnosis Steps	Intervention Steps
3 Decide whether, how, and why to intervene	**4** Describe behavior *Test for different views*
2 Infer meaning	**5** Share inference *Test for different views*
1 Observe behavior	**6** Help group decide whether and how to change behavior *Test for different views*

Explain reasoning and intent

---

3 I think it's important for Ellis to test this out because it affects the project deadline.

2 I'm inferring that Ellis has inferred that the group will drop the temporary employees from the project after the peak season ends and that bringing on new people will delay things.

1 Ellis said, "Don, we have to extend the project deadline because we'll need to restaff the project after peak season."

4 "Ellis, I want to check something out. I think you said, 'We have to extend the project deadline because we'll need to restaff the project after peak season.' Yes?" [*if yes, continue*]

5 "It sounds like you're inferring that the temps will be laid off after peak season even if they are working on the project. Are you inferring that, or something else?" [*if Ellis agrees, continue*]

6 "Would you be willing to test that out with Don, since he handles temp layoffs?"

Figure 9.2. Testing an Inference You Are Making

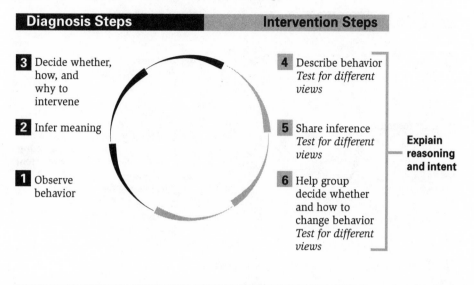

Diagnosis Steps	Intervention Steps

3 Decide whether, how, and why to intervene

2 Infer meaning

1 Observe behavior

4 Describe behavior
Test for different views

5 Share inference
Test for different views

6 Help group decide whether and how to change behavior
Test for different views

Explain reasoning and intent

---

3 I want to test this out because eliminating it at all sites is very different from doing it at just one.

2 I'm inferring that she means the group needs to eliminate the customized service at all sites if it eliminates it at one site.

1 Claire said, "Eliminating the customized service will make us less attractive."

4 "Claire, I want to check something out. I think you said, 'Eliminating the customized service will make us less attractive.' Did I get that right?" [*if yes, continue*]

5 "I inferred that you think the group would need to eliminate the customized service at all sites if it eliminated it at one. Have I inferred correctly?"

6 [*step six is not needed if the person with whom you are intervening is also the person about whom you are making the inference*]

Figure 9.3. Testing an Inference You Think Someone Is Making About You

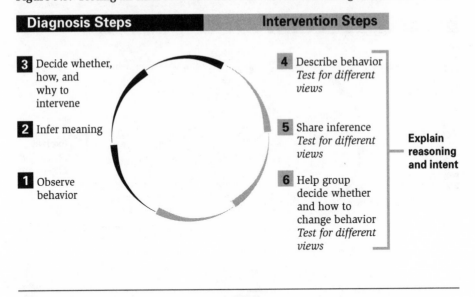

Diagnosis Steps	Intervention Steps

3 Decide whether, how, and why to intervene

2 Infer meaning

1 Observe behavior

4 Describe behavior
Test for different views

5 Share inference
Test for different views

6 Help group decide whether and how to change behavior
Test for different views

Explain reasoning and intent

---

3 I need to test this out because my effectiveness depends on their perceptions.

2 I'm inferring that Drew thinks my facilitating is slowing the group down unnecessarily.

1 Drew said, "We wouldn't be so far behind if we didn't have to look at everything we're saying."

4 "Drew, I want to check something out. When you said, 'We wouldn't be so far behind if we didn't have to look at everything we're saying . . .'" [*skipped test for different views*]

5 ". . . I inferred that you think it's my facilitation that is unnecessarily slowing the group down. Are you thinking that?"

6 [*not needed*]

SHARE ALL RELEVANT INFORMATION

Figure 9.4. Sharing All Relevant Information

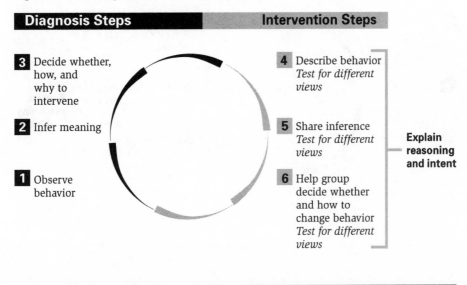

3 I want to test this out because if the data are not monolithic that may change people's views.

2 Amy presents the data in an overall conclusion. I'm wondering whether it is conclusive at the subgroup level.

1 Amy says, "The data we collected and analyzed support my view; people think we need to focus more on our core business."

4 "Amy, you said that the data support your view that people think we need to focus more on our core business." [*skip test for different views*]

5 [*skip*]

6 "Can you tell people what the variance is between and within the subgroups so that they can get a better picture of the responses?"

Figure 9.5. Asking About a Group Member's Silence

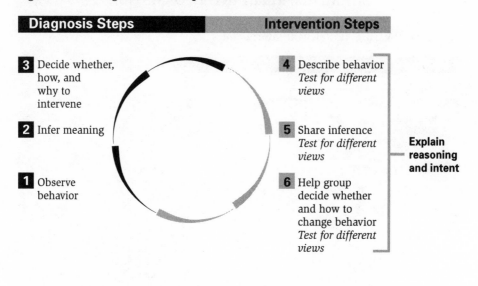

| Diagnosis Steps | Intervention Steps |

3 Decide whether, how, and why to intervene

2 Infer meaning

1 Observe behavior

4 Describe behavior
Test for different views

5 Share inference
Test for different views

6 Help group decide whether and how to change behavior
Test for different views

Explain reasoning and intent

---

3 I want to check this out because if it is related to Julie's comment, that may identify an important issue. Even if it's not related, they may still be withholding relevant information that the group could benefit from.

2 I'm wondering what led them to become silent. I'm inferring that it may be related to Julie's comment.

1 Jennifer, Ted, and Sue have been silent for a period of time after speaking. They have not spoken since Julie, their manager, stated, "It is important that the group exceed the third-quarter revenue projections."

4 "I want to share an observation and get your reactions. Jennifer, Ted, and Sue, I noticed that you haven't spoken for the last ten minutes, since Julie said, 'It is important that the group exceed the third-quarter revenue projections.' Do you see any of this differently?" [*if no, continue*]

5 "I'm inferring that you have had additional thoughts to share since Julie spoke. Is my inference off?" [*if members agree with inference, continue*]

6 "Would you be willing to say what led you not to share the information?"

USE SPECIFIC EXAMPLES AND AGREE
ON WHAT IMPORTANT WORDS MEAN

Figure 9.6. Asking for Specific Examples and What an Important Word Means

Diagnosis Steps	Intervention Steps

3 Decide whether, how, and why to intervene

2 Infer meaning

1 Observe behavior

4 Describe behavior
Test for different views

5 Share inference
Test for different views

6 Help group decide whether and how to change behavior
Test for different views

Explain reasoning and intent

---

3 I think it's important to find out what Bill means, so the group can determine if they see it differently.

2 When Bill says this, he hasn't said who "you guys" are, nor has he said what he means by "taking initiative."

1 Bill said, "You guys aren't taking initiative on the project. If I don't get the tasks started, it doesn't happen."

4 "Bill, you said, 'You guys aren't taking initiative on the project. If I don't get the tasks started, it doesn't happen.' Yes?" [*if Bill agrees, continue*]

5 [*skip*]

6 "Would you be willing to say who you mean by 'you guys' and give some examples of when you thought they didn't take initiative? This way, people can figure out if they see it differently."

EXPLAIN YOUR REASONING AND INTENT

Figure 9.7. Asking One Member to Ask Another Person to Explain Reasoning

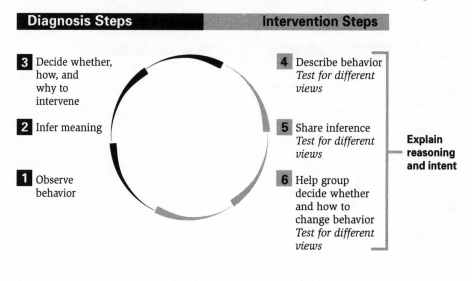

Diagnosis Steps	Intervention Steps

3 Decide whether, how, and why to intervene

2 Infer meaning

1 Observe behavior

4 Describe behavior
Test for different views

5 Share inference
Test for different views

6 Help group decide whether and how to change behavior
Test for different views

Explain reasoning and intent

---

3 I think it's important for Don to see what Sandy's reasoning is, to find out if it makes sense to him or not.

2 Sandy states her conclusion without sharing her reasoning that led to it.

1 Sandy said, "We won't be able to have all the team members trained in managing conflict by the end of the month, given the new software system that's being installed." Don said, "I totally disagree; the two are completely unrelated."

4 [*combine with step five as a paraphrase*]

5 "Don, you're saying that you don't see any relationship between the software installation and people being trained by the end of the month. Have I got that correct?" [*if yes, continue*]

6 "Would you be willing to ask Sandy how she sees them being related?"

Figure 9.8. Asking a Group Member to Explain His or Her Reasoning

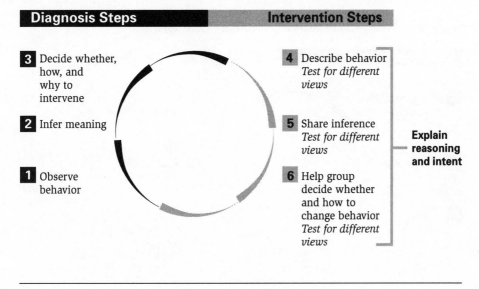

<table>
<tr><td>

3 I think it's important for Erik to share his reasoning so that others can understand it and can see whether it makes sense to them.

2 Erik has stated his conclusion without sharing how he arrived at it.

1 Erik said, "I've thought about everything people have said, and I think it makes the most sense to charge our services back to our internal customers."

</td><td>

4 [*skip*]

5 [*skip*]

6 "Erik, can you share with the group how you arrived at your conclusion? I'm asking because I think it will help people understand how you used their thoughts to reach your conclusion."

</td></tr>
</table>

FOCUS ON INTERESTS, NOT POSITIONS

Figure 9.9. Asking Group Members to Identify Their Interests

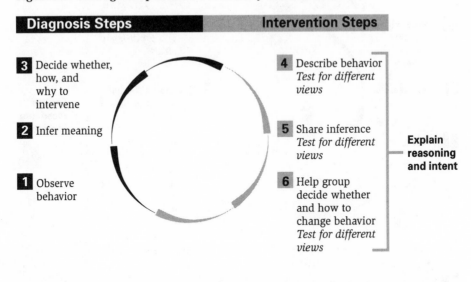

Intervention Steps

3 Decide whether, how, and why to intervene

2 Infer meaning

1 Observe behavior

4 Describe behavior
Test for different views

5 Share inference
Test for different views

6 Help group decide whether and how to change behavior
Test for different views

Explain reasoning and intent

---

3 I think it's important for them to state their interests, so they can find out whether their interests are compatible and, if so, how to craft a solution that meets all of them.

2 When Hal and Ellen say this, they state their positions, but not their underlying interests.

1 Hal said, "I want to outsource the printing rather than do it in-house." Ellen said, "No, we need to keep it in-house."

4 "Hal, you said you want to outsource the printing rather than do it in-house. Yes? And Ellen, you said you want to keep it in-house. Is that correct?" [*if both agree, continue*]

5 "I understand the solution that each of you is proposing, but I don't yet know what your underlying needs are." [*skip test for different views*]

6 "Can each of you say what it is about outsourcing it or keeping it in-house that is important to you? I'm asking because if you know each other's underlying needs, you may be able to come up with a solution that meets both of your needs."

Figure 9.10. Helping Group Members Think About Their Interests

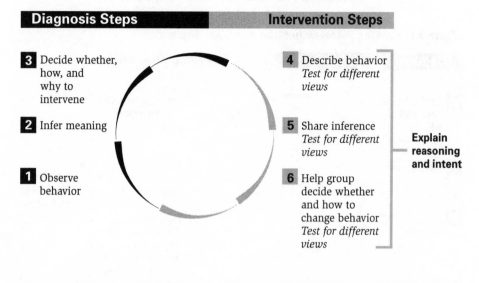

Diagnosis Steps	Intervention Steps

3 Decide whether, how, and why to intervene

2 Infer meaning

1 Observe behavior

4 Describe behavior
Test for different views

5 Share inference
Test for different views

6 Help group decide whether and how to change behavior
Test for different views

Explain reasoning and intent

---

3 I think it's important to intervene because if I'm correct, they will probably need some help thinking about interests.

2 I'm inferring that group members are having difficulty thinking about what an interest is.

1 Group members have repeatedly returned to describing their positions instead of focusing on interests.

4 "I want to share what I've been seeing and suggest a different approach, if it makes sense to you. I've been asking you to identify your interests, and when you responded, I've said that you were still identifying positions. Yes?" [*if group agrees with the paraphrase of behavior, continue*]

5 "I'm thinking that you are not sure what I mean by interests and that it would be helpful for me to walk you through identifying your interests. Am I off the mark?" [*continue if everyone agrees with inference*]

6 "OK. One way to identify your interests is to work backward from your position or solution. Think of the solution you have been proposing for this problem. Now ask yourself what it is about your solution that makes it ideal. For example, you might like the solution because it enables the group to work within its current technology or because it enables you to use your full set of skills. Whatever it is, are there any questions about how to identify your interests?" [*if no, continue*]

"Let's go around the room and find out what interests each of you has."

COMBINE ADVOCACY AND INQUIRY

Figure 9.11. Asking Someone to Make Advocacy Explicit

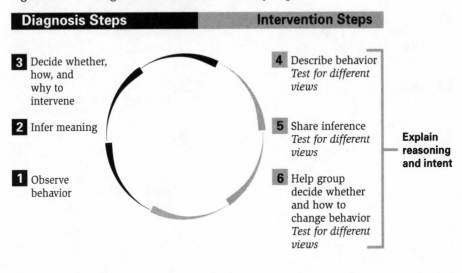

Diagnosis Steps

3 Decide whether, how, and why to intervene

2 Infer meaning

1 Observe behavior

Intervention Steps

4 Describe behavior
Test for different views

5 Share inference
Test for different views

6 Help group decide whether and how to change behavior
Test for different views

Explain reasoning and intent

---

3 If Pat has an opinion on this, I think it's important for her to share that information explicitly and see what others think, so she can get the benefit of the group's views.

2 From the inflection in her voice, I inferred that Pat has her own thoughts about the question.

1 Pat said, "Do you really think September is too late to roll out the new program?"

4 "Pat, a minute ago, when you asked whether people thought September was too late to roll out the new program . . . " [*skip test*]

5 ". . . from the inflection in your voice, it sounded to me like *you* think September would not be too late. Am I correct?" [*if yes, continue*]

6 "Would you be willing to say that, explain your reasoning, and then ask others if they see it differently?"

Figure 9.12. Asking Someone to Add Inquiry to Advocacy

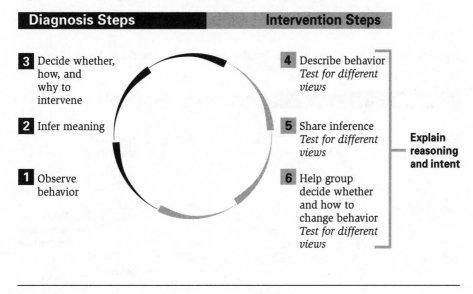

<table>
<tr><td>Diagnosis Steps</td><td>Intervention Steps</td></tr>
</table>

3 Decide whether, how, and why to intervene

2 Infer meaning

1 Observe behavior

4 Describe behavior
Test for different views

5 Share inference
Test for different views

6 Help group decide whether and how to change behavior
Test for different views

Explain reasoning and intent

---

3 If Robin doesn't invite others to comment, he may not get the benefit of their views.

2 Robin shares his position and some reasoning, but he does not invite others to examine his thinking.

1 Robin said, "Here's what I think we need to do. We stop the leadership criteria project until the merger is complete. Developing a set of criteria by working only with our executives won't give us a set of criteria that is acceptable to all the execs in the merged company."

4 [*skip*]

5 [*skip*]

6 "Robin, would you be willing to ask others what problems, if any, they see with your plan? I'm asking because if people see any gaps in it, you may want to revise it to take their ideas into account."

JOINTLY DESIGN NEXT STEPS AND
WAYS TO TEST DISAGREEMENTS

Figure 9.13. Jointly Deciding Whether the Group Is on Track and What the Next Step Is

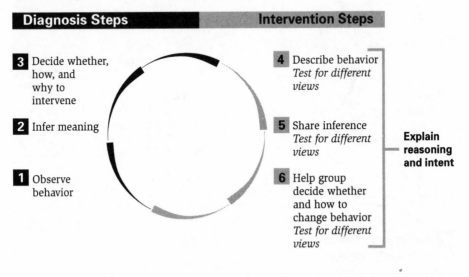

Diagnosis Steps **Intervention Steps**

3 Decide whether, how, and why to intervene

2 Infer meaning

1 Observe behavior

4 Describe behavior
Test for different views

5 Share inference
Test for different views

6 Help group decide whether and how to change behavior
Test for different views

Explain reasoning and intent

---

3 I need to check it out because either Larry has changed the group's focus unilaterally or I am missing the connection between performance standards and his comment.

2 I don't see the relationship between performance standards and Larry's comment. I wonder whether Larry is on the same topic or whether he has switched focus.

1 The group was discussing performance standards when Larry said, "I think we need to figure out who will fill the open position we have."

4 "Larry, I want to check if you've switched focus. A minute ago, the group was discussing performance standards and you said, 'I think we need to figure out who will fill the open position we have.' Yes?" [*if yes, continue*]

5 "I don't see the relationship between performance standards and your comment. But I may be missing something." [*skip test*]

6 "Can you say how your comment is related, or if it's not, can you talk with the rest of the group about which topic you want to discuss?"

Figure 9.14. Asking Someone to Propose a Joint Design for Testing a Disagreement

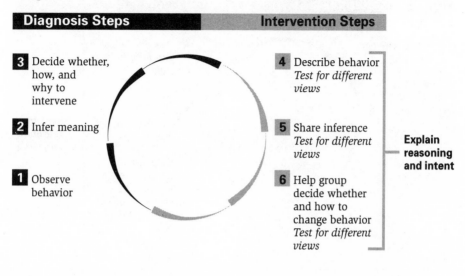

Diagnosis Steps	Intervention Steps
3 Decide whether, how, and why to intervene	**4** Describe behavior *Test for different views*
2 Infer meaning	**5** Share inference *Test for different views*
1 Observe behavior	**6** Help group decide whether and how to change behavior *Test for different views*

Explain reasoning and intent

3 If I intervene, I can help them jointly design a way to find out what the situation is.

2 Both Gareth and Leila seem convinced that their data are valid. Unless they agree on this issue, I don't think they will be committed to a solution.

1 Gareth said, "The product meets our error tolerances." Leila said, "The product is outside the tolerances."

4 "Let's see if you can figure out a way to resolve your difference. Gareth, you said, 'The product meets our error tolerances.' Correct? And Leila, you said, 'The product is outside the tolerances.' Yes?" [*if both agree, continue*]

5 "It sounds to me like the two of you need to agree on this in order to get a solution that both of you are willing to support. Am I correct?" [*if yes, continue*]

6 "Would you be willing to jointly design a way to test out whether the product is within the tolerances?" [*if yes, continue*] "OK. Do either of you have an idea about how you could design the test so both of you consider it a valid test?"

Figure 9.15. Helping the Group Manage Its Time

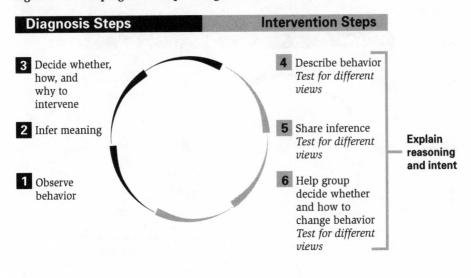

| Diagnosis Steps | Intervention Steps |

3 Decide whether, how, and why to intervene

2 Infer meaning

1 Observe behavior

4 Describe behavior
Test for different views

5 Share inference
Test for different views

6 Help group decide whether and how to change behavior
Test for different views

Explain reasoning and intent

---

3 I need to intervene so the group can make a choice about how it uses its time.

2 [*no inference needed*]

1 The group is about to exceed the amount of time it agreed to spend on a topic.

4 "You agreed to discuss this topic for two hours until ten-twenty. It's now ten-fifteen . . ."

5 ". . . and it looks to me as if you have not yet identified a solution that will meet the interests you've identified. Does anyone see it differently?" [*if no, continue*]

6 "If you continue working on a solution, I think it will be difficult to accomplish the last task on the agenda, given that you have taken about a half-hour longer than we allocated for each issue." [*skip test for different views*] "What are your thoughts about continuing your discussion, moving on to the last topic, or taking some other approach?"

DISCUSS UNDISCUSSABLE ISSUES

Figure 9.16. Identifying a Possible Undiscussable Issue

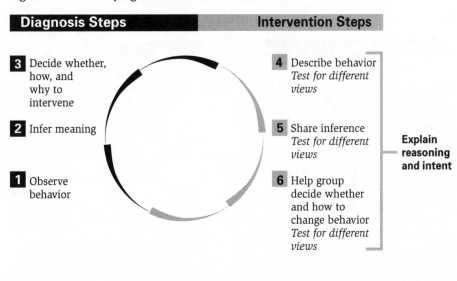

Diagnosis Steps

3 Decide whether, how, and why to intervene

2 Infer meaning

1 Observe behavior

Intervention Steps

4 Describe behavior
Test for different views

5 Share inference
Test for different views

6 Help group decide whether and how to change behavior
Test for different views

Explain reasoning and intent

---

3 I think it's important to raise this because if my inference is right, HR may have a credibility problem.

2 I'm inferring that Stephanie, Bob, or Juan has some concern about HR providing them consultation.

1 During the meeting Stephanie, Bob, and Juan said that their group needs some consultation on improving service quality. Several times, Allison has said her human resource team can provide the service, and each time Stephanie, Bob, or Juan said that the HR team is already overcommitted to other important work. Stephanie and Bob also looked at each other before declining HR's offer.

4 "I want to share some observations, raise what may be an undiscussable issue, and get your reactions. My intent is not to embarrass anyone but to help you create the more effective working relationship you said you need. During this meeting, several of you—Stephanie, Bob, and Juan—have commented that the group needs some consultation on improving service quality. Am I correct?" [*if yes, continue*] "And each time Allison has offered her human resource team to provide the service, at least one of you has said that the HR team is already overcommitted to other important work. Am I correct?" [*if yes, continue*] "Stephanie and Bob, I also noticed one of you looking at the other before declining HR's offer. Yes?" [*if yes, continue*]

5 "From all of this, I am inferring that at least the three of you may have some concern about HR's ability to adequately provide the consultation. Is that what you're thinking, or is it something else?"

6 [*not needed*]

USE A DECISION-MAKING RULE THAT GENERATES
THE LEVEL OF COMMITMENT NEEDED

Figure 9.17. Helping a Group Member Test for Agreement

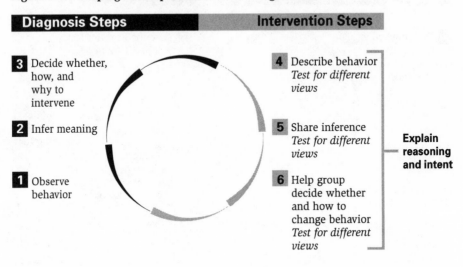

Diagnosis Steps	**Intervention Steps**

3 Decide whether, how, and why to intervene

2 Infer meaning

1 Observe behavior

4 Describe behavior
Test for different views

5 Share inference
Test for different views

6 Help group decide whether and how to change behavior
Test for different views

Explain reasoning and intent

---

3 I need to intervene because if Ian or Leslie doesn't agree and Bart thinks they do, there is a misunderstanding.

2 I'm inferring that Bart did not yet get agreement from everyone.

1 Bart said, "We've got agreement." I didn't hear Bart say what he was seeking consensus on, and I did not hear Ian or Leslie say they agreed.

4 "Bart, you said, 'We've got agreement.' But I didn't hear what you were asking for agreement on, and I didn't hear Ian or Leslie say they agreed. Did I miss something?" [*if no, continue*]

5 [*skip*]

6 "Would you be willing to say what you're asking for agreement on and ask Ian and Leslie if they support it?"

Figure 9.18. Checking Whether a Group Member's Expressed Support Is Genuine

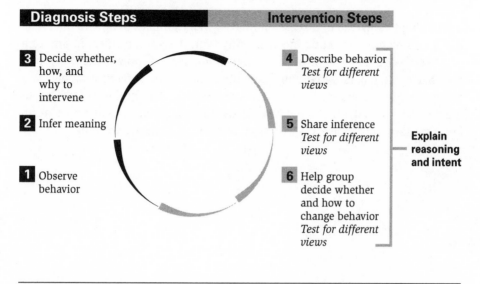

Diagnosis Steps	Intervention Steps
3 Decide whether, how, and why to intervene	**4** Describe behavior *Test for different views*
2 Infer meaning	**5** Share inference *Test for different views*
1 Observe behavior	**6** Help group decide whether and how to change behavior *Test for different views*

Explain reasoning and intent

---

3 I need to intervene because if she is responding to pressure, she is not making a free choice. If she has changed her mind, it would help the group to understand what led her to do so.

2 I'm thinking that she might be feeling pressure to support the proposal.

1 Sue previously expressed concern about the proposal but has now said, "I'll support it."

4 "Sue, in the past hour you have expressed concerns about implementing the proposed program and identified some interests that may not be met by implementing it in its proposed form. Now you just said you'll support it, but I didn't hear you say how your views have changed. Do you see it differently?" [*if no, continue*]

5 and **6** "I'm thinking that either you might be feeling pressure to support the proposal or you have changed your mind. Can you say what led you to support the proposal now?"

SUMMARY

In this chapter, instead of discussion I have given examples of how to intervene if a group member is acting inconsistently with the ground rules, in any of a number of ways. The course of your intervention depends on whether the group member or members agree with your observation and inference. When you choose to skip or combine intervention steps depends on a number of factors. In the next chapter, I describe how you can use these interventions to help a group improve the ability to use any process tools the members are working with.

CHAPTER TEN

Using the
Skilled Facilitator Approach
with Other Processes

In this chapter, I describe how you can use the Skilled Facilitator approach with a variety of other processes, such as strategic planning, process improvement, or conflict resolution. I begin by explaining how these processes can increase group effectiveness and how groups sometimes use the processes in a way that does not produce the most value. Next, I explain the general interventions I make in groups to help them get more value from the various processes. For the remainder of the chapter, I describe how you can use the Skilled Facilitator approach with a common process, a problem-solving model that groups can use to identify and solve problems.

The Skilled Facilitator approach helps a group have almost any conversation more effectively, no matter what the conversation is about. **I think of the Skilled Facilitator approach as being like a computer's operating system software (Microsoft Windows, Mac OS, Unix, or Linux); when used well it increases the effectiveness of any compatible application software that runs with it.** In this analogy, other processes are the applications, like word processing, presentation, or data analysis software.

LEVELS OF PROCESSES

Groups use a variety of processes to perform their work. **A process is a method that includes a set of steps and activities that group members follow to perform some task.** Many groups use some form of problem-solving model to

Table 10.1. Levels of Processes

Designs	Methods	Tools
Problem solving	Five-, seven-, or nine-step problem-solving model	Fishbone diagram Solution matrix
Process improvement	Process mapping	Flowcharting Histogram
Vision, values, mission	Future Search	Time line Mind mapping

Source: Adapted from Davidson and Anderson, 2001.

identify problems; identify criteria for solutions; and generate, evaluate, and select alternatives. Groups engaged in continuous improvement use processes for identifying the root causes of problems. Some groups use systems modeling tools to identify how the various elements of a complex system interact to create certain consequences.

There are three levels of processes, ranging from more macro to more micro (Table 10.1). Process designs, which are more macro, structure the group's time and activities for a longer period of time and are less detailed than the methods and tools that are subsumed by them. At the most macro, level, *process design* structures the group's overall purpose for meeting. For example, a process design may focus on strategic planning, process improvement, or conflict resolution. At the middle level, *process methods* are a way of addressing the process design. Process mapping is one method that a group can use to guide its process improvement. At the most micro level, *process tools* are the most specific and detailed activities. Flowcharting and histograms are two of many process tools that a group would use in process mapping.

When you work with a group, you begin by identifying the purpose of the group's meetings, which identifies the process design. Then you and the group decide together on the process methods to achieve the purpose. Finally, you select a series of tools that define specific activities the group will engage in. You can use the Skilled Facilitator approach to improve processes at any level.

HOW GROUPS REDUCE THE VALUE OF PROCESSES

A process is designed to help a group improve effectiveness, but if the group uses a process in a way that is inconsistent with the core values, then the group

Exhibit 10.1. How Groups Reduce the Value of Process Tools

- Group members select an inappropriate process tool.
- Group members focus on different steps.
- Group members follow steps out of order.
- Group members use a step incorrectly.
- Group members behave ineffectively within a step.

does not obtain the full value. Exhibit 10.1 shows five ways in which a group can lose the value of its processes.

The first category—selecting an inappropriate process—describes a loss that usually results when group members are missing some information about the range of available tools and how they can be applied to their situation. The second, third, and fourth categories—focusing on different steps, taking steps out of order, and using a step incorrectly—describe losses that result from using an appropriate process inappropriately. Not all processes have a prescribed order that group members need to follow; some processes encourage members to move back to a previous step as they gather information in a later step. The fifth category—engaging in ineffective behavior within a step—as the name states describes a loss that occurs from ineffective group process. **Even if group members are following the process as it is intended, if they act inconsistently with the core values of the Skilled Facilitator approach they can lose the value of the process.**

INTERVENING TO INCREASE THE VALUE OF PROCESSES

By integrating the Skilled Facilitator approach with another process, a group can use the process more effectively. You can use the diagnosis-intervention cycle, ground rules, group effectiveness model, and theory-in-use to accomplish this.

Integrating the Skilled Facilitator Approach with Other Processes

Figure 10.1 shows the relationship between a process and the Skilled Facilitator approach. As the group uses the process, I use it as another diagnostic frame, watching for times in which I infer that the group is using the tool ineffectively or acting in a way that reduces their ability to get the full value from the tool. When I make an inference that the group is simply not using the tool effectively, I intervene using the diagnosis-intervention cycle and the ground rules. When I infer that the group is acting in a way that reduces its ability to

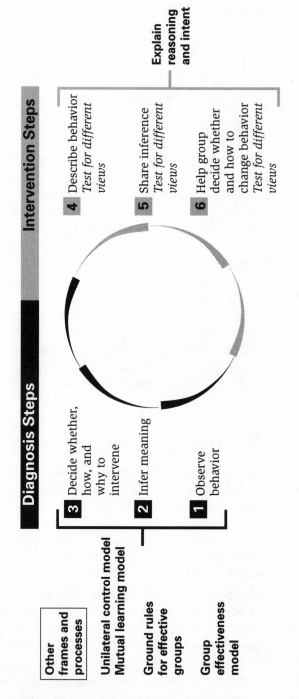

Figure 10.1. Using the Skilled Facilitator Approach with Other Frames and Processes

get the full value from the tool, I use one or more Skilled Facilitator diagnostic frames (that is, ground rules, group effectiveness model, theory-in-use) to identify the aspects of the group's process that are reducing its ability to fully use the tool. Having made the inference, I then use the diagnosis-intervention cycle to test out with the group whether the members agree with my inference; if they do, I ask them if they are willing to change their behavior accordingly.

Depth of Interventions

There are different depths of interventions you can make. As you intervene more deeply, you help the group identify more fundamental causes of its ineffective behavior. The first level uses the ground rules and diagnosis-intervention cycle to help the group redesign its behavior. The second level identifies causes associated with the group effectiveness model. The third level identifies patterns in the group over time. The fourth and deepest level uses theory-in-use to identify the causes of the pattern over time as well as the consequences. In all of these levels of intervention, you use the ground rules and diagnosis-intervention cycle.

Identifying Ineffective Behavior. At the first level of intervention, you use the ground rules and diagnosis-intervention cycle to share your observation and test your inference that members are using an inappropriate process, focused on different steps, following steps out of order, using a step incorrectly, or using ineffective behavior within a step. If the members agree with your inference, you can ask the group to redesign its behavior.

You might do so by saying, "Florence, the group was discussing potential causes of the problem a minute ago when you said, 'Let's put the system in place tomorrow.' When you said that, it looked like you were moving ahead to solutions. Do you see that differently?" If Florence shares your view, you would continue, "Would you be willing to hold off on the solution and come back to the causes?"

Using the Group Effectiveness Model to Identify Potential Causes. At the second level, you use the group effectiveness model with the ground rules and diagnosis-intervention cycle to share your observations and test your inferences about the potential causes of the problem you have just identified. If members agree with your inferences, identify a process for addressing the issue.

For example, you might say, "Jay, as the group was mapping its workflow process, you said that the manuscripts go to production after you give the final editorial approval. Brenda, I think you said that the manuscripts go to production after you sign off. Did I get that correct?" If so, I continue, "I'm thinking that part of the difficulty in the process may stem from lack of clarity about the roles the two of you fill." Is my inference accurate, or do you see it differently?" If they share your view, you can continue: "Does it make sense to address this now, or to hold off discussing the issue until some point after you conclude the map?"

Exploring Patterns in Behavior and Potential Causes. At the next level, you use the ground rules, diagnosis-intervention cycle, and, when relevant, the group effectiveness model to **test your inference that there is a pattern of behavior in the group.** If the group agrees that there is a pattern, you explore potential causes and help the group identify solutions that eliminate the pattern in a way that meets group members' interests.

For example, during a strategic planning session you might say, "I want to identify a pattern that I think is occurring, and get your reaction. You've been discussing strengths and weaknesses as part of the SWOT analysis (strengths, weaknesses, opportunities, and threats). I have noticed that you have different views about whether some element of the organization represents a strength or a weakness. For example, . . . [After several minutes of different views, Sharon, who is the senior member of the team, shares her thoughts on the issue and then no one else speaks on the issue.] A minute ago, after Sharon said X, the conversation stopped. Have I missed anything?" If members agree with your description, you can continue: "I'm thinking that there is something about Sharon's participation that leads you to stop after she has spoken. What are your thoughts?"

Exploring Members' Theories-in-Use as Potential Causes. When appropriate, you can **explore group members' theories-in-use,** using the ground rules and diagnosis-intervention cycle, to help the group identify causes and consequences of the pattern. If they agree that their theories-in-use are contributing to the cause of the pattern, you can help the group begin to make changes in their theories-in-use. Making these changes is a long-term developmental process and is appropriate only when the group has agreed to developmental facilitation.

You might continue the intervention about Sharon's participation by saying, "I'm curious: What were each of you thinking when, after you shared your point of view, Sharon spoke and had either a similar or a different view?" If Howard says he was thinking that he needed to be quiet because otherwise he would be seen as not being a team player, you could continue to inquire by saying, "And what specifically led you to infer that?" On the basis of Howard's response, you can see whether other group members have similar views, and whether Sharon sees Howard as not a team player if he continues to express a different view.

You could also point out some unintended consequences. For example, you might say, "I see some potential unintended consequences of your being silent in order to be seen as a team player. Let me share them and get your reaction. If as a result of your silence the group ends up developing a strategic plan that you privately believe cannot be implemented, I think that increases the chances that you will act in ways such that others will not consider you a team player. What do you think about this?"

You could also help the group reframe what it means to be a team player by saying something on the order of "I'd like to suggest a different way of thinking about what it means to be a team player in developing a strategic plan. You could think of being a team player as sharing all the relevant information you have and carefully explaining your reasoning about why you think something is a strength or weakness. This way, you would be helping your team make a more informed choice. What problems, if any, do you see with thinking about it this way?"

USING THE SKILLED FACILITATOR APPROACH WITH A PROBLEM-SOLVING MODEL

In this section I describe how to use the Skilled Facilitator approach to help a group increase its value by way of a common process: a problem-solving model. There are many versions of problem-solving models; I use the model shown in Figure 10.2.

Much of a group's work involves solving problems—identifying and closing the gap between some desired situation and the current situation. Examples are a department that needs to improve service quality, a group that must reduce the cost of operations, an executive team deciding which new markets to enter, and a city council contemplating a shift from backyard to curbside garbage pickup. A group that solves complex problems using a structured approach is likely to develop a high-quality solution (Hirokawa and Gouran, 1989).

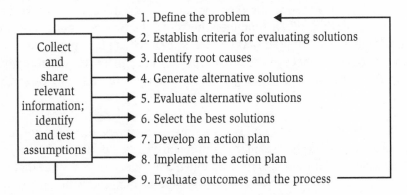

Figure 10.2. Problem-Solving Model

Because each problem-solving step requires certain actions, I envisage the kinds of interventions I may need to make at each step. Here I focus on interventions addressing the fourth type of process problem (Exhibit 10.1): group members using a step incorrectly. For each step, I describe some of the problems that groups encounter and the interventions I would make.

Interventions Throughout the Model

There are several interventions to be made throughout the steps as a group uses a problem-solving model.

First, the model does not have a separate step in which members collect or share the information they need to solve the problem. Instead, as Figure 10.1 shows, the model recognizes that at any point in the process, members may need information from, or need to share information with, non–group members. Here I use the ground rules and diagnosis-intervention cycle to test my inference that the group is making a decision without valid information.

Second, the model does not have a separate step in which members identify their assumptions about solving the problem. Instead, the model recognizes that members make assumptions about how to define the problem, which criteria are appropriate, what the causes of the problem are, and so on. Here I help members make their assumptions explicit so they can test them, if possible, and convey them to anyone who is reviewing or evaluating their work.

If a group does not identify and test assumptions, it reduces its ability to make a valid decision; sometimes the group even prevents itself from finding any workable solution. For example, I facilitated a retreat for a group of physicians who worked for a research hospital. The physicians were interested in adding a member to their group practice, to reduce the waiting time for patients to get an appointment and to lighten the clinical workload on physicians already in the practice. The group made two assumptions: first, the demand for their services was so large that an additional physician would generate enough revenue to pay for the doctor's salary; and second, adding a physician would significantly reduce the waiting time for patients and the clinical workload of the other physicians. When combined, however, the two assumptions seemed invalid. If the first assumption was correct, once hired the new physician would become just as overloaded as the original group, and patient waiting time would remain the same. Without adding other assumptions or changing one of the two, the physicians could not solve their problem.

Step One: Define the Problem. Defining the problem is a deceptively simple, but critical, task. It has been said that a problem clearly identified is half solved. Without a clear definition, the group flounders. Members often assume that they know what problem they are trying to solve and that everyone agrees with the definition of the problem. Once a group has decided to follow a problem-solving model, my first intervention is likely to be helping the group clearly identify the problem so the group can agree on it before they move to other steps.

Defining the problem means identifying a gap between some desired situation and the current situation ("infant mortality is 60 percent above the acceptable rate," or "there has been a two-day lag beyond the guaranteed response time for customer service calls"). A good problem definition implies or states explicitly not only the current situation but also the desired one ("acceptable infant mortality rate," or "no two-day lag beyond the guaranteed response time to customer service calls"). Here I may intervene if the group is making assumptions about the current situation rather than using valid information to define the current one.

A second intervention involves helping the group agree on the desired situation. This often means having the group shift focus from what it does *not* want to what is wanted. This is necessary because the desired situation may not be the opposite of what the group does not want, but some other alternative. To help the group identify the desired situation, I can use the group effectiveness model to see if they have a shared mission and vision that can provide context.

A third intervention involves helping the group define the problem in a way that states only the current and desired situation and no more. An example of a good problem definition is "customers receive responses to billing error inquiries in four weeks, two weeks longer than acceptable." The statement implies no particular solution or potential cause. In contrast, the statement "clerks take ten days to check billing errors" unnecessarily narrows the definition, implying that clerks are a primary cause of the problem. The problem statement "we need more qualified clerks" explicitly states part of the solution. Including the cause or solution in a problem definition diverts the group from exploring all the possibilities and increases the likelihood of the solution not solving the real problem.

The more that individuals have thought about a problem, the more probable they have begun to consider causes and solutions. The facilitator helps the group identify the particular causes or solutions that members implicitly embed in their problem statements.

Step Two: Establish Criteria for Evaluating Solutions. Establishing criteria involves setting standards against which to evaluate alternative solutions. **Criteria are related to interests, so this step focuses largely on the ground rule of focusing on interests, not positions.** In other words, criteria define general characteristics that a solution should have, without describing a specific solution. To take a simple example, recall the group that is deciding to purchase a car for its use; some criteria are good gas mileage, low-frequency repair record, and being large enough to accommodate all group members.

Establishing criteria is difficult because members sometimes cannot think about criteria without the context of a specific solution. Consequently, they may simply suggest specific solutions ("a Chrysler minivan") when asked to develop criteria. I can intervene by asking a member to describe what it is about a Chrysler minivan that makes it a good solution. The intervention is similar to focusing members on interests rather than on positions.

One way to help members develop criteria is to ask them to complete a sentence that naturally leads to identifying criteria: "The solution should be one that _____"; "The solution should be one that does not _____"; "The solution should be implemented in a way that _____." The first example focuses on positive criteria, the second identifies negative unintended consequences, and the third elicits implementation criteria.

Another intervention I make at this stage is to help group members think systemically about the criteria they select. This means helping them think beyond the immediate solution to include criteria about how the solution fits with the rest of the organization. The group effectiveness model can be useful here. Consider a group that is designing a performance-based pay system. One systemic criterion might be that the system must encourage excellent performance in a way that does not promote unhealthy competition among employees, which reduces the ability of the organization to provide excellent service.

Another intervention involves helping the group identify criteria that may conflict with each other. Back to the car example: in general, one large enough to accommodate eight group members is going to get relatively poor gas mileage. It is not necessary that the criteria be nonconflictual, only that members recognize potential conflict and agree on how to resolve it. Here I may help the group reduce conflict among criteria by asking them to distinguish those that the solution *must* meet and those it would be *desirable* to meet.

Members are reluctant to identify or to weight or rank criteria to the extent that it means exposing a hidden agenda. Here I can make several interventions. The first is to reframe a hidden agenda as a legitimate concern to discuss. This involves stating that it is difficult for the group to meet a member's interests if that member does not describe the interests to the group. The second is to identify earlier comments by members that reflect criteria of which they are unaware. For example, in a top management group, I might first point out that earlier, Rebecca had expressed concern that the leader had implemented a program without involving employees. I could then ask Rebecca whether employee involvement is a criterion she has for implementing the solution to the current problem.

Finally, I can help group members by encouraging them to identify only those criteria that are needed or desired to solve the problem. Because each criterion places additional constraints on finding an acceptable solution, each unnecessary criterion needlessly reduces the number of potential solutions.

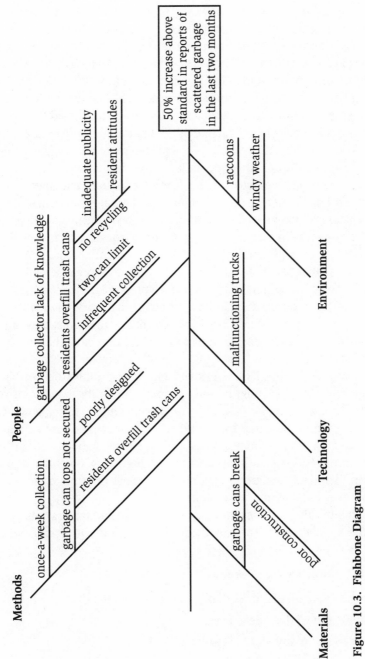

Figure 10.3. Fishbone Diagram

Step Three: Identify Root Causes. In step three, the group identifies the root causes of the problem they have identified. I can simply ask the group to identify potential causes of the problem; however, there are a number of processes useful in this step to structure the discussion of root causes. One tool is often called a *fishbone diagram,* so named because it resembles the skeleton of a fish. The fishbone diagram (Figure 10.3) has a box at the right in which the problem definition is written. In the example, the problem definition is "50 percent increase above standard in reports of scattered garbage in the last two months." Five diagonal lines extend from the backbone, two above and three below. Each line has a label that represents a major category of potential causes. The categories may vary according to the nature of the problem statement, but together the major categories capture the domain of potential causes. In the example I use, the five categories are people, methods, environment, technology, and materials.

After the group has agreed on the comprehensive major categories, I ask members to brainstorm potential causes within each category. One potential "people" cause of the increase in scattered garbage is that garbage collectors do not know how to transfer garbage to their large bins quickly without spills. Another potential cause is that residents fill their trash cans beyond capacity. In the environmental category, two potential causes are a preponderance of windy weather or raccoon activity on the rise. In the technology category, the garbage trucks may be malfunctioning. The rules for brainstorming are simple; they are shown in Exhibit 10.2. Brainstorming continues until the group has exhausted its ideas.

Next, I ask the group to brainstorm about the causes that members have identified; as seen in Figure 10.3, residents may be overfilling their garbage cans because there is no recycling, because a policy limits the number of garbage cans to two per dwelling, or because garbage collection is infrequent. The process continues until the group has identified the root cause of each initial cause. Thus a recycling problem may stem from inadequate publicity about the program, or from residents' attitude about recycling. After potential root causes have been identified, the group may need to collect information to determine which of the causes, if any, are validated.

A group typically attributes the causes of a problem to factors outside of their group; the members miss their own contribution to the problem. Here, I can

Exhibit 10.2. Rules for Brainstorming

- Do not evaluate the ideas that members generate.
- Include the wildest ideas possible.
- Generate as many ideas as possible.
- Combine and build upon ideas already generated.

Source: Osborn, 1953, pp. 300–301.

help the group explore their assumption that they have not contributed to the problem by asking, "In what ways might group members contribute to the causes of this problem?"

If the group has identified the problem statement satisfactorily, the fishbone diagram builds naturally, simply by repeating the question with slight variation: "What is a potential cause of the 50 percent increase above standard in reports of scattered garbage?" However, if the group has incorrectly defined the problem in terms of a solution ("give garbage collectors more training"), members have difficulty using the fishbone technique to generate causes and are likely to become frustrated. The difficulty occurs because it is logically impossible to find the causes of a *solution*. In other words, you cannot answer the question, "What are potential causes of giving garbage collectors more training?"

If a major causal category has no entries, the group may have inadvertently defined the problem in a way that excludes the category. In such a case, I may intervene by noting the group's difficulty, testing the observation, and suggesting that the group redefine the problem.

Sometimes, in brainstorming potential causes, group members identify similar causes under separate categories. For example, in Figure 10.3, "residents overfill trash cans" is a *people* cause that is also a root of the *methods* cause ("garbage can tops not secured"). This occurs because a fishbone diagram artificially separates the causal categories, all of which are related in the real world. It is natural, of course, for a people cause to be the root of a methods cause. Rather than trying to avoid such causal redundancy, I can help the group see how the redundancy creates an important link among the causal categories. By doing this, I help the group develop a more systemic causal map of the problem it is trying to solve.

The purpose of the fishbone process is to brainstorm or make educated guesses about root causes. Still, the group must collect data to determine whether and to what extent each hypothesized cause is in fact a cause. Group members can jointly design ways to collect the data, so that the collection process meets the standards of all members. Once they have completed this step, they have agreed on a causal map of the problem that is based on valid information.

Sometimes a group may find it easier to identify root causes (step three) before developing criteria for evaluating solutions (step two). After members have identified root causes, however, they are naturally motivated to generate alternative solutions (step four) and may not be so interested in developing criteria for evaluating solutions.

Step Four: Generate Alternative Solutions. In step four, the group generates alternative solutions to the problem. Here it is common to experience two problems. First, the members combine generating alternatives with evaluating them. When one member suggests a solution, other members quickly offer reasons it will or will not work. In this case, I can test my inference with the group that they have collapsed steps; if they agree, I can advocate that they separate the steps.

Second, a group sometimes has difficulty identifying a substantial number of potential solutions. This generally results from members prematurely evaluating each other's ideas, which can make group members reluctant to offer ideas. But members can also have difficulty generating ideas because they make assumptions that unnecessarily constrain their own thinking about the solution. As with developing criteria, every unnecessary assumption reduces the number of potential solutions.

I can make several interventions to help the group avoid these problems. First, at the beginning of the step I can ask the group to brainstorm alternatives, using the rules in Exhibit 10.2. Second, I can help the group identify any assumption underlying an alternative solution and help the group assess whether the assumption is necessary. For example, underlying an entire set of proposed solutions might be an assumption that the solution must involve only those who are currently affected by the problem. If the assumption is unnecessary and can be removed, then members could generate entirely new solutions, unconstrained by the assumption. If the assumption is warranted, I can suggest that the group add it as an additional criterion for evaluating solutions.

Third, after the group has exhausted its ideas for solutions, I can encourage members to combine aspects of previously generated solutions. Perhaps one solution is likely to integrate the best aspects of various ideas and also be likely to find consensus in the group.

One choice that members face is whether they should consider the criteria when generating alternative solutions. By considering the criteria, they undoubtedly generate fewer solutions, but those generated probably conform well to the criteria. By not considering the criteria, members may generate some workable solutions that are inconsistent with the identified criteria, thereby calling into question the necessity for some criteria. The latter approach takes more time but can serve as a check against arbitrary criteria.

Step Five: Evaluate Alternative Solutions. In step five, the group considers the alternative solutions in light of the previously established criteria. This can be done with various degrees of structure. In a highly structured approach, members can develop a matrix (see Exhibit 10.3), with each criterion listed on one axis and each alternative solution on the other. The group can weight the criteria if some are more important than others. For each solution, the members assign a score to each criterion (say, from one to ten, with ten the highest score); the score is based on the extent to which this solution meets this criterion. The group score for each alternative solution is determined by following these steps:

Exhibit 10.3. Matrix for Evaluating Alternative Solutions

	Criteria												Solution Scores
	Criterion 1 (x Weight)				Criterion 2 (x Weight)				Criterion 3 (x Weight)				
Solutions	Ann	Al	Jo	Lee	Ann	Al	Jo	Lee	Ann	Al	Jo	Lee	
Solution 1													
Solution 2													
Solution 3													
Solution 4													
Solution 5													

1. If the criteria are weighted, for each criterion, multiply each member's score by the weight of the respective criterion.

2. For each criterion, find the average of the members' scores by adding the results from step one and dividing by the number of members.

3. Add the results from step two for all the criteria.

The group considers solutions that receive higher scores more favorably.

In a less structured approach, every member gives an overall score to each alternative without scoring each criterion separately. The score for the alternative is determined by finding the average of the members' scores for that solution.

It is important to help the group think of the evaluation matrix as a tool to help in making better decisions rather than as a formula that automatically produces a correct answer. Because the results of an evaluation matrix are typically based on the average of members' scores, one or two members may drastically influence the group score by rating one solution very high or very low. Similarly, the solution with the highest score may be one that no member is committed to implementing. Therefore an evaluation matrix should not take the place of group discussion and the group's collective judgment.

In this step, as in every other, I help the group members explain their reasoning to each other—here, so that they understand how members have come to evaluate a single solution differently. If they have reached consensus on the criteria and are weighing the solutions against them, my intervention focuses on what leads them to disagree about the extent to which a particular solution meets a given criterion. However, if the group has reached consensus on the criteria but is not weighing the solutions against them, the intervention focuses on the inconsistency. This occurs when a member is unknowingly applying additional criteria.

Step Six: Select the Best Solutions. Selecting the best solutions means identifying one or more solutions that the group decides to implement. In some cases, the group will select multiple solutions and pilot test them before adapting them. In other cases, the group has to select only one.

Selecting the best solutions requires that the group have some ground rule for making a decision (consensus, majority vote, or some other decision rule). A relevant ground rule here is number nine: to use a decision-making rule that generates the level of commitment needed.

If the group has chosen to make a consensus decision and is having difficulty doing so, I intervene when I think that it will help identify when one or more members are pressuring others to agree instead of allowing each member to make a free choice. I also help the group find an integrative decision by eliciting the specific issue of disagreement, clarifying interests, and then identifying how to integrate similar interests and dovetail divergent ones. As a result of my interventions, the group may identify a new solution.

Step Seven: Develop an Action Plan. Developing an action plan increases the likelihood of the group implementing a solution effectively and on time. Here too, a group can choose from among various action plans. Exhibit 10.4 shows a simple action-planning chart that identifies the steps needed to implement the solution, the objective to be achieved by completing each step, the date each step was assigned, when it is to be started, when it is to be completed, the resources needed to complete it, who is responsible for completing that step, and the current status of each one.

Here, the group effectiveness model is a useful tool for helping the group consider how the action plan affects various elements of the group. For example, I might use the model to help members think about how the plan affects their roles, the design of the group task, and the mission and vision.

I can help the group avoid pitfalls that some groups experience in this step. First, the group's energy and attention may wane during this step (and in subsequent ones) if the members view having agreed on a solution as the culmination of the problem-solving process. By sharing this observation with the group, I can help them refocus or decide to continue at a later date.

Second, the group may underestimate the time or other resources necessary to complete each task in the action plan. This occurs when members do not have valid information or have a fixed deadline for implementation. Although it is not the facilitator's role to unilaterally set a realistic time frame for a substantive decision, I can intervene by asking members to consider how they arrived at the time frame and by sharing my reason for asking. Finally, the group may assign a task to an individual who is not present (and over whom they have no authority), without checking whether the person is available. Here, I can point out that the action plan is not final until the assignment has been agreed to.

Exhibit 10.4. Action-Planning Chart

Step	Objective	Date Assigned	Start Date	Completion Date	Resources	Responsibility	Status

Step Eight: Implement the Action Plan. The group typically implements much of its plan outside the facilitated meetings, so this limits the kind of intervention a facilitator can make in this step. When I am facilitating, I am ready to make several interventions. I can help the group identify how their implementation is consistent or inconsistent with the criteria and interests they identified in step two. I can also inquire whether new, relevant information has become available after implementation that may lead them to reconsider part of the plan. I also use the group effectiveness model to help the group consider how the implementation is affecting the various elements of the group.

Step Nine: Evaluate Outcomes and the Process. Evaluation is probably the step most often underemphasized in a problem-solving model—and some models do not even include it. One reason a group might not conduct adequate evaluation is that it takes additional time, which the group never seems to have. Another reason is that evaluation can be politically unpopular, especially if the group faces negative consequences from surfacing problems in its solution or process. A group could also forgo evaluation to avoid cognitive dissonance (Festinger, 1957), psychological discomfort that, in this case, arises when members are faced with data challenging their beliefs about the effectiveness of the project. In a group in which not all members are internally committed to the solution, uncommitted members may push for evaluation, hoping to find data to support their views. Those who are committed to the solution may be reluctant to evaluate, because they are concerned that negative evaluation results will reopen the entire issue.

All these concerns are understandable. However, some evaluation is essential for a group that desires valid information. If the group does identify problems, it can decide whether to make changes to correct them. I make several interventions in this step. First, I help the group explore its reluctance to evaluate. After identifying the barriers, the group can decide whether they can be reduced sufficiently to conduct an evaluation. As part of the intervention, I may help the group reframe the meaning of evaluation from being a political or psychological threat to a process in which members seek continuous improvement in their work.

Second, I can help the group consider how comprehensive the evaluation should be. The group effectiveness model identifies three criteria for an effective group: performance, process, and personal. Ideally, the group would evaluate how well it meets all three criteria. A particular project may warrant a sophisticated survey or analysis of records, but another might need only a brief conversation with a key individual. Thus I might begin by asking, "What is needed for you to know how well the solution is working, and if it is not working, why it isn't?" Finally, I can ask the group to think about how they solved the problem, enhanced or maintained the ability to work together in the future, and how the process contributed to or hindered individuals' need for professional growth and development.

SUMMARY

In this chapter, I have described how processes can increase group effectiveness. A process is a set of steps and activities that group members follow to perform some task. A group may use a process in a way that does not produce the most value from the tool. It may select an inappropriate tool, perform steps out of order, use a step incorrectly, or act ineffectively in using the tool. I have explained the general interventions I make: (1) using the ground rules and diagnosis-intervention cycle to test my inferences that group members are using the process less effectively than they could, (2) using the group effectiveness model to explore the causes of a problem and to identify patterns in behavior, and (3) using the model of theory-in-use to help group members identify fundamental causes and consequences of the pattern.

In the remainder of the chapter, I have described how you can use the Skilled Facilitator approach to help a group get more value from a common process (here, a problem-solving model that groups can use to identify and solve problems). For each step of the problem-solving model, I explained the type of intervention I might make.

In the next chapter, I describe standard interventions you can make at the beginning and end of meetings to improve the group's process throughout.

CHAPTER ELEVEN

Beginning and Ending Meetings

In this chapter, I describe the relatively predictable interventions I make to begin and end meetings. First, I describe how to set up a room in which facilitating is to be done. Then I describe how I help groups perform such preliminary tasks as agreeing on an agenda and the roles people will play. When I do this, I am making macro interventions that involve managing structure and process. By making these interventions, I help the group create a foundation for an effective meeting.

PREPARING THE ROOM

How the room is arranged is part of the physical environment, which is an element of the group effectiveness model. Arranging the room appropriately reduces potential structural barriers that can hinder effective group process. Three principles (shown in Exhibit 11.1) guide the arrangement.

The first is that **all participants and the facilitator should be able to see and hear each other and any visual information presented (flipcharts, projected images).** As obvious as this principle sounds—and is—I have ended up with room arrangements that were unusable because I had not clearly stated my interests. In one case, I even faxed a picture showing how to arrange the tables and chairs in the U-shaped configuration I wanted so the hotel staff would be able to follow my directions. When I arrived at the meeting room, I found

Exhibit 11.1. Guidelines for Seating Arrangements

- All participants and the facilitator should be able to see and hear each other and any visual information presented (for example, flipcharts, projected images).

- Seating arrangements should distinguish participants from nonparticipants.

- Seating arrangements should be spacious enough to meet the needs of the group but no larger.

everything configured exactly as I had requested—with one significant difference I had not anticipated. In the middle of the U, there were two very large pillars that made it impossible for half of the meeting participants to see all the members! That experience was a good lesson in how focusing only on the solution (position) without clarifying my interests got me what I requested, but not what I needed.

As the facilitator, I often sit in a location that physically distinguishes me from group members, visually reinforcing that my role is different from theirs. Figure 11.1 shows seating arrangements for groups of varying size (*F* indicates the facilitator). For example, in a medium-size group, members often sit around a U-shaped table, with the person managing the group process standing at the opening of the U (or sitting at the center of the bottom of the U). In basic facilitation, this person is typically the facilitator. In a large group, it may not be possible to seat everyone so each person can see everyone else. A series of tables arranged in the chevron pattern shown in Figure 11.1 enables all members to see me and any visual information. In developmental facilitation, I may start out managing the group's process, but over time the role shifts to individual group members, or to all group members simultaneously taking responsibility for managing the process. If all the members take responsibility, a round, square, or rectangular table that does not distinguish a single leader can reflect this decision.

Aside from designating a place for the meeting chairperson (if the chairperson is also managing the process) and for me, I usually do not assign participants to specific seats. Applying the value of free choice and the principle of starting with the group's intents and concerns means enabling participants to sit where they feel comfortable. If all the members of a divided group choose to sit with their subgroup members, that is their choice. (This is also useful diagnostic data.) If I believe it would be helpful for members of various subgroups to sit together, I intervene by suggesting it explicitly and explaining my reasoning.

One exception to not assigning seats occurs with a large group. If I am conducting basic facilitation with a group larger than about forty, I prefer to work with the planning group to assign participants to specific tables. We group

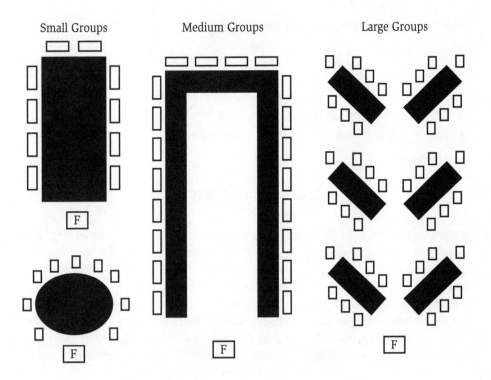

Figure 11.1. Seating Arrangements

people either homogeneously or heterogeneously, depending on the purpose of the meeting and the type of activity members at each table will perform. For example, each table might host representatives of the several functions in the organization. In any event, whenever I assign seats, I share my reasoning so that group members do not make an incorrect inference about my intent.

Second, **use the seating arrangements to distinguish participants from nonparticipants.** A group may invite nonmembers to present information or to just observe a meeting. If there are a number of nonmembers and they are present to observe, seating the non-group members separately from group members enables the group members to attend more easily to one another. It also makes it easier for me to focus on group members without trying to keep track of who is a participant and who is not.

Third, **seating arrangements should be spacious enough to meet the needs of the group, but no larger.** Facilitation involves bringing people together to work. A seating arrangement that leaves empty space between participants creates unnecessary psychological distance that the members then have to bridge.

Exhibit 11.2. Interventions for Beginning a Meeting

1. Make introductions.

2. Bring people up to date.

3. Agree on objectives; identify expectations and concerns.

4. Agree on the agenda and time allocation.

5. Agree on the process, including ground rules.

6. Define roles.

BEGINNING THE MEETING

In the beginning of the meeting, I discuss several issues with the group (Exhibit 11.2) to establish an effective structure and process for the entire meeting. As part of the contracting process, prior to this meeting I have a planning meeting about these issues, either with the full group or else with a representative subgroup. (Chapter Thirteen, on contracting, describes this process in detail.) If there are people in the facilitated session who were not in the planning meeting, beginning the meeting takes more time. If I am meeting with the same group over a series of sessions, after the first session we may not need to spend much time on these issues, except to check for any changes.

In discussing the introductory issues with the group, I tell people about how much time it takes so that they know what to expect. Although it takes time to address these issues, not addressing them takes more time in the long run. In several facilitations, I decided to spend less time at the beginning on issues than I thought was necessary. On every occasion, I was worried that the clients—who made it clear they were very busy and wanted to get right to the substance of their conversation—would see me as taking time away from their business. Unfortunately, in every case, the group later got bogged down because of an agreement we had skipped, whether about my role, the leader's role, or the overall objectives. From these experiences, I learned that as a facilitator part of my responsibility is to use the expertise for which the clients have hired me and be an advocate for effective group process, while still seeking to address their concerns.

Make Introductions

In a small group, I may be the only person who does not know everyone in the room. In a large group, perhaps bringing together individuals from numerous parts of a large organization or from different organizations, many people may be strangers. In any event, I introduce myself and ask others to do the same. Beyond the individual's name, organization, and position, the information I ask others to share about themselves in the introduction varies according to the group's history and its task.

Sometimes facilitators use an icebreaker exercise to have people introduce themselves. I attended a two-day meeting of organizational consultants and researchers in which everyone sketched out their professional history on a piece of flipchart paper, taped it to their body, and milled around the room talking with each other about their background. Then participants formed a human network by standing next to those people with whom they had some connection. Remaining in the configuration, each member made introductory comments to the entire group and explained the connection to her or his neighbor. In thirty minutes, about fifty people were able to learn much more relevant information about each other than if each person had spoken individually to the entire group or if members had formed pairs. The human network also enabled the entire group to see the various links present.

This introduction exercise was effective partly because it was based on the principle that any exercise should be consistent with the group's task. Introductory exercises that are irrelevant to the group's task or inconsistent with the core values can quickly alienate the group from the facilitator. (Resource F offers guidelines for using exercises.)

It may not be feasible for all members of a large group to introduce themselves. One alternative is for people to introduce each other in the small group at their table; a representative at each table then summarizes the table's introductory session. Another alternative is for members to seek out and introduce themselves to at least some individuals they do not recognize. Again, the specific introductory exercise should be based on the group's task and history. Introductions are also necessary whenever a new member joins the group.

Bring People Up to Date

People who have not been involved in planning the facilitation meeting may not have all the relevant information about the background. I ask the person leading the meeting to give a brief history of what led to the meeting. I also describe how I worked with the planning group to reach agreement about the meeting outcomes and process. This leads naturally to the next step.

Agree on Objectives, Identify Expectations, and Address Concerns

I begin by describing the objectives of the meeting. I make it easy for members to raise a question or concern by pointing out that the agreement is tentative and asking, "What problems, if any, does anyone see with the tentative objectives?" If a member identifies a problem, I facilitate the conversation so that the group can make an informed choice about whether and how to modify it.

Even when group members know the tentative agenda for a meeting, they often have differing expectations about what the group should accomplish. Identifying expectations helps the group and me address conflicting expectations and identify those that cannot be met, determine whether the tentative agenda is appropriate or needs changing, and take the steps necessary to meet the agreed-upon expectations.

I might intervene like this: "I assume each of you came to this meeting expecting the group to accomplish certain things. Rather than guess what each of you expects, it would help to know what has to happen for each of you to leave the meeting feeling it was good use of your time. This helps determine whether your expectations are compatible with one another and helps us take the steps necessary to meet the agreed-upon expectations. I'd like to go around the room and ask each person to share his or her expectations. Any questions or concerns about what I'm asking?"

In addition to expectations, members have concerns about things that might prevent the meeting from being successful. In a group struggling with conflict, for example, members may be concerned about the conversation breaking down into personal attack, or the real issues being glossed over, or the group coming to a stalemate. Another group might be concerned about certain members dominating the conversation or not participating, or about the group getting off track and not solving the problem.

Whatever the concerns, identifying them at the outset enables group members and me to pay special attention to the problems and intervene on them as soon as they arise. Here I can say, "You may have some concerns about things that could happen or not happen during the meeting that would undermine the meeting's success. You may also have some ideas about how group members or I can deal with these things. Identifying your concerns about these things helps us watch out for them and, hopefully, prevents them from becoming a problem. What concerns do you have, if any, about these things?" If people identify concerns, I follow up by asking, "What ideas do people have for preventing these issues from becoming a problem or reducing the problem?"

Agree on the Agenda and Time Allocation

Before people arrive at the first facilitated meeting, the tentative agenda is distributed to all attending. For subsequent meetings, I sometimes work with the group at the end each time to establish the agenda for the next meeting. Regardless of the situation, I review and post the tentative agenda at the beginning of the meeting. Then I ask the group whether the tentative agenda remains appropriate, given the participants' expectations and concerns and given any events that have occurred since the tentative agenda was developed.

I say something on the order of "Given your expectations and concerns, and anything that might have occurred since the tentative agenda was developed, does anyone think the agenda needs to be revised?" Once agreed on, I post the revised agenda. This enables all members and me to refer to it throughout the meeting.

The group also needs to decide how much time to allot to each agenda item. I do not treat the time as a deadline that forces the group to automatically move to the next agenda item. Rather, allotting time enables us to monitor the group's use of time and to point out how much time remains for a topic. If the group has not finished an item in the allotted time, I intervene by asking whether the group wants to continue discussing the subject or move on.

I participate in the discussion of how much time to allot to each item, because this is a process issue. As a process expert, I give my estimate of how much time the group is likely to require to deal with each topic.

Agree on the Process, Including Ground Rules

The agenda represents agreement on the content, but the group still needs to decide which ground rules to use. At this point, I advocate the ground rules and inquire into any concerns members have about using them. Chapter Thirteen describes this process in more detail.

As the group comes to each agenda item, I advocate a process for addressing that item (such as a problem-solving model or other macro process) and then check to see what concerns, if any, people have about using the process.

Define Roles

Related to the group process is the question of identifying who assumes each role. If I have managed the contracting process effectively, the group has a good understanding of my facilitator role. In addition, when I introduce myself I briefly describe my role. Then I clarify my role and check for any questions or concerns. For example, in a basic facilitation, I might say, "As facilitator, my role is to help you work together as effectively as possible to help you accomplish what you want to accomplish. To do that, I will help you follow the ground rules. If I think someone is acting inconsistently with the ground rules, I will point it out and see if you agree. If you do, I will ask you if you're willing to make your point again using the ground rules. For example, if you take a position, I will ask you if you are willing to state the interests behind your position.

"I will also help you keep on track and monitor your time, but whether you want to change the agenda or reallocate your time among agenda items is your decision.

"As your facilitator, I will be content-neutral. For example, if you are talking about how best to increase loyalty among customers, I will not share my views on the subject. I will, however, help you have that conversation in such a way that you clearly understand each person's point of view and the reasoning that leads each person to reach this point of view."

Exhibit 11.3. Interventions for Ending a Meeting

1. Review decisions and plans for action.

2. Schedule the next meeting and agenda.

3. Do a self-critique.

(If it's appropriate, I add, "As you may know, I have some expertise in a couple of the subject areas you are working on, but it is not consistent with my role as facilitator to share that information. If, however, someone has a substantive question he or she wants me to answer, and the group agrees that I should answer it, I will temporarily leave my facilitator role, answer, and then return to the facilitator role.")

"If, at any time, you think I am acting inconsistently with what we have agreed is my role, please tell me immediately. Does anyone have any questions or concerns about my role?"

After addressing any questions and concerns, we define the other roles: recorder, formal group leader, nonmember participant, observer. Then we begin to address the content of the facilitation.

ENDING THE MEETING

At the end of the meeting, I help the group perform several tasks (Exhibit 11.3).

Review Decisions and Plans for Action

Reviewing decisions made during the meeting ensures that all members understand the decisions made. Referring to flipchart or other notes that either a group member or I have recorded, I review the decisions or else ask a member to do it ("Let's be sure everyone understands what the group has agreed on. Will someone recap the decisions? If anyone hears something that they believe the group did not agree to, please say so").

Even if the group has not formally engaged in problem solving, it is likely to have made at least one decision that requires some action. At the end of the meeting, planning ensures that members know who is responsible for each task and when it will be completed.

Schedule the Next Meeting and Agenda

If the group is going to meet again, it may be most convenient to schedule the next meeting while all members are assembled. Similarly, building a tentative agenda for the next meeting is easier after members have reviewed the current meeting. The tentative agenda is reviewed and revised, as necessary, at the beginning of the next meeting.

Conduct a Self-Critique

A self-critique is a way to help a group learn from experience and apply the learning in future meetings. Although a self-critique can be used at any time during a meeting, I usually use it at the end.

I begin the self-critique by explaining the purpose and then dividing a flipchart sheet into two vertical columns labeled *What We Did Well* and *What We Need to Improve on or Do Differently Next Time*. I then ask members to reflect on the meeting and use the ground rules to identify specific examples of when they acted effectively (*did well*) and when they acted ineffectively (*need to improve or do differently*). I also ask members to identify times when I acted inconsistently (or consistently) with the approach I have espoused. Members can also identify more complex patterns that contribute to or hinder the group's effectiveness. I participate and encourage members to critique their behavior. In addition, members can evaluate how well they accomplished their substantive goals for the meeting.

I may help the group identify examples by asking members to review the ground rules and think of a situation in which they acted consistently or inconsistently with them. I may also ask members to think of a time they had a strong feeling or thought during the meeting but did not share it.

For the critique to be helpful, members need to give specific examples—a ground rule itself. For example, John might say, "I think Debra helped the group focus on interests rather than positions when she asked Henry what interests led him to oppose flexible working hours. Do others agree?" A general comment such as "I think we all could do a better job of staying focused" does not yield enough information for other members to decide whether the critique is valid. Nor does it help the group identify exactly how they lost their focus or what to do differently. General statements also lead to a situation in which everyone may agree that the group could do a better job of staying focused, but no one believes she or he is responsible for getting the group off track.

Several variations of a self-critique are possible, depending on what kind of critiquing skill members want to develop. The first variation gives members practice in taking responsibility for both functional and dysfunctional behavior. Each person identifies something he or she did well and something he or she needs to improve on. A second variation helps a group in conflict see how other members contribute to the group's effectiveness. In this variation, each member identifies something another member did well.

A third variation helps members learn to give constructive negative feedback (consistent with the ground rules and diagnosis-intervention cycle). Each person identifies something he or she believes someone else needs to improve on, a technique that is useful for a group that tends to avoid or smooth over conflict.

A final variation, which involves a combination of the others, is helpful if members are reluctant to take the risk involved in the other variations, or after they have begun with one of the other variations. Each member identifies something any other member did well or needs to improve on. This variation involves the least risk for members, though it also develops the fewest skills. In a group that begins with this variation, members usually identify things that other members do well.

For all the variations, to maintain members' free choice they can always choose not to participate.

The variations work well for identifying individual actions. However, to identify interaction or a complex pattern, members need to identify how each member contributes to creating the dynamic. Following the ground rule to combine advocacy and inquiry, each member asks the other members of the group whether they see his or her view differently. For each item the group needs to improve on, it is important to also identify specifically how particular members will act differently. To increase the likelihood of the group improving its process, I begin each meeting by reviewing the part of the previous meeting's self-critique that lists what the group must improve on or do differently.

Sometimes a self-critique generates new understanding of something that occurred during the meeting, or a new decision. During a developmental self-critique with a top management group, one member said she did not raise an issue in the group because her supervisor (also a group member) had told her before the meeting that it would be inappropriate to do so. Members then discussed and reached a clear agreement about not preventing any issue from being raised in the group.

A facilitated meeting can be frustrating for a group that is not used to discussing process issues. The dialogue in Exhibit 11.4 shows how a member might express this frustration and how a facilitator can intervene.

Basic and developmental facilitation self-critiques differ. In developmental facilitation, group members take turns conducting the self-critique. Developmental self-critique focuses not only on ground rules but also on the underlying dynamics that lead a group to follow or not follow them, including theory-in-use. Although a self-critique in basic facilitation focuses on the ground rules, it also concentrates on how well the group accomplishes its substantive goals.

Self-critiques give me time to get feedback from the group. To reduce the chance of receiving only positive comments, I might say, "Even though I'm interested in knowing what you think I did that was helpful, my intent in asking about my performance is not to look for compliments but rather to learn how to facilitate better. So I also value comments about what I did that you found not so helpful."

To underscore the point, I can briefly identify something I learned from a self-critique with a previous group, or I can begin by identifying a specific in-

Exhibit 11.4. Facilitating a Self-Critique

Notes	Conversation
	MEMBER: I think we wasted time in the session.
Facilitator seeks to clarify meaning of important words.	FACILITATOR: Can you say specifically what you mean by "wasted time"? For example, are you saying that these topics were not important to discuss in this group? Are you saying that the group could have discussed the topics more efficiently? Or are you saying something else?
	MEMBER: The topics were important to discuss, but I just feel that the discussion should not have taken so long.
Facilitator seeks to find a specific example.	FACILITATOR: Can you give the group a specific example of when you think it was taking too long? I'm asking because I think that will help the group and me better understand what you're saying.
	MEMBER: When we were discussing when to begin the pilot project. I thought we took too long to reach what was a simple decision.
Facilitator seeks to identify how group could have been more effective.	FACILITATOR: Is there anything the group or I could have done in that situation to use the time more effectively?
	MEMBER: No, not beyond the few small things that others mentioned. I can't think of anything. Everything we talked about was important.
Facilitator tests inference.	FACILITATOR: Given that you think the group could not have done anything else aside from the small things mentioned, I'm wondering if you're feeling frustrated because a process you think is important takes such a long time to solve the group's problems. Are you frustrated about this?

Exhibit 11.4. *(continued)*

Notes	Conversation
	MEMBER: Yeah, I am. At this rate, it will take weeks to solve all our problems. That's a long time.
Facilitator reframes the meaning of "a long time" and checks for agreement or disagreement.	FACILITATOR: I agree that it may take weeks. Whether several weeks is a long time depends on how you look at the situation. I would agree that compared to how the group normally works, it's a long time to spend in problem-solving meetings. However, compared to the three years that the group has tried without success to solve these problems, several weeks seems like a relatively short period of time. Do you see it differently?
	MEMBER: I agree with everything you've said. I just don't know whether we can afford all that time in meetings.
Facilitator identifies group issue and checks for members' interest.	FACILITATOR: That's an important question for the group to decide. Do you want to check with the group to see if they want to discuss this issue?

stance when I wished I had intervened differently and then ask other members to comment. In one group self-critique, I identified a specific time when I had let group members continue talking, although I thought they were off the task. When I asked members whether they agreed, several said they had hoped I would intervene sooner.

Finally, self-critique often generates powerful diagnostic information about the group. It can help a facilitator assess how well group members understand their ground rules and whether certain behavior is functional or dysfunctional. Self-critique also enables a facilitator to assess the level of skill among members in an important area: giving feedback to other members.

SUMMARY

In this chapter, I have described structural interventions that I make before the meeting and at the beginning and end. Before the meeting begins, I make sure the room is set up appropriately. At the beginning, I make introductions; bring people up to date; seek agreement on the objectives and identify any concerns; and check for concerns about the agenda and time allocation, the meeting process (including ground rules), and roles. At the end of the meeting, I help the group review decisions and action plans, schedule the next meeting and agenda, and conduct a self-critique.

In this chapter I have explained some relatively easy interventions to make at set times in a meeting. In the next chapter, we explore interventions that are more challenging and that may be necessary at any time with little advance notice: intervening on emotions.

CHAPTER TWELVE

Dealing with Emotions

In this chapter, I explain how to deal with emotions arising in groups, mostly difficult emotions. I begin by describing how people generate emotions and how they express them. Next, we consider how emotional discussion in groups can trigger your emotions and affect your ability to facilitate, as well as how you can intervene to help people express their emotions effectively. The chapter ends with description of how you can respond when group members get angry at you and how you can use this as an opportunity for learning—for the group and you.

Part of facilitating includes helping the group address difficult, conflict-ridden problems. In working on these problems, group members may experience a variety of emotions, expressing anger, fear, disgust, surprise, sadness, or other emotions. *Emotion* refers to a feeling and the distinctive thoughts associated with it, along with the psychological and biological states that, all together, predispose a person to act (Goleman, 1995). **For a facilitator, the challenge is to help group members identify their emotions and the source, and express them in a way that contributes to—rather than detracts from—group effectiveness.**

This is a difficult challenge. Like the groups they are trying to help, many of the facilitators I teach or coach find it hard to deal with an emotional situation. This makes sense if you consider that most people employ a unilateral control theory-in-use when they feel psychological threat or embarrassment. Faced with a group that is becoming emotional, you may have a similar reaction. You may fear the group getting out of control and your not knowing how to help them. You may be overwhelmed by your own feelings and not able to think clearly. Part of the challenge of dealing with group members' emotions is dealing with your own. I address this challenge later in the chapter.

The ability to deal with emotions is what Daniel Goleman calls emotional intelligence (Goleman, 1995, 1998). Drawing on the research of Peter Salovey and John Mayer (Salovey and Mayer, 1990), he describes emotional intelligence as the ability to be aware of and manage your emotions, to use your emotions in motivating yourself to achieve goals, to have empathy for others, and to effectively deal with emotions in your relationships with others.

Fortunately, people are increasingly coming to value emotional intelligence as a key element in the workplace. Organizational leaders are realizing that if a group does not deal with emotion productively, it negatively affects the group's performance, the ability to work together in the future, and the individual's professional and personal development. As a facilitator, you can help a group shift from being afraid of dealing with their emotions to helping them use emotion to improve the quality of their work and their relationships.

Before considering how people generate emotions and how to intervene, it is worth repeating an earlier point: **group facilitation is not therapy. The purpose of dealing with emotions that arise in facilitation is to help the group become more effective at its work, not to change people's personalities or to focus on emotions for their own sake. To be appropriate, your interventions on members' emotional behavior must relate to group effectiveness.**

HOW PEOPLE GENERATE EMOTIONS

Understanding how you and the group members generate and deal with emotions can help you work effectively. Here I present a very simplified version, drawing on Goleman's clear writing on the topic (Goleman, 1995).

A Tale of Two Minds

There is a physiological reason that your emotions sometimes control you rather than you controlling your emotions. The brain has two mechanisms for dealing with emotion: the amygdala and the neocortex. When people say and do things, your eyes and ears convert their sound and speech to neural signals and send them to the thalamus, in your brain. The thalamus sends a signal to the neocortex, the thinking part of the brain. The neocortex (in coordination with the prefrontal lobes it is part of) makes sense of what your eyes and ears perceive, decides how to respond, and then coordinates the response. It does so with the amygdala and other parts of the emotional brain. The neocortex enables us to think about how we feel and allows us to have feelings about ideas, including things that people say to us. It enables us to recognize that we may be making an incorrect inference and decide to test it before acting.

However, at the same time the thalamus sends a message to the neocortex, it sends one to the amygdala. This is part of the limbic system of the brain and deals with emotional matters. When the amygdala gets the message, it figures out whether the situation is potentially threatening to you or something you hate. Sensing that it is, the amygdala instantly mounts a reaction, enlisting the rest of the brain to deal with the threat.

The amygdala's response is immediate but imprecise. It responds on the basis of limited information and without any confirmation. It may lead you to blow up with angry or sarcastic words, give a steely stare, completely shut down in a steamy silence, break down and cry, or storm out of the room. The amygdala responds before the neocortex can and takes over before the neocortex responds. It can even prevent the neocortex from responding at all. Goleman calls this "emotional hijacking."

The amygdala's strength is also its weakness. Quick response has evolutionary survival value, especially for animals like squirrels, which must quickly decide to escape anything that might be a predator. Because the amygdala errs on the side of safety, the cost of misperceiving something as a predator is small. But for you as a human being, the sloppy response of the amygdala can create a huge problem in your natural habitat—encounters with other humans. It means that you might respond angrily and defensively when others are really not threatening you.

Integrating Thought and Emotion

You might logically conclude from this that the best way to handle a difficult situation is to remove emotion from your analysis and decision making. But emotion and rational thinking inform each other. Emotions are an important form of data, even though they are not directly observable. Your emotions can quickly point you in the right direction before your thinking kicks in, and your thinking can assess whether the data match your feeling. With your emotions and thoughts working together, you respond more effectively in a range of situations.

Factors That Contribute to Generating Emotion

Obviously, the amygdala does not drive the reaction to every emotional situation. But even when higher-order thinking is functioning, there are still a variety of factors that that can, in a group meeting, lead you or a member to become emotional and respond in a unilaterally controlling way. Knowing what factors contribute to emotion helps you respond appropriately and, when possible, prepare yourself internally.

Content of the Subject Being Discussed. Certain subjects are likely to be emotionally hot topics because they often evoke feelings of fear, anger, shame, or guilt; consider a performance appraisal, an organizational restructuring or layoff, a merger, violence in the workplace, or sexual harassment.

Nature of Your Relationship with the Group. Even if you have helped clarify what the group can reasonably expect from you, they may still have unrealistic expectations of how you can help them. Combine this with the fact that you are not solving the problems for the group or giving them expert technical advice on how to do so, and this can cause group members to feel ambivalent about you. On the one hand, they may very much want and need your help; on the other, they may resent that you do not solve the problems they need solved.

Depth of Your Intervention. Deep interventions, such as theory-in-use interventions, ask people to reveal information about themselves—their beliefs, values, opinions, and feelings—that is quite private. By revealing the information, they risk making themselves vulnerable. A member may share the fact that his ineffective behavior with a boss is based on his belief that she cannot be trusted. Or, he may reveal that his ineffective behavior results from believing that another member is not competent to do the job. Depending on what the member reveals, he or she may fear loss of support from peers, retribution by a more powerful member, or loss of face. Consequently, the person can feel threatened by and react emotionally to interventions that ask for such information to be revealed.

Experiences That Evoke Past Emotional Responses. An individual's past experience triggers current emotional response. If people perceive the current situation as similar to a past situation in which their emotions were triggered, then even if the situation is dissimilar the emotions are likely to be triggered again. This is true even if the experience was with people other than the current group members.

Cultural Diversity. People of different cultures, races, or genders can make divergent meaning out of the same event and have a range of emotional responses. For example, some Asian cultures place a higher priority on saving face than U.S. cultures do. In a conversation in which group members are not saving face, an Asian member may respond more emotionally than a member from the United States, if each responds in a way stereotypical of the culture.

HOW MEMBERS EXPRESS EMOTIONS

In the *Nicomachean Ethics,* Aristotle defined the challenge of dealing with emotions this way: "Anyone can become angry—that is easy. But to be angry with the right person, to the right degree, at the right time, for the right purpose, and in the right way—this is not easy." The facilitator's challenge is to help group members identify, express, and discuss their emotions so as to increase rather than decrease the group's effectiveness.

People express their emotions in two ways: directly or indirectly. In the former case, they describe what they are feeling: "I am really angry at you," or "I fear that someone will get back at me if I'm honest."

People express their emotions indirectly in two ways: verbally or nonverbally. Indirect verbal expression can take many forms, among them raising or lowering the voice, focusing repeatedly on a particular point or raising unrelated points, immediately changing an opinion when pressured, and verbally attacking someone or denying their actions. Nonverbal examples include glaring at or looking away from other group members, slouching in or perching on the chair, folding or waving the arms, tightening facial muscles, and sighing.

In both indirect methods, a group member transforms the emotion so that other members and the facilitator cannot identify the emotion without asking or making an inference. Again, making an untested inference often creates negative consequences, and this situation is no exception. People do not always express the same emotion in the same way as others (this can be true even of the same person). You may express anger by becoming hostile, while I express anger by withdrawing from the conversation. Further, a given behavior can express different emotions. One person's outburst may reflect anger, while another's is from anxiety. Consequently, you cannot reliably infer a person's emotions from his or her behavior.

Acting defensively—part of the unilateral control theory-in-use—is a common way for a group member to indirectly express emotion. Defensive behavior is a way of trying to reduce anxiety or stress that involves denying or distorting reality (McConnell, 1986). Examples are denial, blaming others, withholding relevant information, and suppressing emotions.

People express their emotions functionally by expressing them directly and in a manner consistent with the core values and ground rules. Whether a person acts functionally does not depend on how frequently or strongly he expresses his emotions.

Just as cultural differences affect how members of a group generate emotions, they also affect how members express them. Some organizations believe that discussing emotions is "touchy-feely" and do not see the relationship between productive discussion of emotion and the group's effectiveness. Consequently, people in such an organization feel pressure to avoid emotional discussion. In contrast, other organizations believe—and the research suggests (for example, Argyris, 1990)—that unresolved issues of negative emotion, especially those that create defensive behavior, reduce the group's ability to maintain its working relationship and consequently the ability to perform tasks. People in this sort of organization feel less pressure to avoid emotional discussion, or none.

The group's culture also influences whether and how members express emotion. Consider, for example, a group comprising members from only one subgroup of the organization, a subgroup with a culture that values discussing emotional issues. The group is likely to do so, even if the discussion is not supported by the larger organizational culture.

The cultural makeup of group members also has an impact on how they express emotion. Although it is dangerous to assume that a person from a particular culture expresses his or her own emotions in a way that is stereotypical of the culture, nevertheless some cultures express their emotions more directly and emphatically, while others express their emotions more subtly. The same holds true for the level of education, class, and position within the organization.

MANAGING YOUR OWN EMOTIONS

You are facilitating a group discussing roles and responsibilities, when Michelle starts to accuse Joe of slacking off. Immediately, Joe angrily tells Michelle that if she were competent the group wouldn't be having problems. Walt jumps in admonishingly, saying that Joe is in no position to complain. With each comment, the group members get angrier.

Many of the facilitators that I teach or coach have a difficult time in a situation like this one, where group members get quite emotional. It is hard to help the members manage their emotions effectively if your own emotions are getting in the way. Should you find yourself starting to get overwhelmed emotionally, you can do several things to manage your emotions and regain your effectiveness.

Slow Down

First, slow down. You do not need to immediately jump in when you see the group getting emotional. Intervening quickly out of fear or anger can be worse than making no intervention at all. By slowing yourself down, you have the chance to use your emotions to inform your thinking rather than to override it. The traditional advice of taking a deep breath and counting to ten is useful. It gives you a chance to interrupt your purely emotional response and integrate your thinking with your emotions.

Treat Yourself with Compassion

Remember that the core value of compassion includes treating *yourself* compassionately. For most people, dealing with an emotional situation is clearly a challenging part of being a facilitator. Compassion for yourself means recognizing that you are also a learner in this process, that there will be times when you feel anxious, overwhelmed, afraid, stuck, and so forth, and that is part of what it means to grow and develop. As a "recovering perfectionist," I can tell you that when things are not working out as you would like, you do not earn extra points for getting down on yourself.

Experience and Name Your Emotions

Name your emotions. Is it anger, fear, shame, surprise, disgust, sadness, joy, or some other emotion—or combination of emotions? These are some basic emotions, but there are hundreds of them, and blends of emotion as well. Anger includes frustration, resentment, and annoyance; fear encompasses anxiety, nervousness, and wariness, to name a few (Goleman, 1995). Increasing your emotional vocabulary makes it easier to clearly name your emotions, which makes it easier to work with them.

To name your emotions, allow yourself to experience them without judging. It is natural to have a range of emotions when facilitating; do not berate yourself for having them. If you think to yourself *I'm feeling anxious and that's bad,* you add another layer of emotion, which makes it more difficult to identify your initial emotion and generates distraction. Instead, try reframing your thinking so that you are curious and compassionate with yourself: *Hmmm, this is interesting; what am I feeling here?*

Identify the Source

Identify the source of your emotion. By continuing to remain curious and compassionate, you can reflect, *I wonder where my reaction is coming from?* Ask yourself what specifically people have said or done that generated the emotion for you. Is it something that has happened in the present conversation? Is it something from a previous conversation with group members? Is it something from a relationship with other people that you are carrying over to this group?

Also ask yourself if something is happening that is triggering some of your own issues. Knowing what your own issues are helps you identify this quickly. For example, if you generally set unrealistically high standards for yourself and keep on raising the bar, you may react emotionally if a group member begins to discuss this topic emotionally. Ask yourself: *Is the level of my emotion in proportion to the situation, or not?* Getting annoyed with group members is different from being outraged at them. Here too, remaining curious and compassionate with yourself helps you identify the source of your emotion.

Use the answers to your questions to help diagnose the situation. Consider that your own emotions may be mirroring what one or more group members are feeling. For example, if you are annoyed at a team member's comment and think that it has something to do with an interaction between group members, consider the possibility that other group members are also annoyed; look for observable data that confirms or disconfirms this idea. If you conclude that your emotions are unrelated to what is happening in the group, then it helps to reflect on your reaction. (This is why having a cofacilitator is important; it enables the other to take the lead for a while.) If you are facilitating alone, recognize that you have become part of the problem. If you've already reacted, let the group know that your own emotions have clouded your judgment. Owning your mistakes and publicly apologizing can also be a vital learning experience for the group.

Remind Yourself of Your Skills

One reason my facilitation students feel anxious is that they do not know what to say or do when group members get emotional. The elements of the Skilled Facilitator approach that you have already learned give you a way of helping members deal with emotions. Thus, by using the diagnosis-intervention cycle and the ground rules, you can test your inferences about whether people are feeling a certain emotion and inquire into what has happened that led them to feel that way. Knowing that there are some standard interventions you can make when a group member expresses emotion can help a lot.

DECIDING HOW TO INTERVENE

There are a number of things to consider when deciding how to intervene.

Look for the Gift

Recently I took some courses in improvisational theater. In improv, you work with others to create a scene or play or song on the spot. If you and I are doing an improvisational scene, you might begin the scene by sitting down at the controls of an imaginary airplane and, while setting the various controls, turn to me in you best professional pilot voice and say "I sure am glad you're able to fill in as copilot for this flight. My regular partner had an awful time on the last flight." I then respond, having had no idea you were going to say that and no idea what you will say or do after I respond. We continue our spontaneous conversation, each of us building on the other's comments to create a scene that is meaningful—and maybe even funny.

What I learned from my improv instructor is that for improv to work, you need to accept the gift that you are given. The lines the person gives you are the lines you have to work with and respond to. You can build on them and play with them, but you have to work with those lines. If you refuse to play with them, the improv ends. By framing the lines a person gives you as a gift, you can look for ways to build on them.

The same is true for facilitation. **The lines that group members say are the lines you have to work with as a facilitator. You can comment on them and ask the members about them, but you need to accept them as the basis for your interventions if your interventions are to be related to their conversation.**

With the Skilled Facilitator approach, by listening carefully and curiously to what group members say you receive the material for your next lines. If Lola says in a loud voice, "Tony, I've had enough of your games. You're always putting yourself before the team!" I might respond, "Lola, you sound angry, yes? Are you willing to look at what you're angry about?" If she agrees, you can continue: "What's happened that led you to feel this way?"

Unfortunately, if you grow fearful, angry, or embarrassed and focus exclusively and extensively on your emotions, you stop attending to the group. Then you miss what people are saying and the gifts they are continuing to give you for intervention. A colleague and I were working with a group when she made what I thought was an inadvertent pejorative comment about a particular race, members of which were in the group. I got embarrassed and put my head down, thereby missing the group members' reactions (which I could have used as data to intervene). A few minutes later, when I recovered from my embarrassment, I did intervene. I said to the group that when she made the remark I felt embarrassed and as a result missed their reactions. I then asked them how they felt about the remark. The group, my colleague, and I discussed it; some group members said they had stopped paying attention after she made the comment, because it bothered them. After talking about it, the group, my colleague, and I were ready to return the group's task.

Part of the difficulty is that when group members become emotional, the diagnostic and intervention gifts they give you are not nicely wrapped. They may come in loud, angry, or sullen packaging. But if you accept the gift, you may help the group unwrap some important issues that are hindering its effectiveness.

Move Toward the Conflict

As conflict arises in a group and people get emotional, you may want to avoid it. You can try to switch the subject, squelch it, or defuse the situation, perhaps by calling a break. But moving away from conflict means you miss an opportunity to help the group.

I learned this lesson by facilitating for a nonprofit volunteer service organization. The organization was in trouble because the leadership was burned out. The leadership had been providing almost all the services because they could not recruit other volunteer members to do so. As a result, the leaders were planning to resign their positions en masse but could not find anyone to replace them. They believed that if they stepped down, the organization would die. They called a membership meeting to deal with this issue.

Unfortunately, my concern about the members' emotions and my ability to handle them led me to intervene in a way that steered the group away from the conflict rather than into it. The group did not get to discuss the essence of the issue; the meeting ended without any agreement.

A principle of the Skilled Facilitator approach is to move toward conflict. By publicly identifying the conflict in the group and engaging people in a conversation about it, you can help the group explore how people contribute to the conflict, how they are feeling about it, and how to manage it.

Follow Through on Interventions

Interventions are not magic. Even if you move toward conflict and intervene, your initial intervention may not have the impact you intend. It is natural to have to make a series of interventions to help the group explore a particular issue.

Sometimes you may drop an intervention because you become frustrated as the group members remain silent or respond only indirectly to your questions. Sometimes you may drop an intervention because a group member responds angrily or tearfully. Faced with restating the intervention or dropping it, you choose the latter.

When I ask facilitators what leads them to not follow through on an emotionally difficult intervention that they consider important and appropriate, they usually explain that they inferred the member or entire group would be embarrassed and could not handle it. They also say they are uncomfortable when pursuing such an intervention. They recognize that by dropping the intervention they are unilaterally protecting their clients and themselves.

It is important that the group members make a free and informed choice to respond to your interventions. If you think that others are growing embarrassed and want you to stop, ask them about it. You can also explain that your intent is not to embarrass them but to help them address some issues that they have said are important. If they are feeling embarrassed or defensive, you can ask what, if anything, you have done to contribute to their reaction. You can also ask them if they would like to continue, and what would need to happen for them to continue. Still, **after you explain your intent for making your intervention and explain the potential consequences for the group if they choose not to pursue the issue, if the members decide not to pursue it, then you have preserved their free and informed choice.**

You can also reframe your thinking about the situation. I often tell myself that the group is paying me to facilitate because they are not able to pursue these difficult issues themselves. If I back off when my initial intervention is not working, I may reinforce their belief that these issues are too difficult to handle. I may also lead them to infer that the core values and ground rules—on which my interventions are based—are not effective in a difficult situation. By pursuing interventions in a way that also maintains the group members' free and informed choice, I model what is possible and also give them hope that they can address their difficult issues.

If clients do not respond directly to your initial intervention or respond defensively, rather than repeating the same intervention you can follow up with a meta-intervention. *A meta-intervention is an intervention that refers to a previous one.* Meta-interventions enable the group and you to talk about interventions. In a meta-intervention, you explore with the group what it was that led members not to respond to the initial intervention.

Consider, for example, a member who remains silent when you intervene to ask the member to identify her interests. You may respond with the general meta-intervention, "Jill, when I asked you what your interests were, you remained silent, yes? [If yes] Can you say what led you to be silent?" The meta-intervention enables Jill and you to identify why the initial intervention did not work as you expected. Once you identify and address the cause, you can change your intervention accordingly.

Sometimes a group member believes she is addressing your question but you think she is not. In this case, your meta-intervention might be, "Andrea, when I asked what your interests were in combining the two departments, you said that people have been concerned about the high turnover in these departments. Is that what you said? [If yes] I don't understand how what you said identifies your interests. Can you explain it me?"

Sometimes a member responds indirectly to avoid discussing a difficult or undiscussable issue. If you have observed behavior that leads you to infer this, you can share the inference with the member and test it.

Of course, making a meta-intervention can surface undiscussable issues that require deeper intervention. A meta-intervention may prompt members to discuss how they disagree with the goals of a program, or how they question other members' performance. I do not become concerned if the group abandons my initial intervention to pursue the issue uncovered by the meta-intervention. In fact, I consider this a success. Meta-intervention issues often help the group move beyond discussing symptoms, to explore underlying problems and causes.

INTERVENING ON EMOTIONS

To repeat an earlier point, the facilitator's role is to help the group identify, express, and discuss emotions in a way that increases group effectiveness. To do this, you can intervene in two ways: by helping members express their emotions effectively or by helping them learn to think differently so that they can manage their emotions effectively themselves. The first approach is appropriate for both basic and developmental facilitation; the second is suited only to developmental facilitation.

Helping People Express Emotions Effectively

You help group members express their emotions effectively by having them do so in manner consistent with the core values and ground rules. In basic facilitation, you accomplish this by encouraging them to name their emotions, identifying comments that may upset other members, and rephrasing for members how they have expressed their emotions. The example in Exhibit 12.1 shows a basic facilitator intervention with a group of department heads who are discussing potential budget cuts.

Exhibit 12.1. Intervening on Emotion, Using Basic Facilitation

Notes	Dialogue
	DAN: I don't think Paul needs all his people because he's increased efficiencies significantly. I think we can cut some people in his area, meet the budget, and not reduce our productivity.
Facilitator observes loud voice, pointing at Dan, and the phrase "I'm sick and tired" and infers emotion. Facilitator decides to intervene on the larger issue of Paul's emotions rather than the unexplained phrase "you're like a little kid," which seems part of the larger issue.	PAUL: (*to Dan in a very loud voice*) I'm sick and tired of hearing this line from you. You talk as if every other department has to justify its existence except yours. Well, we've got real good reasons for our staffing numbers. (*waving his finger at Dan*) You know that, but you're more concerned about your own little kingdom instead of the bigger picture. You're like a little kid.
Facilitator describes the observable behavior, checks for agreement, and simultaneously inquires what Paul is feeling.	FACILITATOR: Paul, You raised your voice, waved your finger at Dan, and told him you were "sick and tired of hearing this line." Yes? I'm wondering what you are feeling.
Facilitator notes that Paul describes a type of anger: being ticked off. Paul has also identified this issue as a pattern, which he attributes to "Dan looking out for Dan."	PAUL: I'll tell you what I'm feeling: ticked off. It's like this all the time. Dan is looking out for Dan.
Facilitator asks Paul to describe his thoughts that led him to be ticked off.	FACILITATOR: OK. What I don't understand exactly is what Dan said that ticked you off. What were you thinking before you told Dan you were "sick and tired"? Can you say specifically?
Facilitator notes that Paul is attributing to Dan that Dan knows that what he is saying is not true and is just trying to protect his people.	PAUL: Dan knows the whole point of increasing efficiency wasn't to cut people in the department. It was to be able to redeploy people on more profitable services. There was never any intention of cutting people once we achieved the efficiencies. He's just trying to protect his own people—it's typical Dan.

Exhibit 12.1. *(continued)*

Notes	Dialogue
Facilitator clarifies the source of Paul's anger and checks for agreement about the attribution.	FACILITATOR: So are you angry because you think Dan knows this but is trying to use that reason to cut your people?
	PAUL: That's exactly what I'm saying.
Facilitator inquires into whether Paul's inferences and attributions are tested or untested.	FACILITATOR: OK. Can you say what leads you to believe that Dan knows this? I'm asking because I'm wondering: Are you inferring it, or has Dan said this explicitly to you?
	PAUL: I'm inferring it from a number of comments he made.
Facilitator asks Paul to test his inference with Dan.	FACILITATOR: Are you willing to share with Dan what data you used to make your inference and find out if he sees it differently?
	PAUL: OK.

In developmental facilitation, you intervene to help members learn how to express their emotions consistently with the core values and ground rules, rather than relying on the facilitator to do it for them, as in basic facilitation. The intervention in Exhibit 12.2 continues essentially from where the earlier conversation ends, illustrating how you can move from a basic intervention to a developmental intervention.

Helping People Reduce Defensive Thinking

The basic and developmental interventions in the example help members express their emotions but do not help them alter their underlying defensive behavior, because neither intervention addresses the source. Instead, the facilitator helps members bypass the defensive behavior instead of "helping the group learn to [discuss these defensive behaviors] in order to get rid of them" (Argyris, 1990, p. 102).

To address the underlying defensive behavior, you can help members change how they think about an experience, so that they perceive less of a threat and therefore do not experience the emotion so overwhelmingly or as a trigger to their defensive behavior. This kind of developmental intervention involves helping people explore and redesign their theories-in-use at a deep level and re-

Exhibit 12.2. Intervening on Emotion, Using Developmental Facilitation

Notes	Dialogue
Facilitator clarifies the source of Paul's anger and checks for agreement about the attribution.	FACILITATOR: So are you angry because you think Dan knows this but is trying to use that reason to cut your people? PAUL: That's exactly what I'm saying.
Facilitator describes the two issues, one content-related and the other emotion-related, and separates the two initially.	FACILITATOR: I think it can be useful to be angry in certain cases and then appropriately express your anger. I see two related issues here. One is whether Dan does know about the purpose of increasing efficiency and whether he was trying to protect his own people. The other issue is how you responded to Dan, given your thinking about the first issue. I'd like first to focus on how you responded, because I think your reaction created some unintended consequences. Then I'd like to come back to the first issue. Any concerns about doing that? PAUL: No, that's OK.
Facilitator identifies Paul's intent, to see if it will match the consequences he got.	FACILITATOR: When you got angry with Dan, what was your intent when you yelled that he was only concerned about his own little kingdom instead of the bigger picture and that he was acting like a little kid? PAUL: I was so ticked off that I wanted to get his attention. FACILITATOR: I think you definitely got Dan's attention. I also think you may have gotten some other consequences that you hadn't intended. Would you be willing to find out from Dan how he reacted to your comments? PAUL: OK. Dan, how did you react when I told you that?

Exhibit 12.2. *(continued)*

Notes	Dialogue
Facilitator chooses not to intervene on Dan's reaction based on Dan's untested inference about Paul.	DAN: I got angry with you because you unfairly accused me and I didn't think you wanted to hear what I had to say. At that point, I just shut down. I wasn't willing to hear what you had to say.
	FACILITATOR: Paul, can you let Dan know what you heard him say, so that he's sure you got it as he meant it? What did you hear Dan say?
	PAUL: Dan, what you're saying is that you got annoyed at me because you thought I was accusing you unfairly and that I wasn't going to listen to your view of the situation. You basically turned me off at that point. Yes?
	DAN: You got it.
Facilitator declares his willingness to share his thoughts and explains why he wants Paul to go first.	FACILITATOR: Paul, earlier I said that I thought you not only got Dan's attention but also got some other consequences you didn't intend. I'm willing to share my thoughts about what the consequences are, but I'm interested in seeing if you can identify any. What do you think?
	PAUL: Well, I guess that in trying to get Dan's attention I got it initially but then lost him completely because I got his attention by ticking him off.
Facilitator agrees with Paul and then asks Paul to redesign his comment.	FACILITATOR: I agree with you completely. You got the opposite of the very thing you intended. Can you think what you could have said to Dan that would have let him know how you were feeling without contributing to his shutting you off?
	PAUL: I'd say something like, "Dan, I'm angry at you. You said that my depart-

Exhibit 12.2. *(continued)*

Notes	Dialogue
	ment could be cut without any loss of productivity. But when we talked about increasing efficiency, you agreed that my department would use the increased efficiency to redeploy people to higher-profit services. Now you're saying something different than what you said before. Do you agree, Dan?" Assuming Dan agreed, I'd continue, "Well, that makes me angry."
Facilitator confirms Paul's statement and checks with the group for problems facilitator may not have seen.	FACILITATOR: I think that's consistent with the core values and ground rules. Anyone see any problems with Paul's revised statement?
	(Members shake heads, say no)

quires a highly skilled facilitator. Again, the conversation in Exhibit 12.3 begins by returning to an earlier part of the last example.

Dealing with Hot Buttons

A *hot button* is a characteristic or situation that has a particularly strong meaning for you and that leads you to respond defensively. For some people, a hot button might be perceiving they are not afforded the respect, deference, or attention they believe they deserve. Other people have a hot button pushed when they believe someone is questioning their ability, commitment, intelligence, or integrity. For still others, it is being manipulated or otherwise controlled. Because your own hot buttons lead you to misperceive others' remarks and actions, you often respond ineffectively even if others have acted effectively.

As a developmental facilitator, you can help group participants respond effectively by reducing the defensive thinking associated with their hot buttons. This involves first working with them to identify the trigger and then reframe their thinking. Some people I have facilitated for find it difficult to respond effectively when a person—especially someone with less power or authority—raises his or her voice at them in anger. Granted, raising your voice or yelling is not a particularly skillful way of communicating, but these people believe that a person yelling at them is showing disrespect for their official position, or their personal dignity. They also believe that allowing a person to raise his voice gives him too much control.

Exhibit 12.3. Using Developmental Facilitation to Identify Defensive Thinking

Notes	Dialogue
Facilitator confirms Paul's statement and checks with the group for problems facilitator may not have seen.	FACILITATOR: I think that's consistent with the core values and ground rules. Anyone see any problems with Paul's revised statement?
	(*Members shake heads, say no*)
Facilitator returns to the first issue he identified.	FACILITATOR: Paul, I'd like to go back to the issue of whether Dan knows about the purpose of increasing efficiency and whether he was trying to protect his own people. Can we return to that?
	PAUL: OK.
Facilitator begins to determine whether Paul contributed to his emotional reaction by making untested inferences about what Dan knew.	FACILITATOR: I'm wondering whether you are inferring that Dan knows his two statements are different. Assuming you're correct that Dan knew this, I can understand how you would feel angry. How do you know that Dan knows the purpose of creating efficiencies wasn't to cut people? Have you checked this out with Dan, or are you making an inference?
	PAUL: Everybody knew it. We talked about it in a lot of meetings.
Facilitator clarifies Paul's response in terms of the facilitator's question.	FACILITATOR: Are you saying that you checked out your inference directly with Dan, or are you saying something else?
	PAUL: No, I didn't check it out. I just think you would have had to be totally out of the loop not to know it.
Facilitator shares observations and inferences and tests them with Paul.	FACILITATOR: Let me identify a pattern that I think led to your angry response and get your reaction. Dan suggests that with the new efficiencies, people in your department can be cut. You infer that Dan knows this wasn't the purpose of increasing

Exhibit 12.3. *(continued)*

Notes	Dialogue
	efficiency, and you respond by getting angry with him. You attribute his actions to protecting his turf and then suggest that this is Dan's typical behavior. But you don't test your inference with Dan. Rather, you assume your inference is true and use your untested inference as the justification for your anger toward Dan. Have I accurately described what happened?
	PAUL: Yeah, that pretty much captures it.
Facilitator identifies a pattern of behavior common to several group members. The facilitator then suggests the value of changing the dysfunctional pattern and asks the group to make the choice.	FACILITATOR: One thing we can spend some time on is talking out how you can reduce this kind of thinking. I raise this because you've had several occasions in which different members—Dan, Amy, and Paul—have experienced similar negative consequences resulting from their thinking. I think this would help your ability to deal with some of the difficult issues you still want to deal with, such as equitable workloads and coordination between departments. But the choice is yours. What do you want to do?

In developmental facilitation, I help them respond effectively through reframing how they think about the person raising his voice. First, I ask them to reframe how they think about the other person's interests—perhaps to think of him not as being disrespectful but as having limited skills; the person yelling is not trying to make someone's life miserable but is trying to solve a problem without the ability to do so. In other words, the person is not interested in raising his voice for its own sake.

Next, I ask the participants to consider reframing how they think about their own role. Because they seek to manage conflict effectively, I ask them to think of themselves as being in the position of helping people who are less skilled at managing conflict.

Part of the reframing involves asking the participant to consider adopting a curious, compassionate response to the person raising his voice. This means inquiring what the participant has done that contributed to the other person feeling the need to raise his voice. Reframing at this deep level can help change the theory-in-use, but it often takes many facilitation sessions and much skill to accomplish this. Because this is a deep level of intervention, it is especially important that you **continue to offer group members a free and informed choice to stop the intervention whenever they wish.**

HELPING THE GROUP EXPRESS POSITIVE EMOTIONS

Although many groups struggle with addressing such emotions as fear, anger, regret, and embarrassment, some groups also have difficulty handling positive emotions—happiness, joy, pride, satisfaction, and kindness. Emotions are neither positive nor negative in the sense of being good or bad; I use the term *positive emotion* to refer to those we typically associate with a positive experience. Helping group members learn to express their positive emotions is also important. As a facilitator, you can help group members accomplish this in several ways.

Help the Group Celebrate Progress

One way to help people in a group express positive emotions is to bring them to recognize and celebrate their achievements (Cuellar, 1986). A group working through a difficult issue using new facilitative skills is in itself cause for recognizing their accomplishment. This does not necessarily require a party to celebrate, but asking members to express their feelings about the achievement creates a group memory about their ability to work together effectively. Marking the accomplishment builds momentum that helps the group to move on to the next steps.

You can also help the group members compassionately reframe the meaning of their experience when they feel frustrated or disappointed because they are not yet able to act consistently with the core values and ground rules. You can remind them that learning to act this way is difficult work that takes time. You can help them shift from frustration to satisfaction by focusing on how they have improved their group process skill set and mind-set, rather than focusing on what they have not yet accomplished.

Find the Humor in Being Human

Being a facilitator does not mean being stoic or humorless. When group members say and do things that are genuinely funny, I laugh accordingly. I do not join in a group's humor if it is at the expense of a member or seems to be a defensive reaction to a genuine issue in the group; but I do bring my sense of humor to my work.

To me, part of being human is laughing at my own ineffectiveness. Yes, group facilitation is serious business, but not so serious that I think we should lose sight of the comic absurdity of our ineffective behavior. Laughing with a group about how it creates the very unintended consequences it tries to avoid does not make the issue less serious; it just gives people more than one perspective. When we laugh at ourselves, we treat ourselves with compassion. Humor can be a powerful way to help people learn.

Look for Missing Positive Emotions

Some groups have a group or organizational culture that does not value or believe in expressing positive emotions. A number of years ago, as a member of such a group, I heard the leader announce that one member had just received a prestigious award; the members agreed it was deserved and were delighted he had received it. Yet, when the leader made the announcement, no one applauded or cheered. In fact, no one said anything. My untested inference was that members felt awkward in openly expressing their positive feelings about another member.

If you observe that group members are not expressing positive emotions, you can share your observation and infer what meaning people make of this. Your intervention may lead to an important conversation about group values and norms.

Help Members Who Misattribute Positive Emotions

When members do express positive emotions, others can misinterpret them. You can reduce misinterpretation by helping group members clarify the meaning of their expressions. Members can easily misinterpret an expression of positive emotion if it seems inappropriate for the situation. Consider, for example, Valerie describing how stressed she feels about the increase in demands on her time. If she does not make some changes to get more control over how she spends her time, she will not accomplish her long-term goals for the group. While Valerie is sharing this, Pat, a more senior group member, starts to smile. As Valerie becomes more frustrated, Pat's smile grows and Valerie sees her smiling. At this point, you might intervene by saying, "Pat, as Valerie has been sharing her frustrations, you've been smiling. Would you be willing to share what you are thinking or feeling?" Pat responds, "I'm smiling because, in a way, I'm happy for Valerie. I know she has felt stressed out for a long time, but this is the first time I've seen a resolve on her part to make some changes that will improve things for her. It's great to see that."

WHEN PEOPLE GET ANGRY WITH YOU

Sometimes you are the subject of the group's emotions; they will get angry with you. They can become angry or frustrated with you either because you have acted ineffectively or because they are redirecting their emotions toward you. As soon as you infer that a group member is feeling negatively toward you, it is important to test your inference. If the inference is correct, then it is difficult to go on facilitating effectively if you do not address this issue in the group.

By using the ground rules and diagnosis-intervention cycle, you can test the inference that the member's emotion is directed at you. You might say, "I'm inferring from your frown and head shaking that you're frustrated with me; am I correct?" If the member agrees, you can start to identify the cause of the frustration: "I don't mean to do anything that will frustrate you, but I might be doing something I'm not aware of. Can you tell me what I said or did that led you to get frustrated with me?" After the group member describes your behavior, the members and you can jointly decide whether you have in fact behaved as the member described; if so, decide whether your behavior was inconsistent with the core values and ground rules.

If you have acted effectively, then you can help the group member explore what leads to his emotional reaction, as I described earlier in this chapter.

If you have acted ineffectively, then you contribute to generating the member's emotional reaction. In this case, you can acknowledge this and, if possible, redesign your behavior to be consistent with the core values and ground rules. If a member is frustrated with a comment you have just made because it is an untested assumption about him, you can simply restate it and test the assumption. In some cases, however, you cannot easily reduce the negative consequences of your ineffective behavior. Perhaps a member is frustrated because you have repeatedly failed to identify when members are getting off task. In basic facilitation, you can simply identify what you will do differently in the future.

In developmental facilitation, after you apologize, you can also ask the group member what led him not to say anything after seeing the group repeatedly go off task. By pursuing this, you are not trying to reduce your own responsibility. Rather, you are helping the group become more independent by exploring why members do not intervene in the group when they believe it is necessary ("Sheryl, if you noticed that several times the group was off task and I did not intervene, and you thought it would be helpful to intervene, I'm curious what led you not to intervene?").

LEARNING FROM YOUR EXPERIENCES

Facilitators are not omniscient. If you have not yet started facilitating, expect at times to be stumped. If you are already a facilitator, you surely know the feeling. There are times when your intuition tells you that something is wrong, but you cannot identify any group behavior to make a diagnosis. Or, having identified the problem, you may be uncertain about how to intervene. When this happens, consider asking the group for help: "I'm stumped. I think the group is having a problem, but I can't figure out what it is, and I also can't point to any behavior that leads me to conclude this. Does anyone else see something?" Although it is not helpful to the group if you intervene like this frequently, using it occasionally can use the group's skills to allow you to see things you are missing.

Even when you act ineffectively, you can create a learning opportunity for the group and yourself. By asking group members about the consequences of your behavior, you learn more about your own behavior while you show group members how to practice diagnosing behavior and its consequences. By publicly acknowledging how you have acted ineffectively, you model accountability without defensiveness. I try to not act ineffectively, of course, but I have been surprised to find that some group members' most memorable learning has come from my publicly reflecting with the group on my ineffective behavior.

Through facilitation, we come to know ourselves by reflecting on how we react to certain situations, understanding the source of our emotion, and learning how to work productively with our feelings. In doing so, we not only help ourselves but also increase our ability to aid the groups with which we work.

SUMMARY

In this chapter, I have explored how to deal with emotions that arise in facilitation—for the group members and for you. Dealing productively with emotion is difficult because there are physiological reasons for emotion overriding rational thinking. Helping a group deal with emotion means showing group members how to use their emotions and thinking to inform each other, rather than avoid emotions or allow them to control the conversation; it also means helping group members express their emotions productively. Because the facilitator is susceptible to the same emotional reactions as the group members, you can do a number of things to manage your own emotions during facilitation.

When you intervene on group members' emotions, you can help them both express their emotions effectively and learn to reduce the defensive thinking that is associated with ineffective emotional response. You can also improve learning on how to express "positive" emotions as well. Finally, managing your own emotions includes responding effectively should a group member get angry at you, and being able to frame the situation as an opportunity for learning—for you and the group. Clearly, it is important to have an explicit agreement with the group about what kind of intervention you will make regarding emotion. In the next chapter, I describe how to develop an explicit agreement with the group about how you will work together.

PART FOUR

AGREEING TO WORK TOGETHER

CHAPTER THIRTEEN

Contracting

*Deciding Whether and
How to Work Together*

In this chapter, I discuss the stages that my clients and I go through to develop an agreement on how to work together and what they will accomplish. During the contracting process, the client and I also develop the foundation of our working relationship. **This contracting approach rests on the premise that only the primary client—the group I will be facilitating—has the valid information to contract with the facilitator.** It also involves investing time in the contracting process, recognizing that ineffective contracting almost invariably leads to problems later in the facilitation.

Before I agree to facilitate a group, I want to understand who is asking for help, what they want to accomplish, what might prevent them from achieving those objectives, and how they see me helping them. Similarly, the group often wants to know about my experience as a facilitator and how I think I can help them. **Through the *contracting* process, the client and I explore these questions, develop a working relationship, and reach an agreement about whether and how to work together.**

In this chapter, I identify the contracting stages and the issues that often arise in each one, principles for dealing with these issues, and the elements of an effective facilitation contract.

WHY CONTRACT?

Contracting occurs generally between the time I initially speak with someone from the client organization and the time the client group and I reach agreement about the goals of the facilitation and the conditions under which the facilitator and group are to work together. Additional contracting may, and often does, occur at any time during the facilitation process.

Contracting has several related purposes. First and most obvious, it ensures that the group and I understand and are committed to the conditions that govern our working relationship. This involves clarifying expectations each of us has for the other: the objectives and boundaries of the facilitation, the ground rules for the group, issues of confidentiality, the roles of the facilitator and group members, how decisions are to be made, and when the facilitation ends.

Second, because contracting is like a microcosm of the larger facilitation, it gives the group members and me an opportunity to observe the other party work and to make a somewhat informed choice about whether we want to work with one another. Members can observe how I intervene in the group, and I can observe how they interact with each other and with me. These data help me anticipate some of the issues arising in the facilitation and the kinds of interventions I may need to make.

Third, the contracting process enables the group and me to develop the trust necessary for me to facilitate. Group members may wonder whether I will treat them fairly and if I can help them with the difficult conversation they have not been able to carry on effectively on their own. I ask members to describe the problems their group faces, the solutions they have tried, and sometimes how individuals have contributed to the problem as well as reduced it. These questions make group members vulnerable. Trust develops as they find that I can help the group discuss these topics in a way that does not place blame and that encompasses empathy and support, even while recognizing the ineffectiveness of the group's behaviors.

The contracting process also helps the client and me become comfortable with each other. When I begin contracting with a new client, I have a number of feelings. I am usually excited to be working with a new group, eager to see how I can help them, and a little anxious about whether I will like the client group members and they will like me. Client group members may be feeling wary about whether I am able to help them, excited about the possibility of improving their group, and vulnerable both for needing help in the first place and for my asking questions about problems within their group. As I learn about their situation and they learn about my approach, and as we reach agreement about how to work together, typically my concerns about whether I can help them and whether they will find my approach useful dissipate.

I have found that many of the problems I face during a facilitation stem from my not having addressed an issue in contracting. **Ineffective contracting almost invariably results in problems later in the facilitation process.** Or, as my colleagues and I like to remind each other, no bad contracting goes unpunished.

STAGES IN CONTRACTING

Contracting occurs in the predictable stages shown in Table 13.1, beginning with a discussion between some member of the client organization and me and ending with discussion between the entire client group and me. **Because the agreement sets conditions under which the group and I will work together, ultimately all members involved directly in the facilitation need to agree to the terms of the contract.** Their agreement ensures that members develop a contract that is based on valid information and free and informed choice. To

Table 13.1. Contracting Stages and Major Tasks

Stage	Major Tasks
1. Initial contact with a primary client group member	• Identify member of primary client group • Conduct initial diagnosis • Discuss approach to facilitation • Agree on whether or not to proceed; if so . . . • Set up meeting for stage two
2. Planning the facilitation	• Send letter to planning group about purpose and agenda for planning meeting; conduct diagnosis with full group or representatives of primary client group • Agree on facilitation objectives, agenda, ground rules, and other elements • Send tentative agreement to full client group • Check for any changes in conditions before actual facilitation occurs
3. Reaching agreement with the full primary client group	• Agree on objectives, identify expectations, and address any concerns • Agree on the agenda and time allocation • Agree on the process, including ground rules • Define roles
4. Completing and evaluating the facilitation	• Evaluate facilitation, using self-critiques • Evaluate contract

accomplish this, I first have to determine who the primary client is, meaning, what group I am facilitating.

In developmental facilitation and in long-term basic facilitation (that is, basic facilitation lasting more than a few sessions) in which the group is making a significant commitment of time, it is important that all members of the client group be involved in the contracting process after the initial contact. In short-term basic facilitation, it is often not feasible to include the whole primary client group in the entire contracting process. It is not necessary that all members participate in the full process. However, until the whole group concurs, all agreements between the primary client group representatives and me are tentative.

Stage One: Initial Contact with a Primary Client Group Member

The initial contact has a number of purposes. First, it lets me determine whether the contact person is part of the group asking for help and, as a result, whether and how to continue the initial discussion. Second, it helps me understand the client's situation, the extent to which the client contact can articulate the results the group wants, and the degree to which the client has already identified ways to solve the problem. Third, the initial contact gives the potential client information about my approach so the client can make an informed choice about whether to commit to using my services. Fourth, I decide whether I have the skills and interest and am available to help the client. Finally, I use the discussion to assess whether any conditions exist that would prevent the facilitation from being effective.

Determining Who the Client Is. I consider my *primary client* to be the group that has accepted responsibility for working on the issue—the group that I may eventually facilitate. **To ensure that the primary client group and the facilitator have valid information about the situation and that this group can make an informed free choice about working with the facilitator, only the primary client group can agree to work with the facilitator.**

However, as Edgar Schein (1987) has noted, the facilitator comes into contact with other kinds of clients who may or may not also be members of the primary client group (Figure 13.1). The *contact client* makes the initial contact with the facilitator. The contact client may be a staff member or a secretary who is not a member of the primary client group but who has been asked to contact a facilitator on behalf of the primary client. An *intermediate client* serves as a link between the contact client and the primary client and is involved in the early part of contracting; I might get a call from a secretary (contact client) who asks whether I am available to help her manager work with a group experiencing conflict. In conversation with the manager, it becomes clear that he is not seeking help for himself but for a group of employees. Human resource managers frequently serve as the intermediate client as they help find a consultant for another manager.

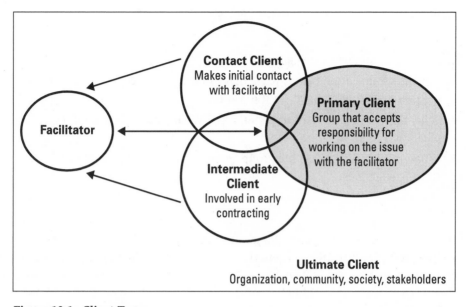

Figure 13.1. Client Types

Source: Adapted from Schein, 1987.

Finally, the *ultimate clients* are "stakeholders whose interests should be protected even if they are not in direct contact with the consultant or manager" (Schein, 1987, p. 125). The ultimate clients include the organization as a whole, the customers who use the services of the organization or buy its products, and the larger community or society. As Figure 13.1 shows, an individual may fall into more than one category.

Working with the Contact Client. Because only the primary client group has the information necessary, and the ability to contract with, the facilitator, I quickly determine whether the contact client is a member of the primary client group. I ask what group would be using my services and whether the caller is a member of that group. After I have determined this, I then ask a series of questions and share relevant information. Exhibit 13.1 lists the questions that I ask a contact client.

If I learn that the contact client is not a member of the primary client group, I ask who the primary client group is, explain why I need to talk with a member of that group, and give the contact client sufficient general information about me to share with the primary client, who can decide whether to contact me.

Who Is the Primary Client? Determining the identity of the primary client is not always easy. In one case, Ken, a county manager, called me to seek help for his public works director, Harris; some employees felt Harris had acted in a racist manner when he fired an African American employee. Ken stated that

Exhibit 13.1. Questions for the Initial Contact

1. Who is seeking the services?

2. Are you a member of this group?

3. Has the group committed to particular times for the work? How much has the group already planned for this work?

4. What does the group want to accomplish? What leads you to want to accomplish this?

5. What problems, if any, is the group experiencing? Can you give some specific examples?

Harris was interested in getting help and asked if I would come in, interview people, and give him (Ken) a report. I described my role and explained how giving him a report would be inconsistent with my role as facilitator. I then said that if Harris was interested in working with me, I would be happy to talk with him. I stated that if I did work with Harris, Ken was, of course, free to talk with Harris about the facilitation, but I would not discuss the content of the facilitation with Ken. Because Ken had described Harris and his staff as having the problem, I defined my primary client as the group that included Harris and his employees.

In another case, Warren, a human resource executive from a global bank, called to see if I could help Eduardo, a senior executive, and Helene, one of Eduardo's direct reports. The employees who reported to Helene and Eduardo considered Helene autocratic. Eduardo also believed he needed to improve his own relationship with Helene. In this case, Eduardo was a primary client because he had expressed responsibility for part of the problem—his relationship with Helene. Helene's employees were also primary clients because they were willing to discuss their ineffective relationship with their boss. However, Helene was only potentially a primary client, because she had not yet expressed an interest in working on the problem identified by her boss. The principle here is that **individuals are not primary clients until they have made a free and informed choice to ask for the facilitator's help.**

When There Is No Primary Client. In some cases, the contact client may represent a primary group that does not yet exist. The executive director of a health care foundation called to ask whether I would be interested in facilitating a large commission to deal with health policy. The commission would comprise public and private leaders, and its report would be used to draft legislation. The foundation would appoint the commission, but no members had yet been appointed, nor had the commission chair been selected. Further, no member of the foundation, including the executive director, would be a member of the commission, so there was no primary client.

I talked with the executive director about how I could work with the commission but stated that the commission members, when appointed, would need to decide whether they wanted to work with me.

The situation is not unusual. Organizational planners, working on projects that may use a third-party facilitator, often try to identify a facilitator who can be available to the group immediately after it is formed.

After determining that the contact client is not a primary client, I might say something like, "I'd be glad to talk with you in general about what I do as a facilitator. However, to figure out whether I can be of help to your organization, I need to talk with the person who heads the group I'll be meeting with. This gives the person and me a chance to make sure that we clearly understand the situation. Do you see any problem in doing this?"

On the basis of the principle that **the primary client is responsible for seeking help,** I prefer that primary clients call me if they are still interested. This reduces the chance that I will call a primary client who is not ready to pursue the conversation with me.

When the Contact Client Is a Primary Client Group Member. When the contact client is a primary client, I use the initial conversation to begin to understand the client's situation, identify factors that might affect the success of the facilitation, determine whether I have the skills and interest to facilitate, and discuss my approach to facilitation.

Some primary clients are not sure what kind of help they need. Others have already defined the problem or opportunity, have identified a specific process for me to facilitate, and want to know whether I can deliver the service requested. In the latter case, I am more useful in exploring with the client how they reached their diagnosis and proposed process, so that I can make my own judgment about the issue, and talk with the client about how our views may differ.

A manager asked that I work with him and his board to develop funding priorities for the county. According to the manager, the board had functioned by funding projects piecemeal, without a consensus on a larger set of goals to be accomplished. In our conversation, the manager also said that his relationship with the board was strained. The board had circumvented his hiring authority and did not involve him in other important decisions. It became clear to me that the strained relationship between the manager and board would make it difficult for the group to set funding priorities. The manager agreed with me but was reluctant to discuss the relationship, fearing that the situation would become worse. After discussing what could be done to reduce his concerns, he agreed to discuss the relationship with the board. Had I accepted the manager's definition of the problem, I would have worked with the board without understanding the full problem and thereby hindered the chance of their accomplishing the task.

So that clients do not misinterpret the reason for my questions, I share my reasoning with them. After the client briefly describes the situation, I might say, "To figure out whether and how I can help you, I'd like to ask you some questions that improve my understanding of your situation and how you see it. Then I can share my thoughts with you and get your reaction. How does that sound as a next step?"

Diagnosing the Situation and Pertinent Factors. Sometimes a person seeks help to solve a problem with how a group is functioning, that is, to close a gap between what they are currently doing and some desired situation; as an example, perhaps they are managing a conflict or attempting to improve service quality. At other times, a group seeks help not because the members face a problem but because they are creating something new (a division, direction, or plan). Exhibit 13.2 lists questions that I ask in the initial conversation with the primary client. The questions aid in identifying the client's problem or opportunity, the impact on the group, and the potential causes of the issue or change. The questions also explore the client's motivation and resources for change, as well as experience the client has had with facilitators and how the current re-

Exhibit 13.2. Questions for the Primary Client Group Member

Problem-Focused Issues

Identifying Problems

1. Describe to me the problems the group is having. What are some specific examples?

2. What do members in the group do (or not do) that you see as a problem? What are some specific examples?

3. How widespread are the problems? Do they occur all the time or only under certain conditions or with certain individuals?

4. When did the problems begin? What else was occurring at that time or shortly before the problems began?

5. How do members contribute to the problems? How do you contribute to the problems?

Consequences for Group Effectiveness

6. What are the consequences of these problems? How do the problems affect the group's ability to produce quality products or deliver quality ser-

Exhibit 13.2. *(continued)*

vices? work together? meet individual members' needs? What are some specific examples?

Potential Causes: Process, Structure, Organizational Context

7. What do you think are the causes of the problems? What have you seen or heard that leads you to think these are the causes?

8. How does the group solve problems and make decisions? communicate and manage conflict? coordinate its work with others in the organization? Do any of these seem related to the problems you described? If so, how?

9. Does the group have clear goals? Are members motivated by their tasks? Does the group have the right kind of members to do its work? Do members understand and agree on their roles? Do they have enough time to do their work? What kinds of behavior do members expect of each other? What are the core values and beliefs that members share about work? Do any of these seem related to the problems you described? If so, how?

10. How does the organization help or hinder the group? Is there a clear mission and a shared vision? Is the culture supportive? How are group members rewarded? Does the group get enough information to do its work? enough training and other resources? appropriate physical space to work in? Do any of these seem related to the problems you described? If so, how?

11. What is the history of the group? How has the membership and leadership changed?

12. How do you think other people in the group would identify the problems and their causes? Would others see things differently? If so, how?

Opportunity-Oriented Issues

13. What are you trying to create? Does this exist in some form currently? If so, what does it look like?

14. What has led the group to create this now? How will creating this have an impact on people and on things that are happening in your group and organization?

15. What barriers do you or others anticipate facing as the group seeks to create this? What is in place in your group or organization that will help the group create this?

Motivation and Resources for Change

16. What, if anything, have you tried to do to improve the situation or create this? What were the results?

Exhibit 13.2. *(continued)*

17. What are the sources and degree of members' motivation to work on this issue? What leads members to want to work with a facilitator?

18. What are the group's strengths? How does the group act effectively?

Experience with Consultants and Current Request for Help

19. Have you used other facilitators in the past, either for this situation or others? What role did the facilitator play? What were the results? What did the facilitator do that members found helpful and not helpful?

20. What has led you to contact someone now? What has happened or is about to happen in the group or organization?

21. How did the idea to call me in particular come about? Who initiated it? How was it received by other group members?

22. How do you see me helping the group accomplish its objectives?

quest for help came about. I do not ask all of these questions for each client, but rather select them according to the client's situation. You may need to modify some questions according to the specific purpose of the facilitation.

My goal is not to develop a complete diagnosis of the client's situation—that is impossible to achieve in one conversation—but rather to begin the diagnosis and determine whether facilitation is an appropriate method for helping the client. A skilled facilitator is flexible enough to begin diagnosing where the client begins the story, rather than forcing the client to respond in an order predetermined by the facilitator. In fact, **a general principle underlying diagnosis and intervention is to begin with the client's interests and concerns.**

Identifying Problems, Consequences, and Potential Causes. Together, the questions about problems, consequences for effectiveness, and potential causes focus on the elements of the group effectiveness model discussed in Chapter Two. The questions about problems do not correspond to a particular element in the model. Instead, they give clients a chance to begin describing the problem as they see it.

Motivation and Resources for Change. A group needs a threshold level of motivation to change behavior. In other words, the group needs to experience a certain level of pain (Levinson, 1972) or aspiration before its members are willing to devote energy to changing their behavior. The motivation may be internal or external. One major premise of this book is that members are more committed to action taken when they are internally motivated. Not all motivation for change, however, stems from dissatisfaction with past or current performance. Some groups that are satisfied with their current performance are motivated to improve their effectiveness because they anticipate future conditions requiring a higher level of performance.

A group seeking help is not necessarily interested in changing its behavior (Blake and Mouton, 1983). A group may seek a facilitator, hoping that person will take responsibility for actions that the group finds threatening. For developmental facilitation, identifying the level and source of the motivation for change can help determine whether the group is able to sustain the energy to change its behavior and to maintain new behaviors.

Sometimes, a critical incident has occurred and is the immediate motivation for change. For example, the chief operating officer (COO) of a medical clinical research organization contacted me after one of her key direct reports left the organization because a long-term conflict between divisions was not addressed. With this incident, the COO realized how much of a negative impact the conflict was generating.

A group needs resources to change, including time and organizational support, which means information, training, and money. As with other significant group changes, a group's performance level is likely to decrease temporarily as it learns the new behaviors resulting from developmental facilitation. This requires that the group have enough organizational slack (Cyert and March, 1963)—some unused capacity—to buffer it from negative consequences that might otherwise flow from decreased performance.

A more subtle resource is a group's strengths. When a group approaches a facilitator for help, it is easy to focus only on its weaknesses, ignoring its strengths. Understanding the group's strengths, however, helps me assess the foundation upon which the group can design new behavior.

Experience with Other Facilitators and Current Request for Help. The group's experience with other facilitators creates expectations about future efforts. By learning how previous facilitators worked with the group and how the group found those facilitators helpful or not helpful, I can identify what the group might expect from me and what issues are likely to arise. In addition, I can ask directly what kind of behavior the group expects from me.

Understanding how the client came to contact me is also useful diagnostic information. Knowing who referred the client to me is information about the client's expectations. Finding out whose idea it was to contact me, how the idea was received, and who was involved in deciding to make the contact can also offer information regarding support for me and for facilitation in general.

Describing Your Approach to Facilitation. At some point during the conversation with the primary client group member, I describe my approach to facilitation so that the client can make an informed choice about whether to use me.

This includes identifying the core values and beliefs that guide my behavior, distinguishing between basic and developmental facilitation, describing my role as facilitator, and explaining how all this translates into working with the client. The challenge is to describe my approach without using the jargon of facilitation.

By describing my approach in the latter part of the conversation, I can use my own behavior in the conversation to describe how I would work with the group. I might say, "Let me briefly describe how I work as a facilitator and get your reaction. As a neutral party, I do not offer my opinion about the content of your discussions, but I will help the group have an effective conversation. I use a set of core values to guide my work: valid information, free and informed choice, internal commitment, and compassion. In plain English, this means that I will help the group discuss the issues in such a way that they can share all the relevant information, agree on what is occurring, understand and appreciate each other's needs and concerns, and reach decisions in a way that all members are committed to.

"I also use a set of ground rules that make the core values concrete and help the group increase its effectiveness. Let me give you a few examples. One ground rule is to test assumptions and inferences. I used that ground rule a few minutes ago; I asked if you had asked Alan whether he thought you were micromanaging the group or whether you were just guessing that he felt that way. Another ground rule is to explain reasoning and intent. I was using this ground rule when I explained earlier why I wanted to ask you a series of questions. Another ground rule is to keep the discussion focused.

"In short, when I work with a group, if I think people are saying or doing something that makes the conversation less effective than it could be, I will point out what I am seeing, ask if people see it differently, and if they do not, then I ask if the group member or members would be willing to say it in a way that is consistent with the ground rules. What are your thoughts about how I would work with your group?"

If the group is seeking developmental facilitation, I offer a much more detailed explanation and have a conversation with the client group about whether they want to learn this approach to build their own capacity.

Assessing Your Interest and Ability to Help. Assuming that facilitation is appropriate for the client's request, during the initial conversation I let the primary client know whether I have the ability to help and whether am interested. I usually decline requests for what my colleague Peg Carlson calls "Vanna White facilitation" (named after the "Wheel of Fortune" game show cohost, whose onstage role largely involves turning letters on a large game board), in which the facilitator helps the group move through a very structured agenda with set presentations or exercises that prevent members from surfacing and dealing with difficult issues. I prefer to facilitate groups in which I have more opportunity to use my skills to help members address difficult issues.

Some facilitators are not interested in working with a group that seeks to accomplish objectives at odds with their own strongly held values and beliefs. If you believe strongly that women have the right to control their reproductive lives, you may not be interested in facilitating a group that is seeking ways to make abortion illegal. Similarly, if you believe that life begins at conception and that the rights of that life take precedent over a woman's right to control her reproductive life, you not be interested in facilitating a group that is seeking ways to increase women's access to abortion. Whether a facilitator's interest in working with a client should be influenced by such personal values is an individual choice. In any event, being aware of your personal values and how they may affect your interest in working with particular client groups is an important step in becoming a skilled facilitator.

The initial phone call with a member of the primary client group may take from fifteen minutes to more than an hour, depending on how complex the situation is, and on how much the client understands about facilitation in general and the Skilled Facilitator approach in particular.

Summarizing and Agreeing on Next Steps. Once I have enough information to make an initial diagnosis, I share it with the primary client group member and determine if he or she sees things differently. Assuming the issues are appropriate for facilitation and I am interested and able to help, I describe how I think I can be most effective with the group, and then I ask for the client's reactions.

I also identify any decisions or tentative decisions the client group has made that are likely to reduce its ability to achieve stated objectives; I ask whether the client group is willing to reconsider those decisions. For example, I may note that the time the group has allocated is insufficient for the objectives it wants to accomplish. Or I may point out that excluding certain individuals is likely to reduce the group's ability to actively discuss the issues on which it seeks consensus. If any group decision is likely to reduce the group's effectiveness to the point where I am unwilling to facilitate unless the decision is changed, I state that, share my reasoning, and ask for the client's reaction.

Finally, the client and I agree on the next steps. If the client is interested in pursuing my help, the next step is for the client to discuss our conversation with representatives of the various parts of the primary client group. If these members are interested, the contact client can arrange a conference call or meeting with the primary client group representatives and me.

Stage Two: Planning the Facilitation

In the planning stage for basic facilitation, I meet either with the entire primary client group or a subset of the group, including the group member who made the initial contact. In developmental or long-term basic facilitation (or, when possible, in short-term basic facilitation), I meet with the entire client group. This planning meeting frequently lasts about two hours. If the facilitation issues are complex, or if there are significantly different points of view about how the facilitation should proceed, the meeting can take longer.

The purposes of this stage are to (1) continue to explore the client's request for help and the factors that affect facilitation, (2) tentatively plan the agenda, and (3) agree on conditions for the facilitation. In the planning session (or sessions, if we need more than one), the client group and I discuss the same kind of information that the primary client member and I discussed in our initial conversation (see Exhibits 13.1 and 13.2), but in greater depth. We also discuss and agree on the conditions of the facilitation and logistical issues, questions for which are listed in Exhibit 13.3. (Resource B describes issues to consider for some of the questions in Exhibit 13.2.) Ideally, the planning meeting is face-to-face, but I also conduct meetings by video or teleconference, depending on what is feasible.

Before the planning meeting, I send a brief letter to the primary group members (through the initial primary group contact) asking that it be distributed to

Exhibit 13.3. Questions for Developing an Effective Contract

1. Who is the primary client, and who will attend meetings?
   a. Will there be others who provide expert information?
   b. Will there be any other observers?
   c. Will any media reporters attend?
   d. Do the participants include those necessary for identifying and solving the problems?
   e. Are any participants included who are not necessary for identifying and solving the problems?
2. What are the objectives of the meetings?
   a. Is the facilitation basic or developmental?
   b. Do the objectives meet the needs of all participants?
3. What are the agendas for the meetings?
   a. Do the agendas meet the needs of all participants?
   b. Do the agendas make effective use of the facilitator's skills and the presence of all participants?
4. Where and how long will the group meet?
   a. Do the location and facilities encourage full, uninterrupted attendance, without distraction?
   b. Is the location considered a neutral site by all participants?
   c. Are the facilities informal enough to encourage open discussion yet formal enough to permit concentration on the work?
   d. Is the location consistent with the image the organization wants to project?
   e. Is the amount of time allocated sufficient to accomplish the objectives?

all members invited to attend the planning meeting. (Resource A presents a sample letter.) In the letter, I explain the reason for the planning meeting, state the objectives, and offer a proposed agenda. I usually include copies of two articles for each person: "A Consumer's Guide to Hiring and Working with a Group Facilitator" (Schwarz, 2002a), which explains the Skilled Facilitator approach to working with groups, and "Ground Rules for Effective Groups" (Schwarz, 2002b), which describes the ground rules of the Skilled Facilitator approach. (Both articles are available through the Roger Schwarz & Associates Web site at www.schwarzassociates.com.)

By including all the members or representatives of the client group, I learn how members' views are similar or differ. This also enables me to watch (or listen to) the group in action—a rich source of diagnostic data. It also ensures that if there are differing views about what the facilitation process and my facilitation role should be, we resolve them before the actual facilitation meeting.

Exhibit 13.3. *(continued)*

5. What are the roles of the parties?
   a. Facilitator?
   b. Leader?
   c. Members?
6. What ground rules will the group follow?
   a. What ground rules do participants commit to following in the meetings?
   b. Will the group make decisions? How?
   c. What limits, if any, will the facilitator and members put on confidentiality?
7. How will the group assess its progress?
   a. Will the group critique its meetings?
   b. What other methods will the group use to assess progress?
8. How will the facilitator's performance be assessed?
   a. Will the facilitator do a self-critique?
   b. Do members agree to give the facilitator feedback at the time of the behavior?
9. What are the facilitator's fees and other charges?
10. How long will the contract be in effect?
11. When and how is the contract changed?
    a. Will each party discuss changes in the agreement before unilaterally changing it?
    b. What does the facilitator require of the client before discontinuing the contract?
12. How and when will the tentative contract be conveyed to all parties?

Who Should Be Involved? In basic facilitation, if the entire group is unable to plan the facilitation, then I ask for a subset of the group to be selected. A subgroup includes any formal group that is represented within the larger group (say, several functions within a division, or people at a number of physical locations) as well as any group of members who see themselves as distinct in some way that is related to the group's task (members who have the same race, sex, or professional background). This includes members who hold similar views regarding a particular group issue.

Finding a Representative Subgroup. If the planning group includes members who can represent the relevant formal and informal subgroups, it increases the chance of the facilitator understanding divergent views on the issues and helps the group craft an agenda that everyone can support. A board of education and its superintendent once asked me to facilitate a discussion regarding the superintendent's performance after the board had voted (four to three) to reduce the superintendent's salary supplement. In this case, the formal subgroup representatives included the superintendent and the board chair. However, it was critical to involve two informal subgroups for planning: the groups voting for and against reducing the salary. Because the chair had voted to reduce the salary, we included an additional member who had influenced others to vote against reducing the salary. Together, the three members represented the relevant subgroups and points of view reflected in the full group.

The definition of the primary client often shifts, typically to become more inclusive, as the facilitator finds out more about the issues facing the group. In contracting with a group of school administrators and faculty members who were in conflict over the form of school governance, I saw that the group did not adequately represent the range of opinions among the faculty and administration. At my suggestion, the group decided to expand its number, thereby increasing the size of the primary client group.

It is not always feasible to include representatives of all subgroups or points of view in the planning stage, particularly if the number would be large. However, if a significant representative of a formal or informal subgroup is absent, this can have negative consequences later in the contracting stage, during the facilitation, or even afterward. A member who is excluded from (or is invited to but does not attend) the planning process may decide not to participate in the facilitated sessions, may disagree with the agenda when it is discussed with the full client group at the first meeting, or may not attend the facilitation and then fail to support the decisions in it. I facilitated a meeting of a religious organization's board of directors. The entire board was invited to the planning meeting, but one long-time member who many board members found difficult to work with did not attend the planning session, stating that retreats were "not my thing." By the end of the retreat, the board had agreed to significant changes in how they would operate, but the directors then expressed concern that the absent board member might not agree to the changes because he had not been part of the process.

The Problem with Delegating Planning. In some cases, a problem arises when the formal leader of the primary client group delegates the planning to others. The secretary of a state agency had delegated the planning for a facilitated retreat to a deputy secretary and a planning manager, both of whom were members of the primary client group. After the initial contact with the planning manager, I reluctantly agreed to plan the retreat with the planning manager and deputy director, with the condition that we would jointly meet with the secretary for the final planning session. In the first two planning meetings, the planning manager and deputy director emphasized that the secretary wanted the retreat to focus on long-term planning. However, in the final planning meeting, in which the deputy secretary, planning manager, and I presented the tentative plan to the secretary, the secretary emphasized the need to focus on team building, given a recent reorganization. As a result, we had to redesign the sessions.

This case raises the general question, Under what conditions can the leader of a primary client group delegate responsibility for planning the facilitation? The question engages the facilitator in the dilemma of choosing between direct access to the top executive and accepting the legitimacy of the organization's natural decision-making process. If the top executive delegates the planning, the facilitator is unable to directly understand her goals and expectations. Also, the top executive's role is likely to require her to take certain personal risks, to which others cannot commit her. However, requiring the top executive to be involved in the planning process may be inconsistent with the organization's normal delegation process. A solution to the dilemma lies in satisfying the interests that drove the decision to delegate, in a way that also meets the facilitator's needs. For example, the top executive may be involved briefly in the planning process initially and then again near the end of the planning process—or at the end of planning, as in my case.

Whether to Meet in a Group or Individually. Sometimes the client asks me to meet individually with group members or with a subgroup before I meet with the full planning group. I usually receive this type of request when the group is experiencing conflict. Once I was asked to facilitate a meeting of the executive director and key individuals in a public health research organization. The executive director asked for my help in part because several incidents in the organization had led her to believe that people were concerned about trusting her. Even before the planning meeting, the executive director told me that individuals would prefer to meet with me individually to discuss the retreat.

In another case, I was asked to facilitate resolution of a dispute between a developer and a town council that was being sued by the developer for not approving a subdivision plan. If the facilitation was successful, the developer would withdraw the lawsuit. The town council wanted to meet with me individually (in a session legally closed to the public) to assess my acceptability to them and to share their concerns with me. The attorney for the developers also wanted to talk with me privately to see whether I was acceptable to her client.

The Dilemma of Individual Meetings. Situations of this kind create a dilemma. If I meet with group members individually or in a subgroup, they may be forthright with information about issues that concern them, especially if I agree to keep their comments confidential. However, if the conversation is to be confidential, I cannot share this useful information with the full group. In addition, I may find myself suggesting a process without being able to share my reasoning, because it involves information I agreed to keep confidential. Even if I have permission to share information from an individual session, I risk leaving the facilitator role by shifting the responsibility for raising group issues away from the group and on to myself. This could lead to a situation in which I raise an issue that was shared in an individual meeting, only to have group members state in the full group that this is not an issue.

If I do not meet with individuals or a subgroup, I avoid these problems, but the potential is high for creating others. If members are reluctant to share information in the full group, I may not find out about important group issues or dynamics until I begin the actual facilitation, and some issues may not be raised at all. Though all of this may slow the group's progress, members are making a free and informed choice about what relevant information they are willing to share.

Managing the Dilemma. In a situation like this, I typically ask to talk at first with the members as a group, if they are willing. This gives me an opportunity to discuss the dilemma that the group and I face, talk with the group about the concerns they have about sharing information in the planning session or facilitation, and inquire about what leads to these concerns. If members are willing to share some of their concerns, I then ask, "What would need to happen for you to be willing to raise and address these concerns?" If group members agree to these conditions (for example, no retribution for raising an issue), they can then discuss issues that they previously chose not to discuss. This was the outcome in the example of the public health research organization.

Whenever members' concerns about sharing information in the full planning group were discussed, I have never had a group state they were unwilling to continue planning in the full group. If it were to happen, however, I might agree to talk to individuals or a subgroup if the planning group (1) agreed on how the information discussed in the private meeting would be shared in the full group and (2) agreed that the responsibility for raising issues remained with group members.

On a few occasions, I have agreed to meet individually with parties before meeting as a full planning group. One instance was the town council–developer case; others were union-management meetings in which the parties had a long-term adversarial relationship and members would not meet together first. This is a difficult situation for the client. They want the relationship with the other parties to be different, but they are concerned about taking the risks involved in changing the relationship. I listen to the parties' concerns, showing compassion for their situation without suggesting that they are right and others are wrong. I may also point out how their behavior contributes to the kind of reaction in others that they are concerned about. I help them explore how they can raise the issues they want to discuss, including their concerns about doing so. I may even role-play with them to find the words to do this. In this situation, I let members know that I cannot raise their issues for them, but once they do so I will use my facilitating skills to help them have as constructive a conversation as possible.

Underlying all of my choices to meet as a full group whenever possible is the principle that **the facilitator seeks to create the conditions in which members can publicly share as much information as possible in a way that permits each member to make a free and informed choice about the risk of sharing the information.**

Deciding What Ground Rules to Use and How. A central part of the Skilled Facilitator approach is the core values and ground rules. I use them as the basis for diagnosing and intervening in the group, and I ask group members if they are willing to commit to using them as well. In the letter I send to members before the planning meeting, I include copies of the "Ground Rules for Effective Groups" article, describing the core values and ground rules. I state that the ground rules are an important part of my facilitation and that I will advocate that they also use the ground rules, if they are willing. I ask them to read the article so that at the planning meeting we can discuss their questions and concerns. On the belief that group members will support what they have developed, some facilitators ask the group to develop a set of ground rules. Because some of these facilitators also have their own ground rules, they privately hope that group members will identify ground rules that coincide with their own. If this does not happen, sometimes these facilitators may even put their ground rules in place, either by rephrasing group members' suggestions for ground rules or by suggesting some of their own.

I believe that group members do not have to develop their ground rules to be committed to them; rather, they need to make a free and informed choice to use them. As group process experts, we should have a clear idea what kinds of ground rules lead to more effective group behavior. Sharing this expertise is consistent with our facilitator role. By discussing the ground rules, I make explicit the kind of group behavior that I consider effective and that I will be helping group members use. Because the ground rules are so central to my approach to facilitation, in the planning meeting I advocate for the set of ground rules that I have developed, explain the reasoning underlying them, and encourage members to raise questions and concerns they have about using these ground rules.

Group Choices. The group has several choices to make regarding the ground rules. First, the members must decide whether they are willing to have me use the ground rules to intervene with the group. Because the ground rules are central to my approach, if the group chooses not to have me use them, then they are also choosing not to use me as their facilitator. If this occurs (and it has not yet), I would find out what the group's concerns were, and if I could not meet the concerns then I would help the group find another facilitator. The second choice the group has to make is whether to commit to practicing the ground rules during the facilitation. The group can revisit this choice if, after practicing the ground rules and understanding them better, members have new concerns about using them.

In the course of making the first two decisions, the group and I make a third decision: whether to add, delete, or modify any ground rules. A group might add a ground rule about whether the information discussed in the meeting is confidential (this is fairly common). Here, my interests are that any change in the ground rules be consistent with the underlying core values; if ground rules are deleted, it does not entirely limit me as the facilitator from intervening on behavior that is decreasing the group's effectiveness.

Putting the Tentative Agreement in Writing. If by the end of the planning meetings the planning group and I have agreed to work together, we reach tentative agreement about the issues discussed in Exhibits 13.1, 13.2, and 13.3. Following the planning meetings, I send a memo of understanding to all members of the group, stating my understanding of the agreement that the planning group and I have reached. I include a copy of my article on ground rules, explaining that I will use them to facilitate and (if we have agreed) will ask them to use the ground rules also. Finally, I ask members to contact me if their understanding about the facilitation differs from mine. Resources C and D are sample agreements for basic and developmental facilitation, respectively.

For two reasons, I find it helpful to put the tentative agreement in writing. First, the full client group often does not participate in the planning stage, but the agreement remains tentative until the full group gives its consent. Putting the agreement in writing enables all group members to read the agreement before the facilitation and raise any questions or concerns they might have. Second, a written agreement enables the client group and me to easily check back if at a later date there are questions about what we agreed to do or how we agreed to do it. If you are concerned that your clients may see a formal agreement as rigid or unchangeable, you may want to state clearly in the tentative agreement that it is open to modification and that you encourage members to review the agreement and suggest modifications during the course of the working relationship. I also regularly ask clients how the current contract is or is not meeting their needs.

Meeting Briefly with Planning Representatives. The final step of the planning stage is a brief conversation between planning representatives and me. Shortly before the facilitation is to begin, I check with the planning representatives to see whether anything has changed that might affect the contract or the facilitation. For developmental or long-term basic facilitation, the conversation is relevant each time the group is about to meet. Both conversations are based on the principle that **the facilitator regularly seeks to determine whether conditions that might affect the contract or the facilitation have changed.** I might say, "I'm wondering, has anything happened or changed since we last talked that might affect the facilitation, including how people feel about it?" If not everyone who is expected to attend has arrived, I share that observation, ask whether someone is unable to attend, and find out the reason.

These simple questions help me determine whether to change how I intervene in the group or even whether to reach a new contract agreement. For example, in working with a group of school administrators and faculty who were trying to resolve a difficult conflict, I asked someone before a meeting if anything was new. I was informed that the executive director—who was a focal point of the conflict—had announced his resignation, effective at the end of the school year. Given this, I began the session by asking the group in what way his resignation affected our work together and whether we should change the contract.

In the premeeting conversation, the client and I also clarify who will handle each of the initial meeting functions: starting the meeting, introducing me as the facilitator, introducing other participants, describing the events that led up to the meeting, and the like. (Chapter Eleven addresses these initial meeting functions in detail.) These decisions may seem detailed and trivial, but by clarifying and coordinating the clients' role and mine, we reduce any anxiety that comes from wondering how the meeting will begin and ensure that it begins how we want it to.

Stage Three: Reaching Agreement with the Entire Group

In the third stage of contracting, the facilitator and the entire primary client group reach agreement on the key elements of the contract. In short-term basic facilitation, this conversation occurs in the beginning of the meeting after all the clients and I have introduced ourselves, and a planning group representative and I have described the planning process that has led to the current meeting.

I review each key element of the tentative agreement and for each one ask whether anyone sees any problems.

If the entire primary client group has attended the planning meeting, this stage of contracting is a quick review of the tentative agreement. If, however, some primary client group members have not been involved in the planning stage, or if the planning group has not represented the range of members' interests, this process may take more time and be more difficult as these members raise questions and concerns about the tentative agreement.

In Chapter Eleven (the sections on beginning and ending a meeting), I described in detail the steps I take and items on which I ask the group to agree at this point:

1. Make introductions.

2. Bring people up to date.

3. Agree on objectives, identify expectations, and address any concerns.

4. Agree on the agenda and time allocation.

5. Agree on the process, including ground rules.

6. Define roles.

Agreeing on the Ground Rules. If the entire primary client group attended the planning meeting, I quickly remind them of the ground rules and our agreement to use them. If the entire client group did not attend the planning meeting and the facilitation is a basic one, I find out whether participants have read the article on ground rules that was attached to the memo of agreement sent to them, and if so, what questions or concerns they have about using the ground rules. I then respond to their questions and concerns and briefly describe the ground rules, including how I would use them and how they might use them. Then I ask if people are willing to commit to using the ground rules during the facilitation. I also post a copy of the ground rules and give each participant his or her own pocket card version. (Both of these items are available at www .schwarzassociates.com.)

In my years of using the ground rules, few client group members have ever expressed concern about using the ground rules. (This may be partly because clients who hire me often know of my work and the ground rules.) If a member does express concern, the person generally sees the value of using the ground rules but worries that others may get defensive or that he or she would experience retribution for sharing real thoughts and feelings, including raising issues that have been undiscussable in the group. If a member raises these concerns, I find out more about them, which often leads me to correct a misunderstanding about what the ground rule means or illustrate how the person could use the ground rule to raise an issue while reducing the chance that others might react defensively. I make it clear that their choice to use the ground rules is a free one.

I also ask, "What, if anything, would need to happen in order for you to be willing to use the ground rules?" Sometimes participants are worried they will not use the ground rules effectively and must be assured that the group gives members the benefit of the doubt. At other times, a participant wants to be assured that there is no retribution for raising a difficult but relevant issue. Sometimes a member wants to add or modify a ground rule. After participants identify what has to happen for them to use the ground rules, I ask the group if they are willing to create these conditions for using the ground rules.

When I work with a group meeting to resolve a difficult conflict among members, I contract to spend more time discussing the ground rules. A city council that had recently expanded in size and was made up of several factions that were in conflict wanted to resolve things. They agreed to spend several hours learning how to use the ground rules and then begin the facilitation to resolve the conflicts. During the facilitation, council members used the ground rules, and afterwards they reported that the miniworkshop of several hours enabled them to work more effectively and efficiently during the facilitation. In a case like this, spending time initially helping group members learn the core values and ground rules can pay off in the long run.

Addressing Members' Concerns. Psychologically, this is a critical time in the facilitation for members who have not been involved in planning the facilitation. Having seen the tentative agreement in writing, they may wonder whether the objectives and agenda can be changed, whether they can influence the process, and if their interests are to be addressed. They may also wonder whether I, as the facilitator, will help them meet their interests.

Sometimes members are eager to get to the substantive topics of the facilitation and want to shorten or eliminate this beginning-of-meeting contracting with the full primary client group. They may feel frustrated spending time on what they consider unnecessary issues that everyone agrees on, or they may be worried that if I inquire about people's concerns with the tentative agreement, members will raise all kinds of objections and the group will never get to the content of the facilitation.

I respond to these concerns by pointing out that if the full group has no concerns about the tentative agreement, then the conversation will be very brief. If, however, there are concerns and the group does not identify or address them, they are likely to come out either during the meeting or, worse, after the meeting, as members voice their lack of commitment to the process. Spending the extra time in the beginning of the meeting reduces the chance that the group will need to invest even more time later.

Stage Four: Evaluating and Completing the Facilitation

In stage four, the client and I evaluate and complete the facilitation.

Evaluating the Facilitation. There are two separate but related foci for the evaluation: the actual facilitation and the underlying contract. Evaluating the actual facilitation involves exploring how the group members and I have acted to either enhance or reduce the group's effectiveness. Evaluating the contract involves assessing the extent to which the terms of the contract (which members should be involved, how frequently the group meets with the facilitator, and so on) meet the client's needs and mine.

Although I discuss it in the final stage, evaluating the facilitation or contract can occur at any time during a facilitation. Still, for long-term facilitation it is useful to set times for evaluating the contract regularly so the client and facilitator can decide how well it is serving their needs and make any necessary changes.

To evaluate the facilitation, I contract with the client to spend time at the end of each meeting to conduct a self-critique (or a plus-delta, as it is sometimes known). I begin by explaining that it helps the group and me to systematically learn from our mistakes and incorporate our successes in future meetings. In Chapter Eleven, I describe how to conduct a self-critique.

Completing the Contract. Deciding when a basic facilitation contract has been completed is relatively easy and can usually be determined before the actual facilitation begins. A basic facilitation contract, especially a short-term one, is normally designed around a specific date or set of dates on which I will work with the client. After I have worked with the client on these dates, the contract work has been completed. If I have contracted to help the group until it reaches decisions on some specified issues, the work is complete when the group has made the decisions.

Deciding when a developmental facilitation contract has been completed is more difficult and can rarely be identified before the facilitation begins. The client typically does not know enough about group process to specify in advance the level of skill they want to achieve. The group can make an informed choice only if they understand what effective group process is and how its own process falls short. Consequently, as a developmental facilitator I need to periodically help the group consider how much further it wants to improve its process skills.

At times, a facilitator or client wants to terminate a contract before the other party believes the agreed-upon work has been completed. The client may shift priorities or become dissatisfied with the facilitator's ability to help, or the facilitator may infer that the client is not sufficiently committed to the facilitation.

In contracting with a developmental client, I ask that I be allowed to meet with the client group one more time if it decides to prematurely terminate the contract. (If I have decided to prematurely terminate the contract, I discuss my decision with the client.) The debriefing meeting helps me understand why the client is terminating the contract, provides me with feedback about my own behavior, and allows the client and me to publicly test some assumptions about each other. Although my purpose for meeting is not to reestablish the contract, I do not rule out that possibility.

Whether it is you the facilitator or the client who wants to terminate the contract, you both may have strong feelings about what has led up to this situation. Client group members may feel angry because they believe their needs have not been met. You may feel angry because you believe the client was not committed enough to the facilitation. You may also feel shame because you did not know how to help the client address their issues. Whatever the feelings, exploring them with the client is important. Your feelings may stem from your inferences about what has happened and your attributions about why people have acted as they have. By sharing your feelings and exploring those of your clients, you can learn about how you and your clients have contributed to creating a situation neither wanted. By voicing and addressing the feelings, you can reach closure on them, and move on with your new learning.

SUMMARY

In this chapter, I have described the process that a client and I use to agree on whether and how we will work together. The four contracting stages are (1) initial contact with a primary client group member, (2) planning the facilitation, (3) reaching agreement with the full primary client group, and (4) completing and evaluating the contract.

Many problems that occur during facilitation are caused in part by ineffective contracting. The contracting process establishes an effective relationship between the client and the facilitator and greatly increases the chance that the facilitation will be effective. In the next chapter, we explore a factor that can significantly influence whether and how to work with another party: the option of using a cofacilitator.

CHAPTER FOURTEEN

Working with Another Facilitator

This chapter considers how two facilitators can work together with the same group. In the first part, I describe the advantages and disadvantages of cofacilitating and when it is beneficial. The second part of the chapter describes how cofacilitators can divide and coordinate their work. The last part discusses how the partners can reflect on their cofacilitation to improve it.

Facilitating a group is mentally challenging work. You need to simultaneously pay attention to content and process, verbal and nonverbal behavior, those who are speaking and those who are not, and what is apparently happening in the group compared to what has happened in the past and what will likely happen in the future. While considering all this, you also have to think about whether to intervene, what interventions to make and how, when to intervene, to whom to address the intervention, and the effects of the intervention on the group once made. Then you intervene. Quite often, you have to do all this in less time than it takes to read this paragraph.

Because of the high demands of the work, facilitators sometimes work together with the same group. In cofacilitation, both people are usually with the group at all times.

DECIDING WHETHER TO COFACILITATE: MANAGING TENSION

When cofacilitators work well together, both they and the group benefit; when they don't, everyone suffers. In this section, which is drawn largely from the work of J. William Pfeiffer and John Jones (1975), I describe tensions that cofacilitators need to manage. They arise from differences between the cofacilitators and from the simple fact of having two facilitators. **The underlying principle in choosing to cofacilitate is that together the cofacilitators can intervene in a greater range of situations and with greater skill than either facilitator can manage alone. Either their approaches need to be similar or they must be able to use their differences to benefit the group rather than hinder it.**

Congruent Versus Conflicting Theories-in-Use

Perhaps the most important factor in deciding whether to cofacilitate is the matter of the two theories-in-use. Facilitators with conflicting theories-in-use make fundamentally differing interventions with a group and will have a difficult time coordinating their work to help the group.

I discovered this in an early cofacilitation, when a colleague and I worked with a city council and the city manager. At one point early in the meeting, there was some disagreement among group members about which issues to address. My colleague called a break and then explained to me that he hoped to see how the manager wanted to proceed, explaining that it was the manager's choice. I saw the situation differently and explained that I considered the group as a whole to have the relevant information; I felt the choice was to be made in the group. My explanation raised more concerns for my cofacilitator, and in the minute that we had to resolve our difference, we reached a compromise to talk with the manager and then raise it in the full group. Yet, the solution compromised core values and assumptions for each of us. This turned out to be the first of many differences my cofacilitator and I had during the facilitation, most of which resulted from our contrasting theories-in-use; we turned our attention away from helping the group and toward working on our own conflict.

Incongruent theories-in-use can show up in an infinite number of ways. To take a simple example, facilitators who seek to unilaterally control the group may enforce a predetermined time frame for discussing agenda items, while those who seek to jointly control the process may ask group members if they want to alter the schedule as they proceed; this simple illustration points out the potential implications for the group's decisions. A facilitator who assumes that how he sees things is correct considers it unnecessary to test his inferences and may act on relatively high-level inferences without publicly testing them, whereas one using the Skilled Facilitator approach tends to make low-level inferences that she tests with the group before acting on them. Finally, a facilitator who values minimizing expression of negative feelings will craft interventions designed to bypass group member emotions, whereas a facilitator using the Skilled Facilitator approach tends to engage group members in exploring the roots of these emotions. In a study of coleaders of therapy groups—a role relationship similar to the cofacilitator's—difference in orientation (values and beliefs) was the reason most cited for not wanting to work together again (Paulson, Burroughs, and Gelb, 1976).

There are times when you may choose to work with another facilitator precisely because you have differing theories-in-use; the contrast can help both of you learn. Still, it is important to determine whether the differences between you and your potential cofacilitator's theories-in-use are great enough that your learning will come at the expense of helping the group.

Complementary Versus Competing Focus and Style

Even facilitators who share a theory-in-use may focus on different things in a group. Some focus more on helping individual members improve their communication skills; others focus more on improving group structure. The individual-level facilitator believes that the group is effective when individual members act effectively; the group-level facilitator believes that an effective group is more the result of group structure, such as group norms or a motivating task. Similarly, facilitators also have favorite interventions that follow from their preferred focus; as a result, they may make these interventions when some other one might be more appropriate.

When individual-level and group-level facilitators work together, they might compensate for each other's blind spots and misplaced interventions, rather than reinforce them, which occurs when cofacilitators have the same orientation.

Facilitators also have differing styles—the particular way in which they conduct themselves in applying their theory-in-use and focus. Style varies along many dimensions, including the facilitator's degree of seriousness versus humor, inclination toward confrontation, and the pace of intervention.

Here too, different styles can help the group so long as they are not incompatible. Cofacilitators can use the difference in pacing or sense of humor as the situation calls for it. However, largely divergent styles may lead group members to feel disjointed by having to continually adjust to two opposed styles (Paulson, Burroughs, and Gelb, 1976).

Being Overwhelmed Versus Overintervening

As a facilitator working alone, you may sometimes leave a session overwhelmed, feeling that much more was occurring in the group than you could even perceive, let alone intervene on. In addition, you may wonder whether your perception of the situation was realistic or distorted, even if you have checked out your inferences with the group. This often happens when there is a high level of overt activity or energy in the group; things are occurring at several levels simultaneously and at a fast pace; a high-conflict situation is one example. But you can also be overwhelmed by a level of activity that is not observably high, if every interaction seems laden with interpersonal issues in the group. Cofacilitating reduces the chance of being overwhelmed and gives you an opportunity to use your cofacilitator for reality checks. Cofacilitating is also useful when a group is large or the plan is to work part of the time in subgroups.

The extra capacity to intervene that cofacilitators can bring to the group can become a liability if it leads to excessive intervention. Facilitators have a need to feel useful, and we usually fulfill that need by intervening. However, at times one cofacilitator may have little opportunity for intervening because the partner is already making a necessary intervention. If facilitators attempt to meet their own needs rather than their clients', they may intervene unnecessarily and slow the group's progress. The problem can be reduced or prevented so long as each cofacilitator places the group's needs first and divides the labor so that each has ample opportunity to intervene. Finally, each facilitator can reframe the meaning of being useful to include refraining from unnecessary intervention.

Learning and Support Versus Competition and Control

Cofacilitation enables you to develop your professional skills by learning from and with a cofacilitator who has her own approach, technique, or style. During breaks and after the cofacilitation, you can converse with her about various interventions, inquiring what led her to make a particular intervention. If you would have intervened differently, you can share your reasoning and ask for her thoughts. In this way, you can use specific data to reflect on and learn about your facilitation.

In facilitation, the relationship between your personal development and professional development is strong; in cofacilitation, you can work on both simultaneously. To diagnose, intervene, and cofacilitate effectively, your personal issues should not distort your observations and inferences or inappropriately influence your actions. Personal issues include problems dealing with authority, ambiguity, control, commitment, status, and intimacy. A facilitator who has problems with authority, for example, may inappropriately confront (or avoid) the formal leader of a group. A facilitator who has problems with control may frequently interrupt while the cofacilitator is intervening.

When cofacilitators are willing to share their personal issues with each other, they can help each other become aware of how these issues affect their facilitation and explore how they might change their behavior as well as the values and assumptions that generate it. For example, through cofacilitating and coteaching facilitation, I have learned how my own seemingly well-intended interventions actually reduce my cofacilitator or coteacher's ability to establish a relationship with the group; similarly, my colleague has learned how she designs interventions that reduce group members' ability to disagree with her. In helping each other in this way, we are really serving as mutual developmental facilitators.

Paradoxically, the issues that are your food for learning are the same ones that can undermine your ability to cofacilitate and learn from the practice. Your unilateral control theory-in-use, mixed with your personal issues, can lead you to view cofacilitation as competition with your partner, instead of as an opportunity for colearning. When this occurs, the group loses as well.

Internal-External Versus Same-Role Cofacilitation

An internal facilitator is employed in the same organization as the group he facilitates. An external facilitator works for herself or another organization. An internal facilitator may seek an external cofacilitator to help with a large or difficult assignment; an external facilitator may seek an internal facilitator to build facilitation capacity in the organization and to better understand the organization's culture.

Although it is often inaccurate and generally inadvisable to classify people by groups, my experience and that of other consultants suggests that internal and external facilitators do have divergent perspectives given their position vis-à-vis the client organization. An internal facilitator is in a position to know the organization's culture and the unwritten rules about how things are done. He may even know some members of the client group and the problems they face. The group also has more access to the internal facilitator.

An external facilitator has the power of independence. She considers it less difficult to challenge the client and to raise important issues, even if it makes the group uncomfortable. She feels less pressure to evaluate clients, collude with them, play messenger, or act in any other way that weakens her ability to facilitate. Whereas the external facilitator may lose her client, the internal facilitator may lose his job.

An external facilitator may wish she had the internal facilitator's local knowledge, while the internal facilitator may wish he had the external facilitator's independence. As cofacilitators, they can have both.

But the reasons for collaborating are also sources of tension. When there is disagreement, the external facilitator may think the internal facilitator does not focus enough on process issues, is too deferential to authority, or is inhibited by the culture of the organization. He, conversely, may think she is too idealistic and challenging and does not appreciate the culture of the organization and the need for the group to get its work done. Because the tension stems from the role each facilitator has with the organization, it is likely to exist even between facilitators who have the same orientation, style, and cultural background.

Are the Benefits Worth the Investment?

In addition to the energy that every facilitator expends working with a group, cofacilitators expend energy coordinating their work with each other. First, they have to spend time talking with each other to determine whether they are compatible enough to cofacilitate. Second, if they decide to cofacilitate, they must plan how to manage differences in orientation and style. Third, they should divide the facilitation labor between themselves and develop a way to coordinate their division of labor. Some of this can be done "offline."

For example, before a session, the cofacilitators can plan how to divide up the opening remarks and how to hand off the lead role to one another during the session. Less predictable aspects of coordination can be partially planned but must also be partially coordinated online (that is, at the time of the intervention and in front of the group). As a simple illustration, if one facilitator agrees to write at the flipchart while the other intervenes (division of labor), both need a way to ensure that what (and when) one writes on the flipchart is congruent with the other facilitator's intervention (coordination). A much more difficult and frequent problem is to coordinate the interventions each cofacilitator makes so that together they help the group make progress, rather than take the group in opposing directions. Coordination is difficult because it can only be done online and must be continuous.

Aside from expending energy dividing and coordinating their labor, cofacilitators burn up psychological energy. Each one commonly worries that the partner will make a significant mistake, that it will be he or she instead who makes a mistake, or both. Finally, they can use psychological energy struggling with a tension inherent in collaboration: each person must temporarily yield some identity to the collaboration so that together they can become something neither alone can be (Smith and Berg, 1987).

A good way for cofacilitators to find out about each other's similarities and differences is to discuss the issues directly. You can use the questions and statements in Resource G to guide your conversation with a potential cofacilitator to decide whether you can work effectively, and to reach agreement about how to work together. Keep in mind that to obtain useful information, you need to go to the level of directly observable behavior. This means describing what each of you would think and say in specific instances.

At the end of the conversation, you and your potential cofacilitator can jointly decide whether to work together. But each of you must also decide whether the greater benefits from cofacilitation are worth the extra energy needed to coordinate the work.

DIVIDING AND COORDINATING THE LABOR

If you have decided to cofacilitate, you still need to decide how you and your cofacilitator will divide the work and coordinate your roles during the facilitation. Exhibit 14.1 lists six options; here we discuss the coordination challenges that arise from them. Although I present the possible division of labor as if each

Exhibit 14.1. Dividing the Facilitation Labor

- Intervener-recorder
- Primary-secondary
- Online-offline
- Task-relationship
- Intervention-reaction
- No explicit division of labor

pair were completely separate, that is not the case. By keeping an eye on your partner's domain, each cofacilitator facilitates coordination.

Intervener-Recorder

In the intervener-recorder arrangement, one facilitator intervenes while the other writes on the flipchart or uses some other technology to record the data. The technique is useful if the group is generating many ideas—as in brainstorming—and does not want to be slowed down by the facilitator's writing each idea before asking for the next one. Still, either the intervener or the recorder has to check that the written statements represent what the members have said.

Coordinating the two roles also requires that the cofacilitators and members agree on when a member's idea is to be written on the flipchart. This can be as direct as saying, "Let's write down all the potential causes of the delays." The issue is simple, but it can create problems if not addressed. Writing a member's idea on the flipchart symbolizes that the idea is valuable. A member whose contributions are not written down and does not know why may feel discounted and begin to distrust the facilitator and recorder. So if the recorder decides not to write down an idea, a brief explanation is appropriate. For example, the recorder might say, "Dan, I was asking for causes and your comment looks like a solution. Do you see it differently? [If not] Can you think of any causes?" In this way, the recorder temporarily becomes the intervener.

Primary-Secondary

In the primary-secondary arrangement, one facilitator is the primary facilitator for all interventions, while the other plays backup, intervening only when necessary. This works well if the group process is easy enough for one facilitator to manage or if the facilitators are concerned about intervening too much. It also gives the secondary facilitator a chance to rest.

The coordination problem here is that the secondary may intervene on some behavior that the primary intentionally avoids. For example, the primary facilitator may avoid clarifying an off-track disagreement among members and instead try to get the group on track. If the secondary facilitator jumps in and clarifies the disagreement, the clarification would continue to take the group off track. Although coordination problems can occur with any division of labor, here the problem is significant because the secondary facilitator is actively looking for opportunities that the partner missed. To reduce this problem, cofacilitators should understand each other's intervention orientation well enough so that they have a shared understanding about the conditions under which they would choose not to intervene.

Online-Offline

In the online-offline division of labor, one facilitator intervenes (online), while the other silently works on some task associated with the facilitation. The task could be how to describe a complex group pattern, how to spend the remaining facilitation time if the group has fallen behind schedule, or simply setting up an activity. This arrangement is useful when the cofacilitators need to solve a problem that is difficult to attend to while observing and intervening, and that is either not appropriate to raise with the group or not a good use of the group's time.

Task-Relationship

In this arrangement, both facilitators actively observe and intervene, but one focuses on what is referred to as task process while the other concentrates on relationship (or interpersonal) process (Schein, 1987). If, for example, a group is setting performance goals, the task-process facilitator focuses on the content by helping the group keep on track, think logically about what goals are needed, and establish clear goals. In contrast, the relationship-process facilitator pays more attention to the group's social and emotional interactions, by silently asking herself, *What do the members' words, style, and nature of discussion say about how they are feeling about the task, each other, and the two of us?* (Yalom, 1985).

Task-relationship is often a natural way for cofacilitators to divide the labor. Research shows that some people are predominantly task-oriented and others relationship-oriented (Bales, cited in Yalom, 1985; Blake, 1964). Task and relationship orientations are relative. Whether a cofacilitator is task- or relationship-oriented depends on the nature of the other's orientation. For example, I have two colleagues with whom I have cofacilitated. One is task-oriented and the other, though capable of being the same, also has a keen eye for relationship issues. My ability to diagnose relationship issues falls between those of my two colleagues. Consequently, when we divide our roles along this dimension, I assume the relationship role with one colleague and the task role with the other. This approach lets cofacilitators take advantage of their strengths. It works well when the group generates many task and relationship issues simultaneously.

Because a group—especially in basic facilitation—generally views task intervention as more appropriate than relationship intervention, the relationship cofacilitator often needs to clearly show how the relationship issue affects the group's ability to complete its task.

Intervention-Reaction

In the fifth division of labor, one facilitator concentrates on intervening with one or a few members, while the other pays attention to the rest of the group. The division is useful should one member be the subject of much intervention and other members are reacting strongly to the member's comments (or to intervention). A facilitator may have to spend several minutes questioning and supporting one member who hesitates to express strong dissatisfaction with the group, the organization, and the facilitation. Knowing the other members' reactions yields important diagnostic data.

The coordination challenge here involves knowing whether, and when, to shift the focus of the intervention from one member to the others' reactions. Should the second facilitator immediately point out the reactions, or wait until the first facilitator completes the intervention?

No Explicit Division of Labor

Having no *explicit* division of labor does not mean there is no division of labor. It means that each cofacilitator pays attention to what appears to need attention, without first talking with the other. Using this approach, they can instantly switch roles to adjust to the group's needs and the needs of the partner. The approach can respond quickly and potentially make the best use of the cofacilitators' skills.

As the least structured way to divide the labor, it is also the most difficult to coordinate. The cofacilitators risk intervening on the same issues while ignoring others, failing to capture members' ideas on the flipchart, and both going offline at the same time, thus temporarily abandoning the group. The approach works if the cofacilitators have worked together long enough and in enough situations to anticipate each other's moves and adjust automatically, just as improv actors respond to each other's lines.

It is not necessarily desirable for cofacilitators to use only one division of labor throughout an entire session. Skilled cofacilitators shift among the divisions of labor to meet the changing needs of the group.

ALLOCATING ROLES WITHIN A DIVISION OF LABOR

After selecting how you will divide your labor (intervener-recorder, task-relationship, and so on), you and your cofacilitator can decide who will play which role. In making this decision, you should consider a number of factors.

Skill with Potential Interventions

You and your cofacilitator can divide your roles so that the one who has primary responsibility for intervening is the more skilled at interventions. Even if it is not possible to predict the kinds of interventions you will have to make, you may quickly be able to identify a pattern in the kinds of interventions that you and your cofacilitator are making in a given session. Knowing this pattern, you and your partner can decide who is better suited to take the lead on these kinds of interventions.

Knowledge of Substantive Problems

Cofacilitators vary in their knowledge about the substantive problems their clients face. For example, I used to cofacilitate with a colleague who knows a lot about finance. When we cofacilitated a group that was discussing financial issues, he usually took the first role in the intervener-recorder, task-relationship, intervention-reaction, or primary-secondary divisions of labor. He could keep up when the discussion became so technical that I would have to slow the group's pace by frequently asking for definition of terms. (Here I am assuming that members agree on the definitions and would be clarifying them only for me.) Still, if a cofacilitator's knowledge about and interest in an issue tempts the facilitator to stray into the content of the discussion, the less-knowledgeable partner may choose the active intervention role.

Internal-External Differences

Similarly, the internal facilitator can often intervene easily in a highly technical discussion. In contrast, if the cofacilitators want to confront the group—especially about members' core values and beliefs—without raising the issue of the internal facilitator's credibility or seeming disloyal, the external facilitator may actively intervene. But in a developmental group, having the internal facilitator confront the group about its assumptions is powerful precisely because it can raise the issue of credibility and disloyalty. Done well, the cofacilitators can use members' reactions to the internal facilitator to discuss why members who challenge the assumption of the organization are seen as disloyal.

Pace

Cofacilitators can switch roles for each to assume the less active role when one gets tired. Cofacilitators can also take advantage of their contrasting pace by matching the needs of the group. For example, the faster-paced partner can actively intervene when the group is behind schedule and nearing the end of the session. The slower-paced partner can actively intervene when members are struggling to understand each other.

Training and Development

At times, a cofacilitator may choose to play a role to develop particular skills. This is a legitimate way to temporarily select a role, so long as the cofacilitator seeks feedback about performance from the partner and does not attempt intervention so far beyond his or her ability as to harm the client.

DEVELOPING HEALTHY BOUNDARIES BETWEEN COFACILITATORS

In a good cofacilitator relationship, you and your partner agree on when and how to modify each other's interventions, correct one another, reinforce the other's interventions, and help when one gets tangled in a conflict with the group. You do this in a way that integrates your skills while preserving your individual identity. It is a matter of setting boundaries (Alderfer, 1976). If you and your cofacilitator routinely interrupt and modify one another's interventions, both of you lose your individual identity, in addition to confusing the group. Conversely, if you never respond to each other, you do not get the full benefit of collaboration. You can discuss and agree on several issues before working with a group.

The Zone of Deference

An important part of intervening is knowing when not to. Organizational theorist Chester Barnard (1938) used the phrase "zone of indifference" to refer to the range within which employees obey orders without considering the merits of the order. I use the phrase *zone of deference* to describe the area in which one cofacilitator lets the other's interventions stand, although the former would intervene differently. Without an agreed-on zone of deference, cofacilitators may constantly correct each other's interventions, confusing the group in their attempt to make things clear. Or, to avoid being seen as nitpicking or overbearing, the cofacilitators may fail to modify any of the other's interventions, which deprives the group of the benefits of cofacilitation.

Here are some questions indicating issues that are outside the zone of deference and that typically lead me to intervene with my cofacilitator.

- *Will the client suffer harm?* The most elementary responsibility the facilitator has is to do nothing that harms the group. An intervention that causes harm might be deceiving or demeaning a member, cheating, breaking a promise, or disobeying the law (Gellermann, Frankel, and Ladenson, 1990). Making an intervention that is beyond the cofacilitators' skills can also harm the group.

- *Is the intervention inconsistent with the core values of facilitation or the ground rules?* Any intervention that is not based on valid information or that does not enable the group to make a free and informed choice that leads to internal commitment reduces the cofacilitators' effectiveness and integrity. Acting inconsistently with the ground rules has the same effect, because the rules are based on the core values.

- *Does the intervention change the facilitator's role?* Leaving your role of facilitator is inconsistent with the client-facilitator contract, unless the group
and cofacilitators explicitly agree that a cofacilitator will temporarily leave
the role. Examples are acting as a group member, a group decision maker,
a content expert, or intermediary between the group and others.

- *Will the intervention prevent or hinder the client group from accomplishing
its goals?* Interventions that prevent or hinder the client group from accomplishing its goals might be taking the group off track; establishing agenda
items in an order that requires everyone to return to items members have
already discussed; or employing exercises that, although interesting, neither contribute to the task nor meet the group's maintenance needs.

Supporting an Intervention

In contrast to the zone of deference, in which one cofacilitator makes an intervention that the other cofacilitator might not, supporting an intervention occurs
when one cofacilitator emphasizes the other's intervention. Here conflicts can
occur when the one who makes the initial intervention expects support, while
the other, believing the first does not need it, fails to provide it. In the reverse
situation, a cofacilitator offers support when the initial partner thinks it is unnecessary. Again, to avoid discrepancy in expectation, the partners can discuss
when and how to support each other's interventions and how each one can ask
for support.

Rescuing a Cofacilitator

Sometimes a cofacilitator gets into conflict with the client group. For example, she
might intervene in a way that divides the group and causes part of the group to attack her. Or a group may draw her into its own conflict, without her recognizing it.

What should her partner do when she is in conflict with the group? A natural reaction is to intervene and protect or rescue the partner from the conflict
with the group. This saves the partner and relieves his concern about becoming a victim of her conflict with the group (Steiner, 1974). Unfortunately, this
discounts the partner and can reinforce the group's belief that the rescued cofacilitator is ineffective. Group members may reason that if she cannot extricate
herself from the conflict without his help, the group's negative assessment of
the cofacilitator in conflict must be accurate.

A more effective response—one that avoids reinforcing the group's negative
views—is to wait for the cofacilitator in conflict to ask for help. Waiting increases
the chance that she will manage the conflict with the group and may simultaneously enhance the group's image of her. Allowing her to choose when to receive
help increases the facilitator's free choice and reduces the image of the cofacilita-

tor as helpless. If, however, she is acting inconsistently with the core values, principles, or ground rules, the other cofacilitator has a responsibility to intervene.

In some cases, a conflict between one cofacilitator and the group becomes known to the other cofacilitator first. Suppose a manager in a top management retreat approaches a cofacilitator during a break and says, "Listen, Tina, your cofacilitator Victor is a nice guy, but he's stirring up issues the group doesn't need to deal with, and people are getting upset with him. Don't tell him I said anything, but just steer the conversation back when he starts challenging the group, OK?" To avoid rescuing Victor, colluding with the client, or acting as an intermediary, Tina can explain that unless Victor talks directly with those who are concerned, he will not have valid information to make a free and informed choice about whether or how to change his behavior. This is true whether or not Tina believes Victor is acting ineffectively. Ideally, the conversation with Victor occurs with the entire group, because it involves all members. Once the conversation is raised with the entire group, Victor can ask Tina for help.

Coordination and Openness with Clients

Because intervention is based on diagnosis, to coordinate their work cofacilitators have to discuss with each other what is happening in the group. Aside from telepathy, I know of only two ways for cofacilitators to coordinate their work in front of the group: they can either talk openly or try to hide their discussion by using some secret language.

Kurt Lewin and the T-Group

The genesis of the training group (T-group; Benne, 1964; Marrow, 1969), which is a source of many group facilitation techniques, reveals the advantages and risks of the open approach. The principles of the T-group were developed in the summer of 1946 by social psychologist Kurt Lewin and his colleagues. Lewin, then a professor at the Massachusetts Institute of Technology (MIT), was asked to help the Connecticut State Commission, which was troubled by the staff's inability to help communities overcome bias and discrimination. Following his motto of "no action without research; no research without action" (Marrow, 1969, p. 193), Lewin proposed a two-week workshop that would simultaneously train three groups of commission staff members and provide research data on what produced the changes. A psychologist led each of the three groups, and a researcher observed each one.

Every evening, the researchers met with the group leaders to discuss and record on tape their process observations of the groups and the leaders. One day, a few workshop participants asked to attend the evening meetings. Most researchers and group leaders feared that it would be harmful for the participants to hear discussion of their behavior. But Lewin, an advocate of feedback, saw no reason the researchers and leaders should withhold data from the participants and believed the feedback could be helpful.

The evening sessions had an energizing effect on everyone involved. When leaders and researchers analyzed an event in a group, the actual participants interrupted with their interpretation. Members found that when they participated nondefensively, they learned important things about their behavior, how others reacted to them, and how groups in general behave. Together, the researchers, leaders, and participants had found a powerful method of learning. By watching leaders discuss their work, group members learned how a group acts and how leaders can create change. By participating in the discussion, members clarified leaders' diagnoses and helped the leaders select appropriate interventions.

Openly Coordinating in Front of the Group

Lewin's findings suggest that when developmental cofacilitators openly coordinate their work in front of the group and encourage members to participate, the group members and cofacilitators increase their learning. A goal of developmental facilitation is for members to facilitate their process. Cofacilitators take the first step in the shift when they allow members to observe and question the "backstage" part of their cofacilitation.

There are risks in open coordination. If the group is angry with the cofacilitators, members may use the cofacilitators' openness to suggest that the facilitators are not competent. In some situations, cofacilitator openness does not help the members achieve their goal. If cofacilitators intervene with each other at a depth much greater than their intervention with the group, the group may consider it a waste of time. Another problematic situation is when cofacilitators disagree with each other without using effective behavior (Dies, Mallet, and Johnson, 1979). In the first few meetings, the lack of group cohesiveness can lead to divisiveness if cofacilitators disagree with each other, even by doing so appropriately (Yalom, 1985). But cofacilitators have to be careful not to discount members' ability. It is easy to justify not being open with members by claiming they are not ready to handle it or would consider it a waste of time.

In basic facilitation, even if cofacilitator openness does not help the group directly achieve its primary goal, it can enhance trust. Members are more likely to trust cofacilitators when they coordinate their work openly rather than use ambiguous gestures such as a nod, frown, or hand motion. Like whispering or note passing, a secret signal may lead members to question whether the cofacilitators are withholding relevant information from them.

Yet there are times when signals are useful, not because the cofacilitators want to hide what they are saying but because openly coordinating would simply be a distraction. How to solve the problem?

One approach, based on the ground rule of sharing all relevant information, is to tell members about the coordinating actions they might observe (such as nodding or a hand signal) and to point out that the purpose is to avoid distracting the group, not to keep secrets from people. As assurance, the cofacilitators can promise to share their private discussion whenever a member asks. Finally, members can agree to tell the cofacilitators if the secret coordination becomes distracting. The approach maintains or enhances trust in the cofacilitators. The underlying principle is that **cofacilitators coordinate their work in a manner consistent with the core values and the client's goals.**

COFACILITATOR SELF-CRITIQUE

After each facilitation session, it is helpful for cofacilitators to conduct their own debrief or self-critique. I find that I can remember many more details of the conversation if my cofacilitator and I have this conversation immediately after the facilitation.

In addition to discussing what has happened in the group, the cofacilitators can discuss how they worked together well and where they need to improve. One approach is to analyze the critical incidents of a session, comparing how they handled them with their cofacilitation agreement. After one facilitation session, I asked my cofacilitator whether I was adding to his interventions too frequently. I said I was concerned that he might see my additions as intrusive. He saw them as appropriate and consistent with our agreement, and he wanted me to continue them. On another occasion with another facilitator, I asked the same question and found that my interventions were causing my cofacilitator to lose her focus.

Cofacilitators can also discuss their behavior, feelings, and thoughts toward one another, identifying the causes and dealing with them so they do not contribute negatively to the group's dynamics. Issues such as status, control, competence, and support are all important to discuss. The principle is that **the cofacilitators' effectiveness depends partly on their ability to constructively talk about and manage the issues that affect their working relationship.**

In developmental facilitation, the cofacilitators may also share some of their own self-critique with group members to understand how the participants responded to cofacilitator behavior or to share their own learning with the group.

SUMMARY

This chapter has considered how cofacilitators can work together to better serve their group and improve their own skills. I began by considering the potential advantages and disadvantages of cofacilitating. In deciding whether to use it, the underlying principle is that together cofacilitators should be able to diagnose and intervene in a greater range of situations and with greater skill than one facilitator can manage alone. Cofacilitators can work together effectively to the extent that their theories-in-use are congruent.

I have also described how cofacilitators can divide and coordinate their labor and, after selecting a division of labor, factors that they should consider in deciding who will fill which role. The final section of the chapter has also dealt with how cofacilitators maintain boundaries and how they coordinate their work in front of the group. Finally, we discussed how cofacilitators can use self-critique to improve their effectiveness.

In the next chapter, I describe how facilitators can use their facilitation skills to help their own organization.

PART FIVE

USING FACILITATIVE SKILLS IN YOUR OWN ORGANIZATION

CHAPTER FIFTEEN

Serving as Facilitator in Your Own Organization

This chapter examines the issues that you face when you facilitate a group in your own organization. We look at the advantages and disadvantages of the role of internal facilitator, how the internal facilitator's role develops, strategies for shaping the role, and how to improve the facilitator role when not actively facilitating.

If you are an internal facilitator and have read this far, you may be thinking, *"The Skilled Facilitator approach could really improve my organization, but how do I apply it as an internal facilitator? I don't have the freedom or power of an external facilitator, and I can't say what an external facilitator can say—the risks are greater than I can take."*

I believe that **there is essentially no difference between what constitutes effective behavior for internal facilitators and for external facilitators. Core values guide the behavior of internal and external facilitators alike. These are the same core values that generate effective behavior for all members of an organization.** Although internal and external facilitators start with some different challenges, they both seek the same behavior.

If you are not an internal facilitator, you may want to skip this chapter. However, if you work with internal facilitators, this chapter can help you understand their challenges and how to work effectively with them.

ADVANTAGES AND DISADVANTAGES OF THE INTERNAL FACILITATOR ROLE

When I talk with internal facilitators about their role, they often tell me about the limitations they feel. Many of these limitations are real. But an internal facilitator also enjoys some advantages compared with external colleagues. Drawing heavily on the work of Fritz Steele (1982), I try in this first section to put the internal facilitator role in perspective by considering a few of the structural differences between internal and external facilitators and the advantages and disadvantages they create.

Accessibility

Internal facilitators have a different kind of access to their organization than an external facilitator does, and the same goes for the organization's access to them.

Access and Information About the Organization. As an internal facilitator, you know a lot about your organization's history, structure, dynamics, and people. Sometimes you know a lot about the potential client group. All this information helps you quickly understand the client group's situation and encourage the group to analyze its decisions in the context of the culture of the organization. However, familiarity with the group's situation can lead you to presume that information, assumptions, and inferences are valid, even if they have not been tested. To the extent that you are part of the culture, it is difficult to see the assumptions embedded in it.

Access and Continuity of Work. Because you are an internal facilitator, it is usually easier for a group to get access to you than to an external facilitator. It can be as simple as giving you a call or stopping by your office. You can more easily become involved in a project from beginning to end and see the long-term results of the project. Typically, a group views an internal facilitator as being more available for ongoing support than an external counterpart; you may also have a better opportunity to build on earlier efforts.

However, this relatively easy access can create conflict. The group may expect you to be available to facilitate on a moment's notice and without adequate contracting. You may be expected to devote more time than you can allot to a particular group. This can be especially difficult if your manager expects you to devote less time to facilitation. Because you are available for ongoing support and design of follow-up projects, it is difficult to determine when a project has ended and whether the terms of the project agreement have been fulfilled.

It may also be difficult for you to work with or maintain credibility with certain levels of the organization. More than the external facilitator, an internal facilitator is identified with a level in the organization's hierarchy. Consequently, a group significantly above your hierarchical level may wonder whether you are up to their facilitation task, and one significantly below your level may wonder whether you are there to meet the organization's needs.

The Insider Image

There are several potential advantages to being considered an insider. The group may consider you "one of us." The members are likely to value your insider knowledge of the organization and of them. For these reasons, the group may be comfortable with you from the beginning of a project. If you have modeled your facilitative skills in your own nonfacilitator roles, the group may consider you credible, especially if they have observed you directly in those roles. If you are part of an internal staff group that provides facilitation services, this reputation may allow client groups to feel some confidence in you, even if they have not worked with you personally.

At the same time, being one of us is a liability if the client sees you as either too close to the problem to be neutral or blind to their assumptions and unable to challenge their thinking.

Internal facilitators tell me they have a difficult time establishing credibility compared with external facilitators, whom they bring in to help with a specific situation. This can be especially true when you raise issues that challenge the culture of the group or organization. One of the most subtle but powerful expectations of group members is that people act consistently with the culture of the organization. Although members may not agree with certain aspects of the culture, at some level they value the culture because it is predictable and meets some of their needs. Consequently, if you identify how group members contribute to the dysfunctional aspects of the culture, people may see you as going too far.

Job Security

As an internal facilitator, you have the security of a regular paycheck and many potential clients are available without much marketing effort. In theory, however, the increased security that comes from working for a single organization also brings increased risk whenever that security is threatened. If a significant project experiences major problems, an external facilitator may lose a client; but you may lose your job or your influence. Consequently, the internal facilitator has more financial security to lose in confronting a group or supervisor.

In practice, I have never met a skilled internal facilitator who was fired or forced to resign simply because he raised difficult issues with the client (if you are out there, let me know). However, I have worked with internal facilitators who decided to leave the organization because they felt they could not help it effect significant change.

HOW YOUR INTERNAL FACILITATOR ROLE DEVELOPS

Many of the challenges that the internal facilitator faces stem from how the role has developed in the organization. Fortunately, you can shape your facilitator role to address these problems. To understand how, we first need to understand how it develops.

You and Others Create Your Role

Like any organizational role, **your internal facilitator role develops through an iterative process in which you and those who work with you share expectations about and attempt to influence how you will do your work.** These people include your manager and subordinates and peers, your primary client groups, and those that the primary client groups report to. Because each of these people depends on you in some way, each has some stake in and expectation of how you should fill your facilitator role.

These individuals may attempt to influence you, either directly or indirectly. Your manager may tell you directly that you cannot work with certain groups in the organization. Or she may simply imply through actions that you should evaluate client-group members for purposes of a merit increase. Similarly, someone may tell you directly, "Do not turn down any assignment from a client group high in the organizational hierarchy." Or the expectation can be vague: "We want you to be available when we need you."

Of course, you also have expectations about how you should fulfill your facilitator role and you convey that to people, directly or indirectly. You may tell client groups that you cannot mediate between the group and the manager, but that you can help the client group figure out how to raise a difficult issue with the manager. Or you may tell your own manager that the rules of confidentiality in the group prevent you from sharing specific comments that members make in their meetings.

Your role develops as the people you work with communicate their expectations to you, and vice versa, as to what kind of work you will do and how to do it. The more similar the expectations, the less role conflict between you and these people.

One reason it can be difficult to fulfill your internal facilitator role is you are working with a large number of people, most of whom have expectations for how you will fill your role. As the number of people sharing expectations increases, so does the likelihood that some of their expectations for you are incompatible and that conflict results.

To make matters more complex, **the expectations that develop for your role are influenced by organizational, interpersonal, and individual factors.** The size and number of hierarchical levels, the available technology, and reward systems are all organizational factors that influence how your role develops.

The nature of your interpersonal relationships with others influences how your role develops, as do your own personal preferences (such as how you use humor, or how formal you are).

Your Other Roles Influence Your Facilitator Role

Finally, **your internal facilitator role may be complicated by the fact that you fill at least one other role in the organization.** Serving as a facilitator may be part of your larger role as a human resource manager, OD consultant, or trainer. **But any organizational member can also serve as an internal facilitator, regardless of his or her other organizational roles.**

Role conflict arises when the people you are working with as a facilitator expect you to take on elements of your nonfacilitator role. For example, if your nonfacilitator position is higher in the organizational hierarchy than your clients' position, the group members may expect you to convey their message to people above them in the hierarchy. Your manager may expect you to evaluate the group members' performance as part of the performance appraisal process. If you are the human resource director, the client group may expect you to make decisions on HR matters. If you are the budget director, the client group may expect you to pass judgment on budget matters.

The problem arises partly because the people you are facilitating typically do not think of your work in terms of a role. They simply think of you as someone who performs a variety of tasks and who can and should be able to perform any task or behavior in any context. **The challenge is to help the people you work with learn to think in terms of roles and to explain that while serving as facilitator, you create problems by engaging in nonfacilitator role behavior that conflicts with the facilitator role.**

SHAPING YOUR FACILITATOR ROLE

You can change your facilitator role to make it more effective. People develop expectations of your facilitator role on the basis of their values, beliefs, and interests. By exploring this with others and sharing your own values, beliefs, and interests, you can shape your role. In this section, I describe strategies for improving your role, some of which are from the work of Fritz Steele (1982).

The strategies in Exhibit 15.1 seek to increase your effectiveness as a facilitator. This means that your primary task is to define your role consistently with the core values. This creates a paradox; in the short run, you may have more opportunity to help groups if you agree to act inconsistently with the core values. Yet by doing so, you become less able to model effective behavior and help groups. The strategies deal with this paradox by helping to create conditions that do not require you to act inconsistently with the core values. Most of the

Exhibit 15.1. Strategies for Shaping Your Facilitator Role

- Decide which facilitative role is appropriate
- Discuss potential role conflicts before they arise
- Seek agreement to switch facilitative roles
- Discuss problems in your past relationships with client groups
- Be willing to give up the facilitator role
- Use the contracting process
- Honor core values and principles; tailor the methods

strategies (they are also principles) can be used continually, not only when you are actively facilitating a client.

Decide Which Facilitative Role Is Appropriate

An easy way to get into difficulty is to serve as a facilitator when that role is inappropriate. Unlike an internal facilitative consultant or facilitative leader, an internal facilitator is substantively neutral. In Chapter Three, I gave the example of an HR manager attempting to serve as a facilitator to a group discussing HR issues. Because the manager had a stake in the group's discussion and because the group knew the manager had relevant information about (and could influence) the HR issues they were discussing, the group found it difficult to accept the manager in the facilitator role.

Substantively neutral is a relative term; you wonder as an internal facilitator if you can ever be totally neutral about issues within the organization. However, there are two working criteria for judging neutrality: (1) you believe that personal views about the substance of the facilitation do not significantly affect your facilitation, and (2) the client group believes that your personal views about the substance of the facilitation do not significantly affect your facilitation. **Unless you have little interaction with the group you are working with, serving as a facilitative consultant or even a facilitative leader is probably a more appropriate role than the facilitator role.** In these two roles, you can offer essentially the same help as a facilitator, and at the same time share the views and expertise that the group understands you to have.

Discuss Potential Role Conflicts Before They Arise

It is easier for people to discuss differing views about their expectations of your facilitator role before conflict actually arises than after they are engaged in conflict with you. For example, it is easier to discuss whether you should serve as an intermediary between a client group and its manager before the manager asks you to do so. This requires anticipating the role conflict that is likely to arise. The challenge is to reach agreement with all constituents so that everyone's expectations are compatible. This conversation is best held during the contracting process.

Because you typically also hold nonfacilitator roles in the organization, you may experience pressure to use information you receive in the facilitator role to act in a nonfacilitator role. This includes taking responsibility for the group, which can easily create role conflict.

Conflict may arise if, for example, your manager asks you to act outside your facilitator role. Consider a situation in which you are an OD manager who also serves as a facilitator. You are facilitating an organizational task force that reports to your manager. Your manager tells you that she is concerned the task force is not making progress quickly enough. In an effort to address your manager's concern, you act as a mediator and convey the message directly to the group. Or you attempt to speed the group's progress by making content suggestions. Both of these actions are outside the facilitator role.

To remain consistent with the role, explain to your manager your interest in having her convey the message directly to the task force. If you are concerned that your manager thinks you are not doing your job effectively, you can test this with her. In doing so, you may learn that she either has an unrealistic expectation for the facilitation process or is unclear about your facilitator's role.

Another source of role conflict is being pressured to obtain information in your facilitator role that is relevant to a nonfacilitator role. What should you do if you learn something in your facilitator role that you would act on if you had obtained it in a nonfacilitator role? Consider the example of my colleague who is an internal facilitator and HR director for his organization. While facilitating a quality improvement group, a discussion began about departmental policy on overtime. The facilitator quickly realized that if the members' comments were accurate, the departmental policy was in violation of the organizational policy. Had he heard the discussion when he was acting in his HR role, he would have contacted the department head to discuss the apparent violation. The question is, should the HR director take different action because he obtained the information in his role as facilitator and in the context of a confidentiality agreement?

The situation poses a dilemma because part of the clients' trust in you as a facilitator stems from the fact that, theoretically, you have no influence over what happens to the members outside the facilitated group. But if you act on the information in your nonfacilitator role, you do have influence. In this example, the influence would benefit the group members, but in another situation it may disadvantage them personally. If the facilitator does not act on the information and neither does the group, the facilitator may be in the position of knowing that some HR policies are being violated but not able to act on that knowledge. On the other hand, if the facilitator acts on the information in his director's role, group members may in the future withhold relevant information, concerned that the facilitator will act on it in his other role.

One approach to the dilemma lies in the core value of generating valid information. In an organization that acts consistently with this value, members would consider it appropriate for you to act on the information in the nonfacilitator role. This suggests that a client group that espouses the core values would act accordingly.

However you decide to deal with this kind of dilemma, clearly contracting with members about how you treat such knowledge gives them valid information with which they can then decide whether to share or withhold certain information in their discussion. Anticipating a conflicting issue means contracting about it before it arises.

Seek Agreement to Switch Facilitative Roles

Most internal facilitators facilitate as part of their larger role, or in addition to their regular organizational role. If this describes your situation, there may be times when you have subject-matter information to share with the group that would take you out of your facilitator role and into your nonfacilitator organizational role. To leave the facilitator role, you need to have agreement from the group.

Consider a group that is discussing how to establish self-managing work teams in its department; team members are deciding how to plan, divide, and coordinate the work among them. To fully implement the change, the group may need to modify the means by which team members' performance is assessed. If you are the facilitator for this group and also serve as HR director, you may know how the group can change its performance appraisal system. In this situation, if you have the agreement of the group, it is appropriate to temporarily leave your facilitator role and in your HR director role describe the process by which the client group can modify its performance appraisal system.

You could do this by saying: "You've raised an issue of HR policy that I have relevant information about as the HR director, and I think you might find it useful. I'd like to share this information. Does anyone have any concerns about my temporarily stepping out of the facilitator role to share this information?" After sharing the information, you clearly identify when you return to the facilitator role by simply saying, "I'm back in the facilitator role."

Offering information to the group without their asking for it can create a dilemma. If you wait to be asked by the group, you may increase the likelihood of the group making a poor decision without the information. However, if you volunteer it, you may inappropriately increase the group's dependence on you. Resolving the dilemma means weighing the negative consequences of withholding the information against the risk of increasing the group's dependence.

Discuss Problems in Your Past Client Relationships

If you have been using a unilateral control approach, your current and potential client groups may have become acquainted with you as unilaterally controlling and may have less-than-full trust in you. **Redeveloping trust with potential**

and current clients is essential. You can begin doing so by asking potential or current clients directly whether anything has occurred in the working relationship that prompts them to mistrust you, explaining your reason for asking.

Also, if you are aware of times when you acted inconsistently with the core values and ground rules, you can share the relevant information, explain why you consider your behavior ineffective, and tell them how you would act differently now. Volunteering the information shows the group that you are aware of your own ineffective behavior and are capable of changing. Sharing the information also demonstrates that you can discuss your own behavior without getting defensive. This makes it easier for potential clients to raise concerns that they might have considered undiscussable with you. Through such discussion, potential clients begin to increase their trust in you.

Be Willing to Give Up the Facilitator Role

Being willing to give up your facilitator role if you cannot fill it consistently with the core values makes it easier to take the risks necessary to openly confront role conflict, even with those having more power and authority than you. Ironically, your willingness to step aside may lead to a set of role expectations that remove your need to give up the role.

Still, in some cases you may find that despite your efforts it is not possible to fill your facilitator role without repeatedly acting inconsistently with the core values. For some people, giving up the internal facilitator role may also mean having to leave a job, and an organization. Financially, this is the most serious consequence an internal facilitator faces. Yet continuing to facilitate while acting inconsistently with the core values leads back to the problem that opened this section. By acting that way, you grow ever less able to help groups.

Use the Contracting Process

Using the contracting process is a direct way of shaping your facilitator role and mitigating the potential problems I have discussed. As an internal facilitator you may want to (or be pressured to) cut short the contracting process. You might assume that you are familiar enough with the members of a client group, or that the client group seems to agree on what it needs to accomplish. Or you may feel pressured by a client group saying they do not have time for the planning meeting. Unfortunately, cutting short the contracting process almost always creates problems later in the facilitation because the client does not adequately understand your role or you and the client are unaware that you disagree on some aspect of the facilitation.

When talking with internal clients about the planning meeting time, you can explain that your interest in the planning meeting is to increase the prospect of the group's facilitation time being used effectively and efficiently. If the client insists that the planning meeting time is unnecessary because the group agrees on the objectives and other issues, you can inquire as to why he considers it unnecessary and explain that if the client's assumptions are correct then the meeting will certainly be brief. Still, sometimes the client does not find your reasoning compelling and does not agree to a full planning meeting. In this case, you have to decide whether the risk of carrying out a (presumably not very effective) facilitation is greater than the risk of not agreeing to do it at all.

Even if the client is unwilling to agree to a full planning meeting, you may be able to meet some of the interests underlying the planning meeting through an abbreviated planning process. This might include meeting with a few representatives, or conducting some of the planning immediately before the facilitation.

One of the most important people with whom to reach agreement is your manager. Having your manager understand your facilitator role and the importance of contracting with a group can ensure that your manager supports rather than hinders your work. Resource H offers a series of questions that you and your manager can discuss to support your facilitator role.

Honor Core Values and Principles; Tailor the Techniques

The core values and principles are the essence of the Skilled Facilitator approach. The methods and techniques are a way of operationalizing the core values and principles. As an internal facilitator, you may find that some of the methods or techniques in this book do not seem to fit, and your organization will not change to adapt to them.

The methods and techniques that I describe throughout this book are not the only ones consistent with core values and principles; they are ones that I have used with good results. Using the Skilled Facilitator approach entails adapting and discovering techniques and methods that fit your organization and that are congruent with the core values and principles.

CHANGING YOUR FACILITATOR ROLE FROM THE OUTSIDE IN

How you act outside your facilitator role can improve your effectiveness within it. Here are some ways to improve your facilitator role while not actively facilitating.

Educate Others About the Facilitator Role

Role conflict often arises simply because people who work with a facilitator do not know what a facilitator is or does. In fact, many people equate facilitators with mediators or arbitrators (see Chapter One for a discussion of the mediator role). Consequently, the expectations for a facilitator are borrowed from another role. You can avoid or reduce these conflicts by creating opportunities to educate others about the facilitator's role. This also helps others reframe the meaning of a facilitator's actions. Once someone understands the facilitator's role, he may no longer necessarily consider the facilitator remiss upon hearing that she allowed a client group to make a "poor" decision. Educating others also generates future clients, as employees understand how a facilitator can help them. But education is a process, not an event; it means constantly finding ways to help others understand the role and its benefits.

Become an Informal Change Agent

By becoming an informal change agent, you can attempt to influence the group contextual factors that make it difficult to effectively fulfill your facilitator role. If your organization has a strict hierarchy, potential client groups may not be permitted, or may be reluctant, to contact you directly. In some cases, the organizational factors that hinder you from fulfilling your role of facilitator are the same ones that contribute to the client group's problems and lead them to ask you for help.

As the group effectiveness model in Chapter Two indicates, one contextual factor is organizational culture. Culture has a strong and pervasive influence on the behavior of members; it is very difficult to change. However, beginning to influence a group or organizational culture can lead to significant change—in your facilitator role as well. Of course, it is essential to use the core values in the role of informal change agent.

Model the Way

Gandhi said, "be the change you want to see in the world." At the heart of being a change agent is modeling the way. As an internal facilitator, you ask others in your organization to follow the core values and ground rules—to suspend their normal behavior and to take a risk with new behavior, expecting that these risks generate more effective behavior that leads to high-quality decisions, greater learning, and better relationships.

If you have modeled this behavior in your own nonfacilitator roles, then clients see you as credible, especially if they have observed your behavior directly. If you have not, clients may reasonably ask how you can advocate that they use the core values and ground rules when you have not.

Modeling the way is essential. People look to a facilitator to see what is possible. Group members know how to act in accordance with the status quo. What is not clear to them is how they can change their thinking and behavior to help create the kind of work relationship they say they desire. When you model this behavior in your nonfacilitator role(s), you become a facilitative leader, creating the kind of relationship that others seek.

If you are concerned that modeling the Skilled Facilitator approach as a facilitative leader is a risk, the feeling is natural. Many of my clients and colleagues who are internal facilitators are initially worried that if they use the approach—particularly with their managers—others will see their behavior as inappropriate or challenging. The risk may exist. However, in general my clients and colleagues have found that they can reduce the risk in part by being explicit about their intentions, stating their concerns about how others might interpret their behavior, and inquiring whether others do see their behavior as ineffective. It is easy to overlook the risks of *not* using the facilitative skills—the risks of not testing an inference, withholding relevant information, and not inquiring. **Using the Skilled Facilitator approach does not require that you get rid of your concerns, or even make believe they do not exist; it requires only that you move forward with your concerns, making them part of the conversation when relevant.**

SUMMARY

As an internal facilitator, you face various issues as you facilitate groups in your own organization. The issues are the advantages and disadvantages of your internal facilitator role, how the role develops, strategies for shaping it, and ways to improve your role when not actively facilitating.

Although the expectations that organizational members have for you as an internal facilitator often differ from those for an external facilitator, a basic principle underlies this chapter: there is essentially no difference between what constitutes effective behavior for you as an internal facilitator and as an external facilitator. The core values of valid information, free and informed choice, internal commitment, and compassion guide the behavior of both. These are the same core values that also generate effective behavior for all members of an organization. By modeling the Skilled Facilitator approach as a facilitative leader, you increase your credibility with groups and help your organization see what is possible using this approach.

In the final chapter, I explore the role of the facilitative leader—using the Skilled Facilitator approach when you are also involved in the content of the conversation. The facilitative leader role enables a group to use the Skilled Facilitator approach on its own without a facilitator. Anyone can serve as a facilitative leader, whether or not in a formal leader role. For an internal facilitator, the facilitative leader role is a natural extension.

CHAPTER SIXTEEN

The Facilitative Leader

The facilitative leader uses the core values, assumptions, and principles of the Skilled Facilitator approach to create effective groups and organizations. In this chapter, I describe problems with traditional philosophies of leadership, how facilitative leadership differs, and how as a facilitative leader you can begin to create fundamental change in your group and organization.

WHY THE FACILITATIVE LEADER?

Facilitative leadership is a values-based, systemic leadership philosophy founded on the core values and assumptions, principles, and methods of the Skilled Facilitator approach. The facilitative leader helps groups and individuals become more effective through building their capacity to reflect on and improve the way they work. Ultimately, like a developmental facilitator, a facilitative leader helps others learn how to learn.

Informal Leaders as Facilitative Leaders

You can be a facilitative leader even if you are not the formal leader of a group or organization, and even if you have no supervisory authority. The influence of the traditional leader or manager has stemmed largely from formal authority. But as a facilitative leader, your influence stems from a mind-set and skill set that enable you to work with others so as to address people's interests and help people learn. This means practicing the core values and principles, including those of group effectiveness, even if others choose not to do so. In this respect, **you can be a facilitative leader regardless of your position in an organization.** Ultimately, the core values, assumptions, and principles represent not only a way to facilitate and lead but also a fundamental choice about the kind of life people create for themselves and others in their organization.

Creating Empowered Employees, Self-Managing Teams, Learning Organizations, and Partnerships

In recent years, organizations have begun to recognize the need to change from a management philosophy based on the values of unilateral control and compliance, moving instead toward a philosophy based more on the values of learning, empowerment, and commitment. But for many leaders—you may be among them—the change has been slow and the results have been inconsistent.

Whereas in the 1960s and 1970s leaders began using participative management approaches, more recently leaders have sought to have members become even more highly involved in and committed to their organization.

To this end, organizations have engaged in a variety of approaches and programs. They have adopted total quality management programs, established continuous improvement teams, and used reengineering, to name a few. They have attempted to empower employees by giving them more decision-making authority and by developing self-managing work teams.

All of these approaches attempt to take advantage of the enormous resources that people bring to the organization. When people are empowered, they are responsive to customers, and the organization adapts quickly to changing conditions. At the same time, as people have more choice about how to do their work, their work becomes motivating, and they are likely to be committed to their work. They also bring their creativity to bear on workplace problems and ideas.

Each of these approaches has something to offer the organization, but in many of those I have worked with people view each new approach as the management flavor of the month and wait for it to pass. In some cases, the approach was used with good short-term results, but over time it never became integrated into the framework of the organization. I believe that this results partly from the unilaterally controlling way in which the leader introduces an approach to the organization and partly from the unilateral control values and assumptions that are embedded in the approach itself. To the degree that the leader introduces any new approach embedded with unilateral control features, I expect there will be similar unintended results and the flavor-of-the-month reaction they hope to avoid.

At a fundamental level, some organizations are seeking to become learning organizations capable of identifying, challenging, and changing the very assumptions that undermine effectiveness. In doing so, they hope to turn their ability to reflect and redesign into a competitive advantage. Insofar as they transform themselves congruently with the core values I have discussed in this book, they can be successful. However, if they attempt to create this transformation using a unilateral control approach, I expect they will encounter the same results as with the other types of organizational changes.

At the same time the organization is changing, its leaders are increasingly finding that they cannot adequately address the problems they face by working only within their organization. Instead, leaders are learning that by developing a partnership with suppliers, distributors, customers, and the community in which they do business, they can synergistically increase their effectiveness and that of their partners. Similarly, in the public arena, government, private sector, and nonprofit organizations are increasingly working together to solve difficult social and economic problems; no single organization has control over the process. Here too, leaders have struggled to create the kind of relationship necessary to achieve this synergy.

The Need for a New Kind of Leader

Underlying all these changes lies a question: What kind of leaders are needed in this new breed of organization? It seems logical that the role and philosophy of the manager needs to change as people become more empowered and take on more responsibility for managing their work and improving the organization. As Charles Manz and Henry Sims have put the question (1984, p. 410), "How does one lead employees who are supposed to lead themselves?"

Clearly, the leader who uses a theory-in-use of unilateral control and compliance cannot fill the role. His values are inconsistent with the direction in which the organization seeks change. In the past, many organizations espoused this type of leadership and rewarded their leaders for it. Now they are seeing the unintended consequences of unilateral control leadership, and many are struggling to develop an alternative approach to leadership. Each new model they adopt becomes another version of what is fundamentally still unilateral, controlling leadership.

Even visionary heroic leaders may not be completely up to the task (Manz and Sims, 1993). A visionary heroic leader paints a vivid and compelling picture of the organization's mission and vision. The leader's inspirational and persuasive manner enrolls people in helping to create the leader's vision. To be sure, such leadership is energizing, and organizations have achieved much through it.

Yet the strengths of heroic leadership are also its limitations. The source of wisdom, direction, and inspiration is the leader, and people act according to the leader's vision (Manz and Sims, 1993). However, as Peter Senge has noted, the only vision to which an individual can truly be committed is the one "rooted in an individual's own set of values, concerns, and aspirations" (1990, p. 211).

This does not mean that the leader cannot shape a vision; the leader must. It does mean, however, that for the vision to motivate and provide purpose for people's work, they must genuinely share the vision, not just adopt it. Finally, the power of visionary, heroic leadership, though inspirational, lies with the leader (Manz and Sims, 1993). In short, the focus of visionary heroic leadership is on the leader. As Peter Block has written, "To put it bluntly, strong leadership does not have within itself the capability to create the fundamental changes our organizations require. It is not the fault of the people in these positions, it is the fault of the way we have all framed the role" (1993, p. 13).

THE FACILITATIVE LEADER

Organizations need the type of leader who works from a set of core values consistent with the concepts of empowerment, commitment, collaboration, learning, and partnership. The core values and principles underlying the Skilled Facilitator approach constitute a foundation for becoming such a leader—what I call a *facilitative leader*.

As I described in Chapter Three, your role as a facilitative leader differs from your role as a facilitator in several important ways (see Table 16.1). First, as a facilitative leader you share your point of view about the content of the discussion. At times, you may be deeply involved in the conversation and feel passionately about the outcome. Second, you are involved in the substantive decision making. Depending on the situation, you may be the sole decision maker, be part of a group making a decision, or even delegate the decision.

Table 16.1. Comparing Facilitative Leader and Facilitator Roles

	Facilitative Leader	Facilitator
Group membership	Group leader or member	Third party
Content	Nonneutral; may be content expert	Content-neutral
Process	Skilled in process; uses skills to help group increase its effectiveness	Process expert; uses skills to help group increase its effectiveness
Decision-making role	Participates in substantive discussions; involved in decision making	Does not participate in substantive discussion or decision making

Third, you can be a facilitative leader even if you are not a member of the group. Similarly, you can be a facilitative leader even if you are not a formal leader. **As a facilitative leader, you may not be a process expert like a skilled facilitator, but you have enough process skills to model the core values and ground rules, and to help others learn them if they choose.**

Being a facilitative leader is more difficult than being a facilitator. As a facilitator, you are a content-neutral third party, so you can focus entirely on helping the group improve its process. But **as a facilitative leader you are participating in the substance of the conversation at the same time that you are helping improve the group process.** The challenge is to participate in the subject matter of the conversation in a way that enhances the group process.

In essence, being a facilitative leader means always asking yourself, *How can I increase my group's effectiveness, that of my organization, and my own by living the core values and assumptions in this situation?*

FACILITATIVE SKILLS AS A CORE COMPETENCY

Over the years I have been consulting to organizations, leaders have changed their thinking about the value and need for facilitative skills. In the past, they saw facilitative skills as ancillary leadership skills. When leaders and managers thought they needed these skills (usually in a difficult situation), they would typically call on a facilitator, or OD and HR people to help.

Now, many organizations consider possession of the skill set and mind-set of the facilitative leader approach as a core competency for leaders—even if they have never heard of this approach. Some of the phrases they use to describe this are *authenticity, building relationships,* and *creating a learning environment.* They realize that this way of thinking and acting is essential for creating and sustaining the kinds of performance outcomes the organization seeks. Even a highly successful organization realizes that in the long run it cannot sustain high performance without effective process. One client of mine, a Fortune 100 company that owns the majority of its market, recently found in an employee survey that the biggest issue facing the organization was poor working relationships. The leaders recognized that unless the organization addressed the issue, it could lose some of the competitive edge it had gained over others in the market.

Even though organizations increasingly espouse the need for what I call facilitative leadership, many still lack a compelling picture of what it looks like in action and how to develop these leaders. In the previous chapters, I described the facilitative skill set and mind-set and what they look like in action. In the remainder of this chapter, I suggest how you can use the same skill set and mind-set as a facilitative leader.

THE FACILITATIVE LEADER VALUES IN ACTION

As a facilitative leader, you design your actions on the basis of the core values and assumptions of the mutual learning theory-in-use. In this section, I describe how using the core values and assumptions guides your actions.

Valid Information

Valid information is the foundation for an effective decision. For information to be valid, at a minimum people must feel free to disagree with each other without retribution, regardless of any difference in authority or power. Better yet, people have to believe that you are as genuinely interested in understanding their point of view as you are in having them understand yours. This means holding the core assumption that you have some information, others have additional information, and you may be missing things that others see. As a facilitative leader, you can model this by asking others how they see things differently from you, or what problems or gaps people see in your thinking; when people respond with different ideas, you inquire into their reasoning, rather than simply advocating your view or responding defensively.

Ultimately, undiscussable issues need to be discussed. Too many of the critical but uncomfortable conversations that people should have with each other take place instead in their minds, with their families, or with friends, or behind closed doors with people they trust to take their side but who cannot resolve their problems. Either the problems remain or people attempt to solve them without having to deal directly and honestly with those they consider the problem, thereby creating more problems and more undiscussable issues. You can interrupt this downward spiral by raising the undiscussable issues directly with those involved and by helping others learn to do the same.

Free and Informed Choice

Valid information becomes important only when people can use it to make a free and informed choice. With free and informed choice, you change the distribution of power from being held largely by the formal leader to being shared by the formal facilitative leader and other group members. Shared power in turn makes possible joint control. Without shared power and joint control, it is difficult to sustain empowerment, a self-managing team, partnership, and genuine organizational learning.

Free and informed choice recognizes a basic truth that leaders in general seem to know deep down but also seem reluctant to accept: "essentially all control over employees is *ultimately* self-imposed" (Manz and Sims, 1989, p. 5). Regardless of the controls and standards that you set, in the end each person chooses whether to be influenced by them. The most powerful control comes not externally but when people freely choose their course of action. As a facilitative leader, you understand that although external controls generate *compliance,* internal controls generate *commitment.* Consequently, you seek to increase the extent to which group members make their own choices about their work. Instead of spending time designing ways to control others' behavior, you can help group members develop their own internal controls, which are necessary for managing themselves effectively.

Like the other core values, free and informed choice is an ideal worth striving for. As an ideal, there are times when it is not possible for everyone to have full free and informed choice. Because almost all organizations use some form of hierarchy, when someone at a higher level makes a decision it can constrain your choices at a lower level. If, for example, the top executive team sets the strategic direction for your organization, then your choices are limited within that strategic direction.

Free and informed choice does not ensure that everyone (including the facilitative leader) gets *all* of what they want all the time. As Peter Block has noted, there are limits: "In any community there will always be different levels of authority. The boss will have 51 percent, the subordinate 49 percent. This means that when all is said and done, others will have the right to tell us what to do. This has no effect on our right to say no, even to say it loudly. The notion that if you stand up you will get shot undermines partnership. Partnership does not mean that you always get what you want. It means you may lose your argument, but you never lose your voice" (1993, p. 30).

The challenge is to reduce unnecessary constraints on creating as much free and informed choice as possible.

Internal Commitment

Internal commitment occurs when people make free and informed choices that fully meet their interests. With internal commitment, people take responsibility for their actions and initiative to do what they need to do to make their choices work. You do not need to engage in over-the-shoulder monitoring to ensure that people are doing what they say they will do. With internal commitment, people get the job done because they *want* to do it. Instead, you can serve as a resource to and partner with group members, helping them diagnose and address problems in implementation. Being a facilitative leader means understanding the paradox that to generate internal commitment in others, you must first give up unilateral control.

Compassion

When I added compassion as the fourth core value, I was concerned that my clients would find it too touchy-feely (to use a pejorative phrase from the 1960s and 1970s). I was particularly concerned about my clients from science- or engineering-based organizations whose professional disciplines emphasize the rigor of generating valid information. To my pleasant surprise (and relief), these leaders told me that that without compassion the first three core values seemed hollow. They saw compassion as a foundation, container, or spiritual force that integrated the core values and imbued them with a larger purpose. They came to the same conclusion that I did: compassion is not at odds with the first three core values; rather, compassion strengthens them.

Compassion means adapting a stance toward others and yourself in which you temporarily suspend judgment. It involves having a basic concern for the good of others that leads you to be concerned about their suffering. By suffering, I mean simply the pain that people feel when their needs are not met.

Unfortunately, some leaders have confused the notion of compassion with unilaterally protecting or rescuing; in doing so, they have reduced accountability. This leads them to help and protect others in a way that in the long run is not helpful and that leaves people even less protected. This is the kind of misplaced compassion that may have led you to withhold some feedback because you did not want to upset or put another person on the defensive. You may have even taken on some of the person's responsibilities instead of addressing a difficult performance issue with him. In predictable systemic fashion, withholding valid and relevant information makes it difficult for him to make an informed free choice to change behavior. Without specific feedback, he is unlikely to change; the problem gets worse. If you continue to unilaterally protect the person, at some point you may feel you need to take serious action, such as firing him—not a particularly compassionate response. The person will never fully understand how his behavior was ineffective, how he might have changed it. In this way, misplaced compassion creates the very lack of compassion that you attempted to avoid.

The kind of compassion I am describing enables you to have empathy for others and for yourself in a way that still holds people accountable for their actions rather than unilaterally protecting others or yourself. With a systemic view, this involves understanding how people, presumably acting in good faith, each contribute to creating or sustaining a problem, rather than placing blame. It means exploring what other people see that you are missing, rather than assuming that they do not share your view, "just don't get it," or have questionable motives.

CREATING STRUCTURES, POLICIES, PROCEDURES, AND PROGRAMS

The facilitative leader approach goes beyond creating effective group process and conversation to creating a group or organization with effective structures, policies, procedures, and programs. Essentially, the approach helps you answer the question, "What would my team and organization look like if they were designed on the basis of core values and assumptions?"

Effective group process is necessary but not sufficient for creating an effective group and organization. Even if you and your team become highly skilled at using the facilitative leader core values and assumptions, ground rules, and diagnosis-intervention cycle, you will probably be frustrated by structures, policies, procedures, and programs in your organization that are inconsistent with this approach and that create unintended consequences.

The reason this occurs is **people design organizations, and they generally do so using structures, policies, and procedures intended to avoid past or anticipated threats. Because almost everyone uses a unilateral control theory-in-use under conditions of threat, the structures, policies, and programs typically contain unilateral control theory-in-use elements.**

Here are a few examples of unilateral control organizational designs and how they can be redesigned using the core values and assumptions of the facilitative leader approach.

Structures and Processes: Performance Feedback

Many organizations use a type of 360 degree feedback in which you get feedback not only from your immediate supervisor or manager but also from those who report directly to you, your peers, and your customers (internal or external). Typically, each person completes a survey rating you on a number of items. Sometimes they add written comments. The completed survey scores are combined so that for each item you get a separate averaged score for your peers, subordinates, and customers. Your direct supervisor or manager's score is identified for you to see. Then your manager or an HR person reviews the survey results with you. Except for those from your immediate supervisor or manager, all of the scores and comments are anonymous. Those who design these systems normally use anonymity because they believe that the people rating your performance may not be fully honest if you identify them from what they said.

Creating Problems. As someone trained in survey research and development, and having helped organizations use survey data to improve their groups, I find a number of problems with this approach. First, anonymity prevents you from learning who gave you which rating and what led them to do so. As a result, you have no way of knowing whether the people rating you are using valid information. Second, without specific examples (including names, places, and events), you cannot learn which of your specific behaviors people think need improvement or are commendable. Third, because the feedback is anonymous, it is difficult to ask those who provided it to continue to give you feedback on the issues they have said you need to work on. Consequently, although people stress that performance feedback systems are developmental tools, this design makes it difficult for you to develop.

A Facilitative Leader Approach. What would performance feedback look like with the core values and assumptions of the facilitative leader approach? One of my clients—I'll call her Cathy—redesigned her organization's system for herself after she attended a facilitative leader workshop. In addition to her manager, Cathy asked several peers, direct reports, and internal customers to complete the survey. She asked each of them to bring the completed survey to a meeting with her. At the meeting, the group discussed the survey items, with each person stating how they rated Cathy on that item and giving some examples to illustrate what led them to choose the rating. When Cathy invited people to the meeting, she shared her approach and her reasoning for it so each could make a free and informed choice about whether to be involved.

Several things happened as a result of the new feedback design. First, Cathy learned the specific behaviors that people saw in her that were effective and ineffective. Second, at times, when a person shared his example, Cathy remembered the situation differently, and so the two talked and jointly reconstructed it. Having new information sometimes led the person to modify a particular rating. Third, together the group was able to identify patterns of behavior across the examples they shared. This enabled them to help Cathy see clearly the behaviors they wanted her to work on and to identify the situations under which they occurred. Finally, she was able to use the group to support her development. Whenever she was working with one of them, she could ask how she was doing on the issues she needed to work on; alternatively, the person could initiate the conversation. Consequently others could continue giving her feedback and reinforce her improvement.

In a follow-up session on facilitative leadership, Cathy told me that the meeting felt quite risky for her, partly because she would be so vulnerable. A peer who was part of the feedback group said she also felt vulnerable. Both said that the session generated more usable information than any other feedback session they had been involved in.

The group could have done something else to reflect the systemic nature of their relationships. Because an individual's performance is partly a function of relationships with others, the group members could have explored how each of them contributed to both helping and hindering Cathy's ability to perform well.

Organizational Policies

As I mentioned above, organizational policies are often designed either in response to or in anticipation of a potential threat or embarrassment. To take a simple example, some organizations have a travel policy that prevents people from staying additional nights either before or after a required trip. The policy is designed to avoid unnecessary travel expenses being paid by the organization; it is often created after someone has stayed additional nights on the organization's tab. But many airline fares are significantly lower if you stay over a

Saturday night. If you choose to arrive on Saturday instead of Sunday for a meeting that begins on Monday, you save your organization hundreds of dollars, even with the additional expenses for lodging and meals. Yet the policy prevents you from saving the money.

This example illustrates how, by focusing on positions, an organization can design policies that undermine its own interests. Many policies I have seen are written as positions and do not explain the interests that give rise to them. Using the facilitative leader approach, the organization clarifies its interests regarding a particular issue, using the core values and assumptions of the facilitative leader approach. This enables people to design a variety of solutions and still honor the interests and intent of the policy in all cases.

Training Programs: The "Sandwich" Feedback Technique

Sometimes clients ask me to review with them their organization's training programs to determine how they are congruent or incongruent with the facilitative leader approach. They recognize that it creates problems when people are unaware that two or more training courses are not only different but also incongruent. Some organizations intentionally offer courses that have conflicting values and beliefs, in part to stimulate conversation and thinking. This is not a problem if people are aware of this and have the opportunity to explore the inconsistencies and the effects that each approach generates, and if they are allowed to make choices about the approach they adopt. Otherwise, people feel that the organization is giving them a mixed message and they have difficulty figuring out which approach to use and why. Worse, if people don't recognize the inconsistencies and try to apply techniques from two inconsistent approaches, they can be ineffective and create conflict rather than improve the situation.

As an example, many of my clients have been taught the "sandwich" technique of giving negative feedback, which is inconsistent with the core values and assumptions of the facilitative leader approach. Using the sandwich technique, you would begin the feedback session by sharing some positive things about the person's behavior, then share some negative aspects of the person's behavior, and finally share again some positive aspects. People are taught that the positive-negative-positive order is designed to first put the person at ease and make her receptive to the negative feedback; then there follows positive feedback to reduce the chance she will disagree with your negative assessment of her behavior and become defensive.

There are a couple of problems with the sandwich technique. First, it is based on the assumption that the person is best able to receive the feedback when it is given in that order. In a facilitative leader approach, you would let her know that you have some negative feedback to give (and some positive feedback if that is also the case) and then jointly design a way for her to receive the feedback.

Second, for the sandwich technique to work, you must withhold your strategy from the person (or she has to agree to play along). To see what happens if you make your sandwich strategy transparent, imagine saying something like this: "Alice, I have some negative feedback to give you. To get you receptive to the negative feedback, I'll begin by giving you some positive feedback. Then I'll give you the negative feedback—the main reason I wanted to talk with you today. Finally, to reduce the chance of your becoming angry, I'll end by giving you some more positive feedback."

People laugh when they hear this, because they realize how absurd it sounds. They recognize that once you reveal the unilateral control strategy to protect yourself and others, it no longer works. By revealing the strategy, you are also revealing yourself. In addition, after the organization teaches people the approach, people recognize when it is being used on them, they feel manipulated, and they resent it. Also, people do not tend to find the positive feedback credible, which makes it difficult to genuinely reinforce behavior that is effective and valuable to the organization. As a result, people sometimes stop doing the very things you want them to continue or increase. Whereas unilateral control strategies become less effective as more people learn them, mutual learning strategies become more effective as more people learn them.

PRINCIPLES IN ACTION

Whether you are having a one-on-one conversation, helping your group address a difficult situation, or developing new structures, the facilitative leader approach offers you several principles that stem from your core values and assumptions.

Being Transparent

Part of being a facilitative leader is being transparent. This means you share the reasoning and intent underlying your statements, questions, and actions (ground rule four). Another way to think about being transparent is sharing your strategy. Being transparent reduces the need for people to make inferences and attributions about what you are saying and doing. When you share your strategy and the strategy matches your actions and is consistent with the mutual learning model, you build trust.

When I described the problems with the sandwich approach, I mentioned that for a unilateral control strategy to work, you need to withhold your strategy from the person receiving feedback (or else the person has to agree to play along). **One way to test whether your strategy is unilaterally controlling is to imagine yourself saying it to the person you are working with.** If it sounds unilaterally controlling or face-saving, it probably is. Of course, in order to do this test, you need to be aware of your strategy. This involves using the skill set and mind-set I describe throughout the book.

Being Curious

Being curious includes a genuine desire to understand how others think about a situation, especially when they think about it differently from you. This includes a desire to understand how you contribute to a problem in a way that you are unaware of. Being curious requires the ability to suspend judgment and embrace the mutual learning assumption that you understand only part of the puzzle. Together with compassion and transparency, genuine curiosity enables you to inquire into others' reasoning without generating defensive behavior, and to invite others to explore your reasoning.

Thinking and Acting Systemically

Throughout this book, I have emphasized that a group or organization is a system in which everything is ultimately related to everything else. Consequently, you cannot change just one thing without changing others. Being a facilitative leader in a system means thinking and acting systemically.

Becoming a Steward. To think systemically means to be a steward for the system as a whole, not just your part of it. This involves thinking simultaneously about the interests of individuals, the group, and the larger organization, as well as stakeholders outside the organization. It may mean spending time on issues that are more important to others than they are to you, or in meeting interests that are more important to other divisions than they are to yours.

Knowing You Do Not Know. Once you see yourself as a steward for the system, one of the first steps to thinking and acting systemically is recognizing that you cannot understand the entire system by yourself. In the language of mutual learning, it means assuming that you have only some of the information about how the system works and that other people who fill other roles in the system may see things that you miss. If you act in the system without fully understanding the dynamics, you are likely to create unintended consequences for others, for yourself, or both. You begin to act systemically by bringing together people who represent the whole system, so that you can plan for changes in a way that reduces unintended consequences. You can ask who and what might be affected by actions you take or changes you make. You can also ask what other changes have to be made to reduce unintended consequences.

The group effectiveness model that I first described in Chapter Two can help you think about how the changes may affect the three criteria for group effectiveness and any of the elements that contribute to it. You can use the group effectiveness model to have a conversation with your group about which elements are aligned and which are not working effectively. You can also use the group effectiveness model to help design a new group or team, making sure that each element is in place and that each is congruent with the others. As a facilitative leader, you help the group have a productive conversation in which everyone shares their views and the group generates a common understanding of the system and the changes needed.

Recognizing Your Contribution to the System. Thinking and acting systemically includes thinking in a feedback loop, asking yourself how changes that someone initiates lead others to make changes that affect others that—eventually—come around to affect the person who initiates the changes.

One form of this is recognizing that you are part of the system—even the systems you complain about—and that you make a contribution to maintaining the system in its current state. **If you think that those higher up in the organization do not understand the problems they are creating for those of you lower in the organization, you contribute to maintaining the system if you withhold information from them about the consequences they are creating that you think they are unaware of.** Thinking systemically means understanding that even if you cannot change the system yourself, at a minimum you can begin to influence it by providing new information to others in the system about how their actions affect other parts of the system. Similarly, if you are concerned that those who report directly to you are not building their capacity to solve problems, you are contributing to maintaining the system if you agree to handle issues they cannot solve without teaching them along the way. As a result, you may find that over time your ability to complete your own work suffers.

Thinking systemically means thinking simultaneously about short-term and long-term interests, and honoring the systems-thinking principle of going slow to go fast. If you have ever found yourself repeatedly solving problems for direct reports instead of helping them build their capacity, you have probably done so because there was a deadline to meet. This strategy makes sense in the short run but exacerbates the problem in the long run. Acting systemically here means taking more time in the short run to help people learn to solve problems so that in the long run their capacity is greater and so is yours.

Shifting from Blame to Contribution. Finally, thinking and acting systemically means shifting from a focus on placing blame to a focus on understanding how various people's behaviors interact and contribute to generating a problem, and how the problem continues despite the sincere efforts of many people to solve it. You can easily convince yourself that the cause of your problems lies in others' actions—those of other group members, groups, or organizations. But in system problems, the causes result from the interaction of behavior rather than individual actions. Looking for others to blame does not help the group understand the system; it obscures how you may contribute to creating, maintaining, or even escalating the problem.

To learn about your own contribution, you can ask group members, "How do you see me contributing to the problem? What are some things that I have done or not done? I'm asking because I don't see my contribution, but I realize I may be missing it."

Increasing Accountability and Ownership, Not Dependence

One of the goals of facilitative leadership is to develop the capacity of those who report to you to manage their own work relationships. Over time, group members become ever less dependent on you and instead create a self-managing group.

The Problem with Solving Others' Problems. A common way in which you can reduce accountability and create unnecessary dependence is to act as intermediary for your group members. Consider a common example in which one group member, Ellen, privately approaches you as the formal group leader and expresses concern about the behavior or performance of another group member, Peter. Ellen asks you to talk with Peter about how his inconsistent performance is affecting her work and the group's overall performance. In a traditional leadership role, you would take responsibility for resolving this problem.

If you agree to do so, you create several problems. First, when you talk with Peter you are likely to find that he has a different view of the situation from Ellen. Because you are not Ellen, you do not have all the relevant information you need to address his comments and questions. This makes it impossible to generate valid information on which to solve the problem. Second, even if you could have all the relevant information, you are now entering into a conversation in which you represent Ellen's perspective for Ellen. This may lead Peter to infer that you are siding with her. It also reduces Ellen's accountability for her behavior. Third, it reduces the opportunity for Ellen and Peter to begin to develop their skills in managing their own relationship.

Building Capacity. As a facilitative leader, your role is to help Ellen and Peter have the conversation they need if they are to adequately address the problem—not to solve the problem for them. This means using your facilitative skills to help them with conversation that is consistent with the core values and ground rules. It means using the diagnosis-intervention cycle to intervene if they are acting less effective than they could be. As a facilitative leader, you are not content-neutral; using specific examples, you share your point of view about how each has contributed to the problem, and you inquire about how they see it differently.

Keeping It in the Group. This issue applies to the group as a whole. Many of my clients have been taught to praise in public but criticize in private. They are taught that it is not relevant for the rest of the group to know about the criticism and that criticizing in private maintains the person's self-esteem.

Following this advice also creates unintended consequences. First, the concept of criticizing stems from a unilateral control frame in which the person criticizing believes he has all the information and that he is right and the person being criticized is wrong. It unilaterally saves face for the other person and for him. However, as a facilitative leader, you would start with the assumption that you have some information, the other person has other information, and you may be missing things that the other person sees. One of the things you may be missing is your own contribution to the person's behavior.

Second, you focus on creating valid information about the situation. If the person's behavior has had an effect on the group, addressing the issue outside of the group cuts off relevant information that group members have about the issue. This makes it impossible to construct a common understanding of what happened and how; it increases the chance of the person being criticized or blamed.

Third, it creates the very consequence you are trying to avoid: it shifts the person's accountability from the group to you. Finally, it prevents the group as a whole from being able to reflect on and learn from their experiences and be less likely to create the situation again.

As a facilitative leader, your role here is similar to that in the example with Ellen and Peter: to use your facilitative skills to have a productive conversation that addresses the issue. The difference here is that you initiate the conversation, so you are more deeply involved and invested in the content of the conversation.

Creating Conditions for Mutual Learning

To develop the kind of group and organization I have discussed in this chapter, facilitative leaders need to create the conditions for mutual learning. By mutual learning, I do not mean simply improving performance or learning new tasks. I mean the fundamental learning that occurs when members identify the core values and beliefs that guide their behavior (Argyris and Schön, 1974), understand how some values and beliefs undermine their effectiveness, and learn how to act consistently with a more effective set of values and beliefs.

As a facilitative leader, you help create the conditions for mutual learning. You can share the core values, principles, and ground rules with others and discuss what they mean, how they work, and what the barriers are to using them. In doing so, you can model the facilitative leader approach and tell others this is what you are doing. You can ask for specific feedback and explain that you will try not to get defensive if it is negative. You can encourage others to tell you if they are responding defensively to the feedback.

You can develop trust with group members by talking about how you have acted ineffectively in the past. Without this conversation, people may infer that you have a new, sophisticated strategy for maintaining unilateral control and compliance.

Finally, **as a facilitative leader you cannot lure, demand, manipulate, or coerce others to use the core values and principles discussed throughout this book. I hope it is obvious that to do so is inconsistent with everything for which the core values and principles stand.** Yet even if others choose not to use the core values, you still can. **By modeling the approach, you give people experience with it so that they may later make an informed and free choice to embrace it.**

SUMMARY

In this final chapter, I have described the facilitative leader approach, which is based on the same core values, assumptions, and principles as the Skilled Facilitator approach. You can serve as a facilitative leader even if you have no formal supervisory authority. The facilitative leader approach makes it possible to create groups that have the ability to manage their own relationships and to have increased accountability to the group as a whole.

Facilitative leadership is also a way to develop structures, policies and procedures, and programs that contribute to, rather than undermine, the group and organization's goals. Together with the core values and assumptions, the principles of transparency, curiosity, thinking and acting systemically, increasing accountability and ownership while reducing dependence, and mutual learning enable you to achieve the group's goals and those of the organization.

RESOURCE A

Current and Previous Ground Rules

There were sixteen ground rules in the previous set, in the first edition of *The Skilled Facilitator.* The current set, in this second edition, has nine ground rules. I have incorporated several interests in changing the ground rules.

First, I (and many of my clients who use the sixteen ground rules) wanted a shorter list because sixteen items are too many to hold in our short-term, or working, memory. Research shows that the number of items we can generally hold in short-term memory is seven plus or minus two.

Second, I have tried to keep the ground rules behaviorally specific so that people can still use them to guide their behavior. I have attempted to shorten the list yet maintain behavioral specificity.

Finally, I have made some changes that reflect my thinking in the years since the rules were published in the first edition.

Table A.1 shows how the previous ground rules relate to the current set of ground rules.

Table A.1. Comparison of Current and Previous Ground Rules

Current Ground Rules	Previous Ground Rules	Explanation
1. Test assumptions and inferences.	1. Test assumptions and inferences.	
2. Share all relevant information.	2. Share all relevant information. 7. Disagree openly with any member of the group. 13. All members are expected to participate in all phases of the process. 14. Exchange relevant information with non–group members. 16. Do self-critiques.	Previous ground rules seven, thirteen, fourteen, and sixteen are all specific ways of sharing relevant information.
3. Use specific examples and agree on what important words mean.	4. Be specific; use examples. 5. Agree on what important words mean.	Previous ground rules four and five typically need to be used together.
4. Explain your reasoning and intent.	6. Explain the reasons behind your statements, questions, and actions. 12. Do not take cheap shots or otherwise distract the group.	The cheap shots described in previous ground rule twelve are a specific way in which people make comments without explaining reasoning or intent.
5. Focus on interests, not positions.	3. Focus on interests, not positions.	
6. Combine advocacy and inquiry.	8. Make statements, then invite questions and comments.	I have used Chris Argyris's language to reflect the spirit of the ground rule.

Table A.1. *(continued)*

Current Ground Rules	Previous Ground Rules	Explanation
7. Jointly design next steps and ways to test disagreements.	9. Jointly design ways to test disagreements and solutions. 11. Keep the discussion focused.	Keeping the discussion focused (previous ground rule eleven) is one example of jointly designing the next steps in the conversation.
8. Discuss undiscussable issues.	10. Discuss undiscussable issues.	
9. Use a decision-making rule that generates the level of commitment needed.	15. Make decisions by consensus.	Consensus is typically required for decisions that need internal commitment from the group, but not all decisions require internal commitment. The new ground rule emphasizes the match between the decision-making rule and the level of commitment needed.

RESOURCE B

Sample
Planning Meeting Letter

ROGER SCHWARZ & ASSOCIATES

MEMO

To: ABC board members and CEO
Through: Ken Ahera, CEO, ABC
From: Roger Schwarz, President
Re: Planning meeting for board retreat
Date: September 16, 2001

I am looking forward to meeting with you on November 5, 2001, from 9:00 A.M. to 11:00 A.M. to begin planning for the ABC board retreat on December 4 and 5, 2001. Ken Ahera called me last week and asked if I could facilitate the retreat. Ken described the board's current situation and its needs, and I explained how I could help the group accomplish its retreat goals.

I requested the planning meeting in order to (1) give you enough information to decide as a group whether you want me to facilitate the retreat; (2) gather enough information for me to decide whether I can provide the facilitation help you need; and (3) if we decide to work together, identify the retreat objective, a general agenda, how we will work together, and logistical issues. Below is my proposed agenda for the meeting; please see if there are any changes you want to make so that we can address them at the beginning of the meeting.

I have enclosed copies of two articles: "Hiring and Working with a Group Facilitator" and "Ground Rules for Effective Groups." The first article briefly describes my approach to working with a group; the second article describes a set of ground rules that I use to help group members work together effectively. Please read the articles before the meeting so that we can explore any questions or concerns you have about how we would work together.

If you would like more information about Roger Schwarz & Associates, our approach to facilitation, or me, you may want to visit www.schwarzassociates.com.

Proposed Agenda for Retreat Planning Meeting
November 5, 2001

Introductions

Explanation of and changes to the agenda

1. What are the objectives of the retreat?
    *   What opportunities and problems exist that lead people to want a retreat now?
    *   What does the group need to accomplish to consider the retreat a success?

2. What will be the general retreat agenda and schedule?
   - What topics will the group discuss, and for about how long?
   - What are the starting and ending times?
   - Where will the retreat be held?

3. Who will attend the retreat?
   - Who needs to attend the retreat in order for the group to have the relevant information and support necessary to achieve its objectives?
   - What preparation is necessary in order for members to use their retreat time efficiently and effectively?
   - Under what conditions will we agree to reschedule the retreat?

4. What will be the facilitator's and others' roles?

5. What ground rules will the group follow?

6. Do you want to use me as the facilitator?

7. Next steps

Guidelines for Developing an Effective Contract

WHO IS THE PRIMARY CLIENT?

The primary client is the group being facilitated. For example, in a top management team that includes a CEO and the direct reports, it is important to specify whether any "assistant to" positions are part of the primary client group. The contract should also specify who else will attend group meetings and what role they play. The facilitation may also include individuals who provide budget or legal information to the primary client group. The role of these individuals may be to respond to primary client group member's requests for information but not to actively participate in discussion or decision making. Other individuals may also be invited to observe the sessions without participating.

I use two principles to consider who should attend and participate. First, **the group is more likely to accomplish its objectives if it does not include unnecessary members.** A group that is larger than what the task requires takes more time to accomplish its work and may end up with low-quality decisions. This does not mean that only those who are responsible for making the decision should be present. Generating valid information and commitment may require that the primary group include individuals responsible for implementing the decision (and who may be affected by it), as well as those making the decision. Second, **when it is necessary to discuss issues of high conflict or something that members find difficult to discuss openly, the group process is more effective the fewer people outside the primary client group are present.** The presence of additional members can create pressure on primary group members to withhold and distort information or to "play to the gallery" (Svara, 1990). For example, if observers include the primary group members' constituents, then members who privately agree with each other may be reluctant to say so if they believe their constituents would disapprove.

Still, it is important that the group not exclude potential participants solely because some group members want to avoid conflict with those individuals. In contracting with a group of physicians, for example, I raised the question of whether one physician, who was loosely connected with the group and about whom some members had concerns, should attend the planning and expectation-setting retreat. One physician remarked, "Well, if he comes, we can't talk about him." I responded: "I agree. But, if he comes, you can talk *with* him." I explained that if members of the group have problems working with this member, the retreat would be an appropriate forum for exploring their unmet expectations, and my cofacilitator and I could help the group discuss the issue constructively. I also mentioned that I believed the group members could not resolve the conflict with that person unless they talked directly with him about the issue. As it turned out, the planning group decided to exclude this person, ostensibly for other, legitimate reasons. My untested inference was that the group members would not have excluded him if they had not seen themselves in conflict with him.

Because the excluded person's presence was not necessary for the group to accomplish its retreat goals, I did not press the issue with the planning group. However, I mentioned that if, during the retreat, this individual's behavior became the subject of group discussion, I would raise the question of the validity of any group decisions made on the basis of untested inferences or assumptions that members made about him.

WHERE AND HOW LONG WILL THE GROUP MEET?

Deciding how much time the group needs depends on several factors: (1) what objectives the group wants to accomplish, (2) how much work is required for the group to accomplish the objectives, (3) the group's initial skill level, and (4) my skill in helping the group accomplish its objectives. It is beyond the scope of this—and probably any—book to describe how long it takes a group to accomplish certain objectives such as clarifying role expectations or resolving a particular conflict. A group's ability to work effectively varies widely; I can have only a limited understanding of one group's strengths and weaknesses before I begin working with it.

For short-term basic facilitation, how long the group meets is often constrained by the block of time the group has available. A group may press you to help it accomplish the objectives in what you consider an unrealistically short time. If you acquiesce because you want to work with the group, feel pressured by the client, or want the income, you are contributing to preventing the group from achieving its objectives.

When scheduling work, match the objectives with the time available and avoid compressing work to fit the time allotted (Schwarz, 1991). A major risk in allotting less time than needed is that the group fails to make sufficient progress and becomes less motivated to continue working in subsequent sessions, or it comes to consider consensus decision making a waste of time. When the group is attempting to resolve a difficult conflict, for example, insufficient time may leave the group in more conflict than if it does not address the conflict at all.

In these situations, I suggest to the group that we do the math to figure out if the allotted time is realistic. For example, I might say, "The agenda has five major items in it, each of which has at least two subparts, and there are fifteen people in the group. Let's assume that for each subpart each person shares his or her thoughts for two minutes and at the end of that time the group is able to reach a decision without any further discussion. I think it is very unlikely to happen, given the views we have heard on the subject; but even if it does, it will still require five hours. You are suggesting allocating four hours for the entire discussion. I think a more realistic estimate is two days. This would permit the kind of conversation in which members can share their reasoning, identify differences in views, examine how those differences occur, and develop solutions that they can commit to. What are your thoughts about what I have said?"

Sometimes I agree to jointly test out how long the process will take. A council-manager group that once asked a colleague and me to facilitate their evaluation of the manager's performance wanted to complete the entire evaluation in three hours. By doing the math with the group, we suggested it would take at least six hours, but we agreed to work with the group for three hours—without rushing the process. We also agreed that after three hours the group would evaluate itself and our effectiveness, including how well we used the time, and then decide whether to continue the process. At the end of three hours, the council group realized its estimate had been unrealistic and agreed to allot more time. Again, the group allotted less time than we thought realistic, and again we reached the same agreement with the group. In this way, the group was able to make a free and informed choice about how much time to spend, and my colleague and I did not have to compress our work in a way that we considered ineffective.

This approach does not work if the initial amount of time scheduled is likely to result in unprocessed issues that would harm the group. This will probably occur if the group is faced with a difficult conflict or if personally threatening or undiscussable issues end up being raised. In these situations, **if the client is likely to be harmed or if the facilitator believes the client is not able to make** an informed choice, the facilitator has an ethical responsibility to explain this to the client and decline to facilitate under those conditions.

WHAT ARE THE ROLES OF THE PARTIES?

Clients often seek a facilitator without clearly understanding what the facilitator will do. In addition, adding a facilitator to a group changes the roles that group members normally play and how they interact with each other. Therefore it is important to agree on the roles that each will play.

Facilitator Role

In this section, I include the basic approach that I use in facilitation, briefly describing how I help the group and the kind of behavior I do not engage in that the client might otherwise expect of me. For example, clients sometimes expect the facilitator to provide expert information or to raise issues for group members who feel uncomfortable doing so themselves. If I believe another facilitative role—such as facilitative consultant—is more appropriate, I will discuss this with the group.

Concern About the Facilitator's Qualifications. The client may have questions about my qualifications. The client may want to know if I have worked on similar problems or with similar organizations, or want to talk with some of my other clients, or see a résumé. Underlying all of these requests is the question of whether I can help the client.

I can address the client's concern in two ways. First I can describe my credentials and facilitation experience, highlighting especially relevant past work. If I do not have experience with the current client's type of organization or problem, I will share that relevant information and explain how my lack of experience may or may not hinder my effectiveness.

Another way to address the client's concern about qualifications is to explore it directly. I might say, "You've asked me a number of questions about my facilitation experience, and I'm happy to answer them. I think it's important that you have an accurate view of whether and how I can help you. I'm wondering, what in particular leads you to ask? Are there particular questions or concerns you have that lead you to wonder whether I will really be able to help?" By discussing the concern, I learn more about the client's problem, assist in determining whether they think I can help, and in the process demonstrate the Skilled Facilitator approach.

Concern About the Facilitator's Neutrality. Sometimes you may be asked to help a group that is in conflict over a controversial issue in the organization or a public controversy such as gun control. A question for the client and you is whether you can serve as a content-neutral third party, regardless of your personal views on the subject. If the clients ask your views, it is consistent with the core values to describe them. At the same time, it is helpful to ask the client group how your personal views affect their views about your facilitating the group.

Facilitator-Leader Roles

Without a facilitator, the formal group leader typically manages the process when the group meets. The leader sets the agenda, decides when to change the topic of the conversation, and in a formal group recognizes those who want to speak. My addition as the facilitator raises the question of who will lead the meeting and monitor and intervene in the group process.

In one approach, the leader continues to lead the group, including management of the process, and I facilitate by intervening when necessary. This approach is most like a regular group meeting. In a second approach, I can manage the process while the leader continues to play a formal role distinguished from other group members. This is the flip side of the first method. Third, the leader can play the same role as other group members and I can manage the process. This approach is useful in short-term basic facilitation, when the leader wants to reduce her influence in the group discussion and increase that of other group members. Finally, all group members can take responsibility for managing the process, including the leader and me. This is the most effective method for developmental facilitation because it decreases the group's dependence on the facilitator.

Member Roles

Changing the relationship between two of the three roles—leader, member, and facilitator—can easily affect the relationship with the third role. For example, if I manage the group's process instead of the leader managing it, the other group members may relate differently to the leader and me. This has two implications. First, **the new group roles and relationships must be defined (or redefined) as a system, so they do not cause role conflict.** Second, **all members have to understand every role and relationship in the group.**

I experienced the consequences of ignoring these principles when I facilitated a city council-manager group. A colleague and I observed that the mayor called on council members to speak in a way that led to a series of unrelated monologues rather than a dialogue. We had clarified our facilitator role vis-à-vis the group members, but not with the mayor. As a result, when we tried to intervene to encourage a dialogue, we found ourselves engaged in a conflict with the mayor as to who should manage the process. We later compounded our error by reaching an agreement with the mayor regarding our respective roles, without including the rest of the group in the discussion. Consequently, when the mayor began playing his agreed-upon role, certain council members inferred that he was abdicating his leadership position, because they had had no involvement in the agreement and did not know what roles we and the mayor had agreed to play.

WHAT GROUND RULES WILL THE GROUP FOLLOW?

Ground rules are an essential part of the Skilled Facilitator approach. I prefer to discuss and tentatively agree on the ground rules in the planning meeting, reviewing them, modifying them if necessary, and finally agreeing on them at stage three of contracting (see Chapter Thirteen). This helps the client group better understand my role and agree on expectations for the members' own behavior. The contract may identify the specific set of ground rules the group will use, or identify that a set of ground rules will be agreed upon at the facilitation.

Ground Rules for Attendance

Unlike the ground rules that members agree to follow within the group discussion, it is important to include ground rules for attendance in the contract, especially for a single-session facilitation. Under what conditions should the facilitator decide not to facilitate? It is important to have all members present if the group has to make a decision that requires the full commitment of all members to implement effectively, or if the absence of a member significantly reduces the information available to make a quality decision. A group's reluctance to commit to full attendance may foreshadow problems during the facilitation.

For example, a county asked me to facilitate a joint meeting of the board of social services and the board of county commissioners. For several reasons, I was ambivalent about requiring full attendance. I had conducted a similar retreat for the same groups the previous year, in which we had set a minimum number for attendance (not full attendance). Although that number was not met, I continued to facilitate the retreat. Thus I anticipated that attendance would be a problem again, but I did not raise the issue because I was concerned about alienating the initial client contact, who was very influential with similar groups that were also my clients. In a conference call to plan the retreat, the social services director (the initial contact) mentioned that the chairperson of the board of commissioners was not going to be able to participate in the conference call. Again, I thought about but did not suggest we reschedule the call for a time when everyone could participate. As it turned out, the chairperson did not attend the retreat. This left other board members reluctant to make certain commitments, which defeated the purpose of the retreat.

When a group faces a difficult conflict, the member or members who are reluctant to attend are often the ones expressing a minority viewpoint. Sometimes they are concerned that if they attend, the majority will pressure them to concede. The majority often respond by asking to meet without those members, believing that the majority can resolve a conflict without the minority being present. If I agree to meet without the reluctant members, I contribute to the group's not being able to address the problem.

Unfortunately, requiring full attendance can lead to control by the minority, in which the majority feels that its meeting is being prevented by the minority. Once members frame the issue as a power struggle over who controls whether the facilitation occurs, members of the majority are likely to push for a meeting with less-than-full attendance as a way of asserting their power, even if they realize the group's objectives cannot be accomplished with the minority subgroup absent.

With a very large group—perhaps beyond twenty—full attendance is less necessary. A large group makes it difficult, if not impossible, for every member to contribute meaningfully to the discussion and decision. The absence of one or several members may make little practical difference in the process or outcomes. Instead, it is important that each subgroup and set of interests be represented. In a management retreat, for example, that includes the top sixty members of an organization, the absence of just three people can be critical if they are the only representatives of one particular function.

It can be difficult to follow through on the attendance ground rule and tell a client group that has gathered at a site (or even worse, traveled a distance) that I am unwilling to facilitate the session as planned because one or more members are absent. When I face this situation, I remind the client of our reasoning and agreement to require full attendance and check whether that reasoning still makes sense to the client. Assuming it does, I then explore with the group what kind of work, if any, the group can accomplish with me given the absence of the members.

How Will Decisions Be Made?

The choice of which rules will be used for making decisions is a central one. Will the group make decisions by consensus, two-thirds vote, majority rule, or some other way? Will all decisions in the session be made using the same rule, or will the decision rule depend on the type? Even more basic, will any decisions be made in the sessions? These questions should be raised in the contracting stage, but they do not have to be settled until the full group meets.

There is a paradox inherent in this issue. To answer the question of how we will make decisions, we first have to answer the meta-question "How do we make a decision about how we make decisions?" This kind of problem cannot be solved, because the meta-question continues infinitely. To get out of this paralyzing loop, the group must somehow just figure out how to make decisions as if they already had a decision rule to guide them (Smith and Berg, 1987).

Ground Rules for Confidentiality

I must reach agreement with the client about when I will treat information that individual members or subgroups share with me as confidential. Confidentiality has advantages and disadvantages. It enables me to learn things that I may not otherwise find out about the group, or learn it earlier than otherwise possible, but it prevents me from using that information to intervene in the group. Maintaining confidentiality may increase client trust in me, but it maintains the mistrust among group members that led them to want to have the information considered confidential in the first place. Finally, confidentiality maintains the members' ability to work together at some level, but it fails to increase the group's effectiveness by keeping relevant information out of its realm.

Confidentiality creates a dilemma. If I agree to protect the interests of the individual seeking confidentiality, I may fail to serve the interests of the full client group. In this way, agreeing to keep an individual conversation confidential can reduce my effectiveness with the full client group, and thus create a conflict with my professional objectives and ethical values.

The client can bind a facilitator to confidentiality explicitly or implicitly (Golembiewski, 1986), as some examples will show.

A colleague and I met with a mayor and the city manager to plan their expectation-setting retreat. At the end of the meeting, the mayor stood up and casually said to us, "Just don't tell the council members I was involved in planning this retreat. If they knew, they wouldn't support it." For reasons I still do not entirely understand, neither my colleague nor I responded to the mayor's statement; we just let it pass as if he had not said it. The mayor explicitly stated that we should not disclose his participation in the planning process. By not responding, we had implicitly (and inappropriately) agreed.

In other situations, a client does not explicitly request confidentiality, but the facilitator may end up granting it, albeit ambivalently. This occurs when the facilitator infers that the client does not want the information disclosed and the facilitator does not test this inference with the client. Unlike the explicit example just described, here the facilitator is largely responsible for creating the bind. For example, during a break in a meeting the mayor may approach the facilitator and say, "What's really behind this conversation is that some of us think the manager is getting out in front of the council on some issues. He needs to lay low for a while."

Whether the facilitator agrees to maintain confidentiality either as a result of a client's explicit request or implicitly because of the facilitator's untested inference, the consequences are similar. The facilitator limits her ability to disclose the conversation held with the individual "promised" confidentiality. The facilitator cannot say in front of the group, "Mayor, you talked with me about the issue of the manager getting out in front. How is that related to the group's discussion?" The facilitator may also limit herself from making any interventions that even appear to rely on information from a "confidential" conversation.

Dealing with the issue of confidentiality effectively means anticipating the issue and raising it "before we find ourselves being told things that put us in conflicts between protecting our client's interests and respecting our commitment to confidentiality" (Gellermann, Frankel, and Ladenson, 1990, p. 175). One way to accomplish this is to reach agreement with the client early in the relationship. In deciding when to discuss confidentiality, I need to balance the likelihood of awkwardness from raising the issue too early with the probability of finding myself in a confidentiality conflict.

Until an agreement is reached, once a client finishes a sentence that begins "Just between you and me . . ." it is no longer possible to disclose the client's information to the group without the client believing that her confidentiality has been violated. When a person with whom I have no agreement about confidentiality begins to tell me something at the same time that she requests it remain confidential, I stop the person. I explain that by agreeing, in advance, to hear information I will not be able to use, I potentially reduce my usefulness to the group. I can then offer a choice about whether the member wants to disclose the information without any agreement of confidentiality. I can also discuss with the member why he is reluctant to tell the group something he believes it is important for me to know. If I can help him find a way to raise the issue with the group, then as facilitator I have helped the group deal with an undiscussable issue.

Some facilitators specify that unless they explicitly agree to keep something confidential, the client should assume the facilitator will use his judgment in sharing information with the larger group. Others agree in advance on the kind of information they will and will not keep confidential.

The agreement about limits of confidentiality should include more than conversation; a client can bind a facilitator without talking with the person. For example, while consulting to a group of employees, I received an unsolicited letter at my office from one of the members in the group. The letter described some of the problems that were occurring in the group but that had not been discussed openly. I inferred that the writer believed the group was not addressing the important issues it needed to address. I also wondered whether I had been ineffective with the group for not helping surface those issues and whether the client thought the same. Because our agreement on confidentiality did not address this sort of situation, and because I did not talk to the letter writer after receiving it, I implicitly agreed to treat the letter confidentially. Unfortunately, I also did not raise the issue in the group because I was reluctant to take responsibility for raising a group member's issue.

I also identify the conditions under which I will reveal information accepted in confidence to people outside the client group. Facilitators often discuss their work with professional colleagues to increase their own effectiveness. This type of consultation is appropriate "when discussion with them is confidential and compatible with the interests of [the] clients and informants" (Gellermann, Frankel, and Ladenson, 1990, p. 175). Facilitators may use information obtained through work with clients in their "writings, lectures, or other public forums only with prior consent or when disguised so that it is impossible from [the facilitators'] presentations alone to identify the individuals or systems with whom [the facilitator has] worked" (p. 175).

An important group to consider is the news media. One option is not to talk with the media at all. This encourages the client to take total responsibility for working with the media and reduces my risk of violating confidentiality. But it also requires the client to answer questions about my facilitator role, which I am more qualified to do. I prefer to agree to talk with the media, but only about my role of facilitator. This helps the reporter (and ultimately the public) understand the process of facilitation without my discussing the client's situation. For example, I might discuss generally how groups benefit from using a facilitator, without discussing the problems that the client group is trying to solve.

Clients also need to agree on what information they will keep confidential and what information they will share, either in the larger organization or outside.

HOW WILL THE GROUP ASSESS PROGRESS?

A group needs some way to assess progress toward the objectives. In single-session or short-term facilitation, self-critique enables the group to evaluate its progress during and at the end of the sessions. For long-term facilitation, self-critique is still useful, but methods such as a survey or analysis of relevant organizational records give the group other types of data. For example, a group of employees who are meeting to increase the quality of service could survey a sample of customers over time, or measure how long people wait to be served. It is not necessary for the contract to identify the specific ways in which progress is to be measured. The client often does not know what specific changes it wants to create before facilitation begins, and, even if the client did, details are not necessary. However, it is important that the contract identify that progress will be measured and the broad way in which this may be done.

HOW WILL THE FACILITATOR'S PERFORMANCE BE ASSESSED?

I also need some feedback from clients about my performance. This can be addressed in a self-critique conducted at the end of each meeting. By participating in the critique, I model reflective behavior. In addition, I encourage the client to give me feedback at the time the relevant behavior occurs.

WHAT ARE THE FACILITATOR'S FEES AND OTHER CHARGES?

The contract should clearly state your professional fee; whether it is charged daily, hourly, or on a project basis; and whether this includes charges for other expenses, such as preparation time, travel, meals and lodging, and materials. Geoffrey Bellman's *The Consultant's Calling* (2001) offers useful ideas for determining consulting fees.

HOW LONG WILL THE CONTRACT BE IN EFFECT?

For short-term basic facilitation, the length of the contract is obvious. However, as the group seeks to create more significant change, it is usually not possible to determine exactly how long the group needs to meet to accomplish its objectives. In this case, I specify some time period after which the client and I will discuss whether the contract should be renewed.

WHEN AND HOW DO YOU CHANGE THE CONTRACT?

Changing the contract requires that the client and I agree. For example, the client sometimes calls the day before a retreat to see whether I will still facilitate if one member is unable to attend. On other occasions, a client (or I) may need to reschedule or cancel a meeting. In still other cases, a client may ask me to expand the work with the group, or to facilitate additional groups.

The ultimate contract change occurs when the client unilaterally decides to stop using you as a facilitator before the end of the agreed-upon period. If the meeting schedule is set in advance, the client may reschedule or cancel a few meetings before telling you. If the next meeting date is not scheduled until after the most recent meeting has occurred, you may never get a call for the next meeting. The latter situation happened once to a colleague and me. Because we had no agreement with the client about changing the contract, and because we were dissatisfied with the group's progress, we did not discuss the situation with the full client group. Only months later, in an informal conversation with one of the group members, did we learn of the client's reasons for discontinuing the work.

To avoid this problem, a long-term facilitation contract can specify that you be given an opportunity to talk with the client before the latter decides to end the work prematurely. The purpose of the meeting is not to persuade the client to continue the work; that is inconsistent with the core value of free and informed choice. Rather, the meeting enables you to hear directly why the client wants to end the facilitation. This conversation may identify such concerns as lack of progress, your competence, external pressure on the group, or members' fear of dealing with undiscussable issues. A conversation like this enables you to help the client make an informed choice about ending the facilitation and provides you with feedback about your performance.

Cancellation of a contract is often preceded by more subtle changes. The client may delay returning your phone calls, exclude you from planning some meetings, or change their reactions to your interventions. The changes may reflect issues addressed in the contract. They may also refer to implicit understandings or norms that have developed between the client and you. In short, the client begins to treat you differently. This can happen subtly but quickly. **As soon as you sense that the client is treating you differently, raise the issue and explore whether the contract should be modified** (Block, 1981).

In one sense, the client and facilitator are continually renegotiating the contract—if not in print, at least verbally. Over the course of the facilitation, clients become clearer about their objectives, the objectives change, the level of motivation waxes and wanes, and dependence on the facilitator varies as the clients' own skills increase. To serve the client well, the agreement has to reflect the client's changing needs.

HOW AND WHEN SHOULD THE TENTATIVE CONTRACT BE CONVEYED TO ALL PARTIES?

To be useful, the contract has to find its way into the hands of all members of the client group. Especially in short-term basic facilitation, this should occur before the first facilitated meeting.

RESOURCE D

Sample Agreement
for Basic Facilitation

ROGER SCHWARZ & ASSOCIATES

Facilitation Agreement Between ABC Top Management Team and Roger Schwarz, Roger Schwarz & Associates

MEMO

To: Terry Copeland, city manager, City of Livingston
        Anna Macher, director of human resources
        Julius Marks, director of public works
From: Roger Schwarz, President
Re: Top management team retreat
Date: June 13, 2001

This memo summarizes the agreement we reached during our planning meeting regarding the top management retreat.

Time and location: The retreat will be held at the Governor's Club outside of Chapel Hill. The retreat will begin at 9:00 A.M. on June 29, and the group will work until 9:00 P.M. The group will meet from 9:00 A.M. until 5:00 P.M. on June 30. Meals will be served at the center.

Attendance and rescheduling: The top management team members will participate in the retreat: Terry Copeland, Anna Macher, Julius Marks, Kathy Washington, Lee Robeson, Vance Forsyth, Charlotte Umstead, and Dale Rosenbaum. To enable full discussion of all participants' views and to ensure adequate support for any decisions reached in the session, the participants agree to attend the full session, without interruption. We have agreed to reschedule the retreat if any member is unable to attend.

Tentative objective and agenda: The objective of the retreat is to help the group improve its functioning by clarifying its roles and working relationships. To accomplish this objective, the group will discuss these general issues: (1) the general role of the city manager and department heads, and (2) the city manager's expectations for the department heads and vice versa.

We will begin the retreat by introducing participants, agreeing on or modifying the tentative agenda, identifying participants' expectations, and agreeing on ground rules. We will conclude the retreat with a discussion of next steps and an evaluation of the retreat, including the facilitator.

The retreat objective and agenda remain tentative until the entire group of participants either confirms or modifies it.

Third-party roles and fees: I will serve as a substantively neutral facilitator for the group. I will not provide expert information on issues the group is discussing nor make decisions for the group, but rather will help the group use effective process to discuss its issues. This will include helping participants (1) stay on topic, (2) see how their views are similar and different, (3) understand the assumptions underlying their discussion, and (4) identify solutions that meet all participants' interests.

Roger Schwarz & Associates' charges for facilitation are $xxxx for the two-day session, plus expenses for travel, lodging, and meals.

Advance preparation: At the beginning of the retreat, the group will decide on a set of ground rules to guide its discussion. To prepare for making this decision, please read the enclosed article "Ground Rules for Effective Groups," which I wrote.

Notification of changes: Please contact me immediately if this memo is inconsistent with the agreement we have reached in our conversations. Terry Copeland will contact me in the event that any participant cannot attend the retreat. If events or circumstances require modifying our agreement, we will jointly decide how to make the changes.

Distribution of memo: So that all participants will be fully informed about the retreat plans, Terry Copeland will arrange for copies of this memo and the ground rules article to be sent to all participants.

I look forward to working with you on June 29 and 30.

RESOURCE E

Sample Agreement for Developmental Facilitation

ROGER SCHWARZ & ASSOCIATES

Facilitation Agreement Between ABC Top Management Team and Roger Schwarz, Roger Schwarz & Associates

The purpose of this agreement is to clarify and commit to the conditions that will govern the facilitation relationship between the ABC top management team and Roger Schwarz of Roger Schwarz & Associates.

Goals and Objectives of Facilitation

Management team goals. The goals of the facilitation are to develop a management team that (1) manages and leads using a shared set of values and beliefs that are consistent with the mission and vision statement of the organization, and (2) solves problems, makes decisions, and communicates effectively within that set of values and beliefs. This includes top management team members' relationships with each other, other members of the organization, and persons in the organization's environment.

The objectives constituting these goals are to

1. Develop a set of espoused values and beliefs that will guide members' actions
2. Increase members' ability to identify the values and beliefs that underlie their actions
3. Increase members' ability to identify inconsistencies between their espoused values and beliefs and the values and beliefs embedded in their actions
4. Increase members' ability to design problem-solving, decision-making, and communication processes and structures consistent with their espoused values and beliefs
5. Increase members' ability to act consistently with a set of ground rules derived from the values and beliefs
6. Increase members' ability to communicate values and beliefs to other organizational members as well as clients and others in the organization's environment

Consultant goals. The primary goal of the facilitator is to help the management team achieve its goals in a way that, over time, reduces dependence on the facilitator. Other goals are to

- Increase the facilitator's effectiveness by obtaining feedback about how his behavior affects the client
- Contribute to the field of organization development by using the facilitation data to publish research, theory, and practice regarding the facilitation process

Criteria for Deciding the Issues on Which to Work

The management team will give high priority to working on issues whose characteristics are likely to help the group achieve its goals and objectives. Issues have high priority for discussion to the extent that they meet the following criteria:

- The issue is fertile ground for learning about the team's or members' values and beliefs.
- The issue has a relatively high level of emotional content or is usually undiscussable.
- The issue is one in which most of the relevant information resides with management team members.
- The issue is one in which the group's learning may be significantly increased by the facilitator's presence.
- The issue can be discussed without pressure to be resolved immediately. This criterion is based on the premise that when the group must use the meeting to make a decision, there is pressure to reduce the time allotted to examining values and beliefs related to the decision.

Ground Rules

The group has committed to using the ground rules described in the article "Ground Rules for Effective Groups." In addition, the group may develop other ground rules during the facilitation process.

Information shared within the facilitated sessions will be considered confidential unless members agree otherwise. Information shared by one or more group members with the facilitator will not be considered confidential with respect to the other group members.

The facilitator has the right to use data from the facilitation process for professional writing, research, and presentations if the identities of the organization and management team members are disguised. The facilitator may use the data in undisguised form with the permission of the management team.

Role of Facilitator

The facilitator will serve as a substantively neutral third party for the group. The facilitator will not make decisions for the group but rather will help the group use and learn how to use effective group process, in part by modeling the ground rules. The facilitator will provide expert information on the group's issues only if a member of the group has requested it and the group has agreed for the facilitator to provide it. The facilitator and top management team will jointly control the facilitation process.

Evaluating Progress

The management team and facilitator may use the following methods to measure the team's progress toward achieving its goals and objectives and to assess the facilitator's effectiveness:

- Self-critiques at the end of each meeting
- Tape-recorded facilitation sessions
- Written communications from top management team members
- Decisions made by top management team members
- Dialogues written by top management team members
- Self-reports of top management team members
- Verbal and written feedback from employees
- Surveys or interviews of employees

Facilitator Fees and Expenses

ABC will pay Roger Schwarz & Associates $xxxx for each half day of facilitation provided by Roger Schwarz. In addition, ABC will reimburse Roger Schwarz & Associates for travel, lodging, meals, and other direct expenses incurred.

Duration of, Changes to, and Process for Terminating Facilitation

The parties agree to meet approximately one-half day per week for one year from the date of this contract. At that time, the parties will evaluate their progress and renew, modify, or terminate their agreement as needed.

At any time, either party may suggest changes in this agreement. Any changes in the agreement shall be agreed to by both parties.

Nevertheless, either party may terminate this facilitation relationship at any time. However, before terminating the relationship, the parties agree to meet to discuss the circumstances of termination and to conduct a final self-critique of the facilitation process.

We commit to facilitation services as described in this agreement:

ABC top management team members: Roger Schwarz & Associates:

Herb Daniels   date   Roger Schwarz   date

Carl Hughs   date

Corin Danforth   date

Jill Suiter   date

Katie Breadman   date

Jerry Mathers   date

RESOURCE F

Guidelines for Using Experiential Exercises and Self-Knowledge Instruments

Experiential exercises and self-knowledge instruments are macro interventions. Experiential exercises help a group learn about its process in the course of working on some simulated task. A popular example is the "lost on the moon" exercise, in which the group pretends it is stranded on the moon. The group must leave the spaceship to try to be saved; members have fifteen items they can take along. Each member ranks the fifteen items (for example, a flashlight, a parachute, a box of matches) in order of importance for their trip. Next, the entire group agrees on a single order. The exercise helps group members explore how their group process (problem solving, decision making, conflict management, and communication) influences the group's effectiveness.

Self-knowledge instruments (such as group communication surveys, Myers-Briggs Type Indicator) help a group understand some aspects of its group dynamics or individual differences within the group.

I rarely use experiential exercises or self-knowledge instruments as part of my facilitation. I find that the group members' own experiences trying to solve real problems create more than enough real data for me to help them learn about their dynamics and themselves as group members. Still, I recognize that many facilitators find these instruments and exercises helpful.

If you choose to use experiential exercises or self-knowledge instruments to facilitate group process, consider using ones that are consistent with the core values and principles of the Skilled Facilitator approach. Use the group's time effectively, and in the case of an instrument be sure it is statistically valid and reliable.

CONSISTENCY WITH THE CORE VALUES AND PRINCIPLES

To be consistent with the core values and principles of group facilitation, the instrument or exercise needs to generate valid information, enable participants to make a free and informed choice, lead members to be internally committed to the choice, and engender compassion. Given these values, I consider it *inappropriate* to use an exercise or instrument with any of these characteristics:

• *It requires withholding information or relying on deception.* For example, one personnel selection exercise is designed to identify how well members test assumptions and share information. Each member is given a sheet of paper with what looks like the same description of several job candidates and asked to select the best candidate. In fact, the best candidate can be selected only if members realize that each member's sheet has slightly different information and share that information. For the exercise to work, as a facilitator you must withhold from the group the information that each sheet is different.

The problem with using deception is that it reduces the group's trust and credibility in you. It reduces trust because deception is inconsistent with the core values. It reduces credibility because it sends the message that deception is justified when you are seeking a pure outcome or are driven by pure motives (in this case, learning). However, because individuals almost always consider their motives or outcomes pure, in practice I believe that using deceptive exercises has the effect of endorsing deception in general. Finally, it is difficult to be a credible model of helping a group reduce deception if you rely on deception in working with the group.

The one condition on which I consider it acceptable to use deception is when the group makes a free and (somewhat) informed choice to participate after you have told them that deception is involved.

• *The outcome is predetermined and controlled by you.* There is an exercise that examines conflict by asking a group to put together a puzzle that, unbeknown to members, is missing a piece. Here too, the group can make a free and (somewhat) informed choice about participating in an exercise if it is aware that the outcome is predetermined.

• *It demands a level of personal risk greater than what the group members agreed to.* An example is having members reveal their answers to survey questions about group trust.

• *It is inconsistent with the group's objectives.*

• *You do not have time to process the results adequately.*

• *You do not know what to expect in terms of the range of issues that might be raised by the exercise or instrument and are not confident about handling all the issues that might be raised.*

DECIDING WHETHER TO USE EXPERIENTIAL EXERCISES

Even if an experiential exercise meets the conditions listed, it may not be the best choice for a learning exercise. The purpose of an experiential group exercise is to create an experience on which group members can reflect and from which they can learn about their process. Experiential group exercises are based on a set of assumptions that are consistent with the Skilled Facilitator approach (Hall, Bowen, Lewicki, and Hall, 1982, p. 3); see Exhibit F.1.

Experiential group exercises require a group task and interdependent group members who are trying to accomplish the task. The group task is typically artificial; that is, the group would not normally perform it (or perform it in this way) in the course of their work, or in a training class in which participants do not constitute an intact work group, the task is artificial because the group is artificial.

In group facilitation, however, group members are usually already in an intact work group and interdependent. The group is faced with many real tasks that you can use to help members reflect on and learn from. In fact, this is what developmental facilitation is all about. Given this, I believe there needs to be some additional purpose for using an experiential exercise.

One purpose is to make it easier for group members to examine their process by separating it from real content issues. By reducing the investment members have in the content of the decision, they can reflect on the process more objectively and less defensively. But this interest can conflict with another: wanting the exercise to be credible. A group may discount the exercise results by arguing that it does not adequately represent the group's situation. If one of a group's problems is that members become defensive, using an exercise that reduces defensive behavior limits the opportunity for working on it. In other words, in some situations members learn more when the experience comes

Exhibit F.1. Assumptions Underlying Experiential Exercises

1. Learning is more effective when it is an active rather than a passive process.
2. Problem-centered learning is more enduring than theory-based learning.
3. Two-way communication produces better learning than one-way communication.
4. Participants learn more when they share control over and responsibility for the learning process than when the responsibility lies solely with the group leader.
5. Learning is most effective when thought and action are integrated.

from the group's real tasks and they experience the full consequences of group process (Schwarz, 1985). When deciding whether to suggest an experiential exercise, consider the various interests.

Finally, experiential exercises are generally not an effective use of time for basic facilitation, the purpose of which is not to learn how to develop more effective process.

VALIDITY AND RELIABILITY OF INSTRUMENTS

Self-knowledge instruments should meet a minimum level of validity and reliability. A discussion of test validity and reliability is beyond the purpose of this book, but here is a brief overview of these terms.

There are two major types of validity: internal and external (Cook and Campbell, 1979). If an instrument is *internally* valid, it measures what it is intended to measure. For example, if an instrument is intended to measure a person's intelligence, internal validity means it measures intelligence only and not the person's conflict style, or whether the person is an introvert or extrovert.

If an instrument is *externally* valid, its internal validity holds for a variety of people and settings. When instruments are developed and tested for internal validity, they are tested using a sample of people (say, five hundred first-level supervisors in the banking industry). If the instrument is externally valid for a certain population, it works for that population (managers, elected officials, people in a particular occupation). You can determine whether an instrument is externally valid for a particular population only after the instrument has been used with that population (Cook and Campbell, 1979).

If an instrument is *reliable,* you can depend on it to give roughly the same results when a particular individual takes it more than once over a period of time (assuming no change in the individual). Reliability reflects the consistency of results over time, and nothing else.

Instruments that are not valid or not reliable mislead people about the meaning of their scores. To determine whether an instrument is valid and reliable, first examine it. Some authors of instruments provide the information in an appendix explaining the design of the instrument. Other authors make it available to those who request it.

RESOURCE G

Questions for Cofacilitators

ORIENTATION AND STYLE

1. The major values, beliefs, and principles that guide my facilitation are . . .

2. The major values, beliefs, and principles that other facilitators hold and that I strongly disagree with are . . .

3. When contracting with this type of group, I usually . . .

4. When starting this type of group, I usually . . .

5. At the end of a meeting with this type of group, I usually . . .

6. When someone talks too much, I usually . . .

7. When the group is silent, I usually . . .

8. When an individual is silent for a long time, I usually . . .

9. When someone gets upset, I usually . . .

10. When someone comes late, I usually . . .

11. When someone leaves early, I usually . . .

12. When group members are excessively polite and do not confront each other, I usually . . .

Note: Some questions are from Pfeiffer and Jones (1975).

13. When there is conflict in the group, I usually . . .

14. When the group attacks one member, I usually . . .

15. When a group member takes a cheap shot at me or implies I am ineffective, I usually . . .

16. If there is physical violence or a threat of violence, I usually . . .

17. When members focus on positions, I usually . . .

18. When members seem to be off the track, I usually . . .

19. When someone takes a cheap shot, I usually . . .

20. My favorite interventions for this type of group are . . .

21. Interventions that this type of group usually needs but that I often don't make are . . .

22. In working with this type of group, the things I find most satisfying are . . .

23. The things I find most frustrating in working with this type of group are . . .

24. The things that make me most uncomfortable in this type of group are . . .

25. On a continuum ranging from completely supportive to completely confrontational, my intervention style is . . .

26. My typical "intervention rhythm" is [fast, slow] . . .

EXPERIENCE AND BACKGROUND

1. Discuss your experience as a facilitator or cofacilitator. What group types have you facilitated? What were the content and process issues in the groups?

2. Discuss your best facilitation and cofacilitation experiences. What was it that made them so successful?

3. Discuss your worst facilitation and cofacilitation experiences. What was it that made them so unsuccessful?

4. Describe some of your facilitation behaviors that a cofacilitator might consider idiosyncratic.

5. Describe issues that have arisen between you and other cofacilitators.

6. Describe the areas in which you are trying to improve your facilitation. How would you like the cofacilitator to help you improve?

7. What personal issues do you have that might hinder the ability of you and the other facilitator to work with each other or with the client?

8. Given what you know about the cofacilitator, what concerns do you have about working with that person?

COFACILITATOR COORDINATION

1. Who will sit where in the group meetings?

2. Who will start the session? Who will finish it?

3. Will both of you need to be present at all times? How will breakout sessions be handled?

4. How will you handle the role of flipchart recorder?

5. How will you divide labor (for example, primary-secondary, task-relationship, intervener-recorder)?

6. What kinds of facilitator interventions and behaviors are inside and outside the zone of deference that each of you will grant the other?

7. Where, when, and how will you deal with issues between the two of you?

8. What kind of disagreement between the two of you are you willing and not willing to show in front of the group?

9. How closely should you expect each other to adhere to the designated roles you have jointly agreed on?

10. What is nonnegotiable for each of you as cofacilitator?

Guidelines for Contracting with Your Manager

If you are an internal facilitator or an external facilitator who is not self-employed, it is important to have an agreement with your manager about how you contract with groups. By reaching this agreement with your manager before you begin contracting with a group, you reduce potential misunderstanding between the group, your manager, and you, all of which better serves the group. In this resource I present a set of questions and issues for you and your manager to consider when developing your agreement with each other. Exhibit H.1 gives a list of the issues.

• *How will groups request my facilitation services?* If the client initially contacts you, you are more likely to accurately represent your own facilitation approach and not inappropriately commit yourself. Your manager and you can also agree on how a request that comes directly to your manager will be handled. For example, your manager may generally describe your role to those requesting services and ask that the potential client contact you to discuss the specific situation.

• *Under what conditions may I decline or accept a facilitation request?* There are numerous legitimate reasons for declining a group's request for help. You may not have the skills or time to help the group, or you may not be able to be neutral on the facilitation topic. Or the group may want you to act in a way that is inconsistent with the Skilled Facilitator approach. The group may have insufficient motivation or time to accomplish its objectives, or other factors within or outside the group may significantly reduce the likelihood of success.

Exhibit H.1. Internal Facilitation Issues to Address with Your Manager

1. How will groups request my facilitation services?

2. Under what conditions may I decline or accept a facilitation request?

3. Who will decide whether I can work with a group?

4. What are my limits for contracting and terminating a contract with a group?

5. What group information will I need to share with you or others in the organization?

6. Will I be required to evaluate my client group members' performance?

7. How will my performance as a facilitator be evaluated?

8. What arrangements will we make regarding my other work while I am facilitating a group?

9. What special agreements do we need if I facilitate a group that you (my manager) are a member of?

10. What will each of us do to ensure that relevant individuals understand and honor our agreement?

11. What will we do if either of us believes the other has acted inconsistently with our agreement?

If you cannot decline a request under these or other legitimate conditions, at least tell the group that you will work with them, but explain the factors that you believe hinder the group in accomplishing its objectives.

• *Who will decide whether I can work with a group?* Ideally, you would decide whether to work with the group because you have the relevant information as the facilitator. If not, you and your manager could jointly make the decision.

In some cases, your manager may want you to decline a request that, from your perspective, meets all the necessary conditions for acceptability. Your manager may consider the group relatively unimportant to the organization and not worth the investment. Alternatively, she may want you to accept a request that fails to meet the necessary conditions, in response to pressure to give the group a quick fix.

• *What are my limits for contracting and terminating a contract with a group?* You and your manager need to agree on your limits, if any, for contracting and terminating an agreement. For example, does she need to approve facilitation that requires more than a certain number of hours of commitment? Or does she need to approve facilitation for a certain level or area of the organization? Can you contract for a high-risk developmental facilitation without approval? In some cases, you may need to terminate a contract with the client. What conversation, if any, do you need to have with your manager before terminating work with a group?

- *What group information will I need to share with you or others in the organization?* In considering confidentiality, there are three immediate sets of interests to consider: the client group's, yours, and your manager's. Facilitators are usually interested in a confidentiality agreement that enables them to use colleagues as a sounding board to increase their effectiveness. If your manager is also a facilitator, you may want to be able to get feedback from her. Similarly, she is likely to be interested in information to help evaluate and improve your performance.

- *Will I be required to evaluate my client group members' performance?* You face a role conflict when someone other than the client—such as your manager—wants you to share your evaluation of a group member. Group members trust you as a facilitator partly because you will not exercise any power in the system to affect them. Evaluating members means exercising that power (if you have it), and it changes the dynamic with the group. This is true even if you evaluate the group member positively.

The need to evaluate the process can be especially strong if members of a facilitated group spend a significant amount of their working time in the group. For example, I worked with a federal agency and its national union to establish a cooperative incentive program. A small union-management committee worked almost full-time to administer the program. Managers often wanted the local internal facilitator to evaluate members' contributions. In fact, the managers believed the members were performing well and were looking for more detailed evaluation data to support giving them bonuses.

- *How will my performance as a facilitator be evaluated?* It is difficult to determine how your performance will be evaluated. The assumption underlying group facilitation is that effective group process contributes to high-quality, acceptable group decisions. But because the group maintains free choice over its actions, the group's performance is not determined solely by your performance. You can perform effectively, yet the group may not achieve any of its objectives. Alternatively, you can perform poorly, and the group can still accomplish its objectives.

An effective way to evaluate a facilitator is to observe his performance or review tapes of the facilitation. (This requires agreement from the group and about confidentiality regarding the tapes or group observations.) Both methods use valid information in the form of directly observable data. Tape recordings also enable you and your manager to review the data, which eliminates problems with recall and is of value in using the evaluation developmentally. If facilitation is only a small part of your responsibilities, evaluation may not be as important for purposes of reward.

- *What arrangements will we make regarding my other work while I am facilitating a group?* If you are a part-time facilitator, you can reduce role conflict by agreeing on how your nonfacilitation responsibilities will be handled while you are facilitating. For example, you may delegate those responsibilities if possible, or you and your manager might agree that you will be responsible only for priority nonfacilitation work.

• *What special agreements do we need if I facilitate a group that you (my manager) are a member of?* At some point, you may receive a request to facilitate a group that includes your manager. If you treat her differently from other group members, it reduces your credibility and effectiveness as a facilitator. Even if you and your manager agree that you will not treat her differently, when contracting with the full client group it is important to raise this issue and ask the group to decide if it wants to work with you as the facilitator.

• *What will each of us do to ensure that relevant individuals understand and honor our agreement?* If your manager understands your approach to facilitation, she can help potential clients understand how you work. It is useful to discuss how your manager is willing to do this. Similarly, you have a role in helping key organization members understand your facilitator's role. Together, you and your manager can decide what initiatives to take to accomplish this objective.

• *What will we do if either of us believes the other has acted inconsistently with our agreement?* Finally, you and your manager need a way to talk together should one of you believe the other has acted inconsistently with your agreement. Agreeing to such a process at the time of contracting makes it easier to raise the issue if a conflict does arise.

REFERENCES

Action Design. Workshop materials. [www.actiondesign.com]. 1997.

Alderfer, C. P. "Group Processes in Organizations." In M. D. Dunnette (ed.), *Handbook of Industrial and Organizational Psychology.* Chicago: Rand McNally, 1976.

Alderfer, C. P. "Group and Intergroup Relations." In J. R. Hackman and J. L. Suttle (eds.), *Improving Life at Work.* Santa Monica, Calif.: Goodyear, 1977.

Allport, F. H. "A Theory of Enestruence (Event Structure Theory): Report of Progress." *American Psychologist,* 1967, *22,* 1–24.

Argyris, C. *Intervention Theory and Method: A Behavioral Science View.* Reading, Mass.: Addison-Wesley, 1970.

Argyris, C. "Reflecting on Laboratory Education from a Theory of Action Perspective." *Journal of Applied Behavioral Science,* 1979, *15*(3), 296–310.

Argyris, C. *Reasoning, Learning, and Action.* San Francisco: Jossey-Bass, 1982.

Argyris, C. *Strategy, Change, and Defensive Routines.* Boston: Pitman, 1985.

Argyris, C. "Reasoning, Action Strategies, and Defensive Routines: The Case of OD Practitioners." In R. W. Woodman and W. A. Pasmore (eds.), *Research in Organizational Change and Development, vol. 1.* Greenwich, Conn.: JAI Press, 1987.

Argyris, C. *Overcoming Organizational Defensives: Facilitating Organizational Learning.* Needham Heights, Mass.: Allyn & Bacon, 1990.

Argyris, C. *Knowledge for Action: A Guide to Overcoming Barriers to Organizational Change.* San Francisco: Jossey-Bass, 1993.

Argyris, C., Putnam, R., and Smith, D. M. *Action Science: Concepts, Methods, and Skills for Research and Intervention.* San Francisco: Jossey-Bass, 1985.

Argyris, C., and Schön, D. A. *Theory in Practice: Increasing Professional Effectiveness.* San Francisco: Jossey-Bass, 1974.

Argyris, C., and Schön, D. A. *Organizational Learning II: Theory, Method, and Practice.* Reading, Mass.: Addison-Wesley, 1996.

Bandler, R., and Grinder, J. *Reframing: Neuro-Linguistic Programming and the Transformation of Meaning.* Moab, Utah: Real People Press, 1982.

Barnard, C. I. *The Functions of the Executive.* Cambridge, Mass.: Harvard University Press, 1938.

Bateson. G. *Steps to an Ecology of Mind.* San Francisco: Chandler, 1972.

Beer, M. *Organization Change and Development: A Systems View.* Santa Monica, Calif.: Goodyear, 1980.

Bellman, G. M. *The Consultant's Calling: Bringing Who You Are to What You Do, New and Revised Edition.* San Francisco: Jossey-Bass, 2001.

Benne, K. D. "History of the T Group in the Laboratory Setting." In L. P. Bradford, J. R. Gibb, and K. D. Benne (eds.), *T-Group Theory and Laboratory Method.* New York: Wiley, 1964.

Blake, R. R. *The Managerial Grid: Key Orientations for Achieving Production Through People.* Houston: Gulf, 1964.

Blake, R. R., and Mouton, J. S. *Consultation.* (2nd ed.). Reading, Mass.: Addison-Wesley, 1983.

Block, P. *Flawless Consulting.* (2nd ed.). San Diego: University Associates, 2000.

Block, P. *Stewardship: Choosing Service over Self-Interest.* San Francisco: Berrett-Koehler, 1993.

Bush, R.A.B., and Folger, J. P. *The Promise of Mediation: Responding to Conflict Through Empowerment and Recognition.* San Francisco: Jossey-Bass, 1994.

Cook, T. D., and Campbell, D. T. *Quasi-Experimentation: Design and Analysis Issues for Field Settings.* Chicago: Rand McNally, 1979.

Cuellar, G. "Creative and Survival Behaviors: Assessing a Creative Behavior Model." Unpublished doctoral dissertation, University of Massachusetts, 1986.

Cyert, R. M., and March, J. G. *A Behavioral Theory of the Firm.* Upper Saddle River, N.J.: Prentice Hall, 1963.

Davidson, A., and Anderson, L. *Meeting and Process Facilitation Workshop Notebook.* Washington, D.C.: Development District Association of Appalachia, 2001.

Dies, R. R., Mallet, J., and Johnson, F. "Openness in the Coleader Relationship: Its Effect on Group Process and Outcome." *Small Group Behavior,* 1979, *10,* 523–546.

Eiseman, J. W. "Reconciling 'Incompatible' Positions." *Journal of Applied Behavioral Science,* 1978, *14,* 133–150.

Festinger, L. *A Theory of Cognitive Dissonance.* Stanford, Calif.: Stanford University Press, 1957.

Fisher, R., Ury, W., and Patton, B. *Getting to Yes: Negotiating Without Giving In.* (2nd ed.). New York: Penguin, 1991.

Gellermann, W., Frankel, M. S., and Ladenson, R. F. *Values and Ethics in Organization and Human Systems Development.* San Francisco: Jossey-Bass, 1990.

Goleman, D. *Emotional Intelligence.* New York: Bantam, 1995.

Goleman, D. *Working with Emotional Intelligence.* New York: Bantam, 1998.

Golembiewski, R. T. "'Promise Not to Tell': A Critical View of 'Confidentiality' in Consultation." (Invited commentary.) *Consultation,* 1986, *5,* 68–76.

Graham, P. (ed.). *Mary Parker Follett: Prophet of Management.* Cambridge, Mass.: Harvard Business School Press, 1995.

Hackman, J. R. "The Design of Work Teams." In J. Lorsch (ed.), *Handbook of Organizational Behavior.* Upper Saddle River, N.J.: Prentice Hall, 1987.

Hackman, J. R. "Work Teams in Organizations: An Orienting Framework." In J. R. Hackman (ed.), *Groups That Work (and Those That Don't).* San Francisco: Jossey-Bass, 1990.

Hall, D. T., Bowen, D. D., Lewicki, R. J., and Hall, F. S. *Experiences in Management and Organizational Behavior.* (2nd ed.). New York: Wiley, 1982.

Hayakawa, S. I. *Language in Thought and Action.* (3rd ed.). Orlando: Harcourt Brace, 1972.

Hirokawa, R. Y. "Group Communication and Decision-Making Performance: A Continued Test of the Functional Perspective." *Human Communication Research,* 1988, *14,* 487–515.

Hirokawa, R. Y., and Gouran, D. S. "Facilitation of Group Communication: A Critique of Prior Research and an Agenda for Future Research." *Management Communication Quarterly,* 1989, *3,* 71–92.

Kaplan, A. *The Conduct of Inquiry: Methodology for Behavioral Science.* San Francisco: Chandler, 1964.

Kaplan, R. E. "The Conspicuous Absence of Evidence That Process Consultation Enhances Task Performance." *Journal of Applied Behavioral Science,* 1979, *15,* 346–360.

Katz, D., and Kahn, R. L. *The Social Psychology of Organizations.* (2nd ed.). New York: Wiley, 1978.

Katzenbach, J. R., and Smith, D. K. *The Wisdom of Teams: Creating the High-Performance Organization.* New York: HarperCollins, 1993.

Kerr, S. "On the Folly of Rewarding A, While Hoping for B." *Academy of Management Journal,* 1975, *18,* 769–783.

Levinson, H. *Organizational Diagnosis.* Cambridge, Mass.: Harvard University Press, 1972.

Manz, C. C., and Sims, H. P., Jr. "Searching for the 'Unleader': Organizational Member Views on Leading Self-Managed Groups." *Human Relations,* 1984, *37*(5), 409–424.

Manz, C. C., and Sims, H. P., Jr. *SuperLeadership: Leading Others to Lead Themselves.* Upper Saddle River, N.J.: Prentice Hall, 1989.

Manz, C. C., and Sims, H. P., Jr. "Business Without Bosses: Real-Life Stories About Self-Managing Work Teams." Paper presented at the annual meeting of the Academy of Management, Atlanta, Aug. 1993.

Marrow, A. J. *The Practical Theorist: The Life and Work of Kurt Lewin.* New York: Teachers College Press, 1969.

McConnell, J. V. (1986). *Understanding Human Behavior.* (5th ed.). Austin, Tex.: Holt, Rinehart and Winston.

Merton, R. K. *Social Theory and Social Structure.* New York: Free Press of Glencoe, 1957.

Moore, C. W. *The Mediation Process: Practical Strategies for Resolving Conflict.* (2nd ed.). San Francisco: Jossey-Bass, 1996.

Nisbett, R., and Ross, L. *Human Inference: Strategies and Shortcomings of Social Judgment.* Upper Saddle River, N.J.: Prentice Hall, 1980.

Osborn, A. F. *Applied Imagination: The Principles and Problems of Creative Thinking.* New York: Scribner, 1953.

Paulson, I., Burroughs, J. C., and Gelb, C. B. "Cotherapy: What Is the Crux of the Relationship?" *International Journal of Group Psychotherapy,* 1976, *26,* 213–224.

Pfeiffer, J. W., and Jones, J. E. "Co-Facilitating." In *The 1975 Annual for Group Facilitators.* San Diego: University Associates, 1975.

Salovey, P., and Mayer, J. D. "Emotional Intelligence." *Imagination, Cognition, and Personality,* 1990, *9,* 185–211.

Schein, E. H. *Organizational Culture and Leadership.* San Francisco: Jossey-Bass, 1985.

Schein, E. H. *Process Consultation: Lessons for Managers and Consultants, Vol. 2.* Reading, Mass.: Addison-Wesley, 1987.

Schein, E. H. *Process Consultation: Its Role in Organization Development, Vol. 1.* (2nd ed.). Reading, Mass.: Addison-Wesley, 1988.

Schön, D. A. *The Reflective Practitioner: How Professionals Think in Action.* New York: Basic Books, 1983.

Schwarz, R. M. "Grounded Learning Experiences: Treating the Classroom as an Organization." *Organizational Behavior Teaching Review,* 1985, *9,* 16–30.

Schwarz, R. "A Consumer's Guide to Hiring and Working with a Group Facilitator." Chapel Hill, N.C.: Roger Schwarz & Associates, 2002a. Article.

Schwarz, R. "Ground Rules for Effective Groups." Chapel Hill, N.C.: Roger Schwarz & Associates, 2002b. Article.

Schwarz, R. M. "Consulting to Council-Manager Groups." *Public Administration Quarterly,* 1991, *14,* 419–437.

Senge, P. M. *The Fifth Discipline: The Art and Practice of the Learning Organization.* New York: Doubleday, 1990.

Smith, K. K., and Berg, D. N. *Paradoxes of Group Life: Understanding Conflict, Paralysis, and Movement in Group Dynamics.* San Francisco: Jossey-Bass, 1987.

Snyder, M., and Swann, W. B. "Behavioral Confirmation in Social Interaction: From Social Perception to Social Reality." *Journal of Experimental Social Psychology,* 1978, *14,* 148–162.

Steele, F. *The Role of the Internal Consultant.* Boston: CBI, 1982.

Steiner, C. M. *Scripts People Live: Transactional Analysis of Life Scripts.* New York: Bantam Books, 1974.

Sundstrom, E., De Meuse, K. P., and Futrell, D. "Work Teams: Applications and Effectiveness." *American Psychologist,* 1990, *45,* 120–133.

Sutton, R. I., and Shurman, S. J. "On Studying Emotionally Hot Topics: Lessons from an Investigation of Organizational Death." In D. N. Berg and K. K. Smith (eds.), *Exploring Clinical Methods for Social Research.* Thousand Oaks, Calif.: Sage, 1985.

Svara, J. *Official Leadership in the City.* New York: Oxford University Press, 1990.

Vroom, V. H., and Jago, A. G. *The New Leadership: Managing Participation in Organizations.* Upper Saddle River, N.J.: Prentice Hall, 1988.

Vroom, V. H., and Yetton, P. W. *Leadership and Decision Making.* Pittsburgh: University of Pittsburgh Press, 1973.

Watzlawick, P., Beavin, J. H., and Jackson, D. D. *Pragmatics of Human Communication: A Study of Interactional Patterns, Pathologies, and Paradoxes.* New York: Norton, 1967.

Yalom, I. D. *The Theory and Practice of Group Psychotherapy.* (3rd ed.). New York: Basic Books, 1985.

Zeithaml, V. A., Parasuraman, A., and Berry, L. L. *Delivering Quality Service: Balancing Customer Perceptions and Expectations.* New York: Free Press, 1990.

INDEX